JOURNAL FOR THE STUDY OF THE OLD TESTAMENT
SUPPLEMENT SERIES
263

Sheffield Academic Press

The Chronicler as Author

Studies in Text and Texture

edited by

M. Patrick Graham
&
Steven L. McKenzie

Journal for the Study of the Old Testament
Supplement Series 263

Copyright © 1999 Sheffield Academic Press

Published by
Sheffield Academic Press Ltd
Mansion House
19 Kingfield Road
Sheffield S11 9AS
England

Typeset by Sheffield Academic Press
and
Printed on acid-free paper in Great Britain
by Bookcraft Ltd
Midsomer Norton, Somerset

British Library Cataloguing in Publication Data

A catalogue record for this book is available
from the British Library

ISBN 1-84127-057-1

CONTENTS

PREFACE

This collection of 16 essays deals with Chronicles as literature and is intended as a sequel to *The Chronicler as Historian*,[1] a collection of essays that explored the value of Chronicles for historical information about the pre-exilic period of Israelite and Judean history. The articles in the present volume, however, investigate the Chronicler's (hereafter, 'Chr.' will be used to designate the author of 1–2 Chronicles) work in terms of its literary sources, the techniques by which it was constructed and its perspective advanced, how early readers may have encountered it, and the value of several contemporary reading strategies for making its voice heard clearly once more. Some of these contributions had their origins in papers for meetings of the Society of Biblical Literature, while others are related to research that began with a dissertation. The composition of this book has indeed been an international, collaborative effort and represents some of the latest Chronicles research from Finland, Scotland, Canada, Australia, Denmark, Norway and the United States. The editors are deeply appreciative of the diligent work, scholarly expertise and congenial spirit that each of the contributors brought to this project.

The articles are divided into three groups. 'Overviews of Chronicles' (Part I) includes the pieces that review the history of the source analysis of the book; debate the current status of the redaction-critical treatment of the work; affirm the value of rhetorical analysis (with its roots in the work of Aristotle) for the appropriation of the book; and apply insights from narratological research for a contemporary interpretation. Part II of this collection traces certain themes or topics related to Chronicles: how Chr. functioned as a member of an interpretive community; how Chr. tracked and interpreted the fortunes of Judah's royal and temple treasuries; how Chr. made use of the addresses of foreign kings to

1.   M.P. Graham, K.G. Hoglund and S.L. McKenzie (eds.), *The Chronicler as Historian* (JSOTSup, 238; Sheffield: Sheffield Academic Press, 1997).

advance his theological concerns; how Chr. used foreigners to articulate a view of the identity of Israel; and finally, how Chr. used psalm texts in his work. Part III takes up specific texts from Chronicles (1 Chron. 10; 16; 21; 2 Chron. 10–13; 36.20-23) and shows how they can be illuminated by the variety of literary-critical methods available to researchers.

It is the editors' hope that this volume will not only make the contributions of these 16 researchers available to a wider audience but that it will further stimulate the scholarly investigation of Chronicles. Although this segment of the biblical canon has long been neglected,[2] there has been a resurgence of interest in the postexilic literature of the Hebrew Bible generally[3] and in Chronicles specifically[4] during the last three decades. Consequently, in addition to the increasing number of specialized studies, Chronicles research is now able to take advantage of an excellent bibliography,[5] a selection of synoptic parallels that facilitate the comparison of Chronicles with other parts of the Hebrew Bible,[6] an extensive, systematic treatment of Chr.'s theology[7] and several major commentaries on Chronicles.[8] In light of these resources

---

2.   See M.P. Graham, 'Setting the Heart to Seek God: Worship in 2 Chronicles 30.1-31.1', in M.P. Graham, R.R. Marrs and S.L. McKenzie (eds.), *Worship and the Hebrew Bible: Essays in Honour of John T. Willis* (JSOTSup, 284; Sheffield: Sheffield Academic Press, 1999), pp. 124-25.

3.   Cf. P.R. Davies, 'Sociology and the Second Temple', in *Second Temple Studies*. I. *Persian Period* (JSOTSup, 117; Sheffield: JSOT Press, 1991), p. 12; T.C. Eskenazi, 'Current Perspectives on Ezra–Nehemiah and the Persian Period', *CRBS* 1 (1993), pp. 59-86.

4.   Cf. J.W. Kleinig, 'Recent Research in Chronicles', *CRBS* 2 (1994), pp. 43-76; and K.H. Richards, 'Reshaping Chronicles and Ezra–Nehemiah Interpretation', in J.L. Mays, D.L. Petersen and K.H. Richards (eds.), *Old Testament Interpretation: Past, Present, and Future. Essays in Honor of Gene M. Tucker* (Nashville: Abingdon Press, 1995), pp. 211-24.

5.   I. Kalimi, *The Books of Chronicles: A Classified Bibliography* (Simor Bible Bibliographies; Jerusalem: Simor, 1990).

6.   See the discussion in J.C. Endres *et al.*, *Chronicles and its Synoptic Parallels in Samuel, Kings, and Related Biblical Texts* (Collegeville, MN: Liturgical Press, 1998), pp. xvi-xviii.

7.   S. Japhet, *The Ideology of the Book of Chronicles and its Place in Biblical Thought* (BEATAJ, 9; Bern: Peter Lang, 1989).

8.   See, e.g., S. Japhet, *I & II Chronicles* (OTL; Louisville, KY: Westminster/ John Knox Press, 1993). Three other important commentaries that are in preparation are those by T. Willi in the BKAT series (fascicles of which have already

and the growing interest in and appreciation of biblical literature from the Persian and Hellenistic periods, the editors hope that the present volume will be of some assistance.

Finally, the editors would like to express appreciation to two groups that have made the present volume possible. First, thanks are due to the Chronicles–Ezra–Nehemiah Section of the Society of Biblical Literature. Its program committee and supporters have created a structure and a community that have encouraged and nurtured research on this part of the Hebrew Bible for more than a decade now. In addition, we are grateful to David J.A. Clines and Philip R. Davies of the Sheffield Academic Press for their support of this project and its inclusion in the JSOT Supplements Series.

M. Patrick Graham
Steven L. McKenzie

begun appearing), R.W. Klein in the Hermeneia series and G.N. Knoppers in the AB series.

ABBREVIATIONS

AASOR	Annual of the American Schools of Oriental Research
AB	Anchor Bible
ABD	David Noel Freedman (ed.), *The Anchor Bible Dictionary* (New York: Doubleday, 1992)
ADB	*Allgemeine deutsche Biographie*
AfO	*Archiv für Orientforschung*
AJS	*American Journal of Sociology*
ATANT	Abhandlungen zur Theologie des Alten und Neuen Testaments
ATD	Das Alte Testament Deutsch
ATJ	*Ashland Theological Journal*
BARev	*Biblical Archaeology Review*
BASOR	*Bulletin of the American Schools of Oriental Research*
BBB	Bonner biblische Beiträge
BC	Biblischer Commentar
BEATAJ	Beiträge zur Erforschung des Alten Testaments und des antiken Judentums
BethM	*Beth Mikra*
BETL	Bibliotheca ephemeridum theologicarum lovaniensium
BHS	*Biblia hebraica stuttgartensia*
Bib	*Biblica*
BJS	Brown Judaic Studies
BKAT	Biblischer Kommentar: Altes Testament
BN	*Biblische Notizen*
BS	*Biblische Studien*
BTH	Book of Two Houses
BWANT	Beiträge zur Wissenschaft vom Alten und Neuen Testament
BZ	*Biblische Zeitschrift*
BZAW	Beihefte zur *ZAW*
CAT	Commentaire de l'Ancien Testament
CB	*Cultura bíblica*
CBC	Cambridge Bible Commentary
CBQ	*Catholic Biblical Quarterly*
CBSC	Cambridge Bible for Schools and Colleges
Chr.	The Chronicler
ConBOT	Coniectanea biblica, Old Testament

CRBS	*Currents in Research: Biblical Studies*
CTM	*Concordia Theological Monthly*
DJD	Discoveries in the Judaean Desert
DtrH	The Deuteronomistic History/Historian
EA	El Amarna Letters
EncJud	*Encyclopaedia Judaica*
ErIsr	Eretz Israel
EvQ	*Evangelical Quarterly*
EVV	*English versions*
ExpB	Expositor's Bible
FOTL	The Forms of the Old Testament Literature
FRLANT	Forschungen zur Religion und Literatur des Alten und Neuen Testaments
FTS	Freiburger theologische Studien
GBSNT	Guides to Biblical Scholarship: New Testament Series
GBSOT	Guides to Biblical Scholarship: Old Testament Series
GTS	Gettysburg Theological Studies
HAR	*Hebrew Annual Review*
HAT	Handbuch zum Alten Testament
HCL	Harper's Classical Library
HKAT	Handkommentar zum Alten Testament
HSM	Harvard Semitic Monographs
HSS	Harvard Semitic Studies
HTR	*Harvard Theological Review*
ICC	International Critical Commentary
IDB	George Arthur Buttrick (ed.), *The Interpreter's Dictionary of the Bible* (4 vols.; Nashville: Abingdon Press, 1962)
IDBSup	*IDB*, Supplementary Volume
ILBS	Indiana Literary Biblical Series
Int	*Interpretation*
JBL	*Journal of Biblical Literature*
JBR	*Journal of Bible and Religion*
JBS	Jerusalem Biblical Studies
JETS	*Journal of the Evangelical Theological Society*
JJS	*Journal of Jewish Studies*
JR	*Journal of Religion*
JSOT	*Journal for the Study of the Old Testament*
JSOTSup	*Journal for the Study of the Old Testament*, Supplement Series
JSS	*Journal of Semitic Studies*
JTS	*Journal of Theological Studies*
KAT	Kommentar zum Alten Testament
KHAT	Kurzer Hand-Kommentar zum Alten Testament
KJV	King James Version
LXX	Septuagint
MT	Masoretic Text

NCB	New Century Bible
NEB	*New English Bible*
NIV	New International Version
NJPS	New Jewish Publication Society
NRSV	New Revised Standard Version
OBO	Orbis biblicus et orientalis
OBS	Österreichische biblische Studien
OLP	Orientalia lovaniensia periodica
Or	*Orientalia*
OTG	Old Testament Guides
OTL	Old Testament Library
OTS	*Oudtestamentische Studiën*
OTWSA	*Oud Testamentiese Werkgemeenschap in Suid-Afrika*
PMLA	*Publications of the Modern Language Association*
RB	*Revue biblique*
ResQ	*Restoration Quarterly*
RGG	*Religion in Geschichte und Gegenwart*
RS	*Ras Shamra*
RSV	Revised Standard Version
SAA	State Archives of Assyria
SBB	Stuttgarter biblische Beiträge
SBL	Society of Biblical Literature
SBLDS	SBL Dissertation Series
SBLMS	SBL Monograph Series
SBLSCS	SBL Septuagint and Cognate Studies
SBLSPS	SBL Seminar Papers Series
SBT	Studies in Biblical Theology
ScrHier	*Scripta hierosolymitana*
SJOT	*Scandinavian Journal of the Old Testament*
SNTSMS	Society for New Testament Studies Monograph Series
STDJ	Studies on the Texts of the Desert of Judah
SUNVAO	Skrifter (Norske videnskaps-akademi i Oslo - Hist.-filos. klasse)
TBC	Torch Bible Commentary
TBü	Theologische Bücherei
TDOT	G.J. Botterweck and H. Ringgren (eds.), *Theological Dictionary of the Old Testament*
ThZ	*Theologische Zeitschrift*
TOTC	Tyndale Old Testament Commentaries
TQ	*Theologische Quartalschrift*
TRE	*Theologische Realenzyklopädie*
TRu	*Theologische Rundschau*
TUMSR	Trinity University Monograph Series in Religion
TVG	Theologische Verlagsgemeinschaft
TynBul	*Tyndale Bulletin*

VT	*Vetus Testamentum*
VTSup	*Vetus Testamentum*, Supplements
WBC	Word Biblical Commentary
WMANT	Wissenschaftliche Monographien zum Alten und Neuen Testament
WTJ	*Westminster Theological Journal*
ZAW	*Zeitschrift für die alttestamentliche Wissenschaft*
ZDPV	*Zeitschrift des deutschen Palästina-Vereins*

LIST OF CONTRIBUTORS

A. GRAEME AULD
University of Edinburgh, Edinburgh, Scotland

NOEL BAILEY
University of Queensland, Brisbane, Australia

EHUD BEN ZVI
University of Alberta, Edmonton, Alberta, Canada

ROLAND T. BOER
United Theological College, Parramatta, Australia

RODNEY K. DUKE
Appalachian State University, Boone, NC

M. PATRICK GRAHAM
Emory University, Atlanta, GA

MAGNAR KARTVEIT
Misjonshøgskolen Teologisk Fakultet, Stavanger, Norway

GARY N. KNOPPERS
Pennsylvania State University, University Park, PA

STEVEN L. MCKENZIE
Rhodes College, Memphis, TN

CHRISTINE MITCHELL
Carleton University, Ottawa, Canada

KIRSTEN NIELSEN
University of Aarhus, Aarhus, Denmark

KAI PELTONEN
Institute for Advanced Training, Järvenpää, Finland

WILLIAM M. SCHNIEDEWIND
University of California, Los Angeles, CA

ARMIN SIEDLECKI
Drury College, Springfield, MO

JAMES M. TROTTER
Murdoch University, Perth, Australia

HOWARD N. WALLACE
United Faculty of Theology, Parkville, Australia

JOHN W. WRIGHT
Point Loma Nazarene University, San Diego, CA

Part I

OVERVIEWS OF CHRONICLES

FUNCTION, EXPLANATION AND LITERARY PHENOMENA: ASPECTS OF SOURCE CRITICISM AS THEORY AND METHOD IN THE HISTORY OF CHRONICLES RESEARCH

Kai Peltonen

Terminological Considerations

An inseparable issue of Chronicles research has been the question of what sources the Chr., its author, drew upon.[1] There are two basic reasons for this. First, Chronicles contains a number of explicit references to sources that have allegedly been used in its compilation and/or that offer information supplementary to that already recorded by Chr. Secondly, the source issue has had and still has a functional import. An assumption that Chr. composed his history with the help of some materials whether known or unknown to us often seems to be the most feasible way of explaining certain features of the chronistic historiography.[2] In this article, it is my purpose to draw attention to some general observations about these issues, based on a survey of the history of

---

1.   In what follows, discussion is limited to the question of the sources of the biblical book of Chronicles, despite the fact that in the history of research the books of Chronicles, Ezra and Nehemiah have long been regarded as forming one literary entity (the hypothesis of Chr.'s history work) or at least as written by the same author.

2.   Minute discussions of Chronicles' source citations and their relationship to the older biblical materials can be found in substantial commentaries on Chronicles as well as in most Old Testament introductions, so that a reference to them may suffice for the purpose of the present article. Useful recent discussions of Chronicles' sources include those of R.W. Klein, 'Chronicles, Book of 1–2', in *ABD* (1992), I, pp. 992-1002 (996-97); G.H. Jones, *1 & 2 Chronicles* (OTG; Sheffield: JSOT Press, 1993), pp. 65-85; A.F. Rainey, 'The Chronicler and his Sources—Historical and Geographical', in M.P. Graham, K.G. Hoglund and S.L. McKenzie (eds.), *The Chronicler as Historian* (JSOTSup, 238; Sheffield: Sheffield Academic Press, 1997), pp. 30-72.

research, especially from the point of view of methodology.[3]

In the modern study of the Hebrew Bible, the term 'source' basically refers to a document that underlies a biblical book and that can be detected and separated from it by means of critical analysis. It is in this sense that the term will be used here. Source criticism is the methodological process by which this detection is carried out. The purpose is to determine whether a text is composite or not, and, if it is, what kinds of documents have been utilized in its composition, how the sources should be dated and so on.[4] Source criticism became a serious topic in the investigation of the Hebrew Bible around the end of the eighteenth century, but, as is well known, its 'classical' period was the nineteenth century, when it was applied to the Pentateuch, in particular, with noteworthy success and long-standing consequences.

Source-critical analysis, though, has not been the most important critical method used on Chronicles. The problem of Chronicles' sources can also take a significantly different shape. The close parallelism between Samuel–Kings and Chronicles makes it quite obvious that Chr.

---

3.   When a later methodological criterion (e.g., the concept of source criticism) is imposed on the work of scholars who did not operate with one, at least in the sense we now understand it, there always lurk the problems (1) of misrepresenting their wider ideas and intentions and (2) of misusing the results. Such an imposition unavoidably happens at the expense of a wider historiographical perspective and coherence. After all, history of research is not a sum of a number of methodological or other case histories but a field where numerous factors of a widely divergent nature (historical, theological, exegetical, political etc.) interact and influence each other with the result that research does not always seem to progress in the way that later observers would expect. Therefore, observations derived from an undertaking like the present one should not be misused, that is to say, absolutized with the consequence that value judgments are made of the earlier scholarly work on the basis of rules made during the half-time break, so to speak. In what follows, justice has been done as much as possible to the scholars surveyed, in the sense that their sincere purpose to deal scientifically and constructively with the problems of source criticism has not been questioned or downgraded, whether or not they were successful from the modern perspective. Furthermore, historical surveys of research like the present one should not be misused as a legitimation of some present view at the expense of others. They should be seen more as a map setting recent concerns in perspective and indicating the future tasks and challenges of research.

4.   Serving as virtual equivalent to 'source criticism' in the classical methodology of biblical criticism, 'literary criticism' emphasizes the scholarly interest in literary documents, not in orally transmitted traditions. See J. Barton, 'Source Criticism: Old Testament', *ABD* (1992), VI, pp. 162-65.

drew upon literary source material preserved in some form in the present Hebrew Bible. Analogously, it is possible, if we are to take Chr.'s
explicit references to sources seriously, that he had before him source
material no longer known to us, and it was from this that he received
the non-parallel information of his work. Consequently, much more
scholarly energy in the critical period of Chronicles research has been
devoted to this issue (i.e., the nature of the sources that Chr. cites) than
to source criticism as a literary procedure. This complex of issues,
which is typical of Chronicles research, could be termed 'source criticism as theory' or 'source-critical theory' in contrast to source criticism
understood as a method aiming at the clarification of the literary origin
and development of a biblical book—the terms 'criticism' or 'critical'
indicating in the former respect an aspiration to scholarly argumentation
rather than 'criticism' in the common sense of the word. In Chronicles
research, source criticism as theory has served larger historical and
theological goals than could source criticism in the traditional sense. It
has attempted to solve the questions of why and on what conditions
Chr.'s history has come to take the form it has now and what kind of a
historical and theological assessment one should make of it.

In what follows, we shall start with source criticism as theory,
because its history is extensive, stretching from the very beginnings of
critical study up to the most modern research. In a short article, where
space is limited, it is possible to pay attention to only the most
noteworthy contributions.[5]

Source Criticism as Theory in Chronicles Research

There are two features of Chronicles that have been observed and that
impel source criticism as theory: (1) references to works available to

5.   I have surveyed the history of research on Chronicles, especially from the
standpoint of the book's historical reliability in a work entitled *History Debated:
The Historical Reliability of Chronicles in Pre-Critical and Critical Research*
(Publications of the Finnish Exegetical Society, 64; Helsinki: The Finnish Exegetical Society; Göttingen: Vandenhoeck & Ruprecht, 1996). For a survey dealing
especially with the literary-critical dimension of Chronicles research in the nineteenth century, see J.W. Wright, 'From Center to Periphery: 1 Chronicles 23–27 and
the Interpretation of Chronicles in the Nineteenth Century', in E.C. Ulrich *et al.*
(eds.), *Priests, Prophets and Scribes: Essays on the Formation and Heritage of
Second Temple Judaism in Honour of Joseph Blenkinsopp* (JSOTSup, 149;
Sheffield: JSOT Press, 1992), pp. 20-42.

the author of Chronicles and/or to his original readership; and (2) the similarities between Chronicles and the present text of Samuel–Kings. The latter are occasionally so striking that it becomes necessary to assume some sort of interdependent relationship between Chr.'s work and Samuel–Kings. It is easy to see, further, that sometimes Chr.'s account differs significantly from the older historiography. In some places Chr. also records events that are altogether absent from Samuel–Kings. In their simplicity, these observations have constituted the basis for what has now become two centuries of intense scholarly debate about what source materials Chr. had before him. The basic lines of this debate and the fundamental alternatives took shape in the first half of the nineteenth century and may be traced to the present.

Approach I: There Were Unknown Sources Only
The assumption that Chr. resorted for source material only to documents no longer known to us ruled the day when the critical study of Chronicles began in the early nineteenth century. Essential to this approach was the assumption that Chr.'s source citations be taken at face value. This was the approach of J.G. Eichhorn's (1752–1827) three-volume work, *Einleitung ins Alte Testament*, which has often been regarded as the starting point of the critical isagogics of the Hebrew Bible.[6] Eichhorn's source theory was based on the observation that the canonical accounts of the history of Israel during the monarchy were not in complete harmony with each other. The traditional notion of the Old Testament as the first part of the Holy Scripture and thus as an authentic record of Israel's history allowed little room for critical conclusions from this observation, however. Inconsistencies and discrepancies had to be apparent and explainable, since otherwise it would have been difficult to maintain the authority of Scripture, according to Christian tradition. A convenient means of achieving this goal was Eichhorn's development of a source theory, an accomplishment that was unparalleled and unrivaled in biblical exegesis in his day.

---

6. J.G. Eichhorn, *Einleitung ins Alte Testament* (Leipzig: Weidmann, 1780–83). On Eichhorn and his work on the Bible, see, e.g., H.-J. Kraus, *Geschichte der historisch-kritischen Erforschung des Alten Testaments* (Neukirchen–Vluyn: Neukirchener Verlag, 3rd edn, 1982), pp. 133-51; H.-J. Zobel, 'Eichhorn, Johann Gottfried (1752–1827)', *TRE* (1982), IX, pp. 369-71; R. Smend, *Deutsche Alttestamentler in drei Jahrhunderten* (Göttingen: Vandenhoeck & Ruprecht, 1989), pp. 25-37.

Eichhorn argued that Ezra, the author of Chronicles, quite probably knew the accounts of David and Solomon in 2 Samuel and 1 Kings but did not use them as his actual sources. The canonical accounts of Samuel–Kings and Chronicles originally had a common point of departure in the independent short biographies of David and Solomon. In the course of their transmission, though, these biographies were copied, supplemented and changed. Consequently, the biblical writers were presented with divergent forms of the original accounts. The respective biblical authors had used different versions of the original biographies as their sources, and this fact in turn offered an explanation for both the similarities and the differences between the accounts. In addition to this source material that was also available—though in a divergent form— to the author of Samuel–Kings, Ezra had access to supplementary information from sources available only to him. Regarding the history of the post-Solomonic era, in many instances Ezra's description was, in Eichhorn's opinion, also based on source material that deviated from that used in Kings. Sometimes Ezra had followed the same source as the author of Kings, resulting in identical presentations of history. Often Ezra had gone one step farther, however, and used the source behind the common source that he and the author of Kings had used, or he had drawn upon some other source material (now unknown to us), and this fact explained the divergencies between his account and that of Samuel–Kings. Even though Ezra had occasionally revised his source material slightly and thus left his own mark on the sacred history of Israel, it was clear that all the differences between Chronicles and other biblical histories could be explained away with the help of the observation that behind both of them were old and authentic sources.[7]

Beyond Chronicles' source citations and observations made about its relationship with Samuel–Kings, Eichhorn had no evidence for the existence of the non-canonical sources that he postulated. It was an ingeniously constructed hypothesis, a source theory, the main element of which was the putative, historically authentic extra-biblical sources that the author of Chronicles had faithfully followed. What must be noted here, however, is that the source theory had a critical, functional significance for Eichhorn's historical (and indirectly also theological) interpretation of Chronicles. By supposing that Chronicles was not dependent

7.   For Eichhorn's treatment of Chronicles, see vol. 2 of his *Einleitung* (1781), pp. 630-56. A more thorough discussion of Eichhorn's views may be found in Peltonen, *History Debated*, pp. 56-60.

on the present Samuel–Kings but on trustworthy non-canonical source material, part of which in its original form constituted a common basis for both canonical histories, Eichhorn succeeded in explaining why ultimately there were no real historical problems in Chronicles, even though a casual reading might create the impression of such problems.

We can thus see how in Eichhorn's argumentation a source-critical theory, appealing to a complicated literary process behind the present forms of Chronicles and Samuel–Kings, was aimed at explaining something other than source-critical problems. In this way, Eichhorn answered historical questions—and indirectly, theological ones too, which may have followed awkward historical problems. To understand Chronicles correctly was to understand it correctly from the historical point of view, and the investigation of its sources had a supporting function in the process of historical understanding. One should not claim that it was Eichhorn who created such a functional paradigm for Chronicles' source criticism, because similar sorts of issues had occupied scholars even before Eichhorn in the pre-critical era of Chronicles research,[8] but it was Eichhorn who constructed a scientific theory out of the earlier notions. In it, literary processes that had generated the different versions of Israel's monarchic history in the Hebrew Bible, became processes that had taken place in the sources used by the biblical authors. Thus, Eichhorn's source-critical theory pushed methodological questions (the application of which in modern terms could be called source or literary criticism) a step backwards, out of reach of critical scholarly analysis—that is to say, to the sphere of postulates.

Eichhorn's interpretation of Chronicles' sources was very influential in the history of research. It won considerable support not only among his contemporaries[9] but also among a significant number of later schol-

8. For a survey of Chronicles research before the dawn of the critical era at the beginning of the nineteenth century, see T. Willi, *Die Chronik als Auslegung: Untersuchungen zur literarischen Gestaltung der historischen Überlieferung Israels* (FRLANT, 106; Göttingen: Vandenhoeck & Ruprecht, 1972), pp. 12-32; Peltonen, *History Debated*, pp. 17-68; I. Kalimi, 'History of Interpretation: The Book of Chronicles in Jewish Tradition from Daniel to Spinoza', *RB* 105 (1998), pp. 5-41.

9. Of the early nineteenth-century biblical scholars of renown, we may refer to G.L. Bauer, J.C.W. Augusti and L. Bertholdt as close followers of Eichhorn's position. A basically similar source construction can also be found in the Old Testament introduction of the contemporary Catholic scholar J. Jahn. See Peltonen, *History Debated*, pp. 59-64.

ars who constructed their views of Chronicles' sources along fundamentally the same basic lines. This is the case especially in nineteenth-
century research, when historical perspectives directed scholarly
attention to the extent that the main goal or 'method' of all scientific
work on Chronicles was to determine the veracity of the historical narrative that it presented. To take but one example of this particular, post-
Eichhornian branch of Chronicles research, we may refer to the German
C.F. Keil (1807–88), a staunch supporter of Protestant confessional
orthodoxy in Germany and arguably the most influential conservative
Chronicles scholar in nineteenth-century research.[10]

Keil argued vigorously in his *Apologetischer Versuch über die
Bücher der Chronik* (1833)[11] that critical allegations concerning the
(un-)historical nature of Chronicles, presented by W.M.L. de Wette and
his closest followers (see pp. 36-41 below), were unacceptable both
dogmatically and exegetically. In the former respect, an attack against
the historical reliability of Chronicles was simultaneously an attack
against the authority of the Bible and against the foundations of the
Christian faith. The dogmatic standpoint, in Keil's opinion, gained
considerable support from the historical and exegetical analysis of
Chronicles. One of the main elements of the exegetical analysis was an
examination of the issue of Chronicles' sources. In a lengthy discussion
of this issue,[12] Keil reached a conclusion that approximated Eichhorn's
source theory in its essentials, although Keil did not go to Eichhorn's
lengths in his speculation on the literary processes that had influenced
the form and content of the sources. According to Keil, Chronicles did
not draw on Samuel–Kings; rather, both canonical accounts were independent extracts from a common source. In addition, the author of
Chronicles had the opportunity to draw upon other source material,
especially prophetic writings.

Keeping in mind Keil's theological point of departure, it is not at all
surprising that he was even more adamant than Eichhorn that the now
unknown source material utilized in the composition of Chronicles was
historically reliable. Keil asserted that there was no reason to doubt the
historical value of Chronicles. He admitted (especially in his later

10. Cf. P. Siemens, *Carl Friedrich Keil (1807–1888): Leben und Werk* (TVG
Monographien und Studienbücher, 394; Giessen: Brunnen, 1994).
11. C.F. Keil, *Apologetischer Versuch über die Bücher der Chronik und über
die Integrität des Buches Esra* (Berlin: Ludwig Oehmigke, 1833).
12. Keil, *Apologetischer Versuch*, pp. 149-260.

works on Chronicles)[13] that this book occasionally evinced the author's parenetic aim and a certain rhetorical character. Such subjective purposes did not exactly agree with the best principles of historiography— a similar concession was also made by Eichhorn in his later days[14]—but the historical significance of this was nevertheless much less consequential than the incontrovertible fact that authentic source material had been available to the author of Chronicles. For Keil's more profound, methodological reflections on Chronicles, one must consider this concession and its ramifications concerning Chr.'s method of presentation. For Keil, the source issue was primarily one that was directly connected with history and historical facticity, and its nature and goal were determined by his theological presuppositions.[15]

Other noteworthy Chronicles scholars of the nineteenth century who, like Keil, followed Eichhorn's conviction that Samuel–Kings did not belong to the historically valuable and trustworthy sources from which Chronicles had been compiled, were H.A.C. Hävernick, O. Zöckler, E. Rupprecht and, in England, S. Davidson (originally).[16] What links all these scholars together is precisely the kind of historical and theological conservatism exemplified by Keil. Chronicles' historical unreliability— about which a few critics under de Wette's guidance had spoken in no uncertain terms—was for them as impossible a historical contention as it was fundamentally erroneous from the theological point of view. Source theories provided an efficient (and to all appearances an exegetically justifiable) means of defending this position, since a straight line led from the postulate of historically accurate sources, carefully followed by Chr. in his work despite occasional evidence of his subjective aims, to the historically reliable book of Chronicles, and from there again to the theologically conservative biblical dogma. If need arose, argumentation could naturally run in the opposite direction as well. We

---

13. See Keil's *Biblischer Commentar über die nachexilischen Geschichtsbücher: Chronik, Esra, Nehemia und Esther* (BC, 5; Leipzig: Dörffling & Franke, 1870), pp. 1-390; *Lehrbuch der historisch-kritischen Einleitung in die kanonischen und apokryphischen Schriften des Alten Testamentes* (Frankfurt am Main: Heyder & Zimmer, 3rd edn, 1873), pp. 439-76.

14. See J.G. Eichhorn, *Einleitung in das Alte Testament*, III (Göttingen: Carl Eduard Rosenbusch, 4th edn, 1823), pp. 598-605.

15. For a fuller discussion of Keil's treatment of Chronicles, see Peltonen, *History Debated*, pp.113-21. See also Siemens, *Keil*, pp. 183-89.

16. See Peltonen, *History Debated*, pp. 121-28, 176-84, 553-54.

can observe here the same fundamental phenomenon as in Eichhorn's position: source theories had an important function in the execution of the historically oriented and theologically traditional approach that governed most areas of Chronicles research in these decades. In the framework of such a general concept, source postulates constituted an indispensable link between historical conservatism and theological traditionalism.

The nineteenth-century combination of historical and theological conservatism provided rich soil for the theory that there were non-canonical, historically reliable sources behind Chronicles. Quite naturally then, source criticism received a historically conditioned version of what I have called source criticism as theory. In the twentieth century, historicism has had to loosen its hold on the study of the Hebrew Bible, and the entire field of research has become increasingly varied. This fundamental change is naturally visible in the study of Chronicles, too, but the conservative historical paradigm has, nevertheless, not disappeared altogether. Historically oriented source-critical theories intended to defend Chronicles' relative historical reliability, the basic elements of which derive from the era of Eichhorn and Keil, are still to be found—though with numerous modifications as to their details—in the sector of the early twentieth-century research, where Chronicles was highly regarded as a reliable source for historical information about the pre-exilic period.[17] Likewise, in quite recent research the notion that Chr. based his account on the careful use of trustworthy source material, common to him and DtrH, has won some support, again with conclusions supporting Chronicles' general historical usefulness.[18]

This first approach to Chronicles is to a great extent one that promoted and advanced the theological and historical ideals of its own age. Its motivation grew from assumptions that were anything but methodologically critical. Its crucial aspect is an assumption that the

17. See Peltonen, *History Debated*, pp. 526-76. At this point, reference may be made to Roman Catholic research on Chronicles in the nineteenth and early twentieth centuries. Due to its own specific theological presuppositions, it was in practice mostly along the same lines as Approach I as regards the questions of how Chronicles' sources and their use by its author had to be understood and what conclusions were to be drawn from this concerning Chronicles' historical value (Peltonen, *History Debated*, pp. 576-621).

18. See, in particular, H.R. Macy, 'The Sources of the Books of Chronicles: A Reassessment' (PhD dissertation, Harvard University, 1975).

parallel histories of Israel were connected with each other not directly but via common source material, in addition to which the author of Chronicles had other extra-biblical sources at his disposal. To be meaningful at all, such an assumption requires its adherents to reason that Chr. utilized his sources so that their content as a whole (or at least as far as all important elements are concerned) is now preserved in his work. When Chr. is presumed to have had access to extra-biblical sources and when, as it is necessary to believe, he followed them faithfully, the problem of his history's character and reliability is essentially pushed back from being his responsibility to being that of his sources. Consequently, Chr. himself remains a relatively anemic transcriber of older materials, without any noteworthy literary or theological objectives. This was—and naturally still is—a useful perspective, if one wishes to present Chr. as a well-intentioned and accurate historian. If his work appears to contain problematic features, it can be argued that he was a prisoner of his sources, so to speak, a victim of circumstance, by no means an author who despite his own special purposes would not have striven for truthfulness in his presentation of history. Again, if Chr.'s work has preserved historically valuable information, the credit must given to his historically reliable sources. As can be observed right away, argumentation very easily runs in a vicious circle: Chronicles' reliability was justified by the author's use of reliable sources, and the reliability of his sources was in turn justified by the reliability of the net result of his work. The existence of a source and the trustworthiness of some piece of information in Chronicles were thus corresponding postulates that could be deduced from each other. Consequently, the scholarly positions about Chronicles' sources discussed above were locked in metahistorical speculation with little possibility of addressing the issue on the basis of sound methodological argumentation.

Approach II: There Were Both Known and Unknown Sources

Since the early decades of the nineteenth century, there existed another approach that closely resembled Approach I but also deviated significantly from it in certain respects. The fundamental idea of Approach II, as I shall call it, was that there were behind Chronicles both sources that are no longer extant but whose existence is obvious from Chr.'s source citations (thus also Approach I) and sources that are extant. The latter naturally include Samuel–Kings in the present Hebrew Bible—and, to a lesser extent, other biblical books, too. Similarities between Chronicles and Samuel–Kings were explained in this approach by Chr. having followed Samuel–Kings, while differences attested the use of other source material.

As a matter of fact, Approach II won wider support than Approach I in the nineteenth century. Furthermore, it seems to have survived in its essentials in modern Chronicles research, albeit as a kind of intermixture with Approach III (to be discussed below) and with some important modifications of its basic elements. The best way to describe Approach II is again to take a couple of typical examples from the rich spectrum of the history of research. Though not a widely known figure in the history of research on the Hebrew Bible in general, F.C. Movers (1806–56), a Roman Catholic theologian and orientalist,[19] made significant contributions to Chronicles research in more than one respect: not only was he the first Christian scholar to advocate explicitly the hypothesis of the literary unity of Chronicles and the book of Ezra, but he also played a prominent role in shifting the mid-nineteenth-century paradigm in the study of Chronicles' historical reliability.

In 1834, Movers published a lengthy review of C.F. Keil's *Apologetischer Versuch*. He believed that Keil's attempt to demonstrate the historical trustworthiness of Chronicles was in itself a creditable enterprise. Unfortunately, Keil was fundamentally mistaken in his interpretation of the relationship of Chronicles to Samuel–Kings. Movers argued that the notion that the author of Chronicles had not utilized Samuel–Kings as his source freed Keil from paying proper attention to the similarities and differences between the parallel accounts. What Keil's position achieved was merely to transform problems between Chronicles and Samuel–Kings into a meaningless speculation about Chr.'s possible extra-biblical sources. Such a vague conception of the materials used in the composition of Chronicles did not do justice at all to the character and fundamental elements of Chr.'s historiography, however, and thus Keil's position failed to be scientifically persuasive. Movers himself was of the opinion that one needed no minute analysis of the parallelism between the canonical histories to realize that such a close interconnection could result only from Chr.'s having resorted to the older material in Samuel–Kings in the form we now have it as his main source.[20]

---

19. F.H. Reusch, 'Movers: Franz Karl M.', *ADB* (1885), XXII, pp. 417-18.

20. See Movers's review of C.F. Keil, *Apologetischer Versuch*, in *Zeitschrift für Philosophie und katholische Theologie* 10 (1834), pp. 132-44; 11 (1834), pp. 149-69.

Movers severely criticized the methodology of Approach I and demanded that scholars acknowledge what even a superficial glance showed to be obvious about the relationship of Chronicles to Samuel–Kings. In other words, he drew attention precisely to the methodological vagueness of the approach so conveniently used in the service of theological goals (see the discussion of Approach I above). Movers's own theory of Chronicles' sources[21] held that Chr. had used two main sources when he compiled his history: one was Samuel–Kings and the other a postexilic Midrash of the book of the Kings (cf. 2 Chron. 24.27), a work based on an earlier book of Kings. This latter work used one of the same sources that the canonical Samuel–Kings used: the ancient royal annals of Judah and Israel. Just as Chronicles was a revision of Samuel–Kings, Chr.'s second main source was a revision of its source, the book of Kings, in a postexilic spirit. The Midrash possessed obvious parenetic and didactic propensities, and historical concerns had been subordinate to the work's basic purpose. The midrashic traits were to be seen in Chr.'s work, too, since he had treated his midrashic sources essentially as he had dealt with Samuel–Kings: he had followed them closely, mostly copying their text verbatim. An annalistic writing of history as exhibited by Chr. was, according to Movers, typical not of him alone but of ancient Near Eastern history writing in general.[22]

Once the dependence of Chronicles on Samuel–Kings was recognized, according to Movers, it then became possible to uncover Chr.'s own distinctive contribution to his history. A careful comparison of the canonical accounts of Israel's history from David to the exile showed that while Chr. usually followed the text of his canonical source closely, he occasionally had made certain modifications. These appeared to follow a certain pattern that revealed Chr.'s own share in the transformation of historical traditions: by introducing didactic and parenetic tendencies, an apologetic approach and a predilection for cultic matters, Chr. showed not only his dependence on the conception of history of his own age but also his motivation for addressing himself to acute

21. F.C. Movers's book, *Kritische Untersuchungen über die biblische Chronik: Ein Beitrag zur Einleitung in das alte Testament* (Bonn: T. Habicht, 1834) appeared in the same year as his review of Keil's work.

22. Movers, *Kritische Untersuchungen*. For his discussion of Chronicles' sources, see, in particular, pp. 95-197.

religious and political issues of his day.[23] Such a theory of Chr.'s sources and his use of them in no way endangered Chronicles' historical value, however. Movers argued that since Samuel–Kings had already had canonical status in Chr.'s day, his manner of using them and his midrashic source as historical documents on a par with each other strongly favored the idea that there had been 'an essential agreement'[24] between Chr.'s main sources in historical matters. As Chr. had followed both his main sources faithfully, no real historical problems remained to be solved: Chr.'s account was no less reliable than his historical sources had been.[25]

Movers's interpretation of Chronicles' historical value—the prime issue of his day in Chronicles research—was in all important respects similar to that advocated by other conservative scholars of his day. Precisely as for the latter, a theory about Chr.'s extra-biblical sources was crucial for him. The essential difference between Movers's view and Approach I is that Movers included Samuel–Kings among the sources that Chr. had utilized directly. This very simple contention,[26]

23. See Movers, *Kritische Untersuchungen*, pp. 1-9, 198-336.

24. Movers, *Kritische Untersuchungen*, p. 172.

25. For a more thorough discussion of Movers's views, especially with regard to Chronicles' historical nature and value, see Peltonen, *History Debated*, pp. 128-36. For Movers's interpretation of Chronicles' sources, see also M.P. Graham, *The Utilization of 1 and 2 Chronicles in the Reconstruction of Israelite History in the Nineteenth Century* (SBLDS, 116; Atlanta: Scholars Press, 1990), pp. 49-50.

26. In fact, Movers was not the first conservative scholar who explicitly argued that Chr.'s main source had been Samuel–Kings, in addition to which he had had access to other historically reliable sources for the information now known only from his work. This view was advanced in a lengthy anonymous essay on Chronicles entitled, 'Die Bücher der Chronik: Ihr Verhältniss zu den Büchern Samuels und der Könige; ihre Glaubwürdigkeit, und die Zeit ihrer Abfassung', *TQ* 13 (1831), pp. 201-82. *Theologische Quartalschrift* was a Catholic publication, and it is commonly believed that the author of this essay was the Roman Catholic scholar J.G. Herbst. As for subsequent developments in the history of research, though, Movers's position was much more influential than that of the anonymous author, since the essay's primary goal was not to attain insight into Chronicles' historiographical nature. Instead, it intended to provide incontrovertible proof, in accordance with the 'spirit' of the day, that the author of Chronicles had used historically reliable extra-biblical sources in addition to Samuel–Kings. In the author's view, this position demonstrated that Chronicles contained entirely trustworthy historical information about the monarchical period, in spite of the comments to the contrary by de Wette and others.

accepted as self-evident by contemporary critical scholars (see pp. 49-52 below), provided him with a methodological starting point and apparatus for the evaluation of Chr.'s own contribution. Those scholars who advanced the view of Chronicles' sources articulated in Approach I (e.g. Keil) could surely refer to Chr.'s own emphases and/or characteristic traits, but ultimately, such references held little value, since there was no precise, methodological means to control them. Even though Movers shared the conservative historical paradigm of his day and reached typical conclusions about Chronicles' historicity, his source theory nevertheless introduced a decisive change into this constellation: methodological control of Chr.'s literary procedures. This enabled the researcher to define more clearly how Chr. treated his source material and, consequently, to assess Chr.'s motives and characteristics as a historiographer. In this way Movers's source-critical theory constituted a methodological advance in the argument for Chronicles' historical reliability (characteristic of Approach I) by making a conscious effort to understand the author of this biblical book as an interpreter of historical traditions, and his work as an independent contribution to ancient Israelite historiography.

Movers's view of Chronicles' sources was developed further by Heinrich Ewald (1803–75), one of the most illustrious and controversial biblical scholars and orientalists of the nineteenth century, although from a somewhat different standpoint. Whereas it had been important to Movers to understand the nature of chronistic historiography from both literary and historical perspectives, Ewald's interest was more in Chronicles as a historical source, and his ideal was to picture the history of Israel just as it had taken place in reality, a positivistic ideal that would permeate his work. According to Ewald, this goal could be attained when sources recording this history were subjected to an unprejudiced critical analysis for the purpose of sifting from them every possible piece of useful information for historical reconstruction. Furthermore, he was a priori convinced that objective historical research would demonstrate the strong historical basis of biblical traditions. Thus, the critical investigation of biblical sources was able to produce an abundance of material for the reconstruction of Israelite history 'as it really had been'. Ewald argued further that this reconstruction was a valuable undertaking both historically and theologically, since it not only increased historical knowledge but also revealed the fundamental uniqueness of biblical history among the histories of all other nations as

well as the divine plan that finally led to the realization of the highest
religious ideal in Christianity.[27]

In accordance with these principles, Chronicles' description of
Israel's pre-exilic history was subjected by Ewald to critical investigation in order to find out how much 'real' historical information it contained.[28] Though not as reliable historically as the staunchest conserva-
tives had acclaimed, Chronicles nevertheless offered, Ewald firmly
believed, plenty of information that was extremely valuable for an
objective scientific reconstruction of Israel's history in biblical times. It
should be observed, however, that even though Ewald spoke loudly in
favor of objective and critical investigation of historical sources
generally, in the case of Chronicles he was unable to connect it with the
aforementioned theological view of the nature and significance of
Israel's history without resorting to source theory. First, according to
him, Chr. had used older biblical materials. Samuel–Kings had been
utilized by him like any ordinary source, however, since it was not yet
regarded as possessing canonical authority. This can be seen both from
the fact that Chr. had occasionally made substantial alterations to
Samuel–Kings and the observation that he had represented the general
course of the history of Israel somewhat differently from it. Secondly,
Chr. had made use of non-canonical documents to which he either
directly referred by name or indirectly alluded (genealogical information, etc.) but the contents of which he did not reproduce in full in his

27. See, in particular, H. Ewald, *Geschichte des Volkes Israel bis Christus*, I
(Göttingen: Dieterich, 1843), pp. 3-60. For discussions of Ewald's interpretation of
Israel's history, see, e.g., T.K. Cheyne, *Founders of Old Testament Criticism: Bio-
graphical, Descriptive, and Critical Studies* (London: Methuen, 1893), pp. 66-118;
J. Wellhausen, 'Heinrich Ewald', in *Festschrift zur Feier des 150 jährigen
Bestehens der Königlichen Gesellschaft der Wissenschaften zu Göttingen* (Berlin:
Weidmann, 1901), pp. 61-81 (pp. 120-38 in R. Smend [ed.], *Grundrisse zum Alten
Testament* [TBü, 27; Munich: Chr. Kaiser Verlag, 1965]); T.W. Davies, *Heinrich
Ewald, Orientalist and Theologian: A Centenary Appreciation* (London: T. Fisher
Unwin, 1903); Kraus, *Erforschung*, pp. 199-205; J.W. Rogerson, *Old Testament
Criticism in the Nineteenth Century: England and Germany* (London: SPCK,
1984), pp. 91-103; Graham, *Utilization*, pp. 69-75; J.H. Hayes, 'The History of the
Study of Israelite and Judaean History', in J.H. Hayes and J.M. Miller (eds.),
Israelite and Judaean History (London: SCM Press; Valley Forge, PA: Trinity
Press International, 1990), pp. 59-61; Peltonen, *History Debated*, pp. 141-45.

28. For Ewald's treatment of Chronicles–Ezra–Nehemiah, see *Geschichte*, I, pp.
215-54; on the question of Chr.'s sources, see, in particular, pp. 233-53.

work. He had also drawn upon some works that he had so completely fused into his own history that there was no longer any need to mention them explicitly. For Ewald, precisely as for Movers, then, a proper point of departure for assessing the historical character and usefulness of Chronicles was to assume that non-parallel information in it was derived from older, now unknown sources.

An important element of Ewald's concept of Chronicles' sources was his observation that Chr.'s way of using Samuel–Kings showed him to have been a historian who not only wrote factual history as such—of course, he had done just that by compiling faithfully from his sources—but who also had taken certain liberties in arranging and presenting his materials. Observing, as he clearly did, the history of Israel from a peculiar postexilic priestly viewpoint, Chr. sometimes took great license in using historical events as a medium for advancing his religious purposes. What was of prime importance, however, in Ewald's view, was that when one assessed the historicity of chronistic materials, one should make a clear distinction between a tradition describing a historical event and the historical kernel of this tradition, that is to say, between what the author had taken from his sources and what seemed to be characteristic of him in terms of his conceptual world and manners of expression. Ewald believed that information derived from a source was reliable unless there were compelling reasons to think otherwise. Consequently, the task of objective historical research was to strip from Chronicles everything that appeared problematic in the light of other sources of Israel's pre-exilic history. What remained after this operation was usable material for historical reconstruction, drawn by Chr. from some now unknown source. And, according to Ewald, there was much such usable material in Chr.'s work.[29]

In Ewald's view, then, postulates concerning authentic historical sources at Chr.'s disposal were supported by objective historical research, though a closer examination indicates that these two aspects were intertwined in a circular way, very similar to that in Approach I. An influential background factor was also Ewald's above-mentioned theological scheme of the nature of ancient Israel's history and of the documents describing it. It was not to be endangered by the results of historical research. It is this fact that effectively prevented the critical

29. For discussions of Ewald's treatment of Chronicles, see Graham, *Utilization*, pp. 76-82; Peltonen, *History Debated*, pp. 145-50.

historical evaluation of ancient sources, so vigorously advocated by
Ewald in the name of objective research, from being able to work without traditional source postulates in the case of Chronicles. Compared to
Approach I, however, Ewald's position signified a methodological step
forward in the respect that a more varied concept of Chronicles' sources
made it possible, within the boundaries set by the theological interpretation of Israel's history, to try to understand and define Chr.'s active
use of sources instead of just giving the entire question of Chr.'s
sources a functional role, that of offering support for a preordained
view of Chr. as a trustworthy historian.

Many of those who came after Ewald adopted his views and held that
Chr. had drawn upon both canonical and non-canonical sources and
worked as an independent historian, exhibiting a certain freedom in his
handling of sources. This perspective surfaces in the works on Chronicles by such scholars as E. Bertheau, A. Dillmann (although there is
some vacillation between Approaches I and II in his source conception), F. Bleek, F. Hitzig, J.J. Stähelin and, again in England, in the later
works of S. Davidson.[30] Closer to the turn of the century, such scholars
as S. Oettli, A. Klostermann, C.J. Ball and W.E. Barnes were also basically very close to the Ewaldian understanding of Chronicles' sources.[31]

Compared to Approach I, Approach II advances a more flexible view
of Chronicles' historical value, although it still clearly remains within
the limits of a conservative stance on this issue. Justice was done, at
least in principle, to Chr.'s biases, and from the historical point of view,
Samuel–Kings was usually preferred to Chronicles as a historical

---

30. The views about Chronicles and its sources presented by these scholars have
been discussed by Peltonen, *History Debated*, pp. 150-64, 176-84. Cf. also Graham,
Utilization, pp. 82-91, 95-96, 102-103. Of them, Stähelin and Hitzig could even tell
the reader that the now-lost important source used by Chr. for his non-parallel
information had in fact been compiled by none other than the great scribe Ezra; see
F. Hitzig's review of F.C. Movers, *Kritische Untersuchungen*, in *Heidelberger
Jahrbücher für Literatur* 28 (1835), pp. 135-38; J.J. Stähelin, *Specielle Einleitung
in die kanonischen Bücher des Alten Testaments* (Elberfeld: R.L. Friderichs, 1862),
pp. 139-45, 159-62. The goal for such an assumption was, of course, to associate
Chr.'s non-canonical main source, which threatened to become somewhat vague
and indefinite if the Movers–Ewald view was accepted in an 'absolute' form, with
an authoritative historical figure and thus provide an extra guarantee of the historical trustworthiness of Chronicles' non-parallel sections.

31. See Peltonen, *History Debated*, pp. 482-87, 493-99. Cf. also Graham,
Utilization, pp. 183-86, 187-89, 233-35.

source. An important factor that contributed to this kind of shift in emphasis is the change that took place in the assessment of what had actually been Chr.'s sources. The acceptance of the fact that Samuel–Kings was among Chr.'s sources made it possible to analyze Chr.'s method of utilizing his sources, and this brought with it a methodological corrective that eliminated at least part of the source speculation so typical of Approach I. At the same time, the change in methodological dimension opened entirely new angles to attempts to understand the different aspects of Chr.'s history, not only as history in the traditional sense but also as a religious lesson, for example, in which history had primarily an instrumental value.

The change in methodological dimension does not reflect concrete development in the basic concept of source criticism, however. Rather, it makes a slight concession to the cumulative effect of critical studies in the wake of de Wette (see below) without giving up the conservative perspective on historical issues. It also, however, reflects the influence of new ideological trends in scientific research on the study of Chronicles. Above all, it reflects the combined effort of the positivistic ideal of historical science and historicism to create an objective historical method that enabled one to sift from basically unhistorical ancient traditions as much factual history as possible, by piercing their ideologically conditioned, outward appearances to the historical kernel itself, if there was one. In practice, the issue of Chr.'s sources was treated within the framework of a source-critical theory of some kind, the basis of which was the conviction that the information in Chronicles proved historical by scientific research had been derived from some source that Chr. had utilized verbatim or in some form. Thus we can see that within Approach II, as well, it was the historical aspect that necessarily determined the methodology and goals of Chronicles research: source postulates were needed when one created a portraiture of Chronicles as a generally trustworthy source of history. The reason for this was the nature of the critical study of Chronicles as 'positive criticism'[32] in the circles where Approach II gained the strongest foothold during the period discussed. Idealistic dimensions were attributed to the history of Israel as a whole (see Ewald, in particular),

32. The term has been borrowed from J.W. Rogerson's essay, 'The Old Testament', in J.W. Rogerson, C. Rowland and B. Lindars, *The Study and Use of the Bible* (The History of Christian Theology, 2; Basingstoke: Marshall Pickering; Grand Rapids: Eerdmans, 1988), pp. 1-150, esp. p. 116.

and biblical history was regarded as directed and controlled by an unfolding of some divine purpose. In other words, theology of history set strict limits to the critical investigation of history.

Approach III: Known Sources Are the Only Ones that Matter
In 1806, the twenty-six-year-old W.M.L. de Wette (1780–1849) published a revolutionary work on Chronicles entitled *Kritischer Versuch über die Glaubwürdigkeit der Bücher der Chronik mit Hinsicht auf die Geschichte der Mosaischen Bücher und Gesetzgebung* ('Critical Investigation into the Credibility of the Books of Chronicles with Respect to the History of the Mosaic Books and Giving of the Law') as the first volume of his *Beiträge zur Einleitung in das Alte Testament*.[33] The title indicates what the author had in mind. He was convinced that the traditional notion of the Mosaic authorship of the Pentateuch was false, and the religious and cultic legislation in it was a product of a much later age. He observed that the parallel accounts describing the preexilic cult and religious practices in Israel differed markedly from each other. Chronicles pictured this history as guided by the laws of Moses, whereas one could deduce from Samuel–Kings that such laws were not at all operative. Traditionally this fact had been explained by assuming that Samuel–Kings did not describe history primarily from the religious-cultic viewpoint, while Chronicles was doing precisely that. De Wette argued that this explanation was untenable, since it was obvious that Samuel–Kings did not intend to be a purely 'historical' (i.e. religiously neutral) composition. Consequently, only one of the parallel accounts could be veracious, while the other offered a distorted picture of Israel's monarchic history. De Wette's objective was to demonstrate the lateness of the Pentateuchal legislation by showing that it was the chronistic portrayal of this history that was unreliable throughout.[34]

De Wette naturally had his reasons for such a set of conclusions, but we need not go into them in detail here.[35] For our purposes it is

33. W.M.L. de Wette, *Kritischer Versuch über die Glaubwürdigkeit der Bücher der Chronik mit Hinsicht auf die Geschichte der Mosaischen Bücher und Gesetzgebung: Ein Nachtrag zu den Vaterschen Untersuchungen über den Pentateuch* (Halle: Schimmelpfennig & Compagnie, 1806).

34. See Peltonen, *History Debated*, pp. 76-77.

35. There are a number of thorough discussions of de Wette's work on the Bible and its importance to the history of biblical research; see, in particular, R. Smend, *Wilhelm Martin Leberecht de Wettes Arbeit am Alten und am Neuen Testament*

sufficient to pay attention to the fact that, basically, Chronicles research was for him a case of a proper understanding of history as much as it was for Eichhorn, Keil, Ewald and other eminent Chronicles scholars of this era, despite the differences in their respective points of departure and ensuing results. De Wette intended to prove with his critical treatment of Chronicles that the book was historically unreliable, in order to be able to probe into the real character of Israel's pre-exilic history from the standpoint of the earlier prophets.[36] For him, it should be observed, the demonstration of Chronicles' historical untrustworthiness was merely an intermediate stop on the way to an examination of more important issues in the Hebrew Bible. In de Wette's thinking, analytic and destructive historical criticism of biblical books, of which his treatment of Chronicles is a prime example, was naturally more than just historically 'negative' destruction for destruction's sake. Showing the unhistorical nature of the biblical texts was ultimately a means to a deeper theological and philosophical perception and interpretation of the biblical *Darstellung* of history and its intentions in an appropriate religious and aesthetic framework, that is, as evidence of the religious intuitions of the Jewish nation. Chronicles was not the biblical book that would have offered de Wette the most fruitful possibilities for the explication of such a 'positive' religio-philosophical and theological program, however. On the contrary, Chronicles was more an obstacle to implementing this program on the more important biblical materials, because it totally obscured the true course of the history of Israel's religion and its development.[37] That is why it was only history that concerned de Wette in Chronicles.

De Wette set strict maxims for historical criticism to be methodologically coherent as well as for a document to be regarded as historically

---

(Basel: Helbing & Lichtenhahn, 1958); Smend, 'De Wette und das Verhältnis zwischen historischer Bibelkritik und philosophischem System im 19. Jahrhundert', *ThZ* 14 (1958), pp. 107-19; Smend, *Alttestamentler*, pp. 38-52; Kraus, *Erforschung*, pp. 174-89; Rogerson, *Old Testament Criticism*, pp. 28-49; J.W. Rogerson, *W.M.L. de Wette, Founder of Modern Biblical Criticism: An Intellectual Biography* (JSOTSup, 126; Sheffield: JSOT Press, 1992). The views of de Wette especially in connection with Chronicles research have been discussed in more detail recently by Graham, *Utilization*, pp. 10-34; and Peltonen, *History Debated*, pp. 69-82.

36. Cf. also S. Japhet, 'The Historical Reliability of Chronicles: The History of the Problem and its Place in Biblical Research', *JSOT* 33 (1985), pp. 84-85.

37. Cf. the discussion in Peltonen, *History Debated*, pp. 74-76.

reliable.[38] One thing about which he was adamant (and here we come to
the question of Chronicles' sources) was that a critical historian had to
rely solely upon available sources. Everything that went beyond the
actual sources at hand resulted only in hypothetical constructions. From
this point of departure, de Wette launched a fierce attack on the dominant view of his day that Chronicles was a historically reliable work.
The main target of his criticism was J.G. Eichhorn and especially Eichhorn's source postulates, with which he tried to vindicate Chronicles'
trustworthiness. According to de Wette, one was able to bring forward
no evidence whatsoever that the short biographies of David and
Solomon (as well as other non-canonical sources) postulated by Eichhorn had actually ever existed.[39] He did not regard the idea of Chr.'s
having had some now unknown source material before him as entirely
impossible in principle, but since there was no tangible proof of it, it
was useless to speculate further about it. Hypothetical constructions
could not 'save' Chronicles from historical criticism and its indis-
putable results. De Wette argued that the only concrete fact to which a
historian could safely hold in the study of Chronicles was that its author
had used Samuel–Kings in its present form as his source. The considerable differences between the canonical histories were due solely to Chr.
As de Wette carefully demonstrated, Chr. had altered, embellished and
distorted his sources, since he was not only a careless and ignorant
writer but also tendentious in his predilection for Levites and the
Judean cult and religion and in his hatred for the northern kingdom.
Therefore, one had no alternative but to conclude that Chronicles had
no value whatsoever as a source for historical reconstruction of the pre-
exilic period.[40] The way was now wide open for the assessment of the
Pentateuch and the history of Israelite religion in a new light, free from
the chronistic distortion.[41]

38. See the second volume of de Wette's *Beiträge zur Einleitung in das Alte
Testament* entitled, *Kritik der israelitischen Geschichte. Erster Theil: Kritik der
Mosaischen Geschichte* (Halle: Schimmelpfennig & Compagnie, 1807), pp. 1-18.

39. De Wette, *Kritischer Versuch*, pp. 10-41.

40. De Wette, *Kritischer Versuch*, pp. 42-132.

41. 'So wie die ganze Jüdische Geschichte von ihrer interessantesten und
wichtigsten Seite, nämlich der der Religion und des gottesdienstlichen Cultus, nach
Wegräumung der Nachrichten der Chronik, welche, die Geschichte der frühesten
Zeiten durch das gefärbte Medium später Esraisch-levitischer Jahrhunderte
darstellend, so lange die rechte Ansicht gestört und die Geschichtsforscher irre
geführt hat, eine ganz andere Gestalt erhält; so erhalten auch die Untersuchungen

The 'source' from which the non-parallel materials in Chronicles derived was thus nothing more than the author's religious imagination. This conclusion of de Wette's freed the critical investigation of Chronicles with one crushing blow from the source hypotheses that had enjoyed great popularity before him (and also long after him, for that matter, as we have observed above). Regarding the particular issue of Chronicles' sources, de Wette could easily have taken the decisive step from source-critical theory to source-critical method as a methodologically reflected assessment of the literary nature of Chronicles. This was not the case, however. What was common to both parties of the debate concerning Chr.'s non-canonical sources was that source postulates or the criticism of them were put at the service of a historically orientated formulation of the entire issue. For Eichhorn, Keil and their kindred spirits, the function of source postulates was to uphold Chronicles' historicity, while de Wette's criticism of them aimed at a conclusive demonstration of its unhistoricity. Another feature common to both parties was the significance of a certain theological perspective as an element that supported the status quo of historical orientation, although with drastically different historical conclusions, depending on the party with which a scholar was associated. Whereas Approaches I and II used source-critical theory to maintain a picture of Chr. as a good historian, Approach III made him a historian of the worst kind with the simple claim that the only thing that was certain was that Chr. had used canonical sources with consequences now visible in the Hebrew Bible. De Wette's historically conditioned source postulate criticism thus turned the edifice of the historically conservative source-critical theory upside down, but it was unable to set itself free from the underlying historical paradigm. It follows from this that even after de Wette the critical study of Chronicles could not do without a source-critical theory of some sort or a negation of it.

The closest followers of de Wette with regard to the question of Chronicles' sources and its historical ramifications were C.P.W. Gramberg, according to whom Chr.'s source references were nothing but empty pomp;[42] the English bishop J.W. Colenso, who claimed that

---

über den Pentateuch auf einmal eine ganz andere Wendung: eine Menge lästiger, schwer wegzuräumender Beweise für das frühe Vorhandenseyn der Mosaischen Bücher sind verschwunden, die andern Spuren ihrer Existenz stellen sich nunmehr in ein anderes Licht ... ' (de Wette, *Kritischer Versuch*, p. 135).

42. See C.P.W. Gramberg, *Die Chronik nach ihrem geschichtlichen Charakter*

Chr.'s hypothetical non-canonical source was a mere phantom;[43] B. Stade, according to whom speculation about the non-canonical sources of Chronicles could interest only those who for some apologetic reasons could not accept the fact that one of the canonical books contained a tendentious reshaping of older traditions;[44] and the American C.C. Torrey, who opined that Chr.'s vividness of imagination and power of invention were surpassed by few, if any, of all the biblical narrators.[45] Later, R.H. Pfeiffer would argue that 'the midrashic ghost source of the Chronicler', postulated by a number of scholars, should be relegated 'to the limbo of illusions where it rightly belongs', and Chr. himself, utterly devoid of historical sense, should be regarded not as a mere compiler or redactor of source materials but as 'a writer of great originality, vivid imagination, and granitic convictions', whose fantasy in creating picturesque tales would make him an eligible contributor to the Arabian Nights—were it not for the devout and earnest purpose of his work.[46] In the most recent Chronicles research, the view that one looks in vain for extra-biblical sources behind Chronicles is to be found in the works of R. North and J. Becker, for example.[47] Historical conclusions based on de Wette's interpretation of Chronicles' nature and sources were taken to extremes by Gramberg and Colenso, in particular, who made Chr. with his alleged endless perversions of history and his 'dead' sense of historical truth look like a caricature of a historian. Such allegations demonstrate the consequences of neglecting de Wette's theologi-

und ihrer Glaubwürdigkeit neu geprüft (Halle: Eduard Anton, 1823), pp. 22-66.

43. J.W. Colenso, *The Pentateuch and Book of Joshua Critically Examined*, VII (London: Longman, Green, Longman, Roberts & Green, 1879), pp. 305-306. See also Colenso, *Lectures on the Pentateuch and the Moabite Stone* (London: Longmans, Green, & Co., 2nd edn, 1873), pp. 332-46.

44. B. Stade, *Geschichte des Volkes Israel*, I (Allgemeine Geschichte in Einzeldarstellungen, 1/6; Berlin: G. Grote, 1887), p. 83.

45. See, in particular, C.C. Torrey's essay 'The Chronicler as Editor and as Independent Narrator', in *Ezra Studies* (Chicago: University of Chicago Press, 1910), pp. 208-51.

46. R.H. Pfeiffer, *Introduction to the Old Testament* (New York: Harper & Brothers, rev. edn, 1948), pp. 805-806.

47. See R. North, 'Does Archeology Prove Chronicles Sources?', in H.N. Bream, R.D. Heim and C.A. Moore (eds.), *A Light unto my Path: Old Testament Studies in Honor of Jacob M. Myers* (GTS, 4; Philadelphia: Temple University, 1974), pp. 375-401; J. Becker, *1 Chronik* (NEB, 18; Würzburg: Echter Verlag, 1986); and Becker, *2 Chronik* (NEB, 20; Würzburg: Echter Verlag, 1988).

cal and religio-philosophical motivation for destructive historical criticism and making historical criticism as destructive historical analysis an end in itself. What deserves attention at this point, however, is that a rejection of all sorts of source theories provided an opportunity to emphasize and assess Chr.'s independent contribution as one who transmits historical tradition.

Even though de Wette's views were subjected to heavy criticism (see Approaches I and II), and voices such as those of Gramberg and Colenso may be regarded as representing a diversion in the history of serious research, one can still say with full justification that all critical Chronicles research after de Wette has continued to build on the basic elements of his interpretation of Chronicles' sources and historicity. Significant modifications naturally have been made to several of his views, but a fundamental factor that links later research inseparably to de Wette is the general acceptance of the fact that it is to Chr.'s use of the known canonical sources that one must turn in order to appreciate fully what Chr. was doing when he composed his history. Irrespective of any hypothetical, non-canonical sources he may have had at his disposal and of theories grounded on a speculation about them, an investigation of the relationship between his work and its canonical main source is believed to be the one that provides real insight into the historical and theological intentions and goals of Chr. and his work.

Source Criticism as Theory and Method in Chronicles Research

What emerges from the previous discussion is that due to its historical and theological liabilities the source-critical study of Chronicles did not progress from a construction of source theories—or from a criticism of their construction—to methodological source-critical research. One may naturally claim that all kinds of suppositions concerning documents used by Chr. as his sources constitute as such source-critical observations. It must be strongly emphasized, however, that all the source-critical theories proposed within Approaches I and II, as well as their criticism by de Wette, were not in need of the support of source-critical investigation or methodology, since their main function was to bring forward postulates for 'positive' historical (and, indirectly, theological) argumentation—or, as in the case of de Wette, present a critical assessment of the postulates in order to support historical and theological argumentation of another motivation and purpose. Such functions set history and theology above method: a good theory was not in need of methodological reflection if it succeeded in fulfilling its functional duty.

By drawing attention to Chr.'s independent contribution to the treatment and theological interpretation of historical traditions, Approaches II and III implied that historical concerns began to lose their position as the driving force and prime attraction of Chronicles research. This is true also with regard to de Wette's position in that it did not have much to say (at least nothing positive to say) about Chr. as a historian. When, in addition, the dogmatic historical-theological commitments that were characteristic of Approaches I and II became increasingly obsolete in the critical study of the Hebrew Bible toward the end of the nineteenth century, the fundamental prerequisites of source criticism as method (which up till now had been lacking) became available, at least in principle. One can see this in the development that took place when the central aspects of the approaches discussed above were combined during the first half of the twentieth century to form a generally accepted critical view of the historical nature of Chronicles.

Intermixture of Earlier Approaches:
From Historical and Theological Function to Historical Explanation
In the 1870s, the influential German scholar Julius Wellhausen (1844–1918) gave a classic formulation to the notion that prophets had preceded the law in the history of ancient Israel's religion, and the priestly law should be seen to constitute the ideological basis for postexilic Judaism. In the light of this revolutionary view of the historical development of Israel's religion according to the rules of 'secular' history, it seemed obvious that Chr. had been a faithful follower and, by means of a reinterpretation of history, an eager propagator of the priestly ideals, the religious mainstream of his day. The picture of monarchic Israel painted by this law-crazed author was colored by these ideals to such an extent that it gave only a theoretical record of what should have happened in the times of David and his followers. Thus, in the wake of Wellhausen, critical Chronicles scholars, who believed that de Wette had been correct in his insistence that the literary basis of the chronistic history had been Samuel–Kings and not some hypothetical ancient source(s), were ready to admit that Wellhausen's reconstruction of Israel's religious history showed that de Wette had also presented a basically correct characterization of Chronicles as a historical work. It was not an accurate history but a history distorted in the light of the religious concerns of its era. And Chr. himself had been a bad historian

or, rather, not a historian at all but a midrashist or the like, who had couched his ideology in the form of history. Such a view of Chronicles as an interpretation of history on the basis of its author's religious ideology rapidly gained scholarly support. It is important to observe, however, that even this position did not need, at least in principle, the support of source criticism as method in addition to what de Wette had already offered. The critical interpretation of the historical value of Chronicles was now comfortably set within the framework of a larger critical view of the religious history of Israel, and it followed from this that the earlier debate about Chr.'s sources lost much of its relevance.

Source criticism as theory did not die, however. The typically his-toricist pursuit after factual history did not leave critical scholars alone. Instead, it kept very much alive the questions of how the non-parallel material in Chronicles should be assessed and how one could avoid the possibility that de Wette's harsh verdict on Chr. as a writer of history would result in the failure to notice valuable information for the recon-struction of Israel's pre-exilic history. It was not in accord with the spirit of historicism to exclude the possibility—as de Wette appeared to do—that Chronicles could contain historically reliable information (unknown from other sources) because of a harsh moral judgment on the low quality of Chr. as a historian. Furthermore, despite the fact that the purpose of Chronicles indisputably was a pious interpretation of history rather than a conveyance of historical facts, certain passages in it (e.g. some genealogies and other lists) seemed historically more trustworthy than untrustworthy, particularly in the light of the corroboration of biblical information by the discoveries of Near Eastern archaeology. Many scholars reasoned that it was methodologically more appropriate to subject such passages to an unprejudiced critical investigation in order to clarify their historical nature than just to overlook them on the basis of a preconceived idea of Chr. as a writer of historical fiction.

It was precisely here that many scholars resorted to the idea that was typical of Approach II: Chr. must have had access to extra-biblical source material in addition to Samuel–Kings (see below). This material had been used by him either as such or in a reworked form in accor-dance with his ideological predisposition. Even a source theory suggesting that Chr. may not have used the present form of Samuel–Kings as a source at all (cf. Approach I) received occasional support,[48]

48. See, e.g., E. Reuss, *Die Geschichte der Heiligen Schriften Alten Testaments* (Braunschweig: C.A. Schwetschke & Sohn, 1881), pp. 519-21; Reuss, *Das Alte*

although now with totally different historical conclusions. Source postulates, which de Wette so impressively and openly rejected, surreptitiously crept back in. Their role was different now, however. They had been adapted to conform with the contention that Chr. was an unreliable historian not only in the light of older biblical parallels but also as far as the new scientific view of the historical development of Israel's religion was concerned. Source postulates were thus no longer used to defend Chr.'s historical trustworthiness but primarily to guard him against excessive claims of historical forgery. A general background for this phenomenon at the turn of the century was constituted not only by a historical interest pure and simple but also by a theologically motivated reaction against Wellhausen's masterfully presented reconstruction of the history of Israel's religion, which gained a foothold even in some critical circles, particularly in England and the United States.[49]

Wellhausen himself[50] admitted that his treatment of Chronicles[51] wholly followed the views of de Wette. In practice, however, he deviated from them somewhat when he argued that Chronicles, a Judaization of Israel's history in the light of the late Priestly Code, was not just an arbitrary product of an individual but owed its origin to the

---

Testament übersetzt, eingeleitet und erläutert, IV (Braunschweig: C.A. Schwetschke & Sohn, 1893), pp. 20-36; A. Kuenen, *Historisch-kritische Einleitung in die Bücher des Alten Testaments hinsichtlich ihrer Entstehung und Sammlung* (Leipzig: O.R. Reisland, 1890), 1/2, pp. 155-63; K. Budde, 'Vermutungen zum "Midrasch des Buches der Könige"', *ZAW* 12 (1892), pp. 37-51; G. Wildeboer, *Die Literatur des Alten Testaments nach der Zeitfolge ihrer Entstehung* (Göttingen: Vandenhoeck & Ruprecht, 1895), pp. 405-409; H. Winckler, 'Muṣri, Meluḫḫa, Maʿîn: Ein Beitrag zur Geschichte des ältesten Arabien und zur Bibelkritik', *Mitteilungen der vorderasiatischen Gesellschaft* 3 (1898), pp. 39-42.

49. See Peltonen, *History Debated*, pp. 290-339, 424-44, 458-68, 493-503, 526-50.

50. On Wellhausen, see L. Perlitt, *Vatke und Wellhausen: Geschichtsphilosophische Voraussetzungen und historiographische Motive für die Darstellung der Religion und Geschichte Israels durch Wilhelm Vatke und Julius Wellhausen* (BZAW, 94; Berlin: Alfred Töpelmann, 1965); D.A. Knight (ed.), *Julius Wellhausen and his Prolegomena to the History of Israel* (Semeia, 25; Chico, CA: Scholars Press, 1983); Kraus, *Erforschung*, pp. 255-74; Smend, *Alttestamentler*, pp. 99-113.

51. J. Wellhausen, *Prolegomena zur Geschichte Israels* (Berlin: W. de Gruyter, 6th edn [*Neudruck*], 1927), pp. 165-223. For a discussion of Wellhausen's views on Chronicles, see Graham, *Utilization*, pp. 144-50; Peltonen, *History Debated*, pp. 232-45.

general ideology of the period in which it was written. It was possible, therefore, that the chronistic history of the pre-exilic Israel had been produced on the basis not only of Samuel–Kings but also of some now unknown documents. Wellhausen nevertheless returned immediately to the position of de Wette by stating that this possibility had no concrete bearing on the interpretation of Chronicles' historical nature. This book was historically unreliable and remained so despite claims that there had been sources behind it. Even if these sources had been available to Chr., it merely meant that Chronicles and its sources shared the same intellectual atmosphere and historical tendencies. According to Wellhausen, it was useless to speak about Chronicles' sources except when one attempted to describe the ideological context that had produced the kind of Jewish literature that Chronicles exemplified. Thus, he rejected Chronicles' historical value as bluntly as had de Wette, but in addition he dealt a serious blow to the source postulates elaborated within Approaches I and II by asserting confidently that if it were possible to show that Chr. had drawn upon some extra-biblical sources, they were as unreliable historically as was his own work. We can see that Wellhausen added to de Wette's conception precisely the missing piece that enabled it to destroy completely the scholarly paradigm of Approaches I and II.

Wellhausen was no longer interested in Chronicles after he had demonstrated its historical unreliability and put it into its proper place in the historical development of Israel's religion. Source criticism as method did not inspire him, and an elaboration of a source-critical theory of some sort was, for him, utterly useless. Most contemporary scholars who accepted Wellhausen's reconstruction of Israel's history and his interpretation of the historical nature of Chronicles as a monument from the heyday of postexilic legalistic Judaism were not so categorical. They devoted more energy and space than did he to attempts to clarify what kinds of sources Chr. had used and to what extent he had received pieces of historical information from them. Even before Wellhausen, K.H. Graf had claimed that although Chr. described the history of his people as it was seen from the historically biased standpoint of fourth-century BCE Judaism, he had presumably been in possession of extra-biblical source material from which some of his non-parallel data (e.g. in 1 Chron. 1–9 and 23–27) had been drawn. However, Graf argued (quite like Wellhausen later) that historical significance should be accorded to this observation in occasional small details at the most, since Chr.'s sources did not antedate Samuel–Kings, his main source; their materials had already been embellished freely before Chr.; and they demonstrated the same lack of historical sense that was characteristic of ancient Jewish historiography in general.[52]

Among the Wellhausen 'school', a similar inclination to see some details of Chr.'s work[53] in a historically somewhat more 'positive' light, by accepting a source-critical theory of some kind, surfaces in the works on Chronicles by C.H. Cornill, E. Kautzsch and C. Steuernagel in continental Europe; W. Robertson Smith, S.R. Driver and W.A.L. Elmslie in England; and H.P. Smith, E.L. Curtis and J.A. Bewer in the United States, to mention but a few examples from the golden era of 'Wellhausenianism' in the late nineteenth and early twentieth centuries.[54] Simultaneously, other scholars who held a more or less critical view toward the 'Wellhausenian' reconstruction of the development of Israel's religion and/or the position of Chronicles in it came to accept a similar approach towards the sources and historicity of Chronicles. This group included such scholars as E. Sellin, E. Riehm, W. Baudissin, O. Eissfeldt and the Jewish scholar Y. Kaufmann.[55]

Naturally, there were differences in the source theories that turn-of-the-century critical scholarship developed concerning, for example, the question whether Samuel–Kings was used by Chr. as his main source (see above), and how much historical material should be credited to Chronicles. The general approach was nevertheless uniform: occasional pieces of information in Chronicles seemed historically probable even after the execution of critical analysis, and this state of affairs could best be explained by assuming that some extra-biblical source material had been available to Chr. It was improbable, though, as critical scholars virtually unanimously maintained, that the non-canonical source material would have been more ancient than Samuel–Kings or other-

52. K.H. Graf, *Die geschichtlichen Bücher des Alten Testaments: Zwei historisch-kritische Untersuchungen* (Leipzig: T.O. Weigel, 1866), pp. 114-247.

53. In particular, this concerns certain genealogical sections in 1 Chron. 2 and 4, some lists such as that in 1 Chron. 27.25-31, and occasional 'secular' information about wars, construction works, administrative initiatives etc. of some kings in passages such as 1 Chron. 11.40-47; 2 Chron. 11.5-12, 18-23; 13.19, 21; 14.8-14; 17.7-9, 11; 19.4-11; 20.1-30; 21.2-4; 25.5-16; 26.6-15; 27.3-4; 28.12-15, 17-18; 32.30, 33; 33.11-14; 35.20-27.

54. See Peltonen, *History Debated*, pp. 259-60, 267-69, 280-83, 291-302, 326-29, 335-37, 375-82.

55. See Peltonen, *History Debated*, pp. 365-68, 456-58, 487-93, 513-18.

wise divergent from the general tendency and unhistorical predisposition of Chr. This view led to a reification of Wellhausen's idea of Chronicles as a reflection of the general ideological tendency of late postexilic Judaism in the form of a 'Chronicler before the Chronicler' source hypothesis. It meant that the question about seemingly reliable, historical data in Chronicles was transferred from Chr. to his sources: it was the earlier 'Chronicler', whom the 'real' Chronicler had followed in his own account, who must have utilized older sources of some sort for his authentic scraps of historical information. This transference happened much in the same way as within Approaches I and II but now for a different purpose. Whereas earlier the reliability of Chr. as a historian was defended with the aid of source postulates, now the prime concern was to explain how and why a work coming from the pen of a writer as untrustworthy as Chr. could contain trustworthy data.

What must be emphasized at this point is the fundamental change in the understanding and use of the concept of 'source' generated by the intermixture of approaches discussed above. For Approaches I and II, 'source' had referred to a document that Chr. (as a historian striving for veracity) had incorporated into his work either *in toto* (e.g. genealogies) or copied faithfully in its essentials. De Wette (and, in his wake, Wellhausen) had turned down such a notion as useless speculation.

After Wellhausen, there was no return to source theories characteristic of Approaches I and II with their historical and theological presuppositions, except in the most conservative circles where historical research was and is still controlled by theological requirements. The fact is that mainstream, twentieth-century Chronicles research closely follows the critical shape originally given to it by de Wette and Wellhausen. When, furthermore, biblical documents were stripped of notions of dogmatic authority, source theories simultaneously lost the theological and ideological ballast accorded to them. They were no longer needed to save Chronicles from the waves of historical doubt. While source theories had earlier had an extremely important function, they now qualified for the new task of explaining from one case to another the origin of the occasional historically authentic details in Chronicles. Consequently, it was not necessary to regard 'source' as referring to a literary document used by Chr. Instead, 'source' could also be understood more loosely as 'tradition' that Chr. had known. Even though the literary dimension remained the dominant one in this respect, the difference in principle is important: the origin of some information was no longer a purely source-critical issue but also a traditio-historical one. This was the focal point where Chronicles research could set itself decisively free from the historicist paradigm of assessing this biblical book merely as history and turn to it as one important link in the transmission and interpretation of religious tradition in the biblical world. The change in the concept of 'source' thus made it possible to give up—at least within certain limits—the old notion of Chr. as an annalist or compiler of historical sources and give him due credit as an author who used his sources to create something of his own out of them.

Even if the functional aspect is still alive on a smaller scale when the question of Chronicles' sources is discussed (see below), it is essential to pay attention to the fact that a shift from functional theory to what we may call functional explanation meant that source criticism as theory lost its place as one of the most fundamental elements of Chronicles research. Its function was no longer to provide an explanation of why Chronicles was as it was, but, rather, to explain how one specific historical aspect had to be comprehended in the larger framework of chronistic historiography. Here we can observe how, within the reassessed and reformulated research paradigm of twentieth-century critical study of Chronicles, source criticism as theory is coming closer to what can be regarded as source criticism as method.

Even though in modern research Chr. is regarded first and foremost as a creative religious author with a distinctive message, scholars still seek to explain satisfactorily the nature and usefulness of the historical information unique to Chronicles. Source criticism as theory is still essential for addressing this question. M. Noth[56] stressed that far from being a mere compiler of extracts from his sources, Chr. was an author in his own right and deserves recognition as such. Living probably in

---

56. Noth's seminal work on Chronicles is his treatment of this book in his *Überlieferungsgeschichtliche Studien: Die sammelnden und bearbeitenden Geschichtswerke im Alten Testament* (Tübingen: Max Niemeyer, 3rd edn, 1967), pp. 110-80. For Noth's significance in setting the agenda for the modern era of Chronicles research, see H.G.M. Williamson, 'Introduction', in M. Noth, *The Chronicler's History* (JSOTSup, 50; Sheffield: JSOT Press, 1987), pp. 11-26; Peltonen, *History Debated*, pp. 639-53; S.L. McKenzie and M.P. Graham (eds.), *The History of Israel's Traditions: The Heritage of Martin Noth* (JSOTSup, 182; Sheffield: Sheffield Academic Press, 1994). On Noth in general, see, e.g., Smend, *Alttestamentler*, pp. 255-75.

the third century BCE,[57] he enlivened, illustrated, embellished, reworked and interpreted older traditions—Samuel–Kings in its present form was undoubtedly his main source for the history of the Judean kings[58]—not for the purpose of deliberately distorting history but to make the traditions serve the concerns of the postexilic community in Judea.[59] His source citations were devoid of historical value as testimony to the existence of historical documents at his disposal, since they were merely a literary device imitating the example of his deuteronomistic *Vorlage*.

There were a few cases, however, where a historian had, especially in the light of the results of modern archaeological research, to admit that Chr.'s non-synoptic information was historically authentic and derived from some unknown literary source at his disposal. The pieces of accurate historical information that compelled one to make such a presumption were 2 Chron. 32.30 and 35.20-24. Furthermore, there were other fragments of non-synoptic information in Chronicles that did not look like the author's own inventions, even though they did not allow such a precise demonstration of authenticity on the basis of extra-biblical evidence as the two texts cited above. A reasonable deduction in such cases was, according to Noth, that since Chr. obviously had at his disposal an ancient source other than his deuteronomistic *Vorlage*, other statements that were in all probability historically trustworthy were derived from it. Passages creating the impression of containing accurate historical tradition concerned the fortification projects of some kings, comparable with Hezekiah's waterworks (2 Chron. 11.5b-10aα; 26.9 [possibly also v. 10aα]; 26.15a; 33.14a), and some military accounts (2 Chron. 13.3-20 and 14.8-14 [both in their present form heavily reworked by Chr.]; 26.6-8a; 27.5; 28.18). Noth concluded that since the themes of fortification and war basically belonged together, it seemed that, besides DtrH, Chr. had utilized only one ancient extra-biblical source document for his history of the monarchic period, possibly a kind of unofficial extract from official annals.[60]

One important methodological point must be noted in Noth's argumentation, and that is his insistence that Chronicles' historical reliability be discussed in connection with its sources. This complex of issues

57. Noth, *Studien*, pp. 150-55.
58. Noth, *Studien*, p. 133.
59. See Noth, *Studien*, pp. 155-80.
60. For Noth's discussion of Chronicles' sources and of the historical information derived from extra-biblical source material, see *Studien*, pp. 131-43.

must in no case be confused with the purely literary-critical effort to search for the original form of Chr.'s work.[61] What Noth basically does here is to speak for a source criticism as theory with its own historical sphere and methodological independence from literary issues—an interesting claim indeed in the light of how source criticism is usually understood. Noth believed that he could sustain this claim because in his work it did not lead to wild speculations about Chr.'s sources but, rather, in the opposite direction. According to him, one was allowed to resort to a hypothesis of unknown historical sources behind Chronicles only where there were weighty grounds preferably of an extra-biblical nature for such an assumption.[62] As we saw above, Noth was convinced that passages where such a procedure was justified were few and far between; one was unable to say anything specific about the historical nature of Chronicles as a whole on such a slender basis.

It is obvious that Noth's contention must be seen first of all as a critical reaction against both the complicated literary-critical theories with source-critical conclusions (see below) and, more generally, the excessive source theories of earlier scholars. What it simultaneously did, however, was to buttress precisely the methodological vagueness that had traditionally been part of the source criticism of Chronicles from the historical standpoint. By demanding that historical research be liberated from literary-critical examination, Noth came to legitimate, despite his critical intention, the hypothetical and methodologically uncontrollable historical paradigm of the source theories of Chronicles that all earlier research had reflected. Against the background of the history of research context sketched above, such a claim again set the methodological trap of which de Wette and Wellhausen had implicitly warned. While in the wake of Eichhorn a number of scholars fell into the trap, so to say, Noth tried to avoid it by appealing to archaeology as an external corrective to historical research—and almost succeeded. After him, such methodological circumspection has not become a commonly observed habit, however, undoubtedly due to the fact that even Noth, who was clearly aware of what he was doing, had to resort to a deduction from historical analogy (see above) in order to produce a sufficiently comprehensive explanation of the historical problems posed by Chronicles.

Several scholars of a distinctly critical disposition have in recent

61. Noth, *Studien*, p. 112.
62. See Noth, *Studien*, p. 133.

years also advocated some form of what has been called here 'source criticism as theory' in their interpretation of the combination of questions concerning Chronicles' sources and historical nature. Some—such as P. Welten,[63] whose method of treating Chronicles was in several respects a direct development of that outlined by Noth[64]—have modified Noth's views in a more critical direction, while others have been ready to admit somewhat more historically reliable information in Chronicles, derived by the author from extra-biblical source(s). To the latter group of scholars belong W. Rudolph, J.M. Myers, L. Randellini, F. Michaeli, J.P. Weinberg, R.B. Dillard and G.H. Jones, to mention but a few well-known examples.[65]

The views of two of the most prominent Chronicles scholars in recent years deserve special mention here. Following Noth's methodological solution to see in the source citations of Chronicles a literary device based on the author's canonical *Vorlage*, H.G.M. Williamson asserts that source citation formulae cannot help us in a search for Chr.'s extra-biblical sources. Beyond the observation, then, that Samuel–Kings constituted Chr.'s major source, one had to be content with 'informed conjecture'.[66] Williamson's own informed conjecture is to regard as the most credible view that in which Chr. really had access to extra-biblical sources from which he had borrowed materials suitable for his purposes and reworked them in his history. At least on some occasions Chronicles could thus be cautiously used to increase our knowledge of the

63. P. Welten, *Geschichte und Geschichtsdarstellung in den Chronikbüchern* (WMANT, 42; Neukirchen–Vluyn: Neukirchener Verlag, 1973).

64. See Williamson, 'Introduction', p. 16; Peltonen, *History Debated*, pp. 661-62.

65. W. Rudolph, *Chronikbücher* (HAT, 21; Tübingen: J.C.B. Mohr [Paul Siebeck], 1955); J.M. Myers, *I Chronicles* (AB, 12; Garden City, NY: Doubleday, 2nd edn, 1983); Myers, *II Chronicles* (AB, 13; Garden City, NY: Doubleday, 2nd edn, 1983); L. Randellini, *Il libro delle Cronache* (La Sacra Bibbia, Antico Testamento; Roma: Marietti, 1966); F. Michaeli, *Les livres des Chroniques, d'Esdras et de Néhémie* (CAT, 16; Neuchâtel: Delachaux & Niestlé, 1967); J.P. Weinberg, 'Die "ausserkanonischen Prophezeiungen" in den Chronikbüchern', *Acta Antiqua* 26 (1978), pp. 387-404; Weinberg, 'Das Eigengut in den Chronikbüchern', *OLP* 10 (1979), pp. 161-81; Weinberg, *Der Chronist in seiner Mitwelt* (BZAW, 239; Berlin: W. de Gruyter, 1996); R.B. Dillard, *2 Chronicles* (WBC, 15; Waco, TX: Word Books, 1987); Jones, *1 & 2 Chronicles*; G.H. Jones, 'From Abijam to Abijah', *ZAW* 106 (1994), pp. 420-34.

66. H.G.M. Williamson, *1 and 2 Chronicles* (NCB; Grand Rapids: Eerdmans, 1982), p. 19.

history of Israel, although hasty historical conclusions from the attribution of a passage or its basis to a source must not be made. One has to take into account the fact that Chr., the master of his sources rather than a servant of them, had at times handled his sources freely and with a wide range of techniques, and the sources themselves may sometimes also have reflected postexilic conditions more than the history that they had purported to describe.[67]

While Williamson spoke about 'informed conjecture' as the means to assess the question of Chr.'s extra-biblical sources, S. Japhet has more explicitly attempted to bring methodological—or at least terminological—coherence to the issue.[68] She is of the opinion, too, that it is historically much more plausible to think that Chr. had been able to draw upon some extra-biblical sources in addition to his main source, Samuel–Kings, and other biblical works than to assume that this had not been the case. Just as obvious was the fact that historically trustworthy information not known from elsewhere was incorporated into Chronicles, a work that, in Japhet's opinion, was essentially composed by a single author who had clearly given his theological message precedence over history. These two observations should not be linked together in a facile manner, however. The existence of non-canonical sources did not necessarily vouch for the historical trustworthiness of the final literary production, since their antiquity and authenticity were not always self-evident. Information derived by Chr. from a source may also have reflected some no longer identifiable, historical and social reality, or it may have been used anachronistically in its present context. In the frequent absence of adequate critical means of assessing the historicity of the chronistic data, one had to rely mainly on a case-by-case application of the criterion of historical probability. Was a certain piece of information (or its factual core—cf. the view of Ewald!) probable or not from a historical point of view in the light of all available evidence?[69] Here is Japhet's equivalent to Williamson's informed conjecture.

---

67. Williamson, *Chronicles*, pp. 17-23.

68. For an elaboration of the points briefly discussed here, see, in particular, S. Japhet, 'Chronicles, Book of', *EncJud* (1971), V, pp. 517-34; Japhet, *The Ideology of the Book of Chronicles and its Place in Biblical Thought* (BEATAJ, 9; Bern: Peter Lang, 1989); Japhet, *I & II Chronicles: A Commentary* (OTL; Louisville, KY: Westminster/John Knox Press, 1993).

69. See Japhet, *Ideology*, pp. 513-15.

As for the sources utilized by Chr., one can see from his adaptation of the sources known to us that he had introduced substantial modifications and additions to them with the result that his historical portrayal conformed to his theological aim. Japhet argued that it was reasonable to assume that Chr. had followed basically the same procedure with his extra-biblical sources: with a varying degree of adaptation he reworked and edited materials provided by his sources to accord with his own theological and literary goals. As Japhet points out, Chr.'s fundamental characteristic was to combine two principal modes of literary work in his treatment of source materials, namely, faithful adherence to his sources and freedom to modify and elaborate them.[70] The extra-biblical sources themselves had been of varying genre, scope and origin without any comprehensive unity as to their literary character, historical presuppositions and theology, and it was Chr.'s 'historical method and philosophy' that bound them together into a new work of historiography.[71] The method with which a scholar had to approach the question of Chronicles' sources and historicity was that special attention was to be paid to the factors that were constitutive both in directing the author's treatment of his sources and in giving his work the appearance it now has: the application of his literary procedures, historical views typical of him and his theological motivation.[72] What this meant in practice was that each non-synoptic passage in Chronicles had to be investigated on a case-by-case basis in the light of observations about the nature, intentions and goals of chronistic historiography in order to discover the origin, character and historical value of the sources possibly used by the author. As we can see, there is not much new under the sun, after all, in this respect. As for the results yielded by the application of these principles and considerations, Japhet admitted a historical core or basis in many of the same passages dealing with military, economic and administrative affairs and construction projects that other modern critical scholars after Noth had found, although she emphasized that such material was not a kind of incidental, purposeless patchwork in Chr.'s account but an organic and coherent part of his history.[73]

70. Japhet, *I & II Chronicles*, p. 41.

71. Japhet, *I & II Chronicles*, p. 23.

72. For a discussion of Chronicles' sources and their use, see Japhet, *I & II Chronicles*, pp. 14-23.

73. Japhet, *Ideology*, pp. 510-11. Her position has been discussed in more detail in Peltonen, *History Debated*, pp. 772-84.

Japhet stressed that a consideration of the problems concerning Chronicles' sources and historicity must take into account the fact that this book is indeed a history, as for its literary genre, but it is an idiosyncratic expression of biblical historiography,[74] in which older materials have been reworked in a deliberate and sophisticated way. Nevertheless, an important element of her position was also the recognition that the question of extra-biblical sources behind Chronicles was not one of merely literary interest on the part of the scholar but an inseparable dimension in the evaluation of Chronicles' historical nature and content. Japhet's intention is thus to minimize the hypothetical aspect of source criticism as theory by paying careful attention to the different literary and historical factors and problems necessarily involved in every source-critical treatment of Chronicles. Her approach is unable to remove the hypothetical nature of the problem of Chronicles' sources altogether, but it is nevertheless one in which the explicitly methodological discussion receives more attention than in any other scholarly work on this particular sector of Chronicles research.

Despite Japhet's attempt to bring methodological clarity to the source issue, it is still obvious that every attempt to determine the extent, shape, date and purpose of Chr.'s extra-biblical source(s) is ultimately speculative. The same holds for the historical assessments of Chr.'s unique contributions that are made on the basis of a source theory. The significance of this fact has naturally been generally realized and acknowledged among the scholars discussed in this article. This is probably one important reason why detailed source-critical theories— so typical of the nineteenth century in particular—have not found many advocates among modern scholars. Furthermore, historical explanation, which has replaced historical substantiation or confirmation as the function of source criticism as theory, does not need such theories any more, since one is no longer dealing here with an aspect that would seem to be crucial to the proper understanding and interpretation of Chronicles. Consequently, indefinite references to some sources, whose nature escapes all attempts at more accurate identification, appear to have become a sufficient scholarly explanation for the existence of otherwise unknown historical data in Chronicles. After that, it is more a matter of taste than anything else whether a scholar wants to be more exact about the question of Chronicles' extra-biblical sources. The

---

74. Japhet, *I & II Chronicles*, pp. 31-34.

speculative character of source criticism as theory has thus diminished in that nowadays its speculative nature is recognized, and attempts have been made to control it, but this does not affect the fundamental fact that the speculative element remains.

Source as a Literary Phenomenon in Chronicles Research

We have observed above that both the historical aspect in the interpretation of Chronicles and the strictly historical function in the source-critical treatments of this book have given way more and more to the critical comprehension of the fact that Chr. was not merely a mechanical collector of historical facts but above all a creative author and religious teacher. Consequently, his work as a theological and literary phenomenon within the context of biblical historiography has received increasing attention in its own right during the last few decades, in particular, without historical implications in the traditional sense being drawn after the fashion of the nineteenth century. It has followed from this that the more one attaches importance to Chr.'s independent literary activity, the less the question about sources seems to be significant other than in the respect discussed above, in the function of a historical explanation of occasional details. In this sense, our survey of the history of source criticism in Chronicles research could end here with the statement that an idea of Chr. as a creative and independent author, with distinctive theological aims of his own, needs source criticism to support it no more than the image of Chr. as a forger of history produced by the historical destruction of his work by de Wette and Wellhausen. This would not be the whole picture of the general trends in this particular field of the study of Chronicles, however. Therefore, we shall finally pay brief attention to one particular form of source criticism in Chronicles research, namely, that where 'source' was understood primarily as a literary phenomenon.

It is, of course, true that basically all historical speculation about an extra-biblical source or sources used by Chr. is also an argument for the view that a literary process is necessary for the proper understanding of Chronicles. As we could see, however, for about a century after Eichhorn, a literary reflection of the source issue as such could hardly concern scholars, critical or consevative, since they were busy debating about the historical nature and value of Chronicles. Consequently, the first noteworthy steps in this direction were not taken until early in the present century by some 'Wellhausenian' scholars. The history of

research context of this phenomenon becomes understandable when one
keeps in mind that it was precisely among 'Wellhausenians' that the
traditional historical speculation about Chronicles first began to look
more or less like a waste of time and energy: after all, it was Wellhausen who, in the footsteps of de Wette, had presented a solution to
the question of Chronicles' historical value that was scientifically convincing, historically persuasive and thus virtually 'final'.

For an early twentieth-century attempt of a more detailed nature to
reconstruct the literary composition of the present form of Chronicles,
one may refer to the one that I. Benzinger put forth in his commentary
in 1901. According to him, Chronicles consisted of three literary strata:
material derived from sources, the chronistic redaction and later additions. The second of these reflected Chr.'s ever-present interest in the
status and significance of the Levites, especially the levitical musicians,
and in the legitimate temple cult;[75] while the third was to be found
above all in the additions made to genealogical lists and in the detailed
information about music and singing included in Chr.'s descriptions of
cultic festivals.[76]

It is the first stratum that belongs to the field of source criticism.
Benzinger argued that Chr. had altogether four bodies of source material at his disposal: Samuel–Kings more or less in the present form (his
main source); midrashic writings from which he derived the typically
midrashic features of his work (exaggerated numbers, in particular);
source material from a historical work of probably postexilic origin,
whose historical and theological disposition resembled greatly that of
Chr. himself (from this he had received information such as that in 1
Chron. 11.10-12.40; 2 Chron. 11.18-23; 13.21; 21.1-4; 24.4-14; 26.6-
15; 27.3-9); and finally, different kinds of defective and fragmentary
lists and the like used in the compilation of the genealogies in 1 Chronicles 1–9.[77] Benzinger argued that a comparison between Samuel–Kings
and Chronicles demonstrated that Chr. had been more a 'redactor', a
compiler of materials, than an independent narrator. According to the
ancient Jewish custom, he had followed the text of his sources very
accurately, introducing redactional changes primarily where they had
been necessary in order to accommodate the content and message of the

---

75. I. Benzinger, *Die Bücher der Chronik* (KHAT, 20; Tübingen: J.C.B. Mohr
[Paul Siebeck], 1901), pp. xiii-xv.
76. Benzinger, *Chronik*, pp. xv-xvi.
77. Benzinger, *Chronik*, pp. x-xiii.

materials in his *Vorlage* to the ideas and beliefs of his own day.[78]

Benzinger followed the 'Wellhausenian' critical interpretation of Chronicles' historical value in general outline,[79] but he did not try to substantiate this view with his detailed source-critical theory. Instead, with the assistance of the literary analysis of Chr.'s work, he strove for an explanation of its theologically and historically heterogeneous form and content. According to him, Chr. never attempted to be a historian in the modern Western sense. Above all, he was a midrashist, a teacher edifying his readers morally and religiously. For this reason, the prime task of the study of his work was not to enter into a debate about its historical facticity but to unravel by means of an analysis of its literary composition the aspects that Chr. had regarded as essential for his own purposes and that reflected the theological contribution of some other quarter. In Benzinger's conception, then, Chr. was already clearly a theologian, an intepreter of earlier materials whose disposition was determined by the theological horizon of his sources. In itself, such an idea was by no means revolutionary within contemporary critical scholarship, but what is worth noting is the way in which source-critical arguments were used to justify it. One can say in the light of this observation that whereas earlier discussions about Chronicles' sources had been directed by a historical interest and function, in Benzinger's case the fundamental factors of a source-critical approach were determined first of all by the complex content and theological structure of Chr.'s work. The shift from theory to a more methodological approach is obvious, since the constitutive factors were now controllable. Or one should perhaps say, these factors were made controllable by supposing that the main characteristics of Chr.'s work were in several cases derived not from the author but from his source materials.

Benzinger's approach was followed quite closely by A. Bertholet in his essay on Chronicles in 1909, although in a somewhat more unspecified manner and with special attention to later additions to Chr.'s work. What was important to Bertholet, too, was that the literary aspect of the source-critical issue was directly related to the assessment of Chronicles primarily as a theological document and only secondarily from a historical standpoint.[80] The source criticism of Chronicles along

78. Benzinger, *Chronik*, pp. xiii-xiv.

79. See Peltonen, *History Debated*, pp. 273-77.

80. A. Bertholet, 'Chronik', *RGG¹* (1909), I, pp. 1791-1804. See also Peltonen, *History Debated*, pp. 277-80.

the lines of Benzinger was also endorsed by C. Steuernagel, who stressed that Chr.'s own literary contribution was chiefly that of a close follower of his sources. Noteworthy literary independence was shown by him mainly when his favorite topic, the vicissitudes of the levites, cropped up. With the exception of information derived directly or indirectly from older canonical works, other literary layers in Chronicles (materials adopted by Chr. from midrashic sources, his own compositions and later additions), in Steuernagel's opinion, reflected and followed mostly the characteristic ideology, spirit and typical features of the Jewish midrashic literature of the postexilic times.[81]

Like Benzinger, Bertholet and Steuernagel expressed their views about the literary composition and sources of Chronicles within the 'Wellhausenian' historical paradigm. They were not primarily concerned about proving the historical unreliability of Chronicles, however, since that had already been done by their predecessors. Instead, they attempted to attain a larger scale comprehension of the multifaceted elements of the peculiar chronistic interpretation of history. Their means of reaching this goal was source criticism, the starting point of which was an assumption that the basis of Chr.'s work was constituted by the canonical history in Samuel–Kings and its midrashic interpretation. Chr. himself had been a compiler of biblical and extra-biblical source materials available to him; he carried out this task in accordance with the spirit of late postexilic Judaism. Source criticism was also associated by them with what is now termed 'redaction criticism' by means of the claim that occasional data—for the scholars discussed above, primarily information concerning cultic music—had been added later to Chr.'s original work.[82] What we have here is basically the same 'a Chronicler before the Chronicler' hypothesis that we met above, but it is no longer explicated in terms of source criticism aimed at substantiating some aspect of Chr.'s activity as a historian. It is now a

---

81. C. Steuernagel, *Lehrbuch der Einleitung in das Alte Testament mit einem Anhang über die Apokryphen und Pseudepigraphen* (Sammlung theologischer Lehrbücher; Tübingen: J.C.B.Mohr [Paul Siebeck], 1912), pp. 377-409. See also Peltonen, *History Debated*, pp. 280-83.

82. Wright ('From Center to Periphery', p. 41) has rightly observed: 'The twentieth-century source-critical study of Chronicles originated in the apologetic attempt to salvage the historicity of Chronicles. This apologetic use of literary criticism, however, ultimately developed into the isolation of later literary layers as the results were absorbed within the de Wette–Wellhausen perspective.'

vehicle for illuminating the characteristic features of his work within the framework of a literary process that can be recognized and reconstructed with the help of a source-critical method. 'Source criticism as theory' was thus needed for 'source criticism as method' to work, when one wished to provide an explanation of the historical nature and theological content of Chr.'s work on the basis of a conviction that they did not derive from Chr. himself.

A reconstruction of the composition of Chronicles basically similar to that proffered by Benzinger and others can be found in the commentary on Chronicles by R. Kittel (1902).[83] According to him, literary activity of a midrashic inclination was typical of the period to which Chronicles belonged. The author's account was therefore strongly imbued with this particular manifestation of the postexilic religious spirit.[84] The book of Chronicles had been composed by no less than three successive levitical writers. The first, already close to midrashic writers but nevertheless trying to avoid the kind of exaggeration of traditional material that in the sphere of midrash normally produced legendary features, was active sometime between 500 and 400 BCE. The second writer, a midrashist or a group of them, belonged to levitical circles of the mid-fourth century BCE. Much material in Chronicles derived from this stratum. Kittel regarded it as probable, furthermore, that in this layer we have before us sections from the sources cited in Chronicles; this assumption was quite natural for Kittel, since he argued that the source citations in Chronicles most probably referred to two midrashic works and to Isaiah 1–39. The third levitical writer was then Chr. proper, a 'neo-levite' from around 300 BCE. Like his predecessors, Chr. proper reworked older materials in accordance with the doctrine of retribution and the cultic system of the Priestly Code. A new trait was his special sympathy for the classes within the Levites whose status had begun to improve in his day (singers, musicians, gatekeepers). In addition to the work of these three levitical authors, a number of later additions had been made to Chroni-

---

83. R. Kittel, *Die Bücher der Chronik übersetzt und erklärt* (HKAT, 6/1; Göttingen: Vandenhoeck & Ruprecht, 1902). In this work, Kittel took his analysis of the composition of Chronicles farther than he had earlier in his contribution to what has been called the Rainbow Bible; see Kittel, *The Books of the Chronicles: Critical Edition of the Hebrew Text Printed in Colors Exhibiting the Composite Structure of the Book* (The Sacred Books of the Old Testament, 20; Baltimore: The Johns Hopkins Press, 1895).

84. Kittel, *Chronik*, pp. vi-x.

cles. Furthermore, according to Kittel, Chronicles contained, especially in the genealogical section but also elsewhere, material that apparently went back neither to Chr. himself nor to any of his sources mentioned so far, whether biblical or extra-biblical. A logical deduction from this observation was that either Chr. proper or some of his predecessors also had access to data of various sorts and origins that were more ancient than any of the literary levels recognizable in Chronicles as it is now. For the most part, this data contained historically authentic information that was generally free from the typically midrashic treatment of older traditions. Kittel believed that the value of Chronicles as a source for pre-exilic history was largely based precisely on this complex of ancient traditions.[85]

From the standpoint of source criticism, Kittel's position[86] is an interesting combination of elements that we have come across in the course of our discussion. On the one hand, he presents a clear source-critical theory in order to argue for the historical origin and value of certain materials in Chronicles. On the other hand, he analyzes and assesses the structure and different aspects of the chronistic history by paying close attention to what kind of source-critical observations and conclusions a literary analysis of them warrants. The historical perspective was clearly regarded by Kittel as one that could not be ignored if full justice were to be done to Chr. and his work. But what he quite obviously tries to do at the same time is to minimize the speculative element of the historical perspective by means of literary analysis as a source-critical method. Even though the later history of Chronicles research indicates that Kittel's combination of source-critical aspects was far from successful,[87] it is an excellent indicator of how differently oriented the historical and literary source criticisms basically are: the former cannot manage without a theory, which the latter is unable to provide.

An original attempt to link the question of Chronicles' sources with a

85. See Kittel's discussion of the sources and literary structure of Chronicles in *Chronik*, pp. x-xvi.

86. For a more detailed presentation of Kittel's views, see Graham, *Utilization*, pp. 176-82; Peltonen, *History Debated*, pp. 503-11.

87. Kittel's view of the complicated literary history and structure of Chronicles never became popular among scholars. The most sympathetic response it evoked was in the work on Chronicles by the contemporary British scholar, W.H. Bennett; see Peltonen, *History Debated*, pp. 305-308.

theory of the literary composition of this book was made by J.W. Rothstein and J. Hänel in their commentary on 1 Chronicles in 1927.[88]
According to them, the sources of Chronicles included Samuel–Kings
and the completed Hexateuch as well as the Priestly Code as a separate
entity, the *Vorlage* of Samuel–Kings and several other bodies of non-
canonical source material containing genealogical and historical data.
All these sources had not been used by the author called Chr., however.
Their inclusion in the present chronistic account had taken place in a
complicated process of redaction. 1 Chronicles had undergone a double
redaction, the first soon after 432 BCE and the second around 400 BCE.
The older of the redactors, whom Rothstein and Hänel labeled the
actual author of the chronistic work, had used the separate Priestly
Code. His work was designated as a kind of continuation of the P
stratum in the Pentateuch. Furthermore, this redactor had drawn upon
the *Vorlage* of Samuel–Kings. The second chronistic redactor had for
his part utilized the complete Hexateuch and Samuel–Kings. In addition
to the main double redaction of the chronistic work, some materials
(1 Chron. 15.1–16.3; 22-27) had undergone separate chronistic redactions before the literary development proper reached its terminal point
with the second extensive redaction. After that, numerous additions
were still made to the chronistic work but without any plan that would
cause them to be regarded as a uniform redactional level.[89]

The aim of the conception of Rothstein and Hänel was basically similar to that advanced by Benzinger: the reconstruction of Chronicles'
sources and literary composition served first of all a literary-functional
or a redactional-functional approach, not a historical-functional one. It
sought to clarify the elements constituting the theology of 1 Chronicles[90] and the context for Chronicles within the historical development
of the religion of ancient Israel. Historical issues in the traditional sense
were of secondary importance, since the necessity of the entire conception was neither grounded in nor substantiated by them—although,
logically, the commentators argued that the historical value of 1 Chronicles could not be categorically denied after the fashion of de Wette, for
example, when account was taken of all the source material on which

88. J.W. Rothstein and J. Hänel, *Kommentar zum ersten Buch der Chronik*
(KAT, 18/2; Leipzig: D. Werner Scholl, 1927).

89. Rothstein and Hänel, *Chronik*, pp. xliv-lxix.

90. See the extensive discussion of this topic in Rothstein and Hänel, *Chronik*,
pp. ix-xliv.

the chronistic history was, in all probability, built.[91] The conception of
Rothstein and Hänel was hypothetical both from the historical and the
literary viewpoints, as can easily be seen, and precisely as its predecessors in the works of Benzinger, Kittel and others, it never won widespread scholarly acceptance.[92] Methodologically, however, it was—or
at least was meant to be—less hypothetical than all the traditional
source theories that were built solely on historical postulates.

An approach comparable to that of Benzinger, Kittel, and Rothstein
and Hänel,[93] in which source criticism of Chronicles was discussed
more as an indicator of the process of literary composition and formation than as a historical theory, subsequently surfaced chiefly in the
hypothesis of two continuous chronistic strata or two 'Chroniclers',
proposed by K. Galling (1954).[94] Such theories have not found noteworthy support in modern research, however, and currently literary-
critical work on Chronicles no longer results in scholars separating
from Chronicles its literary precursors. Instead, considerable attention
has been accorded to an aspect that truly cropped up in the works of
scholars discussed in this chapter but only in a somewhat secondary
role, namely, the one that leads from literary criticism to redaction
criticism. Here marks of literary heterogeneity in Chronicles are
regarded as an indication of the existence of later additions and expansions of various types and origin in Chr.'s original work. The original

91. Rothstein and Hänel, *Chronik*, pp. lxix-lxxxii. On Rothstein and Hänel, see
also Peltonen, *History Debated*, pp. 392-96.

92. Wright ('From Center to Periphery', pp. 40-41 n. 60) has aptly observed that
in the works of Benzinger, Kittel, and Rothstein and Hänel 'hypothetical literary
strata proliferated in a manner parallel to the literary-critical investigations of the
Pentateuch, ultimately becoming implausible'.

93. According to Wright ('From Center to Periphery', pp. 40-41), a major
influence upon the works of Benzinger, Kittel, and Rothstein and Hänel was exerted
by A. Büchler's article 'Zur Geschichte der Tempelmusik und der Tempelpsalmen'
(*ZAW* 19 [1899], pp. 96-133, 329-44; *ZAW* 20 [1900], pp. 97-135), even to the
extent that they applied 'Büchler's method' to the entire book of Chronicles. It
appears, however, that Wright somewhat overemphasizes the significance of
Büchler's work. After all, Büchler did not construct a compositional 'method' that
Benzinger and others would then have followed in a slavish way, but mainly
modified the earlier source critical conclusions of K.H. Graf, as Wright himself
observes, in particular, to produce a new insight into one specific theme in Chronicles, the history of the postexilic priesthood and Levites.

94. K. Galling, *Die Bücher der Chronik, Esra, Nehemia* (ATD, 12; Göttingen:
Vandenhoeck & Ruprecht, 1954).

Chronicles itself became a 'source', a catalyst for secondary literary activity based on a variety of ideological motives. Well-known scholars of the earlier generation, for whom this aspect played an important role in the understanding of the literary nature of Chronicles, include M. Noth, W. Rudolph and A.C. Welch.[95] Of more recent scholars utilizing this approach, naturally with widely varying emphases, either on a large or a more limited scale as one of the basic elements for understanding the present form of Chronicles, we may refer to F. Michaeli, T. Willi, F.M. Cross, D.L. Petersen, M. Sæbø, S.L. McKenzie, R.L. Braun, M.A. Throntveit, D.N. Freedman and B.E. Willoughby, E.M. Dörrfuss and G. Steins.[96] Such a fundamental modification of what is traditionally understood as source criticism does not belong to the purview of this article,[97] but one observation may be pertinent here. Many a source-critical theory, be it based on historical postulates or literary observations, tried to provide an explanation of the numerous problems posed

95. Noth, *Studien*, pp. 110-31; Rudolph, *Chronikbücher*, pp. viii, 1-5; A.C. Welch, *The Work of the Chronicler: Its Purpose and its Date* (Schweich Lectures, 1938; London: Oxford University Press, 1939).

96. Michaeli, *Les livres des Chroniques*, p. 12; Willi, *Die Chronik als Auslegung*, pp. 194-204; F.M. Cross, 'A Reconstruction of the Judean Restoration', *JBL* 94 (1975), pp. 4-18 (= *Int* 29 [1975], pp. 187-203; and now pp. 151-72 in *idem*, *From Epic to Canon: History and Literature in Ancient Israel* [Baltimore: The Johns Hopkins University Press, 1998]); D.L. Petersen, *Late Israelite Prophecy: Studies in Deutero-Prophetic Literature and in Chronicles* (SBLMS, 23; Missoula, MT: Scholars Press, 1977); M. Sæbø, 'Chronistische Theologie/Chronistisches Geschichtswerk', *TRE* (1981), VIII, pp. 74-87; S.L. McKenzie, *The Chronicler's Use of the Deuteronomistic History* (HSM, 33; Atlanta: Scholars Press, 1985); R.L. Braun, *1 Chronicles* (WBC, 14; Waco, TX: Word Books, 1986); M.A. Throntveit, *When Kings Speak: Royal Speech and Royal Prayer in Chronicles* (SBLDS, 93; Atlanta: Scholars Press, 1987); D.N. Freedman and B.E. Willoughby, 'I and II Chronicles, Ezra, Nehemiah', in B.W. Anderson (ed.), *The Books of the Bible* (2 vols.; New York: Charles Scribner's Sons, 1989), I, pp. 155-71; D.N. Freedman, 'The Chronicler's Purpose', *CBQ* 23 (1961), pp. 436-42; E.M. Dörrfuss, *Mose in den Chronikbüchern: Garant theokratischer Zukunftserwartung* (BZAW, 219; Berlin: W. de Gruyter, 1994); G. Steins, *Die Chronik als kanonisches Abschlussphänomen: Studien zur Entstehung und Theologie von 1/2 Chronik* (BBB, 93; Weinheim: Beltz Athenäum, 1995).

97. For a convenient brief summary of different theories of Chronicles' *Entstehungsgeschichte*, see G. Steins, 'Die Bücher der Chronik', in E. Zenger *et al.*, *Einleitung in das Alte Testament* (Kohlhammer Studienbücher Theologie, 1/1; Stuttgart: W. Kohlhammer, 1995), pp. 170-71.

by Chronicles by supposing that there had been 'a Chronicler before the Chronicler'. The existence of this phantom Chronicler could then be used as a factor that freed Chr. proper from at least some of the 'chronistic' problems. The literary-critical approach that emphasizes the role of secondary material in Chronicles may basically be used for the same purpose: it frees Chr. from at least some of the 'chronistic' problems by assuming that there was 'a Chronicler after the Chronicler'. It appears, therefore, that whichever way the research proceeds from observations about the literary composition of Chronicles, there is a distinct possibility that it will become source criticism as theory, at least as far as methodology is concerned.

Ultimately, there is one specific area of study where source criticism as theory and method (with both their historical and literary implications) most clearly converge. It is quite simply the relation of Chronicles to its source material known from the present Hebrew Bible. Modern research on Chronicles is virtually unanimous in the conviction, and surely not without good reason, that Samuel–Kings belonged to the sources on which Chr. based his history. The relationship between his work and the older canonical histories may have been indirect as well, but in one form or another Chronicles is dependent on its canonical precursor and should thus be understood on this basis only.[98]

---

98. In recent years, the ancient theory of a common source at the base of both Samuel–Kings and Chronicles has occasionally been revived, too, either with conclusions directly supporting Chronicles' reliability (Macy, *Sources*; see above, n. 18) or with tentative remarks regarding Chr.'s consistent and extensive reliance on the common source; see B. Halpern, 'Sacred History and Ideology: Chronicles' Thematic Structure—Indications of an Earlier Source', in R.E. Friedman (ed.), *The Creation of Sacred Literature: Composition and Redaction of the Biblical Text* (University of California Publications: Near Eastern Studies, 22; Berkeley: University of California Press, 1981), pp. 35-54. However, a directly opposite conclusion has also recently been drawn from the same contention that there is common source material behind Chronicles and DtrH. It has been claimed that this notion really makes it plain how not only in Chronicles but also in Samuel–Kings the common source had been substantially expanded and thoroughly redrafted from the postexilic viewpoint, and how, consequently, both histories as alternative appropriations of an earlier story of Judah's kings should be regarded as historically tendentious and thus unreliable. This view has been energetically advocated by A.G. Auld, in particular; see his *Kings Without Privilege: David and Moses in this Story of the Bible's Kings* (Edinburgh: T. & T. Clark, 1994) and his article in this volume, 'What Was the Main Source of the Books of Chronicles?' (pp. 92-101). For a

Methodologically, source criticism as theory is on as firm a footing here as it can ever be—see, for example, the way in which S. Japhet has recently attempted to systematize this particular issue. Source criticism as method, operating on the basis of literary criticism, naturally attains its most tenable results, too, when the relationships between the two blocks of canonical material are analyzed. The reason for this is obvious: the source is known before any theories are made and conclusions drawn.

The course taken by most modern research on this issue has been significantly influenced by the observation made from Greek translations of the biblical texts as well as from the discoveries at Qumran that, contrary to the general view of many earlier scholars, a textual tradition of the books of Samuel, which was to some extent at variance with the Masoretic tradition, appears to underlie the book of Chronicles.[99] Consequently, scholars have become hesitant, and rightly so, to attribute, after the fashion of de Wette and others, every deviation in Chronicles from the MT of Samuel–Kings directly to Chr.'s historical and ideological biases.

This textual factor has obvious methodological implications for the historical evaluation of Chr.'s use of the older canonical books in numerous details, as well as for an assessment of him as an allegedly tendentious user of source material. What it indicates even more is that the study of Chronicles does not possess an 'absolute' historical and literary method. It seems, therefore, that the area of investigation that can constitute the firmest methodological anchor for the different aspects of source criticism of Chronicles discussed above is an examination of Chr.'s general aim and method of composition in his adaptation of source materials—even though it is somewhat uncertain from the start to what extent insights gained from the comparison of Samuel–Kings to Chronicles are applicable to Chr.'s general purpose and method of adaptation in his use of now unknown source material. A central result achieved by the source criticism of Chronicles at this point is the view—generally accepted today—that Chr. was a creative and sophisticated author with considerable literary talent, who skillfully treated older materials when he created a novel and original interpretation of

similar view, see C.Y.S. Ho, 'Conjectures and Refutations: Is 1 Samuel xxxi 1-13 Really the Source of 1 Chronicles x 1-12?', *VT* 45 (1995), pp. 82-106.

99. On the textual problem, see, e.g., Klein, 'Chronicles', pp. 995-96.

the history of his people.[100] It must be noted, however, that an investigation into the creative theology, ideology and historiography of Chr. is a source-critical issue only indirectly at best. The more one wishes to emphasize this aspect of his work or his own literary achievements or the ideological homogeneity of his work necessitating a kind of synthetic understanding of it, the less there is room for source criticism, theory or method.

Conclusion

By way of a conclusion from the foregoing discussion, especially as regards the most modern research,[101] the following points may be made:

1.   The understanding of the problem of the sources of Chronicles as well as of Chr.'s literary method, historical perspective and theological position as a transmitter of older traditions stands on a firm methodological footing only when it is based on a critical reflection and analysis of the relationship between this book and Samuel–Kings.

2.   For Chr., history was subservient to theology. That is why he used his sources, whatever they were, freely and creatively in order to meet the historical and religious needs of his day. Therefore, one should not speak of an intentional falsification of history in Chronicles. It is of prime importance to discover as thoroughly as possible Chr.'s ideological presuppositions and historiographical method that have determined his use of source materials. At the same time, Chr.'s free handling of sources is in some contradiction with the assumption that his use of extra-biblical sources can still be recognized and assessed by the modern scholar, since in order to do so one must presume that in these particular instances Chr. did not proceed in his typical fashion but followed his source(s) closely enough for the material to have preserved its original shape and content.[102]

100. Most recently, see I. Kalimi, *Zur Geschichtsschreibung des Chronisten: Literarisch-historiographische Abweichungen der Chronik von ihren Paralleltexten in den Samuel- und Königsbüchern* (BZAW, 226; Berlin: W. de Gruyter, 1995).

101. See also the useful summary of recent research on Chronicles' sources by J.W. Kleinig, 'Recent Research in Chronicles', *CR:BS* 2 (1994), pp. 47-49.

102. H.R. Macy has pointedly referred to the danger that methodological incon-

3.   The most recent research on the literary nature of Chronicles is very sparing in producing new source-critical—and redaction-critical—theories, particularly of a detailed nature, and tends to support the compositional unity and literary integrity of Chronicles.[103] Regarding the author's sources, it follows from this that whatever materials he may have had at his disposal, his work is not to be considered a mere compilation of earlier materials, but a deliberate composition of a skillful author who created from earlier tradition a new theological and historiographical synthesis for his own time.

4.   As has been pertinently observed recently by G.H. Jones,[104] the issue of Chronicles' extra-biblical sources and that concerning later additions to or successive editions of it are in a kind of inverse proportion to each other. If the extra-biblical sources are regarded as having been very meagre, the amount of material attributed to secondary expansions is usually considered substantial, and, conversely, an increase in the number of sources admitted tends to reduce the supposed later revision and supplementation.

5.   The two previous points notwithstanding, the idea of extra-biblical sources of varying sorts at Chr.'s disposal and the usefulness of this idea for historical explanation is more widely supported in scholarly circles than the alternative that there were no extra-biblical sources at all. A justification for this idea is found in the character of the non-parallel material of Chronicles, not in the author's source citations, which are generally regarded as being directly dependent on his deuteronomistic *Vorlage* and reflecting his literary goals. At the same time, it is admitted that the traditional supposition, according to which the historical trustworthiness of a piece of information would be guaranteed by the observation that it probably derives from a source, is untenable. It is admitted, further, that source postulates with a large-scale historical

sistency in this respect may make Chr. appear as 'a schizophrenic literary personality who in one instance follows his sources to the letter and in another rewrites them with abandon' (*Sources*, p. 171).

103. See Kleinig, 'Recent Research', pp. 44-46.

104. Jones, *1 & 2 Chronicles*, p. 82.

function lead to unfruitful speculation that does justice neither to the historical nor to the literary character of Chronicles.

6.   An explanation of some historical detail or passage in Chronicles by means of source-critical theory must be supplied on a case-by-case basis with due recognition of the fact that conclusions are mostly tentative and beyond unambiguous methodological control.

7.   Source-critical theory is an inseparable element of Chronicles research as long as at least some weight is accorded to the historical aspect of the source issue. The fundamental problems concerning the relationship between history and an interpretation of history in Chronicles have not yet found a solution that would make obsolete the questions that scholars had already tried to answer in the early nineteenth century. While they still intended to a find a motive or a reason why Chr.—that reliable historian and faithful follower of his sources—sometimes seemed to depart from what was regarded as acceptable writing or interpretation of history, the problem is now to find a motive or a reason why Chr.—that creative theologian—occasionally still seems unable to escape the strong, historical focus of his presentation. It is obvious, therefore, that even today one is unable to provide a satisfactory explanation for all the characteristic traits of Chronicles without resorting to some form of source criticism as theory.

8.   It appears that nowadays we know much less about Chr.'s extra-biblical sources than ever before. Except for the relation of Chronicles to Samuel–Kings, a source theory of some sort representing a scholarly consensus does not exist. In the early days of the nineteenth century, scholars like Eichhorn and Keil were still able to describe the contours of the sources of Chronicles, because the biblical work itself was historically reliable and its author had faithfully copied his sources. Conversely, one could also suppose like de Wette that the historical unreliability of Chronicles indicated that there had been no extra-biblical sources at the author's disposal. Later, it was 'known' that whatever Chr.'s sources had been, they were rooted in precisely the same soil of legalistic Judaism dominated by priestly ideology as Chr. himself. Some observed that postexilic Jewish Midrash was a common denominator of the

literature represented both by Chr. and his sources. Today none of these aspects alone is regarded by scholars as sufficient to create the historical, ideological or literary context into which Chr. and his sources can be set with confidence. The more this general notion is accepted, the more Chr. is seen to have been a sovereign master and interpreter of the biblical world of thought instead of being a mere partisan of some aspect of it, with the result that he becomes a scribe writing for other scribes,[105] for example, or the first theologian of the canon whose work is a *Nachschrift* of the older works, a 're-written Bible'.[106]

9. After a couple hundred years of critical effort, the basic questions are still open: What were Chr.'s sources? What was their historical nature and value? How did Chr. use them? As long as commonly accepted answers to these questions escape us— and perhaps they always will—source criticism of Chronicles will preserve its peculiar nature as a combination of theory and method with a more or less conspicuous functional role determined and legitimated by varying scholarly interests.

---

105. M. Oeming, *Das wahre Israel: Die 'genealogische Vorhalle' 1 Chronik 1–9* (BWANT, 128; Stuttgart: W. Kohlhammer, 1990), p. 206.
106. Steins, 'Die Bücher der Chronik', p. 171.

THE CHRONICLER AS REDACTOR*

Steven L. McKenzie

Introduction

As a good Deuteronomist, I make my point of departure for this topic
Martin Noth's 1943 *Überlieferungsgeschichtliche Studien*.[1] According
to Noth, the respective compositions of Chr.'s history and DtrH were
remarkably similar. He freed both works from the hegemony of the
Documentary Hypothesis,[2] arguing that Chr., like DtrH, was an author/
editor who fashioned an extended theological history. Their respective
sources were different: DtrH assembled a variety of independent traditions, while Chr. had DtrH in front of him. But the two authors dealt
with their sources in similar ways. Noth also found a number of later
additions in each work, without considering either one to be the product
of multiple redactions.[3]

---

*   I am indebted to Ralph Klein, Gary Knoppers and Hugh Williamson, who
all read and commented on an earlier draft of this paper, and to Pat Graham for the
invitation to address this topic in the Chronicles–Ezra–Nehemiah Section of the
SBL.

1.   M. Noth, *Überlieferungsgeschichtliche Studien: Die sammenden und bearbeitenden Geschichtswerke im Alten Testament* (Halle: Max Niemeyer, 1943).

2.   J.W. Rothstein and J. Hänel (*Das erste Buch der Chronik* [KAT, 18/2;
Leipzig: D. Werner Scholl, 1927]) had contended that the basic layer of Chronicles
was a continuation of P. G. von Rad (*Das Geschichtsbild des chronistischen Werkes*
[BWANT, 54; Stuttgart: W. Kohlhammer, 1930]) countered with evidence of both
P and D in Chr.'s history. Then, A.C. Welch (*The Work of the Chronicler: Its Purpose and its Date* [Schweich Lecture, 1938; London: Oxford University Press,
1939]) tried to extend von Rad's conclusion by arguing that Chr.'s initial work
relied on Deuteronomy and that texts dependent on P came from a second redactor.

3.   'Noth never stopped to ask who was responsible for the multifarious additions to Chronicles which he had detected and what was the rationale for their
inclusion.' H.G.M. Williamson, 'Introduction' in M. Noth, *The Chronicler's History* (JSOTSup, 50; Sheffield: JSOT Press, 1987), p. 19. The same could be said of
Noth's treatment of DtrH.

Scholarship since Noth on these two biblical histories has largely been a study of contrasts. Since Noth brought an end to the treatment of the Former Prophets as individual books, subsequent study of DtrH has been preoccupied with isolating redactional levels. Scholarship in Chronicles–Ezra–Nehemiah, on the other hand, has moved from identifying unified authorship to independent books.[4]

As a result, consideration of Chr. as redactor must take place in two arenas: that of the entire Chr.'s history, namely, the books of Chronicles, Ezra and Nehemiah, and that of the books of 1–2 Chronicles only. The former concerns theories of redactional levels—the *who* behind the composition of these books. For 1–2 Chronicles, we inquire about the sources and editorial techniques that they reflect—the *what* and *how* of redaction. These three topics—who, what and how—form the outline for this paper.

1. *Who Redacted?: Theories of Multiple Redactions*

As in DtrH, reconstructions of the composition of Chronicles fall into two categories: *Blockmodelle* (block models) and *Schichtenmodelle* (layered models).[5]

---

4. The two people primarily responsible for this shift are S. Japhet, 'The Supposed Common Authorship of Chronicles and Ezra–Nehemiah Investigated Anew', *VT* 18 (1968), pp. 330-71; 'The Relationship between Chronicles and Ezra–Nehemiah', in J.A. Emerton (ed.), *Congress Volume: Leuven, 1989* (VTSup, 43; Leiden: E.J. Brill, 1991), pp. 298-313; *I & II Chronicles: A Commentary* (OTL: Westminster/John Knox Press, 1993); and H.G.M. Williamson, *Israel in the Books of Chronicles* (Cambridge: Cambridge University Press, 1977), pp. 5-82. For an assessment of their principal arguments see M.A. Throntveit, 'Linguistic Analysis and the Question of Authorship in Chronicles, Ezra and Nehemiah', *VT* 32 (1982), pp. 201-16. Two very recent works that still advocate the unity of authorship of the *Grundschrift* of Chronicles and Ezra–Nehemiah are J. Blenkinsopp, *Ezra–Nehemiah: A Commentary* (OTL; Philadelphia: Westminster Press, 1988) and K.-F. Pohlmann, 'Zur Frage von Korrespondenzen und Divergenzen zwischen den Chronikbüchern und dem Esra/Nehemia-Buch', in Emerton (ed.), *Congress Volume: Leuven, 1989*, pp. 314-30.

5. The terms were coined, I believe, by H. Weippert, 'Das deuteronomistische Geschichtswerk: Sein Ziel und Ende in der neueren Forschung', *TRu* 50 (1985), pp. 213-49.

a. *Cross's Theory of Three Editions*

While scholars, such as Japhet, who posit a single author behind Chronicles fit in the first category, the only example of a redactional *Blockmodelle* that I know is the one initiated by Freedman and amplified by Cross.[6] The delineation of editorial levels in Chr.'s history was one scene in Cross's portrait of the postexilic restoration. In it, Chr.'s initial work, written as a program for the rebuilding of the temple in 520–515 BCE, underwent two subsequent editions, which added the Ezra and Nehemiah materials, respectively. Thus, Chr_1 = 'a genealogical introduction plus much of 1 Chronicles 10.1 through 2 Chronicles 36.21 plus the continuing Hebrew material in Ezra 1.1–3.13 (= 1 Esd. 2.1-15; 5.1-62)'.[7] Chr_2 = 1 Chronicles 10–2 Chronicles 34 + the *Vorlage* of all of 1 Esdras. Chr_3 = 1–2 Chronicles, Ezra, Nehemiah.

This three-tiered edifice rests on two pillars of evidence. The first is the book of 1 Esdras, which is held to preserve a fragment of the second edition of the work, before the Nehemiah Memoir was attached. 'In parallel passages First Esdras proves on the whole to have a shorter, better text, as generally recognized. Its order of pericopes reflects an older, historically superior recension of the Chronicler's work (Chronicles, Ezra).'[8] The first edition is then postulated on the basis of the major themes in Chronicles. Freedman had argued that the themes of Davidic dynasty and temple cult fit best in the setting of the effort to rebuild the temple and reestablish the monarchy under Zerubbabel in 520–515. He dated the initial edition of Chronicles to shortly after 515, suggesting that its original ending had been supplanted by the Aramaic section in Ezra 4.6–6.1. Cross saw the work as more programmatic and

---

6. D.N. Freedman, 'The Chronicler's Purpose', *CBQ* 23 (1961), pp. 436-42; F.M. Cross, 'A Reconstruction of the Judean Restoration', *JBL* 94 (1975), pp. 4-18 (= *Int* 29 [1975], pp. 187-203 and now pp. 151-72 in *From Epic to Canon: History and Literature in Ancient Israel* [Baltimore: The Johns Hopkins University Press, 1998]). Citations are from the 1998 version. Cf. also J.D. Newsome, Jr, 'Toward a New Understanding of the Chronicler and his Purposes', *JBL* 94 (1975), pp. 201-17. In my 1985 published dissertation, *The Chronicler's Use of the Deuteronomistic History* (HSM, 33; Atlanta: Scholars Press) I upheld Cross's reconstruction. I had initially hoped to reaffirm it in this paper, but the evidence has led me in a different direction.

7. Cross, 'Reconstruction', p. 165. Verse numbers throughout this article follow those of the MT for Chronicles, Ezra and Nehemiah, and the Greek (LXX) text for 1 Esdras.

8. Cross, 'Reconstruction', p. 160.

open to the future. He ended it with Ezra 3.13 (= 1 Esd. 5.62) and assigned it a date between 520–515, when the temple was being rebuilt.

There are two components of the first pillar, as indicated in the statement from Cross quoted above: the parallel texts in Ezra and 1 Esdras and the order of pericopes in 1 Esdras as opposed to Ezra. I shall examine the second component first by analyzing the Artaxerxes correspondence in 1 Esd. 2.15-25 = Ezra 4.6-24. The way in which this correspondence demonstrates the dependence of 1 Esdras upon Ezra has not been fully appreciated.[9] In the first place, it falls between portions of 1 Esdras (2.1-15; 5.1-62) that Cross assigns to Chr₁. But the correspondence dates to the reign of Artaxerxes I (c. 465–424 BCE), 50 years or more after the completion of the temple in 515.[10] Cross avoided the contradiction by following the Ezra parallel in 1.1–3.13, which does not

9. The arguments of W. Rudolph (*Esra und Nehemia, samt 3. Esra* [HAT, 20; Tübingen: J.C.B. Mohr (Paul Siebeck), 1949], pp. xi-xiii) and B. Walde (*Die Esdrasbücher der Septuaginta: Ihr gegenseitiges Verhältnis untersucht* [BS, 18; Freiburg: Herder, 1913], pp. 110-18) are useful but can be strengthened. Blenkinsopp (*Ezra–Nehemiah*, p. 106) and Williamson ('Eschatology in Chronicles', *TynBul* 28 [1977], p. 123; 'The Composition of Ezra i–vi', *JTS* 34 [1983], pp. 15-20) both refer to it but do not take note of its full significance for this issue. A. Schenker ('La relation d'Esdras A' au text massorétique d'Esdras–Néhémie', in G.J. Norton and S. Pisano [eds.], *Tradition of the Text: Studies Offered to Dominique Barthélemy in Celebration of his 70th Birthday* [OBO, 109; Freiburg: Universitätsverlag; Göttingen: Vandenhoeck & Ruprecht, 1991], pp. 218-44) has recently reasserted the priority of 1 Esdras based on three comparisons with Ezra: chronological details, lists of adversaries and the question of whether the restoration of the temple or the city is being described in Ezra 4.7-24 and 1 Esd. 2.15-25. The Aramaic correspondence is important in all three. Schenker's reasoning that Ezra's more logical chronology and longer, better organized list of adversaries must be secondary escapes me. Williamson ('The Problem with 1 Esdras', in J. Barton and D.J. Reimer (eds.), *After the Exile: Essays in Honour of Rex Mason* [Macon, GA: Mercer University Press, 1996]) has pointed out the inconsistency of Schenker's argument and the problems with the contrast between city-altar-temple and altar-temple-city that he perceives in the restoration programs of 1 Esdras and Ezra, respectively. My literary observations, which follow, counter Schenker's arguments and point to the dependence of 1 Esdras on Ezra.

10. Past efforts to identify Ahasuerus (Ezra 4.6) and Artaxerxes with earlier Persian kings have proven unacceptable as Williamson (*Ezra–Nehemiah* [WBC, 16; Waco, TX: Word Books], pp. 56-57) and Blenkinsopp (*Ezra–Nehemiah*, p. 111) explain. See H.H. Rowley, 'Nehemiah's Mission and its Background', in *idem, Men of God: Studies in Old Testament History and Prophecy* (London: Thomas Nelson, 1963), p. 220.

include this correspondence. But this move undermines his contention that 1 Esdras retains an older, better arrangement of pericopes than Ezra.

The location of this correspondence is anachronistic in both Ezra and 1 Esdras, since it describes an event from Artaxerxes' reign (and in Ezra, Xerxes' [Ahasuerus'] as well) before Darius (522–486 BCE) takes power.[11] In Ezra, there is a literary explanation for this: it serves as yet another example, along with those in 4.1-5, of the opposition of the 'people of the land' to the reconstruction efforts of the returnees.[12] This is not true of 1 Esd. 2.15-25, however. Here, the correspondence is preceded by the account of the return under Cyrus, led by Sheshbazzar, with an inventory of the temple vessels (2.1-14 = Ezra 1.1-11). Unlike the Ezra version, 1 Esdras does not at this point recount the laying of the temple foundation (Ezra 3.10-13) or the opposition of the 'people of the land', whose offer to join in the work is refused by Zerubbabel (Ezra 4.1-5). As a result, the location of 1 Esd. 2.15-25 makes no sense. The building activity is mentioned for the first time in the letter from the 'people of the land' (1 Esd. 2.17). The text does not inform the reader that building has begun, much less that it is opposed, and certainly gives no motive for the opposition. Without the explanatory foreground in Ezra this letter comes 'out of the blue'. Thus, the reader has to know the Ezra account in order to make sense of 1 Esdras. The only explanation for the placement of the Artaxerxes correspondence in 1 Esd. 2.15-25 is its comparable location in Ezra. 1 Esdras 2.25 even retains the sentence from Ezra 4.24 that is used to resume the narrative after the inclusion of the correspondence. But again, 1 Esdras lacks the literary reason for this shift from Artaxerxes back to Darius.[13]

---

11. Josephus (*Ant.* 11.21), who used 1 Esdras as his source, recognized the problem and resolved it by changing Artaxerxes' name to Cambyses. Some scholars have argued that the correspondence should be attributed to earlier kings, but the names of the kings given in the text militate against their case. For a discussion of other explanations that have been offered, including the well-known 'Tabeel hypothesis', see Williamson, *Ezra–Nehemiah*, pp. 57-59.

12. This holds whether it reflects a technique of the author (*Wiederaufnahme*), as Williamson (*Ezra–Nehemiah*, pp. 56-60) and Blenkinsopp (*Ezra–Nehemiah*, pp. 106, 111) contend, or is an editorial interpolation.

13. J.M. Myers (*I and II Esdras* [AB, 42; Garden City, NY: Doubleday, 1974], pp. 41-42) points to other signs of 1 Esdras's familiarity with Ezra: 1 Esd. 2.15 seems to telescope the names of the authors of the two accusations from Ezra 4.7-8 into a single accusation, and it refers to the building of the temple (2.17, 18) where

The reason for this disarray in 1 Esdras vis-à-vis Ezra is the inclusion of the story of the three youths in 1 Esd. 3.1–5.6.[14] The author or compiler of 1 Esdras divided the accusations of the 'people of the land' in Ezra 4 into two parts (1 Esd. 2.15-25; 5.63-70) in order to explain two separate delays in the reconstruction efforts. Ezra 4.1-5 had to be moved to 1 Esd. 5.63-70 because it mentioned Zerubbabel who is first introduced in the story of the three youths. The Artaxerxes correspondence (1 Esd. 2.15-25 = Ezra 4.6-24), despite its obvious misplacement historically, explains why the temple was not rebuilt under Sheshbazzar but was delayed until the arrival of Zerubbabel. This delay allowed the writer to insert the story of the three youths, which introduces Zerubbabel and explains his leadership role, along with the list of returnees in 1 Esd. 5.4-45 (= Ezra 2.1-70; Neh. 7.7-73). Then, as in Ezra, the writer presented the account of the temple foundation and the hindrance of the 'people of the land', which delayed the rebuilding until later in Zerubbabel's career (1 Esd. 5.46-70 = Ezra 3.1–4.5). The resulting contradiction between 1 Esd. 2.25, which mentions Darius' second year, and 5.70, which speaks of a two-year delay until Darius' reign begins, comes from the writer's preservation of the Ezra *Vorlage*.[15]

The reliance of 1 Esdras 1–6 on Ezra's order of pericopes seriously weakens the case for Cross's view of 1 Esdras as a fragment of a Chr$_2$ recension and adds weight to the arguments for it being a composition in its own right.[16] It is possible to maintain, as Pohlmann does (see n.

the Ezra account mentions only the city walls in this correspondence, though Ezra 4.1-3 had referred to the temple. Cf. also Walde, *Esdrasbücher*, pp. 112-17. Both conclusions are the opposite of Schenker's ('La relation d'Esdras A''). On the first point, see R.W. Klein, 'Studies in the Greek Texts of the Chronicler' (ThD dissertation, Harvard Divinity School, 1966), pp. 141-47, who makes the case that the longer Ezra (MT) text is expansive. Another weakness of Schenker's article is that he does not consider text-critical differences between Ezra and 1 Esdras.

14. Cf. K.-F. Pohlmann, *Studien zum dritten Esra: Ein Beitrag zur Frage nach dem ursprünglichen Schluss der chronistischen Geschichtswerkes* (FRLANT, 104; Göttingen: Vandenhoeck & Ruprecht, 1970), pp. 35-37.

15. For an attempt to explain 1 Esdras's chronological statements cf. Rudolph, *Esra und Nehemia*, pp. xii-xiii.

16. Williamson ('The Problem with 1 Esdras') summarizes six such arguments. Cf. also B. Halpern, 'A Historiographic Commentary on Ezra 1–6: Achronological Narrative and Dual Chronology in Israelite Historiography', in W.H. Propp, B. Halpern and D.N. Freedman (eds.), *The Hebrew Bible and its Interpreters* (Winona Lake, IN: Eisenbrauns, 1990), pp. 81-142.

14), that despite the secondary arrangement of pericopes in 1 Esdras, it still reflects a compositional stage before the addition of the Nehemiah Memoir. But this seems pointless, since there is no evidence for it; 1 Esdras as we have it presupposes Ezra. 1 Esdras 9.37, moreover, seems to presuppose the canonical placement of Nehemiah 8, and therefore the book of Ezra–Nehemiah as we have it.[17] In addition, this position must insist that the story of the three youths is secondary to 1 Esdras. But this runs counter to the integral role that the story plays in 1 Esdras, as described above, and to recently articulated evidence that both the story and its editorial link in 5.1-6 are translations of Semitic originals.[18] The final blow to the fragment hypothesis may now have been dealt by van der Kooij, who has made impressive cases for regarding the present beginning and ending of 1 Esdras—long held to be too abrupt to be intentional—as original.[19]

17. Williamson, *Israel*, pp. 32-35. Pohlmann (*Studien*, pp. 66-71) considered the evidence of 1 Esd. 9.37 to be the strongest argument in favor of the compilation theory. Cf. also S. Mowinckel, *Studien zu dem Buche Ezra–Nehemia. I. Die nachchronistische Redaktion des Buches: Die Listen* (SUNVAO, 2; Oslo: Universitetsvorlaget, 1964), pp. 21-25.

18. Z. Talshir and D. Talshir, 'The Original Language of the Story of the Three Youths (1 Esdras 3–4)', in M. Fishbane and E. Tov (eds.), *'Sha'arei Talmon': Studies in the Bible, Qumran, and the Ancient Near East Presented to Shemaryahu Talmon* (Winona Lake, IN: Eisenbrauns, 1992), pp. 63*-75* (Hebrew). Cf. also Z. Talshir, 'The Milieu of 1 Esdras in the Light of its Vocabulary', in A. Pietersma and C.E. Cox (eds.), *De Septuaginta: Studies in Honour of John William Wevers on his Sixty-Fifth Birthday* (Mississauga, ON: Benben, 1984), pp. 129-47. W. In der Smitten ('Zur Pagenerzählung im 3. Esra [3 Esr. III 1-V 6]', *VT* 22 [1972], pp. 492-95) had earlier argued against Pohlmann's view that this story was interpolated into the Greek text.

19. A. van der Kooij, 'On the Ending of the Book of 1 Esdras', in C.E. Cox (ed.), *VII Congress of the International Organization for Septuagint and Cognate Studies: Leuven, 1989* (SBLSCS, 31; Atlanta: Scholars Press, 1991), pp. 37-49; 'Zur Frage des Anfangs des 1. Esrabuches', *ZAW* 103 (1991), pp. 239-52. He shows that the final two words, καὶ ἐπισυνήχθησαν, in 9.55 are not the fragmentary beginning of a new sentence but the second part of a 'both ... and' construction within a ὅτι clause. It explains the joy of the festival in 9.37-55 as both the result of the teaching they had received and 'because they had been gathered together'. His case for the beginning is based on 1.21-22, which is unique to 1 Esdras. This passage refers to things about Josiah's reign that were recorded earlier. The language of the passage has parallels to 2 Kgs 22.11-20 // 2 Chron. 34.19-28, indicating that 1 Esdras did not include this material, i.e., the earlier account about Josiah. It thus distinguishes its own account of Josiah's Passover ('things that are now

What complicates matters, however, is that the first part of Cross's assertion, 'in parallel passages First Esdras proves on the whole to have a shorter, better text', was based on Klein's study, which is still convincing.[20] The text of Chronicles–Ezra–Nehemiah used by the compiler of 1 Esdras was apparently based on a different type from that of the MT. As Cross points out, textual traditions are not identical with literary editions.[21] The literary evidence indicates that 1 Esdras was a later edition of or composition using the canonical books of Chronicles and Ezra–Nehemiah. The textual evidence indicates that its compiler had access to a better version of those books than preserved in the MT. There is no reason to believe that this version had a different order of pericopes, since the different order of 1 Esdras is the result of the inclusion of 1 Esd. 3.1–5.6 and coordinate changes and of the addition of the reading of the Law from Neh. 7.72–8.12, where Ezra had a leading role appropriate to the 1 Esdras narrative. The reason for the composition of 1 Esdras in the first place remains uncertain,[22] but it does not support a theory of redactional levels in Chronicles.

As for Freedman's connection of Chronicles' interests in David and the temple with the rebuilding efforts of 520–515 BCE, this raises the whole issue of Chr.'s eschatology and the role of the Davidic monarch in it, which has been the subject of intense analysis in recent years. Fortunately, the two just-published dissertations of Riley and Kelly make it possible to survey the matter from contrasting perspectives.[23]

---

told') from the accounts of the earlier part of Josiah's reign in Kings and Chronicles ('things that he had done before', 1.31). The abrupt beginning may be due to translation style and is comparable to the beginnings of Numbers and Leviticus. T.C. Eskenazi ('The Chronicler and the Composition of 1 Esdras', *CBQ* 48 [1986], pp. 39-61; Eskerazi, *In an Age of Prose: A Literary Approach to Ezra–Nehemiah* [SBLMS, 36; Atlanta: Scholars Press, 1988], pp. 159-74) and A.E. Gardner ('The Purpose and Date of 1 Esdras', *JJS* 37 [1986], pp. 18-27) had both previously made cases for the beginning and ending being intact, though on far less convincing grounds.

20. Klein, 'Studies in the Greek Texts of the Chronicler', esp. his reconstruction on pp. 321-22. See the summary in *HTR* 59 (1966), p. 449, and his 'Old Readings in I Esdras: The List of Returnees from Babylon (Ezra 2 // Nehemiah 7)', *HTR* 62 (1969), pp. 99-107.

21. Cross, 'Reconstruction', p. 159.

22. Cf. Gardner ('Purpose and Date of 1 Esdras') and Williamson ('Problem with 1 Esdras') for recent discussions of this matter.

23. W. Riley, *King and Cultus in Chronicles: Worship and the Reinterpretation*

Riley represents the view that Chr. subordinates David and Solomon to the temple. He contends that Chr.'s idealization of the two kings looks not to the future restoration of the dynasty but to Israel's *Urzeit* for their roles as founders of the temple. If this view is correct, it would significantly weaken the possible connection between Chronicles and the restoration effort under Zerubbabel. But even those who, with Kelly, hold that the future restoration of the Davidic kingdom is Chr.'s focal hope also observe that this interest cannot be limited to the early post-exilic period but continues for centuries thereafter.[24] It is still possible, of course, that an initial edition of Chronicles was composed in the late sixth century. But this possibility has yet to be advanced on literary-critical grounds or to explain satisfactorily the indications of a later setting, such as the genealogies and the reference to dariacs (1 Chron. 29.7).

b. *Schichtenmodelle*[25]

Many scholars, in agreement with Noth, have found evidence of later scribal activity in Chronicles, especially in 1 Chronicles 1–9, 15–16 and 23–27. Willi identified this activity as primarily cultic in orientation.[26] A few see enough common features among the additions to posit redactional levels. Williamson perceives a light, pro-Priestly redaction particularly in 1 Chronicles 15–16, 23–27 and Ezra 1–6, to which he attributes the joining of the books of Chronicles and Ezra–Nehemiah.[27] With the exception of Galling,[28] however, no one has attempted to

of History (JSOTSup, 160; Sheffield: JSOT Press, 1993); B.E. Kelly, *Retribution and Eschatology in Chronicles* (JSOTSup, 211; Sheffield: Sheffield Academic Press, 1996).

24. See, especially, Williamson, 'Eschatology in Chronicles', whose conclusions are extended by Kelly.

25. Cf. G. Steins, *Der Chronik als kanonisches Abschlussphänomen: Studien zur Entstehung und Theologie von 1/2 Chronik* (BBB, 93; Weinheim: Beltz Athenäum, 1995).

26. T. Willi, *Die Chronik als Auslegung: Untersuchungen zur literarischen Gestaltung der historischen Überlieferung Israels* (FRLANT, 106; Göttingen: Vandenhoeck & Ruprecht, 1972), pp. 194-204.

27. Williamson, *1 and 2 Chronicles* (NCB; Grand Rapids: Eerdmans, 1982), esp. pp. 14-15, and 'The Composition of Ezra i-vi', pp. 1-30.

28. K. Galling, *Die Bücher der Chronik, Esra, Nehemia* (ATD, 12; Göttingen: Vandenhoeck & Ruprecht, 1954). Galling contended that Chr.'s original work, written c. 300 BCE (Chron), was enlarged about a century later by a second writer

identify a thoroughgoing level of redactional activity in Chronicles until quite recently.

The newly published dissertations of Dörrfuss and Steins[29] appear to represent a significant new trend in Chronicles scholarship, at least on the Continent, akin to the *Göttingerschule* of redaction criticism in DtrH. These two works are quite different from each other. Dörrfuss argues for a late (Maccabean) 'Moses redaction' of Chronicles that criticizes the Davidic monarchy and the Jerusalem temple and holds up Moses and the associated Sinai traditions as the source of hope for theocratic leadership in the future. He specifically calls for the application of literary-critical techniques to Chronicles in the search for discernible redactional levels.[30]

Steins answers the call. Chronicles, Steins contends, is a conscious effort to close the canon, especially the Writings, by recapitulating Israel's history through the lens of Torah. It is a multilayered work, what Steins calls a 'literary process'. Indeed, Steins isolates a *Grundschicht* ('basic composition') followed by three levels of redaction, two of which are themselves multilayered. The first level, concerned with cultic personnel boasts a levitically oriented layer, two musician layers and a 'musician-gatekeeper layer'. The second level is the community (קהל) level. The third level has two main layers, a cult layer and a northern layer, but Steins also includes here late additions, which he admits are really too diverse for a single redactional phase.[31] Thus, a given text could have ten layers or more, and Steins typically finds a half dozen in the texts he analyzes.

The same criticisms that have been leveled at the *Schichtenmodelle* in DtrH apply here. Roberts's review of Spieckermann's work in Kings, for example, applies well, *mutatis mutandis*, to Steins:[32]

(Chron**), who added numerous passages displaying an interest in certain cultic matters (personnel, music, festivals) and the return of what Galling called the Israelite proselytes. Galling's literary-critical judgments are often not compelling, and it is difficult to discern any particular *Tendenz* in the texts he regards as additions that would justify ascribing them to one hand or viewing them as distinct from the rest of Chronicles.

29. E.M. Dörrfuss, *Mose in den Chronikbüchern: Garant theokratischer Zukunftserwartung* (BZAW, 219; Berlin: W. de Gruyter, 1994); Steins, *Abschlussphänomen.*

30. Dörrfuss, *Mose,* p. 277 n. 8.

31. Steins, *Abschlussphänomen,* pp. 429-30.

32. J.J.M. Roberts, review of *Juda under Assur in der Sargonidenzeit,* by

> It is possible, of course, that the composition of 2 Kings is the result of a
> process as complicated as that envisioned by S., but even if it were, one
> may well question whether it would still be possible for modern scholars
> to disentangle all these strands and supplements with the certainty that S.
> and company suppose. Such criticism runs the risk of discrediting the
> discipline in the same way that the splintering of the pentateuchal
> sources ultimately reached the point of absurdity.

The appeal to Pentateuchal criticism is particularly apt as it shows the
importance of form criticism as a corrective to literary criticism.
Dörrfuss's neglect of form-critical matters allows him to engage in the
kind of hypercritical literary division that his work reflects.[33] The same
is even truer of Steins's treatment of individual texts. What is more, his
definition of Chronicles' genre as *Abschlusswerk* seems patently contradictory to his literary-critical method. How could a community have
consciously produced a closing work to its canon and then continued to
add to it? In short, I do not find the application of the *Schichtenmodelle*
to Chronicles studies particularly healthy. Williamson's theory of a
moderate redactional level is more attractive to my mind and his literary judgments much more sober. However, the connections between the
texts that he identifies as additions remain somewhat tenuous, so that it
is not certain that they are from the same hand. Perhaps Noth's view of
the composition of Chronicles, like his view of DtrH, still has much to
commend it.

2. *What Chr. Redacted: Auld's Theory of a Shared Source*

Scholars have long perceived that Chronicles offers a unique opportunity for observing the redactional techniques of a biblical writer—
unique because Chr.'s *Vorlage* does not have to be reconstructed; we
have it in Samuel–Kings. The qualification imposed by the Qumran
discoveries regarding the type of text of Samuel used by Chr. may have
made scholars more cautious but has not changed this basic perception.
However, Auld has now advanced the theory that Chr. did not use
Samuel–Kings as his source but that he shared with the author of

H. Spieckermann (FRLANT, 129; Göttingen: Vandenhoeck & Ruprecht, 1982) in
CBQ 46 (1984), pp. 328-30.
    33. I use the word 'hypercritical' over Dörrfuss's objections in *Mose*, p. 277 n.
8. For further criticisms of Dörrfuss, see the review by G.N. Knoppers, *CBQ* 58
(1996), pp. 705-707.

Samuel–Kings a primary source that covered the history of Judah and that each writer expanded in his own direction.[34] Before we can survey Chr.'s redactional handling of his *Vorlage*, therefore, it is imperative to come to some resolution about the nature of that source in the light of Auld's recent proposal.

Auld seems justified when he contends that, by privileging Samuel–Kings over Chronicles, scholars have tended to overlook interests and biases that shaped the former. But one can cultivate a greater sensitivity to these interests and biases and a greater skepticism about the historicity of the Former Prophets without adopting Auld's view of a shared source. And there are a number of aspects of Auld's theory that render it unlikely or at least in need of further explanation. First, recognizing that Auld's 1994 book (*Kings Without Privilege*) was devoted to sketching the rudimentary case for his postulated shared source, it is not unfair now to request a tighter definition of this document, especially in form-critical terms. If it was a history of the Judahite monarchy, when was it written and for what purpose? In particular, where did it begin? The first text that Chronicles has in common with Samuel–Kings, and the place where Auld begins his survey, is the story of Saul's death (1 Chron. 10 // 1 Sam. 31). But an independent history of Judah could not have begun with this text. It only makes sense a beginning for Chronicles in view of its deuteronomistic *Vorlage*. Chr.'s addition in 10.13-14 explains why he begins at this point—because the kingdom is herewith placed in David's hands. Chr.'s reference to Saul's faithlessness (מעל) and to his inquiry through a medium in this same addition (10.13) presupposes at least the story in 1 Samuel 28, if not those of his rejection in 1 Samuel 13 and 15. Auld observes, 'The Saul stories are largely set north of Judah, yet not very far north.'[35] His ambivalence indicates the problem that the Saul stories pose for his theory. It seems unlikely that a history of Judah would have included them, yet Chr. seems to know them.[36]

---

34. A.G. Auld, *Kings without Privilege: David and Moses in the Story of the Bible's Kings* (Edinburgh: T. & T. Clark, 1994).

35. Auld, *Kings without Privilege*, p. 172.

36. The attempt of Auld's protegé, C.Y.S. Ho ('Conjectures and Refutations: Is 1 Samuel XXXI 1-13 Really the Source of 1 Chronicles X 1-12?' *VT* 45 [1995], pp. 82-106) to address this problem is not successful. His inclusion of a story of Saul's rise and fall (before 1 Sam. 19) in the shared source only exacerbates the question of its genre. A history of the Judahite monarchy would hardly have included Saul.

The mention of Saul's faults in 1 Chronicles 10 is only the tip of the proverbial iceberg where it concerns references in Chronicles to material in the Former Prophets that is not shared by Chronicles. A second major query for Auld concerns these references. How does the theory of a shared source explain them? In other words, how could Chr. know of this material unless he had the Former Prophets, much in their present form, in front of him? Following are a few of the more obvious examples.[37]

1. 1 Chronicles 29.27 mentions that David reigned seven years in Hebron and 33 in Jerusalem, though Chronicles lacks the account of the civil war during the first seven years that is found in 2 Samuel 2–4.[38]

2. 1 Chronicles 15.29 tells of Michal seeing David bring up the ark and then despising him. The Samuel parallel (2 Sam. 6.20-23) is part of a series of stories about David and Michal with apologetic intent (giving David some claim to the throne and explaining why Michal had no children). Since Chronicles does not elsewhere mention Michal or David's marriage to her, the reader has to know Samuel in order to make sense of Chronicles at this point.

3. 1 Chronicles 17.6, 10 // 2 Sam. 7.7, 11 refer to the judges. In v. 6 // 7 Yahweh asks David whether any of the judges were told to build a temple. The question is rhetorical, but the reader would not know the answer without the book of Judges more or less intact. Also, v. 10 // 11 ('from the time [למימים //

Moreover, Ho (p. 99) alludes to connections between 1 Chron. 10 and 1 Sam. 5. If, as such connections would suggest, the shared source began even earlier than Saul, the difference between it and Samuel–Kings all but disappears. Ho notes the allusion of 1 Chron. 10.13-14 to 1 Sam. 15 and 28, but these chapters are probably late additions to Samuel (J. Van Seters, *In Search of History: Historiography in the Ancient World and the Origins of Biblical History* [New Haven: Yale University Press, 1983], pp. 258-64), indicating Chr.'s acquaintance with DtrH essentially as it now stands. Ho makes several astute observations about other connections within Samuel and between 1 Chron. 10 and Samuel, but these can all be explained as Chr.'s authorial changes (see the next section of this paper) under the standard view that Chr. used Samuel as his source, albeit in a better textual form.

37. For more examples and more extensive discussion, see Willi, *Der Chronik als Auslegung*, pp. 56-66.

38. Auld (*Kings without Privilege*, p. 43) includes a translation of the chronological data in 2 Sam. 5.4-5, despite leaving out the verse numbers in the heading.

לִמַן־הַיּוֹם] when I appointed judges') assumes the existence of a period of judges. This is particularly striking if one follows the spirit of Auld's recommendation and understands, as seems proper, the period of the judges not as an era in Israel's tradition history but as the construct of an author.

4. 1 Chronicles 20.5 reflects a deliberate change of 2 Sam. 21.19, so that Elhanan the Bethlehemite (*bêt-laḥmî*) killed not Goliath but Lahmi the brother of Goliath. The obvious reason for the change was to avoid the contradiction with 1 Samuel 17, which is not reflected in Chronicles. Of course, as part of the David story, Auld may well include 1 Samuel 17 in the shared source. But then, in addition to the question raised above about the beginning of this source, one must also ask about the difference between Chr.'s familiarity with this story and his familiarity with other materials in the Former Prophets but not in Chronicles.

5. 2 Chronicles 10.15 // 1 Kgs 12.15 refer to the division of the kingdom as the fulfillment of Ahijah's oracle. But Chronicles does not contain a version of the oracle, so that Auld does not include it in the shared source. The writer of this source would certainly not report the fulfillment of an unknown prophecy, especially one as important as this division. What makes this even more remarkable is that the 'Supplement' in 3 Kgdms 12.24a-z, which Auld would like to see as the shared source's account for Jeroboam, attributes this oracle to Shemaiah rather than Ahijah. Thus, the only possible source for the fulfillment report shared by Chronicles and Kings is 1 Kgs 11.26-40.

6. 2 Chronicles refers several times to Ahab (18; 22.3-5 [and Omri, 22.2]). It assumes that the reader knows about him from another context, since it never introduces him or describes his reign. The story in 2 Chronicles 18 // 1 Kings 22 is especially revealing in this regard. This chapter along with 1 Kings 20 is out of place both historically and literarily.[39] It is part of a

39. A. Jepsen, 'Israel und Damascus', *AfO* 14 (1942), pp. 153-72; S.L. McKenzie, *Trouble with Kings: The Composition of the Book of Kings in the Deuteronomistic History* (VTSup, 42; Leiden: E.J. Brill, 1991), pp. 88-93; J.M. Miller, 'The Elisha Cycle and the Accounts of the Omride Wars', *JBL* 85 (1966), pp. 441-54; 'The Fall of the House of Ahab', *VT* 17 (1967), pp. 307-24; and 'The Rest of the Acts of Jehoahaz (I Kings 20. 22, 1-38)', *ZAW* 80 (1968), pp. 337-42;

whole series of chronological misplacements in Kings.[40] It is also one of a number of northern, prophetic legends that have been added at a post-DtrH level to Kings.[41] The king of Israel in the story was originally not Ahab but a member of the Jehu dynasty. One of the indications of the story's misplacement is the fact that it lies outside of the regnal formulas for Jehoshaphat, yet these formulas typically serve as the rubrics within which the writers include the narratives about individual kings. It is unlikely that the shared source, which focuses on Judah's royal history, would have included a northern prophetic legend, and certainly not outside of the regnal formulas for the featured southern king. The problems with the text can only be explained as the result of phenomena in the development of the book of Kings, yet Chronicles follows Kings faithfully in the placement of the story and in the names of the characters. In short, Chronicles' references to Ahab strongly indicate that Chr. used the book of Kings as it now stands.

7. 2 Chronicles 22.7-8 summarizes the account of Jehu's revolt (cf. 2 Kgs 9–10). The reference to 'Jehu son of Nimshi, whom Yahweh had anointed to destroy the house of Ahab' is dependent on 2 Kgs 9.1-10, which has been revised by DtrH in order to provide a prophetic commission for Jehu to annihilate 'the house of Ahab' in fulfillment of Elijah's oracle in 1 Kgs 21.17-29.[42] Auld apparently recognizes the problem this text presents, for his reconstruction of the shared source lacks the allusion to Jehu's anointing.[43] But it still retains the reference to Jehu, who could only be known to Chr. and his readers from the book of Kings, since without the background of the Kings

---

W.T. Pitard, *Ancient Damascus: A Historical Study of the Syrian City-State from Earliest Times until its Fall to the Assyrians in 732 B.C.E.* (Winona Lake, IN: Eisenbrauns, 1987); C.F. Whitley, 'The Deuteronomic Presentation of the House of Omri', *VT* 2 (1952), pp. 137-52.

40. In addition to the articles by Miller cited in the previous note, see his 'Another Look at the Chronology of the Early Divided Monarchy', *JBL* 86 (1967), pp. 276-88; and J.D. Shenkel, *Chronology and Recensional Development in the Greek Text of Kings* (HSM, 1; Cambridge, MA: Harvard University Press, 1968).

41. McKenzie, *Trouble with Kings*, pp. 81-100.

42. McKenzie, *Trouble with Kings*, pp. 70-73.

43. Auld, *Kings without Privilege*, p. 113.

explanation of Jehu's position in the army and his religious (deuteronomistic!) motive for rebelling, Chr.'s mention of Jehu is incomprehensible.

8. Chronicles' account of events in Hezekiah's reign (2 Chron. 32) is much shorter overall than that in Kings. There are two fairly clear cases of abbreviation by Chr. of the Kings version. The first is 32.24, which summarizes Hezekiah's prayer and sign in 2 Kgs 20.1-11. While the exact nature of Chr.'s *Vorlage* is uncertain, his one-verse sketch of the story is too terse to have been original, as Auld contends. There are good parallels for a king's inquiry in a case of illness that compare to the Kings account (cf. 3 Kgdms 12.24g-nα; 2 Kgs 1), but nothing like the extremely brief version in Chronicles. The Chronicles verse assumes that the reader knows the Kings story. The same is true of 2 Chron. 32.31, a summary of the tale of the Babylonian envoy in 2 Kgs 20.12-19. Auld recognizes the abbreviated nature of this verse.[44] But since it runs counter to his principle that the shorter text was in the common source, he speculates that this may be 'a further case of secondary adaptation in Chronicles from later additions to Kings'. Later on (p. 173), he suggests that the shared source, as well as the current books of Samuel–Kings and Chronicles, developed in stages. The problem, of course, is that if one resorts very often to this notion of secondary cross-referencing, one loses the control for being able to isolate a common source. And if the shared source gradually accumulated the rest of the material in the Former Prophets, as Auld seems to imply, what is the real difference between this model of Chr.'s source and the older view that he had the finished DtrH?

My third and final query of Auld's proposal concerns the language and themes of 2 Samuel 7 and 1 Kings 8, which are widely regarded as thoroughly deuteronomistic. Auld isolates six levels of development of the MT: the first two pertain to the shared source; the next two to the composition of Kings as we know it in both MT and LXX; and the final two to scribal additions in the MT and LXX of Kings.[45] He quite correctly observes that 'deuteronomistic' language alone does not neces-

44. Auld, *Kings without Privilege*, p. 121 n. 3.
45. Auld, *Kings without Privilege*, pp. 150-51.

sarily signal the hand of a DtrH author/editor, since later scribes could copy this style and terminology. Auld limits DtrH writing to the middle levels, denying that the shared source was deuteronomistic. The difficulty is that while later scribes could imitate earlier writers, the reverse, obviously, is not true—earlier writers cannot imitate the style of later scribes. Yet, 2 Samuel 7 and 1 Kings 8, even as Auld has rendered them for his shared source, remain replete with deuteronomistic vocabulary and ideology. In reference to Cross's well known list of deuteronomistic terms in 2 Samuel 7, Auld remarks:

> However, what strikes me most forcibly after scanning his lists of cross-references is not so much the links between Deuteronomy and Nathan's oracle, but just how closely 2 Sam 7 shares language with Solomon's prayer, his two visions ... and to a lesser extent the greetings to Solomon, including praise of Yahweh's wisdom, extended by both Hiram and the Queen of Sheba.[46]

I am baffled by Auld's statement for several reasons. First, of the 24 expressions from 2 Samuel 7 listed by Cross, he finds parallels in 1 Kings 8 to only five (12, 14, 16, 21, 22) and in the rest of 1 Kings 1–11 to only five as well (1, 3, 11, 16, 21), two of which overlap. Since parallels in Deuteronomy are cited much more frequently, I do not see how Auld could conclude from this list that 2 Samuel 7 has greater affinity with 1 Kings 8 than with Deuteronomy. Secondly, Auld does not mention Weinfeld's list, which is more general, not focusing on 2 Samuel 7, and thus contains instances of deuteronomistic language in 1 Kings 8.[47] Finally, Auld is correct in noting the close relationship of 2 Samuel 7 and 1 Kings 8. This is not surprising, since the latter describes itself as the fulfillment of the former. Nor does it undermine the affinities that these two texts share with Deuteronomy and the other Former Prophets. Auld may be correct that the doctrine of election did not originate with DtrH and that the direction of influence for such themes as the promised 'rest' was from monarchy to earlier traditions rather than the reverse. But these themes, like the language that conveys them, still seem integral to both 2 Samuel 7 and 1 Kings 8 and connect these texts at the fundamental level to the rest of what has become

---

46. Auld, *Kings without Privilege*, p. 151. F.M. Cross, *Canaanite Myth and Hebrew Epic: Essays in the History of the Religion of Israel* (Cambridge, MA: Harvard University Press, 1973), pp. 252-54.

47. M. Weinfeld, *Deuteronomy and the Deuteronomic School* (Oxford: Clarendon Press, 1972), pp. 320-65.

known as DtrH.[48] The relationship between these two texts and earlier portions of DtrH is one of mutual influence and dependence because they are all part of a larger whole.

For the time being, therefore, I remain unconvinced by Auld's proposal, though I find his book quite stimulating. Again, to borrow the words of another reviewer:[49]

> Here, then, is a book which courageously sets out a bold hypothesis which flies in the face of much recent work on Chronicles [and DtrH]. That it will stimulate renewed examination of widely held presuppositions is to be welcomed. Such challenges to conventional wisdom are necessary to prevent scholars from forgetting how much that they take for granted is indeed hypothetical and needs to be checked time and again in the light of new evidence and inquisitive proposals. Conversely, we may hope that [Auld] will also look [closely at the queries that other scholars raise] and then ... return with further goads to our complacency.

3. *How Chr. Redacted: Kalimi's Analysis of Redactional Techniques in Chronicles*

If Chr.'s principal source was indeed DtrH, how did he make use of it? This, the real crux of the topic, 'The Chronicler as Redactor', is a frustrating issue to try to cover in an article like this. On the one hand, it seems simple. Chr.'s most forceful redactional moves—the large omissions and changes in order from Samuel–Kings in support of his principal theological interests—the temple, David and Solomon, all Israel—are well known and have been thoroughly explored,[50] so that it is difficult to offer anything new. On the other hand, the topic is extremely complex because of the myriad of small differences in Chronicles vis-à-vis Samuel–Kings that scholars have struggled to explain. The topic of Chr. as redactor truly lies at the heart of Chronicles studies and continues to preoccupy nearly every treatment of this

---

48. On the focal nature of the deuteronomistic themes of rest, election and centralization in 2 Sam. 7, see P.K. McCarter, *II Samuel* (AB, 9; Garden City, NY: Doubleday, 1984), pp. 209-31.

49. H.G.M. Williamson, review of *The Chronicler's Use of the Deuteronomistic History* (HSM, 33; Atlanta: Scholars Press), by S.L. McKenzie, in *VT* 37 (1987), p. 114.

50. See esp. R. Mosis, *Untersuchungen zur Theologie des chronistischen Geschichtswerkes* (FTS, 92; Freiburg: Herder, 1973).

literature, so that merely noting his main interests barely scratches the surface.

Fortunately, my task is significantly facilitated by the new publication of Isaac Kalimi's revised dissertation.[51] This work might be regarded as a reponse to Auld's theory. He treats the differences between Chronicles and Samuel–Kings in a series of categories including changes in order (literary versus historical), historiographic corrections (e.g. to do away with contradictions), additions, omissions, name changes, treatment of difficult texts, harmonizations, characterization by the use of names and titles, reward or punishment in like measure, allusions (e.g. to other biblical texts or episodes), chiastic arrangement both within Chronicles texts and in tandem with parallel passages, narrative resumption (*Wiederaufnahme*), literary framework, antithesis or contrast, comparison, catchword (*Leitwort*), numerical scheme and moving from general to specific or the reverse.

This book should have a serious impact on Chronicles studies and may well alter the direction in which they proceed. Its freshness lies in its careful attention to Chr.'s literary activity within the breadth of the Hebrew Bible. Kalimi claims, correctly to my knowledge, to be the first to have systematically compiled and evaluated the literary techniques evinced in Chronicles.[52] He shows that the variations in Chronicles vis à vis Samuel–Kings are not limited to or automatically associated with theological *Tendenz* but reflect a broader range of literary expression in addition to Chr.'s own creativity. For example, Kalimi's chapter on harmonizations is instructive.[53] In this category he includes not just Chr.'s efforts to harmonize discrepancies within his *Vorlage* but also his use of language that conforms to that of passages in Deuteronomy or elsewhere in the Pentateuch or in Ezra–Nehemiah. Kalimi has also uncovered a whole series of stylistic devices used by Chr. in his minor variations from Samuel–Kings. While I am skeptical of the claims of ubiquitous chiasms, Kalimi's chapter on the topic convinces me that it was a genuine stylistic technique employed in the composition of

---

51. I. Kalimi, *Zur Geschichtsschreibung des Chronisten: Literarisch-historio-graphische Abweichungen der Chronik von ihren Paralleltexten in den Samuel- und Königsbüchern* (BZAW, 226; Berlin: W. de Gruyter, 1995).

52. Kalimi, *Zur Geschichtsschreibung*, p. 319.

53. Kalimi, *Zur Geschichtsschreibung*, pp. 113-48. Cf. also his chapter on Chr.'s allusions to other biblical texts (pp. 172-90).

Chronicles.[54] The same holds true for the structuring devices, such as *Wiederaufnahme* and the building of narrative frameworks, discussed by Kalimi.

At first glance, Kalimi's work may seem to be a return to the pre-Qumran state of Chronicles studies, but this is not the case. Lemke's important 1963 thesis argued that differences between Chronicles and Samuel–Kings should not automatically be ascribed to Chr.'s *Tendenz* but that greater consideration should be given to other factors, especially text-critical ones, as explanations for differences. Kalimi agrees and shows that literary activity is a fertile and heretofore largely neglected arena for explaining Chr.'s variations. In arguing his case, Kalimi tends to undervalue textual criticism and fails to appreciate the independence of the witnesses, especially 4QSam[a]. In my view, he too readily resorts to secondary assimilation as a way of explaining agreements between Chronicles (MT) and 4QSam[a] or even sometimes the LXX witnesses of Samuel,[55] so that one must be cautious in reading

---

54. Kalimi, *Zur Geschichtsschreibung*, pp. 191-234.

55. Kalimi (*Zur Geschichtsschreibung*) discusses the matter on pp. 13-16, citing 2 Sam. 8.8 // 1 Chron. 18.8 and 2 Sam. 24.25 // 1 Chron. 21.28–22.1 as illustrations of secondary adjustment of the LXX of Samuel to readings in Chronicles. However, neither case is as clear-cut as Kalimi implies. (On 2 Sam. 8.8 // 1 Chron. 18.8, cf. Lemke, 'Synoptic Studies in the Chronicler's History' (ThD dissertation, Harvard Divinity School, 1964), pp. 48-51; McKenzie, *Chronicler's Use*, p. 65). Moreover, the examples of 4QSam[a]'s accommodation to Chronicles that Kalimi promises on p. 13 n. 46, are not convincing. This is especially important in 2 Sam. 24 // 1 Chron. 21, where extant 4QSam[a] readings consistently agree with Chronicles against the MT of Samuel. That these are not the result of secondary accommodation is shown by small variations between Chronicles and 4QSam[a] (cf. Lemke, 'Synoptic Studies', pp. 58-75; McKenzie, *Chronicler's Use*, pp. 55-58). The independence of the witnesses is also indicated by the fact that Chr.'s text of Kings was much closer to the MT than was his text of Samuel (McKenzie, *Chronicler's Use*, pp. 119-58). This raises doubts about Kalimi's treatment of this passage (pp. 69, 150-52) along with other cases where he dismisses as secondary the 4QSam[a] reading (e.g. p. 63 on 2 Sam. 6.2 // 1 Chron. 13.6). Cases such as 1 Chron. 14.12 // 2 Sam. 5.21, where Chronicles (MT) agrees with reputable LXX (in this case, the Lucianic) witnesses of Samuel, also require caution. Kalimi (*Zur Geschichtsschreibung*, p. 140 n. 89) may be correct in seeing this as a tendentious change by Chr., to which the LXX[L] of Samuel has been corrected. However, this does not appear to be a common feature of the Lucianic text in Samuel, so that Chr. may have found the pious change already in his *Vorlage* (cf. Lemke, 'Synoptic Studies', pp. 33-34; McKenzie, *Chronicler's Use*, p. 62).

Kalimi and be aware of the possibility of textual corruption as an explanation for the variations in the witnesses. But this caveat only slightly diminishes the value of Kalimi's study for opening our eyes to the potential of literary phenomena for explaining even the smallest differences between Chronicles and its deuteronomistic *Vorlage*.

Conclusion

Kalimi's work brings us back to Noth. What Noth said of DtrH rings equally true for Chr: 'The Dtr was not only "redactor", but the author of a history work…'[56] Noth removed the Pentateuchal shackles from the scholarly understanding of Chronicles' composition. Kalimi has further liberated Chr. from the contraints often imposed upon him by the very term 'redactor'. He has shown that redaction was not opposed to but was part of the process of the creative literary activity of an author. Kalimi refers to Chronicles as an 'old-new literary-historigraphic creation' and a 'new literary formulation' that went beyond small changes in language and ideological adaptations to confer a completely new meaning on the older, deuteronomistic material.[57] The term 'redaction' thus describes the entire creative process in which he was engaged. The Chronicler as redactor is actually Chr. as author.

---

56. 'Dtr war nicht nur "Redaktor", sondern der Autor eines Geschichts-werkes…' Noth, *Überlieferungsgeschichtliche Studien*, p. 11.

57. 'Uns jedenfalls erscheint die Chronik als eine alt-neue literarisch-historio-graphische Schöpfung, die durch ihre raffinierte Durchgestaltung besticht. Bei ihren Abweichungen von älteren Texten handelt es sich nicht nur um geringfügige sprachliche Veränderungen oder um textuelle, ideologisch-theologische Adaptionen, sondern um eine literarische Neugestaltung, die dem älteren Material einen neuen Sinn verleiht und eine andere Bedeutung, als es an seiner ursprünglichen Stelle in den Samuel- und Königsbüchern hatte.' Kalimi, *Zur Geschichtsschreibung*, p. 324.

WHAT WAS THE MAIN SOURCE OF THE BOOKS OF CHRONICLES?

A. Graeme Auld

Steven McKenzie has made several acute observations about my proposal in *Kings without Privilege*[1] that Samuel–Kings and Chronicles were largely independent, diverging amplifications of a shared source. In a number of more recent papers, several of them prepared since I heard McKenzie read a version of his article in the present volume[2] to the 1996 annual meeting of the Chronicles–Ezra–Nehemiah Section of the Society of Biblical Literature, I have sought to develop and also modify my original argument in implicit response. As my title suggested, I was concerned then first and foremost with the composition of (Samuel and) Kings and the implications of my proposal for the other so-called 'deuteronomistic' books. I welcome the invitation to offer in this volume of studies on Chronicles an explicit response to his critique. McKenzie's remarks are offered under three headings. He asks first for a more precise definition, historical and form-critical, of my proposed common source. He then lists eight portions of Chronicles that are best understood on the consensus view that their author[s] knew the Former Prophets substantially in the canonical form we have them. His final challenge is to my remarks about the roots and development of deuteronomistic terminology.

McKenzie may overstate matters when he claims that an independent history of Judah 'could not' have begun with the story of Saul's death. Yet his response has helped me realize that the 'Book of Two Houses' (hereafter, BTH) was in fact no 'independent history of Judah'. Inasfar as I described the material common to Samuel–Kings and Chronicles as a history of Judah, I left a hostage to fortune and demonstrated that I had not sufficiently extricated myself from the 'privileged' categories

---

1.   A.G. Auld, *Kings without Privilege: David and Moses in the Story of the Bible's Kings* (Edinburgh: T. & T. Clark, 1994).

2.   See above (pp. 70-90): S.L. McKenzie, 'The Chronicler as Redactor'.

of the Former Prophets. Challenged (originally by David Clines) to give my common source a name, I have chosen one that does at least suggest a response to McKenzie's request for closer definition, calling it in more recent studies the 'Book of Two Houses' (the houses of David and of Yahweh in Jerusalem). BTH is both less and more than a history of Judah: its focus is on Jerusalem's royal and divine 'houses'; and yet from beginning to end Israel and Israel's god are in view. A non-Davidic, pre-Davidic, failed leadership of Israel is acknowledged at the outset. The concern with the nature of Israel, quite differently explored in both Samuel–Kings and Chronicles, is in each case an extension of an important concern of BTH. This was written in or after the sixth century BCE, in response to the collapse of Jerusalem. As for the challenge to offer a form-critical definition of BTH (and what, pray, would a strictly 'form-critical' account of 'DtrH' look like?): at least one major element in it is a genealogy of the sons of David, king of Israel. BTH seeks to answer the questions: What has become of the Davidic kingship over Israel? and Why?

Saul's death as starting place leads McKenzie naturally to his first example of Chr.'s knowledge of the rest of the Deuteronomist's work. 1 Chronicles 10, but not the parallel 1 Samuel 31, ends with a note explaining Saul's death. Opening with Chronicles' stock complaint of מעל, it continues: 'he had consulted a medium, seeking guidance, and did not seek guidance from Yahweh'. There is no doubting the connection between this note and the narrative in 1 Samuel 28 about Saul's visit to the witch at Endor; yet it is not easy to prescribe just how the link operated. McKenzie, like John Van Seters whom he quotes, has himself contributed to a wave of studies that have excluded from their reconstructed DtrH substantial blocks of the Former Prophets that earlier scholars had reckoned among its sources.[3] There is in recent years much greater doubt that the Former Prophets were brought to substantial completion by Deuteronomists in the sixth century BCE. It is all the more important not to mis-state the evidence from Chronicles.

The main theoretical possiblities would seem to be these:

3.　See most recently S.L. McKenzie, *The Trouble with Kings: The Composition of the Book of Kings in the Deuteronomistic History* (VTSup, 42; Leiden: E.J. Brill, 1991), pp. 81-100; J. Van Seters, *In Search of History: Historiography in the Ancient World and the Origins of Biblical History* (New Haven: Yale University Press, 1983), pp. 277-91.

1. Chr. did, as the consensus holds, possess a text of the Former Prophets (much as we know these books). Some of that text was transcribed with little alteration; some other parts were simply alluded to, on the understanding that they would be familiar to the readership.

2. The main text available as a source for Chr. (in the sense of sitting on his desk) was BTH or something like it. The Former Prophets had already been produced by expanding that main text; and at least some of the contents of that narrative were familiar to Chr., but not necessarily available in a scroll. He knew of Saul and the witch just as he knew of Jeremiah's 70-year sabbath for Jerusalem or some lines from Isaiah; and these were all indeed parts of books. However, he knew them by ear or by repute, and not from a scroll in his scriptorium.

3. Chr. made reference to a discreditable consultation of a medium by Saul that he knew in a form preliminary to its narrative elaboration in 1 Samuel 28.

Given that it is only from evidence within the books of Chronicles that we can deduce the forms in which Chr.'s sources were available, I find it unsafe to prefer option 1 to option 2. And given the fluidity of dating presently canvassed for the completion of the Former Prophets, no less than of Chronicles, together with Van Seters's judgment (cited approvingly by McKenzie) that 1 Samuel 28 is a late addition to the books of Samuel, I find it unsafe to begin with a preference for option 1 over option 3. Similar points could be made about other links in McKenzie's following list of eight; but other explanations may be more appropriate.

1. 1 Chronicles 29.27 // 1 Kgs 2.11 notes that David ruled seven years in Hebron and then 33 in Jerusalem. We are told, in turn, throughout Kings about how many years each of his successors ruled in Jerusalem. The narrative about Israel making David its king at Hebron necessitated an alteration to the first appearance of this formula: David did not simply rule in Jerusalem. The figures 7 and 40 are typical—and indeed 33 may represent one-third of 100. I find it more likely (quite apart from any theory about the relationships between Chronicles and the Former Prophets) that such a computation in round figures provided the chronology for 2 Samuel 2–4, than that it was deduced from these chapters as McKenzie suggests.

2. McKenzie insists that we have to be familiar with the more

expansive story of Michal and David in Samuel in order to understand Chr.'s sole mention of Michal, daughter of Saul, in 1 Chron. 15.29 (// 2 Sam. 6.16). There are many teasingly brief fragments of information in the biblical narratives. This lone verse about Michal at a window despising David makes perfectly adequate sense in (BTH or) Chronicles. Mention of a daughter of Saul after the report of his death at Gilboa, 'he and his three sons and all his house together' (1 Chron. 10.6), suggests either that the report was proleptic or exaggerated, or that as a daughter she was not reckoned in his house—or that she belonged already in another man's house. The stories in Samuel of David, Saul and Michal may quite as well have been inspired by an earlier reader of BTH glimpsing Michal through that same window and turning story-teller himself.

3. Nathan's oracle refers to a former time when Yahweh appointed judges. It is, of course, possible that this is a reference to the familiar (deuteronomistic) book of Judges. Yet a number of scholars are asking in different ways whether Judges was not drafted subsequent to the books of Samuel. And the books of Samuel, of course, depict Samuel and his sons as judges over Israel. McKenzie grossly exaggerates the evidence when he claims, 'The reader would not know the answer [to the divine question whether any of the judges were told to build the temple] without the book of Judges more or less intact'.

4. We cannot be sure how to evaluate the slightly different wording of the notes on Elhanan and Goliath (2 Sam. 21.19 // 1 Chron. 20.5). Some accidental corruption may be involved. The introduction in Chronicles of a brother of Goliath will likely recognize the prior claim of David to Goliath's own head (1 Sam. 17) but may not be part of Chr.'s own [re]draft. And yet, David's claim may be 'prior' only in a very limited sense. I am far from holding (as McKenzie appears to suppose) that 1 Samuel 17, as part of the larger David story in the books of Samuel, was part of the shared source;[4] and I am more persuaded by (my 'protege'!) Craig Ho's defence of the shorter 1 Chronicles 10 as largely prior to the longer 1 Samuel 31 than by his arguments about the

---

4. As I noted in 'The Deuteronomists between History and Theology', in A. Lemaire (ed.), *Congress Volume: Oslo, 1998* (VTSup; Leiden: E.J. Brill, forthcoming), 1 Sam. opens (admittedly at slightly greater length) by removing Eli and his sons by death in favor of a new regime in Samuel. Why should its major source not have started similarly with the deaths of Saul and his sons in favor of David?

wider relations of that text to others in 1 Samuel.[5] I have argued else-where that the note about Elhanan's killing of Goliath—as one of several large Philistines disposed of by 'David and his servants' (2 Sam. 21.18-22 // 1 Chron. 20.4-8)—is prior to the extended narrative in 1 Sam. 17.1–18.5, whether the shorter extension attested in LXX (38 verses) or the still later and longer revision in MT (63 verses).[6] See further under 8 below.

5. The reference in 2 Chron. 10.15 (// 1 Kgs 12.15) to the fulfillment of an oracle of Ahijah, which Chr. has not reported, is admittedly difficult and should only be assessed in the light of the total case.

6a. McKenzie makes a further strong point when he notes that the story of Jehoshaphat, the king of Israel, and Micaiah son of Imlah, 'lies outside of the regnal formulas for Jehoshaphat'. That is simple fact, at least in Chronicles and in Kings (MT)—Kings (LXX) provides the standard summary of Jehoshaphat's reign after 1 Kgs 16.28, hence well before the long prophetic story. However, he appears to me to be on much shakier ground when he affirms the widely held view that the narrative featuring Micaiah and the two kings is a 'northern, prophetic legend'. On the one hand, although the scene is set in the north, Jehoshaphat—who is regularly given his own name—is very much more the hero of the tale than Ahab—who is mostly referred to as 'the king of Israel'. And on the other, I have argued that this story fits very well into the small cycle of prophetic stories in BTH.[7] Whether and how far the story is historical, or historically misplaced (as McKenzie holds), is another matter: the [mis]placement belongs to BTH and func-tions well there.

6b. I am surprised at McKenzie's remark that Chronicles 'assumes that the reader knows about [Ahab] from another context, since it never introduces him or describes his reign'. Ahab and his house are mentioned in Chronicles significantly more often than any other king of northern Israel—not only in the passages cited by McKenzie, but also in

5. Cf. C.Y.S. Ho, 'Conjectures and Refutations: Is 1 Samuel XXXI 1-13 Really the Source of 1 Chronicles X 1-12?', VT 45 (1995), pp. 82-106.

6. A.G. Auld, 'Re-Reading Samuel (Historically): "Etwas mehr Nichtwissen"', in V. Fritz and P.R. Davies (eds.), *The Origins of the Ancient Israelite States* (JSOTSup, 228; Sheffield: Sheffield Academic Press, 1996).

7. A.G. Auld, 'Prophets Shared—but Recycled', in T. Römer (ed.), *The Future of the 'Deuteronomistic History'* (BETL; Leuven: Leuven University Press, forth-coming).

2 Chron. 21.6, 13; 22.6, 7, 8. Chr.'s evaluation of Ahab and of the baleful interconnections between his family and the house of David in Jerusalem is clear. The same was already true for BTH. It is often remarked by students of Kings that the prejudices of that book show through particularly clearly in the treatment of Israel's significant monarchs, Omri and Ahab. Apart from his role in the (legendary) narratives about Elijah, Ahab is hardly 'described' in Kings—simply briefly dismissed in stock vituperation (1 Kgs 16.29-33).

7. McKenzie rightly draws attention to my unsatisfactory treatment of Jehu's revolt. It is entirely understandable that the author of BTH should have ascribed divine motivation to the usurper whom he knew to have toppled Israel's worst king. On reflection, I should simply have proposed 2 Chron. 22.7-9 as part of BTH and hence the source of the legendary treatment in 2 Kings 9–10. The divine 'anointing' of Jehu brought to a close this most distressing period in Israel's kingship. Similarly, the ceremonial anointing of Joash marked a new start after the embarrassing interregnum in Jerusalem of his grandmother Athaliah, herself of the house of Omri. The only other anointing reported in BTH was of David, at the fresh start after Saul.

8. Several aspects of the interrelationships between the narratives on Hezekiah in Isaiah, Kings and Chronicles are particularly contorted. As McKenzie remarks, I had already recognized at least one case for abbreviation by Chr. I am happy in turn to applaud his recognition that 'the exact nature of Chr.'s *Vorlage* is uncertain'. On the more general point of whether a 'one-verse sketch of [a] story is too terse to have been original', I have suggested partial responses at 2. and 4. above, on Michal and Goliath. In fact, comparison between the Philistine Goliath and Sennacherib of Assyria deserves closer inspection. The author of 1 Samuel 17 not only adopted a new opponent for Goliath but also adapted from one of his fellow Philistine victims in the original (2 Sam. 21.21 // 1 Chron. 20.7) the charge that he 'taunted' or 'defied' Israel. This important element in the new story features three times in LXX (vv. 10, 36, 45), and twice more in MT (vv. 25, 26). Only in 2 Kings 19 (and the almost identical Isa. 37) do we find a similar massing of this term (vv. 4, 16, 22, 23); and the link is made all the more interesting because 1 Sam. 17.26, 36 redefine 'armies of Israel' (17.10) as 'armies of the living god', and all four verses in 2 Kings 19 have Israel's deity (and in vv. 4, 16 precisely 'living El') as the butt of Assyrian defiance. The concentration on this theme did happen in stages in 1 Samuel 17

(LXX, then MT) and so may have also in 2 Kings 19. It is all the more dangerous to assume that the briefer treatment of the same theme in 2 Chron. 32.17 represents abbreviation by Chr.

In short: I find that the failure of Chronicles to mention Ahijah's oracle and the Chronicles placement of the Jehoshaphat and Micaiah story unusually early within the stock framework do require further study. However, in an academic environment where the history of the formation of the books of the Former Prophets and the historicity of the story they tell are rightly and properly contested, I continue to find my proposals about interrelationships between Samuel–Kings and Chronicles to be no less robust than McKenzie's counter proposals. And I have welcomed his challenge to comment as I had not done before on the roles of Michal and of Jehu in (BTH or) Chronicles.

Yet why develop a radically new hypothesis in the first place, if it is only 'no less robust' than the consensus? The answer relates to McKenzie's third line of questioning, about the development of 'deuteronomistic' terminology. My brief remarks about Cross and the affiliations of 2 Samuel 7 proved too cryptic. What sparked my comments was Cross's statement that 2 Samuel 7 'fairly swarms with expressions found elsewhere in works of the Deuteronomistic school'.[8] He provides 24 examples. The first thing I note about these is that only 13 are said to occur in Deuteronomy itself (1, 2, 4, 5, 6, 8, 10, 12, 18, 19, 20, 21, 24). By contrast, as many as eight are found again in the much smaller block of material in the Solomon narratives of BTH (1, 3, 11, 12, 14, 16, 21, 22); and four more are part of the larger stock of BTH (2, 7, 8, 9). 2 Samuel 7 is equally connected with Deuteronomy and with (the rest of) BTH. The link with BTH might quite as sensibly attract Cross's judgment 'fairly swarms'.

What are the implications for Chr.? The familiar view, which McKenzie defends, is that Deuteronomy and the Former Prophets were substantially complete in the form we know them before Chr. began his work. Chr. transcribed from these books much of the material on the Davidic house but spliced into this a similar amount of special material of his own. Here and there, he left truncated torsos, as with Michal and with Ahijah's oracle. Here and there, as with Saul consulting a medium, he showed his familiarity with material he chose not to transcribe.

---

8. F.M. Cross, *Canaanite Myth and Hebrew Epic: Essays in the History of the Religion of Israel* (Cambridge, MA: Harvard University Press, 1973), p. 252.

If this view is correct, then Chr.'s word usage is puzzling. I am grateful to McKenzie for urging me to check my remarks against Weinfeld's much more comprehensive lists of 'deuteronomistic phraseology'. Of close to 200 words and phrases listed by Weinfeld[9] (I have excluded the purely Jeremianic usage), less than a tenth are found in non-synoptic portions of Chronicles—and among these are several expressions from the synoptic portions. In fact, the indebtedness of Chronicles to the phraseology of the synoptic portions (BTH) is much higher than that suggests: many of the key interests of BTH, many of its key phrases, do not appear in Weinfeld's lists, which he restricts to specifically 'deuteronomistic' language. My puzzle is this: If Chr. had Deuteronomy and the Former Prophets in book form so that he could transcribe about half of 2 Samuel–2 Kings and allude to several portions of the rest, if he left unchanged and unchallenged the 'deuteronomistic' phraseology of the synoptic portions, then why was he largely uninfluenced by the wordstock of this major source outside the parts he transcribes?

Kings without Privilege has been held to fail the simplicity test of Occam's Razor by positing an unnecessary stage in the relationship between Former Prophets and Chronicles, by inventing a non-existent source common to both instead of recognizing that the one was simply adapted from the other. My first response is that the source requires no 'invention': it simply has to be recognized as being there in two very similar versions. My second response is that the consensus view of how Chr. dealt with the Former Prophets could, of course, be correct, but it is far from 'simple'. Much simpler is the thesis of divergent elaboration into Samuel–Kings in one direction and Chronicles in the other of a shared narrative with its common stock of phraseology. McKenzie concedes that 'Auld may be correct that the doctrine of election did not originate with DtrH and that the direction of influence for such themes as the promised "rest" was from monarchy to earlier traditions rather than the reverse'.[10] If Auld is correct, then surely it is unwise to call chapters such as 2 Samuel 7, 1 Kings 8 and other related synoptic texts 'deuteronomistic', which implies (for Weinfeld as Cross) post-Deuteronomic. Why complicate matters by urging two-way influence and claiming, 'The relationship between these two texts and earlier portions of DtrH is one of mutual influence and dependence because they are all

---

9.　M. Weinfeld, *Deuteronomy and the Deuteronomic School* (Oxford: Clarendon Press, 1972), pp. 320-59.

10.　McKenzie, 'Chronicler as Redactor', p. 86.

part of a larger whole?'[11] Not to recognize these as (pre-deuter-onom[ist]ic) influences on the thought of Deuteronomy and the Former Prophets, and equally of Chronicles, is to fail Occam's test.

In short, I continue to affirm the main thrust of *Kings without Privilege*. Several texts where Chronicles is shorter than Samuel or Kings look odd when viewed from the habitual perspective of Samuel–Kings, but not when read in their own immediate context:[12] in a number of cases the shorter version can cast fresh light on the development of the longer. That situation in a series of microcosms is true at the macro-cosmic level as well: recognition of the BTH eases our understanding of the development of both Former Prophets and Chronicles. And, if an occasional narrative in Samuel–Kings suggested a footnote to Chr. or to a scribe in his tradition, then why not? (I have argued elsewhere that some of the links between Joshua and 1 Chronicles are best explained by mutual influence.)[13] However, I freely admit that it was quite mis-leading to characterize the shared source I 'found again' in the synoptic material as a history of the monarchy of Judah.

11. McKenzie, 'Chronicler as Redactor', p. 87.

12. And the very title of the volume in which this response appears allows and may even require such a fresh perspective.

13. A.G. Auld, 'Joshua and 1 Chronicles', in *idem, Joshua Retold: Synoptic Perspectives* (Edinburgh: T. & T. Clark, 1998).

A RHETORICAL APPROACH TO APPRECIATING THE BOOKS OF CHRONICLES

Rodney K. Duke

1. *Preface to the Task*

a. *The Chronicler as Historian and Chronicles as Literature*

The task I was given was to help the reader better appreciate the books of Chronicles as literature through the presentation of a rhetorical analysis. Without attempting to define precisely the relationship of the current volume, *The Chronicler as Author*, to the editors' earlier work, *The Chronicler as Historian*,[1] it seems worthwhile to note that a rhetorical study of Chronicles serves a 'crossover' function in the relation of these two works. If the books of Chronicles are to be understood as a form of historical narrative,[2] then a rhetorical reading of Chronicles will be concerned with both Chr.'s[3] role as a *historian*[4] and how he expressed himself in the *literature* that he created. A rhetorical approach, at least in the traditional sense, will not bifurcate a work of communication from the communicator, because a rhetorical approach works within the context of the process of communication. This point needs to be clarified further in view of the variety of assumptions the contributors to this volume are likely to make as they present their readings of Chronicles.

---

1. M.P. Graham, K.G. Hoglund and S.L. McKenzie (JSOTSup, 238; Sheffield: Sheffield Academic Press, 1997).

2. See 3.a.2 below.

3. For the purpose of this article, I am assuming the generally held position that there has been one primary author for Chronicles, even though others have probably shaped it further. Also, I am not assuming that the identity of the author is known but will adopt the custom of referring to Chr. with masculine pronouns.

4. By calling Chr. a historian I do not mean to imply that he was not also a theologian, exegete and literary artist. Indeed, I would claim that the act of creating any historical narrative involves interpretation on a philosophical or theological level and literary artistry. See 3.a.3 below.

b. *The Distinct Perspective of a Rhetorical Analysis*

Most basically a rhetorical analysis is concerned with the process by which a 'speaker' purposely creates a 'text' to achieve communication with an intended audience. Viewing the biblical texts in the context of the process of communication runs counter, however, to one modern trend to view biblical literature as 'works of art' for public consumption. In this modern, text-centered trend the biblical texts are viewed outside of the context of deliberate communication, the communicator is left out of the process, and the focus is on the aesthetic or poetic element of the text.[5] The reader arbitrarily divorces the analysis from any interest in the author's original intention, because such a pursuit is viewed as unnecessary and perhaps even misleading for appreciating a work as art.[6]

A rhetorical approach also runs counter to another perspective, a 'postmodern' perspective, which views readings of texts as reflections of the constructs of the readers' interpretive communities. In this reader-centered approach the act of effective communication between an author and an audience through a text is virtually denied. For philosophical and linguistic reasons, the reader believes that the intention of the author is utterly unattainable. (This perspective has led to the postmodern usage of the phrase 'referential fallacy'.)[7]

5.   In the history of literary studies one finds in the seventeenth century the development of a category of imaginary literature, or *belles lettres*, that was seen to exist solely for the sake of art. Later, in the first half of this century one finds the rejection of the historicism that tended to see meaning as caused by the historical setting of an author. This led to a movement that ignored such external factors and located the artistic value of a work in the forms revealed in the artwork itself. See R. Lundin, 'Our Hermeneutical Inheritance', in R. Lundin, A.C. Thiselton and C. Walhout (eds.), *The Responsibility of Hermeneutics* (Grand Rapids: Eerdmans, 1985), pp. 1-29, 115-20; N.R. Petersen, *Literary Criticism for New Testament Critics* (GBSNT; Philadelphia: Fortress Press, 1978), pp. 25-28; M. Sternberg, *The Poetics of Biblical Narrative: Ideological Literature and the Drama of Reading* (ILBS; Bloomington: Indiana University Press, 1985), pp. 7-8.

6.   This perspective led to the modern and original meaning of the phrase 'intentional fallacy'. See the classic statement by W.K. Wimsatt and M. Beardsley, 'The Intentional Fallacy', *Sewanee Review* 54 (1946), pp. 468-88, reprinted in W.K. Wimsatt, Jr, *The Verbal Icon: Studies in the Meaning of Poetry* (Lexington: University of Kentucky Press, 1954), pp. 3-18; and Beardsley's later comments in 'Intentions and Interpretations: A Fallacy Revived', in M.J. Wreen and D.M. Callen (eds.), *The Aesthetic Point of View: Selected Essays* (Ithaca, NY: Cornell University Press, 1976), pp. 188-207.

7.   See C. Walhout, 'Texts and Actions', in Lundin, Thiselton and Walhout

In distinction from the above two trends,[8] a rhetorical analysis will place the biblical text in the context of communication and will not cut off the communicator from the text.[9] Therefore, a rhetorical analysis of Chronicles, if this biblical text is to be understood as historical narrative, will not be a kind of 'literary' approach that views the text as a 'work of art' and ignores what Chr. was attempting to do as a historian. Neither will it take the position that it is pointless to ask what Chr. meant to communicate. It will ask about what Chr. was attempting to communicate as a historian and how Chr. attempted to communicate effectively through a literary medium.

c. *The Basic Goal of our Rhetorical Study*
Rhetoricians, recognizing that communication does take place successfully (not perfectly), as evidenced by the existence of human 'community', explore what makes for successful communication. Ancient rhetoricians recognized that a communicator, usually in their context an orator, had a goal that he wished to achieve through his 'text', a goal of

(eds.), *The Responsibility of Hermeneutics*, pp. 69-77; and Petersen, *Literary Criticism*, pp. 38-40.

8.   The mention above of only two other perspectives is admittedly too simplistic. There is a wide variety of 'modern', 'postmodern' and even 'premodern' perspectives about the relationship of the author to the text, the audience to the text and the text to 'reality'. For instance, a psycholinguistic reading of a text would look for the ways in which the author unintentionally communicated the structures of his humanity.

9.   In defense of seeking the 'authorial intention', see Walhout's discussion of the limits of the literature-as-language model and the principles of the literature-as-action model ('Texts and Actions', pp. 34-49), and see E.D. Hirsch, Jr, *Validity in Interpretation* (New Haven: Yale University Press, 1967), pp. 1-23.

Roman Jakobson stands out as having made a balanced and 'corrective' contribution to literary studies by placing poetics and literary studies within linguistics—all the while applying linguistic analysis to the broad scope of verbal communication—as opposed to, for instance, confining it to grammar. R. Jakobson, 'Closing Statement: Linguistics and Poetics', in T.A. Sebeok (ed.), *Style in Language* (Cambridge, MA: Technology Press of Massachusetts Institute of Technology, 1960). For a communication model adapted from Jakobson and applied to biblical studies, see Petersen, *Literary Criticism*, esp. pp. 33-48. For a student-level work explaining Jakobson's model and providing excellent teaching exercises in biblical criticism, see M.B. Dick, *Introduction to the Hebrew Bible: An Inductive Reading of the Old Testament* (Englewood Cliffs, NJ: Prentice–Hall, 1988), pp. 13-17.

moving the audience to some state of mind and/or action.[10] The rhetoricians described, and often prescribed, for their culture, the means by which the communicator could be most effective. Approached from this perspective, purposeful communication, such as the books of Chronicles, is by definition 'rhetorical' and open to rhetorical analysis.[11] Most basically, a rhetorical approach to the books of Chronicles is going to ask two questions. The first is, 'What are the communicative goals of Chr.?' That is, what does he want the audience to think, understand or do in response to this act of communication? The second is, 'How has Chr. sought to achieve those goals successfully through the literary devices of his text?'

In the following sections my first goal is to address the methodological concerns of applying a rhetorical analysis to Chronicles. The second goal is to provide a brief rhetorical analysis of the whole of Chronicles.

2. Rhetorical Analysis: Methodological Concerns

a. The Nature of Rhetorical Analysis

Acts of deliberate communication, 'rhetorical acts', employ rhetorical strategies. Every rhetorical act involves a speaker or composer, an audience and a 'text' of some sort. Generally some exigency has arisen that motivates the rhetor to communicate. (Readers of Chronicles need to

---

10. Aristotle said, 'The use of persuasive speech is to lead to decisions. (When we know a thing and have decided about it, there is no further use in speaking about it.)'. R. McKeon (ed.), *The Basic Works of Aristotle* (New York: Random House, 1941), pp. 1317-1451; *Rhetorica* 2.18.1391b.

11. G.A. Kennedy (*Classical Rhetoric and its Christian and Secular Tradition from Ancient to Modern Times* [Chapel Hill: University of North Carolina Press, 1980], p. 4) has described how a rhetorical intent pervades most of our acts of communication: 'Rhetoric is a form of communication. The author of a communication has some kind of purpose, and rhetoric certainly includes the ways by which he seeks to accomplish that purpose. The ancient world commonly thought of this purpose as persuasion, but meant by that something much looser and more inclusive than persuasion as understood by a modern social scientist. Purposes cover a whole spectrum from converting hearers to a view opposed to that they previously held, to implanting a conviction not otherwise considered, to the deepening of belief in a view already favorably entertained, to a demonstration of the cleverness of the author, to teaching or exposition. In practice almost every communication is rhetorical in that it uses some device to try to affect the thought, actions, or emotions of an audience, but the degree of rhetoric varies enormously.'

seek to uncover the situation that has motivated Chr. to compose his work, even if we cannot answer such a question with certainty.) The rhetor begins with a goal in mind and must arrive at a strategy of communication that will motivate the intended audience to understand, accept and/or act on the message to be communicated in such a way as to achieve that goal. The rhetorical strategy may be arrived at rather non-deliberately (e.g. by employing language skills that are second nature) or with great deliberation. This strategy involves a multitude of factors that include one's language skills, life experiences and worldview as well as the anticipated audience's language skills, experiences and worldview. More particularly, rhetoricians tend to focus on the decisions the rhetor makes regarding genre, kinds of material included, arrangement of materials, types of arguments, modes of persuasion and word choice.

What then is rhetorical analysis? According to Aristotle, 'Rhetoric may be defined as the faculty of observing in any given case the available means of persuasion'.[12] A rhetorical analysis refers to the attempt to identify the effective means of communication that have been employed in the 'text', partly to appreciate artistic communication, but more importantly to work backwards to re-create the rhetorical strategy employed by the author, and finally, to come to a better understanding of what the author wished to achieve through that particular act of communication.

Such an analysis proceeds by a disciplined method but is still a subjective and creative literary task. A rhetorical analysis employs an understanding of what constitutes effective communication. It looks for universal modes of effective communication. It recognizes universal tasks for which we employ language. It also identifies and classifies a culture's specific rhetorical devices. Nonetheless, when we have only the finished work from an ancient, foreign culture, no contact with the author, no contact with the audience, and in the case of ancient Hebrew, no self-descriptive works of Hebrew literary devices, we must also recognize the subjectivity of a rhetorical analysis of a biblical work.

What then does a rhetorical analysis offer in comparison to other approaches? A rhetorical-critical analysis of Chronicles will certainly build on many of the observations and conclusions of previous critical studies, but its perspective and objectives differ. It is the objective of

12. Aristotle, *Rhetorica*, 1.2.1355b.

this approach to arrive at a better appreciation of Chr.'s artistry, a better understanding of what he wanted the audience to believe and/or do, and a better understanding of how he attempted to effect his purpose through a particular rhetorical strategy. George Kennedy has summed up the particular contribution of a rhetorical analysis in this manner:

> For some readers of the Bible rhetorical criticism may have an appeal lacking to other modern critical approaches, in that it comes closer to explaining what they want explained in the text: not its sources, but its power. Rhetoric cannot describe the historical Jesus or identify Matthew or John; they are probably irretrievably lost to scholarship. But it does study a verbal reality, our text of the Bible, rather than the oral sources standing behind that text, the hypothetical stages of its composition, or the impersonal working of social forces, and at its best it can reveal the power of these texts as unitary messages. The Bible speaks through ethos, logos, and pathos,[13] and to understand these is the concern of rhetorical analysis.[14]

b. *The Utilization of Greek Rhetorical Theory with a Hebrew Text*
Since an understanding of classical rhetoric comes from Greek and Latin sources, one might ask what justifies the application of such rhetorical theory to ancient Israelite, Hebrew texts. Indeed, my under-standing of rhetoric has been heavily influenced by Aristotle's work, *Rhetoric*, an ancient Greek work.[15] The decision to be dependent on Aristotle is grounded on the fact that his work is one of the earliest and most influential *descriptive* works on rhetoric. In this connection, George Kennedy states, 'If one looks back over the first hundred and fifty years of rhetorical theory, Aristotle's *Rhetoric* seems to tower above all the remains ... Its influence has been enormous and still con-

---

13. 'Ethos', 'logos' and 'pathos' are rhetorical terms that refer to modes of persuasion. They are explained and illustrated below in section 3.c.

14. G.A. Kennedy, *New Testament Interpretation through Rhetorical Criticism* (Studies in Religion; Chapel Hill: University of North Carolina Press, 1984), pp. 158-59.

15. Two complete handbooks from the second half of the fourth century BCE have been preserved: *Rhetorica ad Alexandrum* and Aristotle's *Rhetoric*. Although earlier works are referred to, none prior to Aristotle have survived. *Rhetorica ad Alexandrum*, preserved in the corpus of Aristotle, is probably a typical product of early sophistic rhetoric, of which Aristotle disapproved (G.A. Kennedy, *The Art of Persuasion in Greece* [History of Rhetoric, 1; Princeton, NJ: Princeton University Press, 1963], pp. 81, 114-15).

tinues.'[16] The emphasis above on 'descriptive' is essential. Aristotle did not write *Rhetoric* as a prescriptive work, although it was used for training rhetors. Neither did he write it merely to be descriptive of Greek rhetoric. He sought to describe the universal characteristics of effective communication employed by all people.[17] As such, the system as set forth in the *Rhetoric* may be applied at least to some degree to all deliberate verbal acts of human communication. Certainly stylistic features vary from culture to culture, but some of the elements of an effective rhetorical strategy will be universal (e.g., selection and arrangement of material, modes of persuasion, word choice, expectations regarding the audience).

One other question might be raised about applying classical rhetoric to an ancient Hebrew text. Aristotle and the other ancient rhetoricians described the art of rhetoric with oral speech genres in mind, not written compositions. As noted above, however, all deliberate acts of communication serve rhetorical purposes and will employ rhetorical strategies, even historical narratives.[18] Also, one must realize that the modern distinction between written and oral compositions is quite different from the ancient perspective in which written works used oral techniques, because they were often composed orally and because they were composed to be read aloud. Therefore, many of Aristotle's observations about effective communication apply to narratives as well as speeches.[19]

16. G.A. Kennedy, *Art of Persuasion*, p. 123.

17. He stated in *Rhetorica*, 1.1.1354a: 'Rhetoric is the counterpart of Dialectic. Both alike are concerned with such things as come, more or less, within the general ken of all men and belong to no definite science. Accordingly all men make use, more or less, of both; for to a certain extent all men attempt to discuss statements and maintain them, to defend themselves and to attack others. Ordinary people do this either at random or through practice and from acquired habit. Both ways being possible, the subject can plainly be handled systematically, for it is possible to inquire the reason why some speakers succeed through practice and others spontaneously; and every one will at once agree that such an inquiry is the function of an art.'

See also, Kennedy, *New Testament Interpretation*, pp. 10-11; and C.S. Baldwin, *Ancient Rhetoric and Poetic, Interpreted from Representative Works* (New York: Macmillan, 1924), p. 8.

18. See section 3.a.3 below on the genre of historical narrative.

19. For an example of categories of classical rhetoric applied to other biblical narratives, see Kennedy, *New Testament Interpretation*.

c. *The Designation of Chronicles as a Rhetorical Unit*
Another concern that needs clarification is the designation of the books
of Chronicles as a rhetorical unit. Rhetorical criticism looks at a complete work synchronically.

> Rhetorical criticism takes the text as we have it, whether the work of a
> single author or the product of editing, and looks at it from the point of
> view of the author's or editor's intent, the unified results, and how it
> would be perceived by an audience of near contemporaries.[20]

It is quite probable that there were more than one source and more than
one author/editor that contributed to the books of Chronicles as we now
have them.[21] (And, if we had extant, chronologically ordered editions[22]
or if it were possible to reconstruct them definitively, then one could
analyze each edition and ask about the different rhetorical intentions
and shaping of each modification, a goal that is a rhetorical component
of redaction criticism.) However, the mere identification and separation
of sources and layers of redaction is not the focus of rhetorical analysis.
Such sources have become transformed in their rhetorical function to
conform to their current role in the final work.[23] The present study will
work with the text in its Massoretic form and not with hypothetical
reconstructions. It also will be assumed that this final form basically
represents the intent of the major composer/editor who has been
referred to as Chr.[24] Moreover, since Chronicles is found in the Hebrew

20. Kennedy, *New Testament Interpretation*, p. 4.

21. See, for instance, the brief surveys of the issue of unity by S. Japhet, *I & II Chronicles: A Commentary* (OTL; Louisville, KY: Westminster/John Knox Press, 1993), pp. 5-7; or by H.G.M. Williamson, *1 and 2 Chronicles* (NCB; Grand Rapids: Eerdmans, 1982), pp. 12-15.

22. We do have different textual versions of Chronicles, and comparing them can lead to rhetorical insights, but this situation is not the same as having chrono-logically sequential major editions. (One might also note that textual criticism employs rhetorical analysis when it seeks to determine which reading shows evi-dence of deliberate change by a copyist.)

23. I agree with N.R. Petersen ('Literary Criticism in Biblical Studies', in R.A. Spencer [ed.], *Orientation by Disorientation* [Pittsburgh: Pickwick Press, 1980], pp. 25-50 [36]), who has defended the method of analyzing the whole of a text before its parts: 'The authors are, to whatever degree, responsible for the whole. Therefore, to start with the whole makes sense, more sense than starting with the parts that may have no authorially intentional function in the whole but be in it only because they were in the author's sources.'

24. By specifying the final, 'major' composer, I am allowing for later, minor

Bible as a complete work, separate from Ezra–Nehemiah, it will be treated as a rhetorical unit.[25]

d. *Reading Chronicles Synoptically*

The fact that Chronicles not only retells much of the tradition found in Samuel–Kings but also frequently quotes from or alludes to material found in the law, the prophets and Psalms[26] raises the question of how Chronicles is to be read. Some students of Chronicles have come to the conclusion that Chr. was providing an interpretation of the then known 'Hebrew Bible',[27] or of DtrH[28] or of at least parts of that history.[29] So, for instance, if one works with the assumption that Samuel–Kings was the primary source of Chr. that was being interpreted, then one might read Chronicles together with Samuel–Kings for a detailed examination of Chr.'s use and transformation of that material, a pursuit that is unquestionably a legitimate scholarly pursuit. However, I argued above that one needs to read Chronicles as a rhetorical unit in its own right.[30] Do these claims conflict?

The solution, from the perspective of rhetorical criticism, lies in an understanding of Chr.'s rhetorical strategy. The evidence suggests that Chr. was communicating with an audience that, he presumed, would be familiar with much of the Israelite 'biblical' tradition.[31] For instance,

changes, such as extending the genealogies and lists of returnees from the exile, modernizing names, etc.

25. For a survey of the positions defending the separate authorship of Chronicles and Ezra–Nehemiah, see Japhet, *I & II Chronicles*, pp. 3-5; and Williamson, *1 and 2 Chronicles*, pp. 5-11.

26. See Japhet, *I & II Chronicles*, pp. 14-23.

27. M.J. Selman, *1 Chronicles: An Introduction & Commentary* (TOTC, 10a; Downers Grove, IL: InterVarsity Press, 1994), pp. 20-26.

28. T. Willi, *Die Chronik als Auslegung: Untersuchungen zur literarischen Gestaltung der historischen Überlieferung Israels* (FRLANT, 106; Göttingen: Vandenhoeck & Ruprecht, 1972).

29. W.E. Barnes, 'The Midrashic Element in Chronicles', *Expositor*, 5th ser., 4 (1896), pp. 426-39.

30. See on this point the essay in the present volume by C. Mitchell, 'The Dialogism of Chronicles' pp. 311-26.

31. The attempts to recreate to some degree the intended audience and to imagine its reactions to the author and to his account, as well as to compare the role of the narrator with that of the author, are rhetorical concerns that have been picked up by modern 'reader-response' criticism. See W.G. Gibson, 'Authors, Speakers, Readers and Mock Readers', in J.P. Tompkins (ed.), *Reader-Response Criticism:*

his citation of sources—even if fabricated as some scholars have concluded—indicates that he assumed his audience accepted the existence
of other written historical materials and regarded them as authoritative
sources. Also, his narrative makes allusions to events not contained in
his story, but found in material outside of Chronicles. For example, 1
Chron. 11.3 refers to how David became king according to the word of
Samuel, which is found in 1 Samuel 16, and 2 Chron. 10.15 refers to
the fulfillment of the prophecy of Ahijah, which is recorded in 1 Kgs
11.29-39.[32] Such allusions lead to the conclusion that the audience was
expected at least to be familiar with such traditions, which we find in
other parts of the Hebrew Bible, whether they knew our current texts of
the Hebrew Bible or not. (It should be noted that such a rhetorical
setting would present Chr. with the problem of how to draw on the
authority of traditional material and yet re-present it in a manner that
would satisfy or convince his audience.)

On the other hand, to assume that Chr. expected the audience to make
a detailed, synoptic comparison of his work to other texts tends to foist
the methods and concerns of modern scholarship on the ancient audience.[33] Even if Chr.'s listening audience knew of the existence of such
texts, it would be presumptuous to think that they all possessed and
could read such texts, unless his grand, sweeping historical narrative
was intended only for the elite few. In conclusion, it appears that
although Chronicles is a historical narrative in its own right and is to be
read as a unit, it was intended to be read in a loose, synoptic sense with
an 'ear' for echoes, parallels, allusions and even quotations from other
traditional material.[34] It will be difficult, however, if not impossible, to
recognize just how much difference in detail the audience was expected
to discern and respond to.

From *Formalism to Post-Structuralism* (Baltimore: The Johns Hopkins University
Press, 1980), pp. 1-6; G. Prince, 'Introduction to the Study of the Narratee', in
Tompkins (ed.), *Reader-Response Criticism*, pp. 7-25.

32. See also B.S. Childs, *Introduction to the Old Testament as Scripture*
(Philadelphia: Fortress Press, 1979), pp. 646-47; and P.R. Ackroyd, 'The Chronicler as Exegete', *JSOT* 2 (1977), p. 21.

33. So, too, observes M. Fishbane, *Biblical Interpretation in Ancient Israel*
(Oxford: Clarendon Press, 1985), pp. 381-82.

34. See Selman, *1 Chronicles*, pp. 27-45.

3. *Rhetorical Analysis: An Overview of Chronicles*

In another work I have tried to give an overarching rhetorical analysis of Chronicles as a whole.[35] What I wish to do in this section is synthesize or summarize some of those observations and conclusions.

a. *The Genre and a Rhetorical Purpose of Chronicles*
1. *The role of genre recognition.* The first major step of rhetorical analysis involves placing the 'text' into the context of its 'form' or, better, 'genre'.[36] Genres are communally shared patterns of 'speech' with relations to certain roles in human life.[37] Again, it seems to be Aristotle who originated the classification of speech acts into genres.[38] He recognized that addressers used different forms of speech for different rhetorical intentions.[39] The recognition of genre determines the audience's interpretive strategy. It gives them a sense of the general purpose of the communication act and guides them to focus on the expected literary features of a text that associate it with similar texts of

35. R.K. Duke, *The Persuasive Appeal of the Chronicler: A Rhetorical Analysis* (JSOTSup, 88; Bible and Literature Series, 25; Sheffield: Almond Press, 1990).

36. See Hirsch for a defense of the argument that a shared understanding regarding genre is necessary for an addresser to communicate successfully to the intended audience (*Validity*, pp. 68-126). The argument that placing a text into its context of genre is the most important step of interpretation has even recently been advocated in a lay-level reading guide to the Old Testament: D.B. Sandy and R.L. Giese, Jr (eds.), *Cracking Old Testament Codes: A Guide to Interpreting the Literary Genres of the Old Testament* (Nashville, TN: Broadman & Holman, 1995).

37. See M.J. Buss, 'The Study of Forms', in J.H. Hayes (ed.), *Old Testament Form Criticism* (TUMSR, 2; San Antonio, TX: Trinity University Press, 1974), pp. 1-56, for an excellent description and history of the study of forms. He tracks the reductionistic tendency of biblical form critics toward formalism and toward limiting their object of study to oral forms (pp. 49 and 54, respectively). A. Devitt, a non-biblical scholar who approaches the study of genre from the perspective of compositional theory, has argued for a 'new' concept of genre as a 'dynamic patterning of human experience' in 'Generalizing About Genre: New Conceptions of an Old Concept', *College Composition and Communication* 44 (1993), pp. 573-86. In reality, her 'new' concept is not so new (see Buss, 'Forms') but a rejection of the formalism that took place in literary studies, the movement called 'New Criticism'.

38. Kennedy, *Classical Rhetoric*, p. 72.

39. See Aristotle, *Rhetorica*, 1.3.1358a-58b, where he discusses how different genres are used with different audiences who have different roles to carry out.

the same type and distinguish it from texts of other genres. If we understand how a genre functions to communicate an impact, then we can come closer to identifying the meaning intended by the author/ editor.[40] Identifying the genre of Chronicles, then, is the first step toward understanding Chr.'s purposes.

The step of genre analysis, however, is fraught with problems. If we do not possess descriptions of biblical genres, then how do we know that we are not just foisting our forms onto the Hebrew Bible? To some extent we probably are doing just that. We can only read the biblical texts in relation to what we know. However, although the patterns of genres are specific societal conventions, the general communicative functions they carry out are basically universal functions of human communication. Therefore, even if our analysis starts with our contemporary knowledge of genres, we are still on the correct path when we pursue the literary distinctions of the biblical, indeed ancient Near Eastern genres, and ask about the relationship of form to function. We are asking the right kind of questions in light of the communication process.

2. *Chronicles as historical narrative.* The book of Chronicles, although containing many subgenres or forms, is an act of communication in the basic genre of 'historical narrative'.[41] By 'historical narrative' I am referring broadly to narrative texts written from the authorial stance of communicating about the past. I am not imposing modern presuppositional and stylistic criteria that might label such texts as Chronicles as 'history-like' or 'fictionalized history' or 'interpreted history'. The primary criterion that distinguishes historical narrative from fictional narrative is not internal structures (they share the same narrative structures)

40. A genre's function and an author's intention cannot be equated, but they are related. In the composition of an act of communication the author employs various formal elements because of the ways they generally function to create an impact on an audience within a common culture. An exploration of the function of a genre and its particular formal features, as well as the effort to place a text into its total historical and literary context, theoretically can lead back to some insight into the authorial intention.

41. For the purposes of this paper I will not be making a distinction among the proposed subgenres of historical narrative such as 'report', 'historical story', etc. For a thoughtful description of biblical, historical literary forms, see B.O. Long, *I Kings: With an Introduction to Historical Literature* (FOTL, 9: Grand Rapids: Eerdmans, 1984), pp. 2-8.

or subject matter or aesthetic appeal or the citation of sources or even the credibility of the events to a reader. It is the authorial stance that presents the text as referring to the actual past that marks a narrative as 'historical'.[42] In the history of biblical scholarship regarding the emergence of Israelite history writing and the classification of biblical narrative into genres, one finds that this primary distinguishing feature between fiction and history writing was generally overlooked.[43] The authorial stance found in the books of Chronicles is that of historical narrative.

3. *The rhetorical nature of historical narrative.* Historical narratives, like all acts of deliberate communication, function rhetorically. Hayden

42. For further discussion of this point, see P. Hernadi, 'Clio's Cousins: Historiography as Translation, Fiction, and Criticism', *New Literary History* 7 (1976), pp. 245-57; P. Ricoeur, 'The Narrative Function', *Semeia* 13 (1978), pp. 177-202; R. Scholes, 'Afterthoughts on Narrative II: Language, Narrative, and Anti-Narrative', *Critical Inquiry* 7 (1980), pp. 204-12; Walhout, 'Texts and Actions', pp. 69-77; and within biblical studies, Sternberg, *Poetics*, pp. 23-35.

43. As Sternberg notes, biblical narratives have been shaped by three sets of regulating principles or functions: ideological, historiographic and aesthetic (*Poetics*, pp. 41-57). However, the co-working of these functions has often been overlooked in the practice of biblical studies. When historically oriented biblical scholars have identified an ideological or aesthetic function of a text of historical narrative, they have tended, at best, to regard the text as poor historiography, and at worst, to re-label the genre as 'history-like fiction'. To see this trend within the study of Israelite historiography, see the survey by J. Van Seters, *In Search of History: Historiography in the Ancient World and the Origins of Biblical History* (New Haven: Yale University Press, 1983), pp. 209-48. For examples regarding the books of Chronicles, see Duke, *Persuasive Appeal*, pp. 13-18.

On the other hand, with the current trend of focusing on the aesthetics of biblical narrative and on its ideology, the historiographic function is often overlooked. Note how the methodological discussions about literary criticism and rhetorical criticism not infrequently fail to distinguish fiction from history on the basis of the authorial stance. See, e.g., D.M. Gunn, 'Biblical Story and the Literary Critic', in *idem, The Fate of King Saul: An Interpretation of a Biblical Story* (JSOTSup, 14: Sheffield: JSOT Press, 1980), pp. 11-19; M. Kessler, 'A Methodological Setting for Rhetorical Criticism', in D.J.A. Clines, D.M. Gunn and A.J. Hauser (eds.), *Art and Meaning: Rhetoric in Biblical Literature* (JSOTSup, 19; Sheffield: JSOT Press, 1982), pp. 1-19. Moreover, it is sometimes assumed that to read biblical narratives as 'stories' means that one reads them as fiction. See, e.g., D. Robertson, *The Old Testament and the Literary Critic* (GBOST; Philadelphia: Fortress Press, 1977), pp. 1-10.

White defines historical narrative as 'a verbal structure in the form of a narrative prose discourse that purports to be a model, or icon, of past structures and processes in the interest of *explaining what they were by representing* them'.[44] Historical narratives are representational depictions of the world composed for the purpose of conveying 'meaning' to the intended audience. The addresser wishes to persuade the audience to accept her or his story as true, that is, to accept it with its inherent presuppositions, worldview and ideology. Each historical narrative not only 'informs' an audience about the past, but also confronts it with the need to make a variety of decisions: to judge a past act, to assess praise or blame, to accept certain laws of coherence among events, to believe there is a teleology to history.[45] The degree to which the audience accepts the story as 'true' depends on the rhetorical effectiveness of the narrative. The effectiveness of a historical work, namely, what makes it acceptably 'realistic' or 'objective' to one's audience, is rhetorical in nature.[46]

4. *The rhetorical functions of Israelite historical narrative.* I would suggest that the general rhetorical functions of the genre 'historical narrative' in the Hebrew Bible are: (1) to preserve the traditions, and consequently shape the identity, of Israel; (2) to respond to the needs and questions of the intended audience in their given situation; and (3) to present and inculcate a worldview, a description of how the world operates. In our modern Western culture, when asked how one should evaluate historical narratives, the typical reply is that one must determine whether or not the 'facts' of who, what, when and where are correct. Yet when one asks why people 'do history', the answers are usually on a different level: for the purpose of learning from it who we are, how we got here, where we are headed, what mistakes should not be repeated and so on. In other words, a primary reason for doing history is for the 'why' questions that it answers, that is, what it tells us about the way the world works. This rhetorical function was recognized

44. H.V. White, *Metahistory: The Historical Imagination in Nineteenth-Century Europe* (Baltimore: The Johns Hopkins University Press, 1973), p. 2.

45. See below on how narratives communicate meaning, section 5.

46. H.V. White, 'Rhetoric and History', in H.V. White and F.E. Manuel (eds.), *Theories of History* (William Andrews Clark Memorial Library Seminar Papers, 1976; Los Angeles: William Andrews Clark Memorial Library, University of California, 1978), p. 3.

by ancient historians such as Livy and Thucydides.[47] The locus of meaning that we seek when we interpret a historical narrative is not in the who, what, when and where. They are important, but they are just the 'bones'. The flesh and blood of a historical work is what it says about 'why'. When reading Chronicles the rhetorically minded reader should be asking: How might the traditions that are being selected and recorded by Chr. shape the identity of the audience? What questions about their past, present and prospective future situations are being answered? What is the audience being 'told' about the way its world functions?

5. *How narratives communicate meaning.*[48] 'History', conceived and communicated in the form of historical narrative communicates meaning, to some degree in the same manner as all narratives, that is, through the creative act of mimesis.[49] It is, therefore, important that a

47. Livy discusses how one may learn moral lessons through history in the 'Preface' of *The History of Rome* (HCL; 2 vols.; New York: Harper & Brothers, 1875–81). Thucydides saw his work as having abiding value, since human nature, being what it is, would cause events of the past to be repeated in the future. Thucydides, *History of the Peloponnesian War* (Penguin Classics, 139; Baltimore: Penguin Books, 1954), 1.1.

48. For a fuller treatment of how narratives communicate meaning, particularly how biblical narratives communicate theology, see R.K. Duke, 'A Model for a Theology of Biblical Historical Narratives: Proposed and Demonstrated with the Books of Chronicles', in M.P. Graham, W.P. Brown and J.K. Kuan (eds.), *History and Interpretation: Essays in Honour of John H. Hayes* (JSOTSup, 173; Sheffield: JSOT Press, 1993), pp. 65-77.

49. The mimetic quality of narrative has been recognized in literary criticism at least since Aristotle's *Poetics*, although the nature of narrative referentiality is a debated topic in contemporary literary criticism. As noted above, often literary critics, having drawn a false dichotomy between history and fiction, have focused on the mimetic quality of only fictional narrative. However, historical narrative shares the same formative elements of narrative as fictional narrative. In other words, history—conceived of and communicated in the form of narrative—participates in the mimetic function of all stories. See Hernadi, 'Clio's Cousins', pp. 245-57; L.O. Mink, 'History and Fiction as Modes of Comprehending', *New Literary Inquiry* 1 (1969–70), pp. 541-58; Ricoeur, 'The Narrative Function', pp. 177-202; R.E. Scholes and R. Kellogg, *The Nature of Narrative* (Oxford: Oxford University Press, 1966); White, *Metahistory*; H.V. White, 'The Value of Narrativity in the Representation of Reality', *Critical Inquiry* 7 (1980), pp. 5-27; White, 'Rhetoric and History', pp. 3-24.

rhetorical analysis of narrative texts such as Chronicles be sensitive to the basic components of narrative. I would suggest that the following components need to be explored in any rhetorical analysis of narrative. First, the creative selection of subject matter (e.g. characters, events) communicates values by revealing what is worthy of the audience's attention. Secondly, the relationships among events (i.e. how events are perceived as connected or unconnected) communicate the laws of reality operating within the narrative world. Thirdly, the weaving of events into the plot of a narrative storyline with a beginning, middle and end communicates a teleology within the narrative world. Finally, the combination of these components (values, laws of reality, teleology) implicitly communicates an ideology that prescribes the proper course of action within that narrative world.[50]

6. *A basic purpose of the Chronicler.* In much of the rest of this paper I wish to work with the thesis that one of the primary purposes of Chr. was to move his audience to seek Yahweh through the proper forms of the Jerusalem cult. This manner of summarizing Chr.'s main message does not cover all that Chr. intended to do, and certainly not all that the work 'means' to any given reader, but it appears to support and encompass most scholarly theories regarding the purpose of the books of Chronicles.

Students of the books of Chronicles have arrived at various conclusions regarding the purpose(s) of this work. Proposed purposes have included: to present a theory of the return of 'all Israel' from exile (Torrey), to defend postexilic cultic institutions (Curtis and Madsen, Noth, Myers), to write a history of the Davidic dynasty in terms of its religious and cultic accomplishments (Freedman), to defend the realization of the theocracy in the new community of Israel against the claims of the Samaritans (Pfeiffer, Noth, Rudolph), to write a history of Judah and its institutions (Driver), to teach religious values through history (Keil, Welch, Mosis), to maintain religious orthodoxy (Myers) and to interpret to the restored community the history of Israel as an eternal covenant between God and David (Childs, Selman).[51]

---

50. The last three categories, as well as much of my understanding of the nature of how one constructs historical narrative, come from White, *Metahistory*, pp. 1-42. For a fuller development of the implications, see Duke, 'Model for a Theology of Biblical Historical Narrative'.

51. C.C. Torrey, *The Chronicler's History of Israel: Chronicles–Ezra–Nehemia*

First, although the above proposals might seem quite disparate at first glance, they can be reconciled within a rhetorical perspective of historical narrative. Descriptions of Chr.'s intention as 'to write a history' do not necessarily conflict with such descriptions as 'to demonstrate something by historical narrative'. Once one recognizes the general rhetorical functions of the genre 'historical narrative', then one can accept the fact that Chr.'s purpose was not to write the unachievable 'objective' history of modern idealization, but 'to teach' or 'to defend' or 'to encourage' or whatever. Secondly, most scholars defending these proposals hold at least two common observations: (1) Chr. stressed the importance of the institutions of the Davidic monarchy and the Jerusalem cult; and (2) within Chr.'s worldview the Israelite God, Yahweh, was believed to be active in the course of history, effecting blessing and punishment, particularly in regard to matters involving the Davidic dynasty and the temple cultus.[52]

The thesis that I believe best incorporates the above points of commonality was set forth by G.E. Schaefer:

> The primary aim of the Chronicler was to demonstrate from history that a faithful adherence to the 'God of the fathers' results in happiness and blessing and that forsaking the LORD will lead the nation and individual

Restored to its Original Form (New Haven: Yale University Press, 1954), pp. xxiv-xxv; E.L. Curtis and A.A. Madsen, *A Critical and Exegetical Commentary on the Books of Chronicles* (ICC; New York: Charles Scribner's Sons, 1910), p. 9; M. Noth, *Überlieferungsgeschichtliche Studien: Die sammelnden und bearbeitenden Geschichtswerke im Alten Testament* (Tübingen: Max Niemeyer, 2nd edn, 1957), p. 174 (= *The Chronicler's History* [JSOTSup, 50; Sheffield: JSOT Press, 1987], p. 100); J.M. Myers, *I Chronicles* (AB, 12; Garden City, NY: Doubleday, 1965), pp. xxx-lx; D.N. Freedman, 'The Chronicler's Purpose', *CBQ* 23 (1961), p. 437; R.H. Pfeiffer, *An Introduction to the Old Testament* (New York: Harper & Brothers, 2nd edn, 1948), pp. 802, 806; Noth, *Überlieferungsgeschichtliche Studien*, p. 166 (= *The Chronicler's History*, p. 89); W. Rudolph, *Chronikbücher* (HAT, 21; Tübingen: J.C.B. Mohr [Paul Siebeck], 1955), pp. viii-ix; S.R. Driver, *An Introduction to the Literature of the Old Testament* (Edinburgh: T. & T. Clark, 9th edn, 1913), p. 517; C.F. Keil, *The Books of Chronicles* (Clark's Foreign Theological Library, 4th ser., 35; Edinburgh: T. & T. Clark, 1878; Grand Rapids: Eerdmans, repr., 1978), p. 19; A.C. Welch, *The Work of the Chronicler: Its Purpose and Date* (Schweich Lecture, 1938; London: Oxford University Press, 1939), pp. 54, 123; R. Mosis, *Untersuchungen zur Theologie des chronistischen Geschichtswerkes* (FTS, 92; Freiberg: Herder, 1971), p. 223; Childs, *Introduction*, p. 644; Selman, *1 Chronicles*, p. 26.

52. R.B. Dillard, 'Reward and Punishment in Chronicles: The Theology of Immediate Retribution', *WTJ* 46 (1984), pp. 164-65.

to ruin and curse. His highlighting of the reigns of David and Solomon was to demonstrate that one is to seek the LORD through the temple cultus that was established in Jerusalem by them and honored by subsequent kings. The Chronicler's emphasis on 'seeking the LORD' is to be understood as an invitation extended to the people to experience life on its highest plane. His desire was to see the theocracy realized in Israel, with the people giving themselves completely to the LORD and looking to him to meet all their needs.[53]

'Seeking Yahweh' meant a total response of the worshiper to God. The Davidic king and all Israel were to turn to, pray to, inquire of, trust, praise and worship Yahweh and no other god. Most importantly, they were to do so through the proper cult in the proper cultic place, as established and modeled by David, with whom an everlasting covenant had been established. The opposite of seeking was not so much the commission of a sinful action, but an unfaithfulness demonstrated by failing to turn to Yahweh and by neglecting the temple cultus.[54] The resultant blessing or cursing, although often centered on the king, had an impact on the well-being of the whole nation. Blessing took a variety of forms: victory in battle, rest from one's enemies, united support of the people, prosperity, wisdom, healing, the ability to execute building projects or to strengthen one's army and fortifications. Cursing or retribution took the opposite forms: military defeat, illness or death, rebellion of the people and so on.[55]

---

53. G.E. Schaefer, 'The Significance of Seeking God in the Purpose of the Chronicler', (ThD dissertation, Southern Baptist Theological Seminary, 1972), pp. 17-18. S. Japhet seems to be making much the same point when she summarizes Chronicles as 'a comprehensive expression of the perpetual need to renew and revitalize the religion of Israel'. Japhet, *I & II Chronicles*, p. 49. Similarly, W. Johnstone notes that Chr.'s work is essentially theological and 'concerned with the universal relationship between God and humanity, and the vocation of Israel within that relationship'. W. Johnstone, *1 and 2 Chronicles*. I. *1 Chronicles 1–2 Chronicles 9: Israel's Place among the Nations* (JSOTSup, 253; Sheffield: Sheffield Academic Press, 1997), I, p. 10.

54. Schaefer, 'Seeking God', pp. 53-94.

55. Rudolph, *Chronikbücher*, pp. xviii-xx; R.L. Braun, 'The Significance of 1 Chronicles 22, 28, and 29 for the Structure and Theology of the Work of the Chronicler' (ThD dissertation, Concordia Seminary [St Louis], 1971), pp. 169-81, 204; Dillard, 'Reward and Punishment', pp. 165-70; P. Welten, *Geschichte und Geschichtsdarstellung in den Chronikbüchern* (WMANT, 42; Neukirchen–Vluyn: Neukirchener Verlag, 1973); See also the chart in Duke, *Persuasive Appeal*, pp. 78-79, of the indications of blessing and cursing.

The above paradigm of seeking Yahweh was believed by Chr. to be the message the audience of his day needed. Although scholars vary widely on their dating of Chronicles, from the late sixth to the late third century BCE,[56] some aspects of Israel's existence remained constant throughout this chronological range. The 'Israelites' had returned from the Babylonian exile to greatly reduced circumstances. They were reduced in number and territory. They were without their own king and self-government. They had to struggle to survive. Their continued existence as a people depended on their shaping and maintaining a sense of identity and hope. Chr.'s paradigm of seeking Yahweh explained the exile and the return from exile. Moreover, it provided the people with an identity that connected them to the promises of God and institutions of their past. It focused and guided their present actions. It gave them reason to hope for a better future. As Sara Japhet has said:

> For the Chronicler, 'the history of Israel' is the arena in which God's providence and rule of his people are enacted. By unveiling the principles which govern its history, a firm foundation is laid for the future existence of Israel.[57]

b. *The Structure of Chronicles*

My goal in this section is to identify how the macrostructure of Chronicles functions rhetorically. However, it should be at least noted that a rhetorical analysis should also examine the microstructures. Several studies, particularly in recent Chronicles research, have identified various rhetorical, structural devices on the micro level, such as the use of *inclusio*, chiasm, typology, repeated motifs and contrasting motifs.[58]

---

56. See Selman, *1 Chronicles*, p. 70.

57. Japhet, *I & II Chronicles*, p. 44.

58. In addition to the comprehensive study by I. Kalimi (*Zur Geschichtsschreibung des Chronisten: Literarisch-historiographische Abweichungen der Chronik von ihren Paralleltexten in den Samuel- und Königsbüchern* [BZAW, 226; Berlin: W. de Gruyter, 1995]) and K. Strübind's detailed work on 2 Chron. 17.1–21.1 (*Tradition als Interpretation in der Chronik: König Josaphat als Paradigma chronistischer Hermeneutik und Theologie* [BZAW, 201; Berlin: W. de Gruyter, 1991]), see L.C. Allen, 'Kerygmatic Units in 1 & 2 Chronicles', *JSOT* 41 (1988), pp. 21-36; R.B. Dillard, 'The Chronicler's Solomon', *WTJ* 43 (1980), pp. 299-300; Dillard, 'The Literary Structure of the Chronicler's Solomon Narrative', *JSOT* 30 (1984), pp. 85-93; H.G.M. Williamson, '"We Are Yours, O David": The Setting and Purpose of 1 Chronicles xii 1-23', in *Remembering All the Way* (OTS, 21: Leiden: E.J. Brill, 1981), pp. 168-70; Williamson, *1 and 2 Chronicles*, e.g. pp. 46-

For instance, Leslie Allen discovered that various rhetorical devices seemed to subdivide Chronicles into brief units that could be assimilated easily by an audience:

> What emerges from this study is a sense of the Chr.'s literary and homiletic skills. He indulged in widespread usage of the standard techniques of rhetorical criticism and used them as signals of his kerygmatic intentions. By means of such techniques he presented his material in assimilable portions, highlighting various themes in order to communicate his distinctive theological and devotional message.[59]

Such studies have highlighted Chr.'s skill as a communicator and call for the reader to look closely for the devices employed by Chr. My goal, however, is to focus on the macrostructure.

Aristotle recognized that effective communication was structured to have different parts with different purposes.[60] Most commentators have identified major sectional divisions to the books of Chronicles at three points: the genealogical section (1 Chronicles 1–9), the accounts of David and Solomon (1 Chronicles 10–2 Chronicles 9) and the accounts of the kings of Judah (2 Chronicles 10–36).[61] Respectively, these three sections function rhetorically as an introduction, the presentation of Chr.'s argument (i.e. his paradigm of seeking Yahweh) and illustration or further proof of his argument.

1. *The introduction: 1 Chronicles 1–9.* An introduction, according to Aristotle, should give the audience a foretaste of what is to come and clear away any obstacles regarding the addresser, audience or subject

---

47, 49-50, 96-97; M.P. Graham, 'Aspects of the Structure and Rhetoric of 2 Chronicles 25', in Graham, Brown and Kuan (eds.), *History and Interpretation*, pp. 78-89. For a thorough form-critical study of the structure in Chronicles, see S.J. De Vries, *1 and 2 Chronicles* (FOTL, 11; Grand Rapids: Eerdmans, 1989).

59. Allen, 'Kerygmatic Units', p. 4.

60. Aristotle, *Rhetorica*, 3.13.1414a30-35.

61. Japhet (*I & II Chronicles*, p. 8); Selman (*1 Chronicles*, pp. 76-84); and R.L. Braun (*1 Chronicles* [WBC, 14; Waco, TX: Word Books, 1986], pp. vii-viii) find just these three major divisions. Rudolph (*Chronikbücher*, pp. 1-5) and P.R. Ackroyd (*I & II Chronicles, Ezra, Nehemiah: Introduction and Commentary* [TBC; London: SCM Press, 1973], pp. 5-7) also subdivide David and Solomon. M.A. Throntveit (*When Kings Speak: Royal Speech and Royal Prayer in Chronicles* [SBLDS, 93; Atlanta: Scholars Press, 1987], pp. 113-20) also subdivides the period of the kings in Hezekiah's reign.

matter.[62] The genealogical section of Chronicles (1 Chronicles 1–9) leads the audience into Chr.'s main subject matter and thesis of the following narrative, as well as disposing the audience to a favorable reception of Chr. as the addresser.[63] Using genealogies and lists, Chr. opens his account with creation and Adam but quickly narrows his perspective temporally, geographically and nationally to focus on the twelve sons of Israel (chs. 2–8). But even within this section greater detail is given to two tribes: the sons of Judah (2.3–4.23), with particular focus on the Davidic line (2.3-17 and 3.1-24), and the sons of Levi (6.1-80), with special attention given to the Aaronic priests (6.1-15, 50-53) and temple musicians (6.31-47). By this means Chr.'s key subjects of Judah, the Davidic monarchy and the Jerusalem temple cultus have been introduced before the narrative proper begins. Interspersed within this section are a few brief narrative statements that play a major role:[64] they reveal the laws of operation within Chr.'s worldview and lay a foundation for the 'seeking' paradigm. They show, for example, that those who are wicked in Yahweh's sight are cursed (2.3; 5.25-26; 9.1), but that those who trust Yahweh are blessed (4.10; 5.20-22).

2. *The Chronicler's argument: 1 Chronicles 10–2 Chronicles 9.* In the narrative that follows the 'introduction', Chr. creates a portrait of David and Solomon as kings who personally and properly sought Yahweh by 'establishing' (note the frequent use of the key word כון) and supporting the Jerusalem temple cultus.[65] Consequently, Yahweh established them

---

62. Aristotle, *Rhetorica* 3.14.

63. See section 3.c.2 below on ethos. On the unity of 1 Chron. 1–9 with the rest of Chronicles, see M. Oeming, *Das wahre Israel: Die 'genealogische Vorhalle' 1 Chronik 1–9* (BWANT, 128; Stuttgart: W. Kohlhammer, 1990).

64. It is not my concern here to address the issue of whether these narrative statements were created by Chr. The fact that he included them shows that they suited his purposes.

65. The unity of the presentation of the period of David and Solomon has also been supported by R.L. Braun ('Solomonic Apologetic in Chronicles', *JBL* 92 [1973], pp. 503-16), W.L. Osborne ('The Genealogies of 1 Chronicles 1-9' [PhD dissertation, Dropsie College, 1979], pp. 10-11), H.G.M. Williamson ('The Accession of Solomon in the Books of Chronicles', *VT* 26 [1976], pp. 356-57) and Throntveit (*When Kings Speak*, pp. 114-15). Mosis, however, argues for the separation of David and Solomon (*Untersuchungen zur Theologie*, pp. 164-204). Tae-Soo Im also sees only David as providing the major paradigm. Im, *Das Davidbild in den Chronikbüchern: David als Idealbild des theokratischen Messianismus für*

in their roles as 'successful' kings of all Israel. Chr. implicitly demonstrates a reciprocal nature between David's actions of establishing the official cultic forms of worship (1 Chron. 15.1, 3, 12; 22.3, 5, 14; 28.2; 29.2, 3, 19; 2 Chron. 1.4; 2.6) and Yahweh's response of establishing the Davidic kingdom (1 Chron. 14.2; 17.11, 12, 14, 24; 22.10; 28.7).

For instance, in 1 Chronicles 15–16 David transported the ark to Jerusalem, appointed levitical singers and ministers, and led the people in worship, arranging everything 'according to all that is written in the Law of Yahweh' (16.40b). These actions are followed by a scene in which David, who desires to build a house for Yahweh, receives the promise from Yahweh to 'establish' (כון) the everlasting Davidic dynasty (ch. 17). Chapters 18–20 then illustrate the further establishment of David's kingdom, as David achieves military success and acquires wealth, which will be used for the construction of the temple (1 Chron. 18.11; 22.14; 29.3-5).[66]

As the portrayal of David is positive and idealistic, so too is the picture of Solomon, who followed in David's ways, carried out the construction of the temple and so completed Chr.'s paradigm of what it means to seek Yahweh. The material on David and Solomon comprises about 42 per cent of the narrative of Chronicles. One might suppose that the unique characteristics of these men were of particular interest to Chr. However, in this material there is very little interest shown in their personalities, thoughts and feelings, in contrast to Samuel–Kings. Rather, the Chr. has created a typological presentation.[67] David is the ideal king who exemplified the correct behavior of seeking Yahweh. He

den Chronisten (Europäische Hochschulschriften, 23rd ser., 263; Bern: Peter Lang, 1985), pp. 104-12.

66. Im (*Das Davidbild*, pp. 180-81) has further observed the connection between the establishment of the kingdom and the establishment of the cult and has noted that the whole story of David was built on this alternating pattern:

1 Chron. 11–12	Kingdom:	support of all Israel, Jerusalem established as capital
1 Chron. 13	Cult:	attempt to transport ark
1 Chron. 14	Kingdom:	Yahweh gives military success
1 Chron. 15–16	Cult:	David transports ark, appoints cultic officials
1 Chron. 17–20	Kingdom:	military victories
1 Chron. 21–29	Cult:	preparations for the temple

67. So, too, W. Johnstone noticed this difference about the biblical portrayals of David. 'Guilt and Atonement: The Theme of 1 and 2 Chronicles', in J.D. Martin and P.R. Davies (eds.), *A Word in Season* (JSOTSup, 42; Sheffield: JSOT Press, 1986), p. 113.

becomes explicitly the model to which the succeeding Davidic kings are compared and implicitly the model for Chr.'s audience.

3. *Illustrations of the argument: 2 Chronicles 10–36.* Having established his paradigm with extensive material on David and Solomon, Chr. then illustrates how the whole of the rest of Israelite history confirms this paradigm. He presents the accounts of the kings of Judah in quick succession. Through narrator comments, he explicitly compares Jehoshaphat, Ahaz, Hezekiah and Josiah to David and/or Solomon (17.3; 28.1; 29.2; 34.2, 3). Other comparisons are implicit. When a king (and people) 'does right in the sight of Yahweh', 'walks in the ways' of a righteous predecessor, humbles himself and preserves the Jerusalem cult (that is some form of 'seeking Yahweh'), then the king is blessed with deliverance from defeat, military success, building projects, and so on. But when the king 'walks in the ways' of an unrighteous predecessor, is proud, relies on an idolatrous king or nation, or ignores the Yahwistic cult (that is, some expression of forsaking God), then he (and the people) meet with a reversal of their fortunes.[68]

For example, Rehoboam began his reign properly: he obeyed Yahweh and was able to establish a strong kingdom (11.1, 5-12, 18-23). However, when he and all Israel forsook Yahweh later, they suffered from an invasion by Shishak of Egypt. When they humbled themselves, the situation was reversed and they were restored (12.1-12). This paradigmatic evaluation of Israelite (Judahite) history continues through the reign of Zedekiah, in whose reign the temple was destroyed and the people were carried off into captivity due to their abominations of forsaking God (36.11-21).

4. *The rhetorical impact of the Chronicler's structure.* Such structuring creates important rhetorical effects. First, the audience has been 'sold' an argument. The seeking paradigm was introduced, developed and illustrated.

Secondly, the audience, in the last section has been shown that that argument holds within short parameters of time. When the story in Chronicles is viewed as a whole, one notices that there has been very little development of plot. There is a rather long story about the founding of the cult and the establishment of Israel under David and

---

68. So, too, Osborne found this section to be highly structured ('The Genealogies', p. 39).

Solomon. That story is followed by several rather independent, short stories about each succeeding Davidic king. Developments of tensions and resolutions occur within each story, but they do not move a greater story along. The portraits of the Davidic kings function much like separate pictures of a slide show. As Von Rad noticed, this portrayal demonstrates that each generation is immediately accountable to Yahweh.[69] The significance of this structure can be seen more clearly when Chr.'s mode of emplotment is compared to that found in Samuel–Kings. The causal laws of reality at work within Samuel–Kings are similar to those in Chronicles, but they operate in a more cross-generational and fatalistic manner. Particularly, from the reign of Manasseh onwards the audience can see that the fate of Judah is sealed (2 Kgs 21.10-15). However, within Chr.'s representation of reality the reversal of negative or positive situations could take place from one reign or generation to the next and even within a given reign.

Thirdly, by structuring his account around material that fits the paradigm of seeking, Chr. has produced reductionistic, typological portraits that can easily be classified. Each king can be classified as one who did or did not seek Yahweh within the various periods of his reign. The simplicity and clarity of the portrayals move the audience to engage in the act of evaluation and yet accept Chr.'s judgment of each past king or generation.

Finally, the impact of such structuring would be to motivate the audience to seek Yahweh. The presentation and development of the master paradigm, which reduced each element in the historical field and compared it to the master paradigm for classification, implicitly invites the audience to judge the past. It also would invite them to evaluate their present situation in terms of the past. They have been shown that there are causal laws operating within reality that can effect the reversal of the situation of each generation.[70]

c. *The Modes of Persuasion in Chronicles*
According to Aristotle the addresser has three modes or means of effecting persuasive communication that are inherent to the act of

---

69. G. von Rad, *Old Testament Theology* (2 vols.; New York: Harper & Row, 1962, 1965), I, p. 350.

70. The audience has been shown further, as Japhet notes, that not only are people always given a chance to repent, but that warning before punishment is a mandatory element in Chronicles. Japhet, *I & II Chronicles*, pp. 44-45.

communication. One, typically designated 'logos', is the appeal made
on the rational level that demonstrates that the argument of the speech
is credible. Another, 'ethos', is the appeal that is made through the presentation of the character of the addresser as acceptable. The third,
'pathos', is the appeal that is made on the 'emotional' level that makes
the communication connotatively acceptable.[71] Analyzing Chronicles
from these perspectives provides the reader with three more tools for
observing what Chr. has done to present his message effectively.

1. *Chronicles and the 'rational' mode of persuasion.*[72] As has already
been noted above, Chr. has an argument to present through his historical narrative, the 'seeking' paradigm. How has Chr. tried to make that
argument credible through a rational mode of communication (logos)?[73]
According to Aristotle, in rhetoric, as opposed to dialectic, there are
two forms of argumentation or demonstration, the 'enthymeme' and the
'example'.[74] The enthymeme is an inferential argument that states some
conviction and gives a reason generally based on probabilities or on
popular opinion as to why this conviction should be accepted. The
example is a form of argument in which a parallel is drawn between
things of the same class.[75] In Chronicles these two forms occur in
different kinds of narrative. Enthymemes occur in material in which an
evaluation is stated in speech material by a character of the story or by
the narrator in 'narrative comments'. Examples occur in what might be
called 'straight narrative', narrative that is reporting an event.

An illustration of the enthymematic form of the seeking paradigm is
found in an important narrative comment following the straight narration of Saul's death (1 Chron. 10.1-12):

> And Saul died for his sin which he sinned against Yahweh on account of
> the word of Yahweh which he did not keep, and even by asking the
> medium to seek. But he did not seek Yahweh, so he killed him and he
> turned over the kingdom to David the son of Jesse (vv. 13-14).

71. Aristotle, *Rhetorica* 1.2.13563-4.

72. For a fuller treatment, see Duke, 'Logos: The Rational Mode of Persuasion',
Persuasive Appeal, pp. 81-104 .

73. For a fuller discussion of this mode, see E.E. Ryan, *Aristotle's Theory of
Rhetorical Argumentation* (Montreal: Bellarmin, 1984).

74. Aristotle, *Rhetorica* 1.2.1356a36-1356b17. In dialectic there are two forms
of demonstration as well: one deductive, the syllogism; and one inductive, called
simply 'induction'.

75. Ryan, *Aristotle's Theory*, pp. 117-27.

This enthymeme, which expresses the seeking argument in negative form, can be restated as a dialectical syllogism:

> The one who does not seek Yahweh will be punished.
> Saul did not seek Yahweh.
> Therefore, Saul was punished (lost kingdom and life).

It is important to examine further the grounds of appeal for this enthymeme. Aristotle examined the construction of arguments in terms of what he called the 'topics', which represent the ways the mind works to generalize, classify, analyze and synthesize that which it perceives.[76] I wish here to pick up on just one of the 'topics'. The premise of the above enthymeme is constituted by one of the 'common topics' that provide a form for making inferences, the maxim.[77] A maxim is a commonly accepted opinion about a generally applicable principle. The maxim here is, 'Yahweh blesses those who act in the manner he prescribes and curses those who do not'. The strength of this maxim was that it was not new. One finds this idea of divine retribution in the Samuel–Kings narrative, in the legal material, in the wisdom literature and in the prophets. Chr. built his enthymeme on a concept he could safely assume his audience accepted as a foundational truth. Aristotle claimed that building an enthymeme on a generally accepted principle invested the act of communication with moral character and gained the audience's favor.[78]

Most importantly, Chr. started with this maxim of divine retribution, qualified it and redefined it in the more specific terms of his complete 'seeking paradigm' in the following account of David and Solomon. Whereas Saul did not keep God's word and literally 'sought' a medium—presumably a tradition known to the audience—David is shown *by examples* as one who fully sought God. 'Seeking Yahweh' implicitly, by examples, becomes connected with the proper cultic forms of worship. Blessing takes the forms of having one's kingdom established, prosperity, favor with the people, building projects, military success, and so on. Further details about the duration of the consequences and how they could be reversed within a single generation are

---

76. E.P. Corbett, *Classical Rhetoric for the Modern Student* (New York: Oxford University Press, 1965), p. 108.

77. Aristotle, *Rhetorica* 2.23-24.

78. Aristotle, *Rhetorica* 2.21.1395b1-17.

taught and illustrated in the narration of Israel's history, particularly in the form of examples.

Further, Chr.'s demonstration of his argument reveals a skillful employment of examples and enthymemes. Aristotle observed that when examples precede enthymemes, the argument takes on an inductive air. For an inductive argument to be convincing, one must provide a large number of examples. However, when examples follow enthymemes they function much like the testimony of witnesses and fewer are needed.[79] It is instructive to see the arrangement Chr. used.

First, Chr. laid the groundwork for his argument somewhat proleptically in the genealogical 'introduction' in which there are a handful of narrative comments that set the stage for a world in which there is divine activity.[80] Secondly, he first clearly states his argument with an example followed by a 'high-risk' enthymeme explaining the death of Saul. It is 'high risk' because the enthymematic form brings to the fore the character and credibility of the speaker who is making the inference. Chr. decreases the risk, however, by basing what he says on an appeal to apparently known tradition about the causes of Saul's demise and on the commonly held maxim regarding divine blessing and cursing. Thirdly, the paradigm is then more fully defined and supported inductively by the examples of the lives of David and Solomon, as Chr. in his role as narrator moves again into the background. Indeed, the seeking paradigm in enthymematic form is found a few times in the material on David and Solomon, but only in the mouths of authoritative characters and not as narrative comments (see below on the ethical mode). Finally, the accounts of the Davidic kings serve as a series of examples showing the results of seeking or forsaking Yahweh. Among these examples, however, Chr. proceeds with more boldness. The enthymeme is more frequently stated, primarily still in the mouths of authoritative characters, but also now in the form of narrative comments. In summary, after cautiously stating his case with an enthymeme, Chr. shifted to an inductive mode that used examples of his two key 'witnesses' (David and Solomon), and having established his case, then shifted back to the more declarative form of argumentation by enthymemes.[81]

79. Aristotle, *Rhetorica* 2.20.1394a9-17.

80. 1 Chron. 2.3; 5.20, 22, 25-26; 9.1.

81. For further support and discussion, see Duke, *Persuasive Appeal*, pp. 95-104, and Lists 1 and 2 in Duke's Appendix, which catalogue the enthymemes in narrative comments and in speech material.

2. *Chronicles and the 'ethical' mode of persuasion.*[82] One of the rhetorical questions that needs to be asked, even if it can only be answered by speculation, is: How would an Israelite audience have perceived and reacted to the character of Chr. as he sought to re-present their historical heritage? That is to ask: What gave his re-presentation the authority that it should be accepted? We have noted above Chr.'s skillful presentation of his argument through enthymemes and examples. However, effective communication is not based on just a cogent presentation; it is also based on the audience's perception of the credibility of the speaker, or on what is called the 'ethical' mode of persuasion (ethos). Aristotle noted that in a practical sense the ethical appeal was the most effective or authoritative mode of persuasion.[83]

How does one go about evaluating the ethos created by Chr.? Aristotle looked for the qualities of good sense, good moral character and good will. Most basically, one can note that Chr. was of the skilled scribal class, was knowledgeable of Israelite tradition and law, presented an argument that was fundamentally consistent with the Israelite worldview found in their scriptures, and composed his account for the benefit of his audience. Moreover, as Fishbane has noted, Chr. wrote with what seems to be the typical authoritative voice of an ancient historian: the narrative voice is omniscient, in the third person and for the most part unobtrusive.[84] One would suppose that Chr. projected a good and proper disposition for a speaker of history and that he induced a favorable disposition from his audience. Still, such general observations do not take us very far. I would propose that the ethical appeal of Chr. is further disclosed by bringing in some other basic concerns of rhetorical analysis: an examination of the types of material he selected and how they were utilized to compose his account.

With what kind of material did Chr. compose his account and how did he shape it? Approximately one-half of Chr.'s history uses material

---

82. For more fully developed arguments and support regarding Chr.'s ethical appeal, see Duke, 'Ethos: The Ethical Mode of Persuasion', *Persuasive Appeal*, pp. 105-38.

83. Aristotle, *Rhetorica* 1.2.1356a.

84. Fishbane, *Biblical Interpretation*, p. 382. As with Greek historiography, it appears that in the Old Testament third-person narration was the expected standard. Scholes and Kellogg (*The Nature of Narrative*, p. 243) note that although the use of first person was avoided in early Greek historical narratives, it was employed in fiction.

parallel with that found in Samuel–Kings. The other half constitutes material that is unique to Chronicles (about 834 verses): genealogies and lists (447 verses), speeches (197 verses) and their narrative framework (100 verses), and additional narrative material (90 verses).[85] The use of each type of material needs to be examined in turn.

i. *The Chronicler's use of traditional material.* It appears that Chr. handled traditional material in a worthy manner. The evidence suggests that Chr. expected his audience to be familiar with traditions found in Samuel–Kings but that he did not expect them to make a detailed synoptic reading of the two histories (see 2.d, above). Much work has already been done comparing these accounts. Thomas Willi has argued that Chr. interpreted the DtrH from a postexilic perspective and created a complementary account, which—while containing contradictory details—did not contradict the traditions as a whole.[86] Brevard Childs came to a compatible conclusion. According to him, Chr.'s technique for re-presenting Israel's story involved: harmonizing the earlier record to other authoritative texts, supplementing it with material normative to Israel's concept of prophetic revelation and typologizing in order to emphasize enduring values and the continuity of God's dealings with Israel.[87] He concluded that Chr. did not feel at liberty to alter tradition at will: 'Rather, on the basis of a close study of the tradition the Chr. sought to explore the outer limits which the texts allowed in order to reconcile differences.'[88] Others, having examined Chr.'s exegetical techniques, have concluded that Chr. employed techniques common to other examples of inner-biblical exegesis and to later Judaism.[89] It

---

85. These statistics were taken from R.O. Rigsby, 'The Historiography of Speeches and Prayers in the Books of Chronicles' (ThD dissertation, Southern Baptist Theological Seminary, 1973), p. 70 n. 107.

86. Willi, *Die Chronik als Auslegung*, pp. 48-66.

87. Childs, *Introduction*, pp. 647-53. For Willi, the authoritative writings to which Chr. was bound were those primarily of DtrH (*Die Chronik als Auslegung*, pp. 55-56, 64-65). For Childs, Chr.'s authoritative texts included other canonical and possibly other non-canonical traditions.

88. Childs, *Introduction*, p. 648.

89. See D. Patte on how midrashic hermeneutic and exegesis were inseparable in the Jewish community that composed the Targum. (D. Patte, *Early Jewish Hermeneutic in Palestine* (SBLDS, 22; Missoula, MT: Scholars Press, 1975), pp. 6-7, 65-76. R. Bloch finds a historical trajectory between rabbinic Midrash and the Hebrew Bible. Chronicles, she finds, shares some of the midrashic characteristics in

appears, then, that Chr.'s handling of known tradition would not have aroused distrust. Rather, it would have communicated to the audience Chr.'s desire to interpret correctly and provide the true meaning of older tradition.

ii. *The Chronicler's use of unique material: external proofs.* The types of unique material that Chr. employed further reveal the ethical mode of his rhetorical strategy. One would suppose that Chr.'s credibility would be most at risk with the introduction of unique material (i.e. material not found in the biblical literature). It appears, however that Chr. has been quite circumspect. Approximately eight-ninths of his unique material has the rhetorical impact of what Aristotle called 'external proof'.[90] External proof is material supposedly not created by the addresser but brought in from external sources and used to support the argument, such as eyewitness testimony, physical evidence, letters, and so on.[91] This material carries its own authority. In Chronicles these 'external proofs' consist of genealogies, lists, the speeches of key characters and the citation of sources. (Whether or not Chr. made any of these up does not matter, since in form they function rhetorically as external proofs.)

The use of genealogies and lists would create a tone of reliability. Over half of the unique material is 'statistical' in nature: lists and genealogies. Employing such 'objective' material would reveal to the audience the addresser's efforts to be credible, since the credibility of his account rested not on personal authority but on external records. But, being credited with drawing on objective records was not the only rhetorical benefit. As was noted in the genealogical 'introduction', Chr. effectively used such material to introduce his main subjects and themes, while remaining personally in the background.

The quotation of direct speech also created the ambiance of reliability and played an important role in Chr.'s rhetorical strategy. Direct speech has the character of external proof, because it purports to be not the

its literary dependence on P and by its interpretation of older narrative material for contemporary purposes. R. Bloch, 'Midrash', in W.S. Green (ed.), *Approaches to Ancient Judaism: Theory and Practice* (BJS, 1: Missoula, MT: Scholars Press, 1978), pp. 37-39. See, too, Fishbane, *Biblical Interpretation*, p. 525; and M.D. Goulder, *Midrash and Lection in Matthew* (London: SPCK, 1974), p. 10.

90. Technically external proofs should be treated separately from the internal mode of ethos; however, the strategy of employing external proofs does reflect on the rhetors' appeal or lack of appeal to their own authority.

91. Aristotle, *Rhetorica* 1.2.1355b36-40 and 1.15.

words of Chr. but the 'testimony' of other persons. It is *their* ethos that gives weight to the contents of the speeches, even if it is Chr. who controls the content of those speeches. Such material allowed Chr. to avoid a blatant dependence on his own authority and yet speak through authoritative characters.[92]

There are some noteworthy characteristics of Chr.'s employment of direct speech. First, Chr. relies more on scenes of direct speech and less on scenes of dialogue than Samuel–Kings. Where scenes of dialogue occur in Chronicles they are usually synoptic. The bulk of his unique speech material is primarily in the form of speeches and isolated comments.[93] Such forms more directly and powerfully address the audience of the text. Scenes of dialogue are useful for revealing the characters of the speakers but they leave the audience as observers. Speeches, however, have the force of direct address to the narrator's audience, particularly when addressed to a vague or unspecified audience within the text.

Secondly, much of the direct speech in Chronicles either implicitly or explicitly presents the seeking paradigm in enthymematic form. Of the 107 incidences of direct speech in Chronicles, 37 of these state the seeking enthymeme, and 28 of these are unique to Chronicles.[94] Chr. heavily relied on direct speech, that is, the authority of others, to present his argument to his audience. No matter how the enthymematic statements functioned internally to the story (e.g. as prophetic rebukes to a king), they also functioned rhetorically to inculcate the seeking paradigm into the minds of Chr.'s audience.

Thirdly, the speech material that does not present the seeking enthymeme (70 out of 107 cases) still often plays a major role. Frequently it supports the seeking paradigm by helping to develop the stereotypical portrayal of the main characters. For instance, some are

92. It has long been noted that the speeches in Chronicles are quite uniform. The nature and uniformity of the speeches prompted G. von Rad to label them as levitical sermons, similar to the sermonic style found in Deuteronomy. (G. von Rad, 'The Levitical Sermon in I and II Chronicles', in *The Problem of the Hexateuch and Other Essays* (New York: McGraw-Hill, 1966), pp. 167-80. Welch thought the unique speeches of the prophets were so stereotypical that the prophets became colorless mouthpieces for the same message. Welch, *The Work of the Chronicler*, pp. 42-54. Rigsby also concluded that the speeches in Chronicles are in the vocabulary, idiom and syntax of Chr. Rigsby, 'Historiography of Speeches', p. 246.

93. Duke, *Persuasive Appeal*, p. 123.

94. Duke, *Persuasive Appeal*, pp. 124-25, and Lists 2 and 3 in the Appendix.

positive statements that show kings praying, repenting, restoring cultic practices, and so on, while others are negative statements portraying a character as one deserving judgment.[95]

Fourthly, the speeches primarily are spoken by authoritative characters: kings (55 times), prophets (18) and God (8).[96] In fact, the first speech in which the enthymeme is implied actually occurs in the mouth of Yahweh in response to David's desire to build the temple (1 Chron. 17.1-15), albeit a synoptic text. Chr. here has built his case on the credibility of Yahweh and on a well-known tradition about David. (It is interesting to note that all of the divine speech occasions are in synoptic sections, although Chr. has unique material in which Yahweh speaks indirectly through the prophets. One might suppose that Chr. felt the freedom to present 'new' speeches of human characters, but not new speeches of Yahweh.)

In regard to prophetic speeches, for instance, one notes further the rhetorical strategy of Chr. Fourteen of the 18 prophetic speeches are in unique material, and 13 of these state or imply the seeking enthymeme. However, in accord with what was noted earlier, all 13 cases occur after the Davidic–Solomonic period in which the seeking paradigm had been established primarily by the inductive means of example. Once the argument had been established mainly by example, it was reinforced by the enthymematic form. These prophetic speeches function as a deductive tool, teaching not only their narrative audience, but also Chr.'s audience, about the divine, cause-effect principle of seeking God. Moreover, these speeches, in contrast to those in Samuel–Kings, emphasize the conditional nature of blessing and judgment. As a result, they highlight Chr.'s theology about the possibility of the immediate reversal of one's state of blessing or judgment.[97]

In summary, Chr. has created an ethos that looks as though it would be quite effective. Where he comes to the fore as the composer of a historical narrative and a handler of known tradition, he seems to fit the

---

95. Duke, *Persuasive Appeal*, p. 125, and List 3 in the Appendix.

96. Duke, *Persuasive Appeal*, p. 127, and see Lists 4-8 in the Appendix.

97. These speeches are: 2 Chron. 12.5-8; 15.1-7; 16.7-10; 19.2-3; 21.12-15 (in part). C. Westermann noted that prophetic judgments of an earlier period were unconditional in nature, whereas in Chronicles some of the prophetic speeches reveal a formal difference in which the announcement of judgment was no longer unconditional. C. Westermann, *Basic Forms of Prophetic Speech* (London: Lutterworth, 1967), pp. 163-64.

acceptable standards of the day. Where he has an argument to put forward through his historical presentation, he does so primarily in ways that put him in the background and that rely on the authority of past examples, 'objective material' and the authority of others.

3. *Chronicles and the 'emotional' mode of persuasion.*[98] 'Pathos', the emotional mode, is the third of the three modes of persuasion. Aristotle stated that:

> the orator must not only try to make the argument of his speech demon-
> strative and worthy of belief [logos appeal]; he must also make his own
> character look right [ethos appeal] and put his hearers, who are to decide,
> into the right frame of mind [pathos appeal] ... [99]

For Aristotle, the emotional appeal was not a play on the audience's emotions that was effected through the orator's delivery and against reason. On the contrary, it was an appeal that, like the ethos appeal, complemented the development of the rational argument.[100] He noted, 'Our judgments when we are pleased and friendly are not the same as when we are pained and hostile'.[101] How then has Chr. told his story in such a manner as to affect the emotions of his audience to be sympathetic to his argument?

First, Chr. sought to evoke a supportive emotional response through the employment of repeated motifs that would induce the desired feelings toward the objects of his focus (e.g. the kings, the cult and the paradigm of seeking). For example, two repeated motifs stand out in association with the cult. The ultimate justification of the cultic institutions is based on divine disclosure made to Moses and recorded in the book of Law (1 Chron. 6.49, 15.15; 22.13; 2 Chron. 8.13; 23.18; 24.9; 30.16; 34.14-21) as well as to David (1 Chron. 28.11-19). Through this association, the audience's respect for and feelings toward Mosaic revelation, as well as toward Chr.'s idealized David and Solomon, is shifted toward the cultic practices of their day. Moreover, although on the whole Chr. rarely portrays the inner feelings of his characters, he

98. For a fuller discussion, see Duke, 'Pathos: The Emotional Mode of Persuasion', *Persuasive Appeal*, pp. 139-47

99. Aristotle, *Rhetorica* 2.1.1377b21-1378a5; the comments in brackets are mine.

100. L. Arnhart, *Aristotle on Political Reasoning* (DeKalb, IL: Northern Illinois University Press, 1981), p. 22; Kennedy, *Art of Persuasion*, pp. 93-95.

101. Aristotle, *Rhetorica* 1.2.1356a13-16.

frequently paints them as carrying out cultic activities with joy and singing.[102] Such pleasant associations draw the audience toward proper cultic participation.

Secondly, Chr. employed a typological presentation of characters both for an authoritative and emotional impact.[103] The major typology within Chronicles is the way in which the Davidic kings are stereotypically presented as seeking or forsaking Yahweh. He painted their portraits in contrasting colors with bold, unambiguous strokes intended to create a clear classification and the right emotional response from the audience toward the good and the wicked. However, scholars have also noted other typologies: that Solomon's succession to David was patterned after Joshua's succession to Moses,[104] that Solomon's and Hiram's roles in the building of the temple have parallels to Bezalel and Oholiab,[105] and that even the account of building the temple follows a stereotypical pattern found in the ancient Near East.[106] This rhetorical device of typology subtly encourages the audience to carry their evaluation of and feelings for the prototypical character or event over to the secondary character or event.

Thirdly, as Chr. illustrated his paradigm of seeking within the reign of each king or generation, he produced a certain kind of storyline or emplotment with an emotional impact. As noted above, each account of a Davidic king had its own emplotment and functioned as a separate portrait. The divine principle regarding blessing or judgment was operative within and virtually limited to each unit. Chr. avoided a fatalistic kind of emplotment that would leave an audience without hope for a better life. Rather, in showing the accountability of each generation and the willingness of Yahweh to bless those who seek him, Chr. created a 'romantic' storyline (in the classical sense), which

102. 1 Chron. 13.6-8; 15.16-29; 29.9, 22; 2 Chron. 5.12-13; 15.14-15; 20.21-22, 27-28; 23.18; 29.25-30; 30.21, 25-26. Braun observed that שׂמח ('rejoice') occurs 15 times in Chronicles without parallel in Samuel–Kings ('Significance', p. 185).

103. See R. Alter, 'Biblical Type-Scenes and the Uses of Convention', in *The Art of Biblical Narrative* (New York: Basic Books, 1981), pp. 47-62.

104. Braun, 'Significance', pp. 30-34; R.L. Brown, 'Solomon, the Chosen Temple Builder: The Significance of 1 Chronicles 22, 28, 29 for the Theology of Chronicles', *JBL* 95 (1976), pp. 586-88; Dillard, 'The Chronicler's Solomon', pp. 293-95.

105. Dillard, 'The Chronicler's Solomon', pp. 296-99.

106. A.S. Kapelrud, 'Temple Building: A Task for Gods and Kings', *Or* 32 (1963), pp. 56-62.

offered the possibility of a happy ending. The audience could always emulate the heroes of the 'Golden Age' of David and Solomon, so that in times of blessing there would be need for steadfastness, and in times of disaster there would be reason for hope.

Fourthly, the manner in which Chr. demonstrated his argument through the enthymeme and example generated an emotional appeal. As noted above, Chr. began to develop his seeking paradigm out of a maxim of divine retribution toward Saul (1 Chron. 10.14), rather than by stating the full deductive form of the implied syllogism. Aristotle argued that to create an emotional appeal it was better to abbreviate the enthymeme and to argue with maxims. That is to say, it is generally more effective to develop an argument out of something one's audience has already accepted as a general truth: '[hearers] love to hear him [the speaker] succeed in expressing as a universal truth the opinions which they hold themselves about particular cases'.[107] The fact that Chr. demonstrated a pattern of divine activity inductively through examples would not only give an aura of authority and credibility to his account,[108] but feelings of anticipation or apprehension also would be generated in the audience as they examined their own generation for manifestations of the pattern. The use of such examples should have elicited a sense of security in the continuity and predictability of divine activity in the ongoing life of Israel.

Finally, the use of speech material creates not only an ethical appeal, but also an emotional one. When speeches are quoted directly, they have the impact of addressing not just the audience within the narrative, but also the narrator's external audience, Chr.'s audience. When David or a prophet exhorts his audience, Chr.'s audience receives the exhortation, too. By this means, Chr.'s audience has been variously encouraged or rebuked throughout the historical narrative with regard to the seeking paradigm.

In summary, as an effective communicator Chr. artfully employed the emotional mode of persuasion. He painted the key subjects, the key characters and his main argument in bold stereotypical strokes with

107. Aristotle, *Rhetorica* 2.21.1395b1-13; material in brackets added for clarification. See also, *Rhetorica* 1.2.1357a17-21; 2.22.1395b20-31; 3.17.1418a12-21.

108. For the use and effect of patterning in the OT, see Alter (*Art of Biblical Narrative*, pp. 47-62, 88-113), and for the use of stereotypical presentation in rabbinic exegesis, see Patte (*Early Jewish Hermeneutic*, pp. 67-74), who prefers to call the device 'telescoping'.

defining colors, playing off the audience's familiarity with past images and concepts. His picture is clear, and the desired and unambiguous emotional responses evoked would support his story.

4. *Conclusion*

The tools of rhetorical analysis, when applied to a deliberate act of communication, such as biblical historical narrative, can provide insight into the artistry, functions and 'meaning' of a text. Applied to Chronicles, one can gain insight into Chr.'s character, worldview, theological perspective, purposes and intended audience. Rhetorical features are not extraneous, cosmetic elements tacked on to beautify or deceive. Rather, they constitute the form and content of an act of communication. It is the rhetorical quality of a work, whether poor or skillful, that determines its ability to communicate effectively. This holds true for historical narratives as well as other forms of communication. Hayden White writes, 'The principal source of a historical work's strength as an *interpretation* of the *events* which it treats *as the data to be explained* is rhetorical in nature'.[109] The rhetorical nature of a historical work is its principal source of appeal to the audience to accept the work.[110] And, as we know, the books of Chronicles became an officially accepted retelling of the traditions of Israel. Chr. was rhetorically effective.

109. White, 'Rhetoric and History', p. 3.
110. White, 'Rhetoric and History', p. 3.

THE FABULA OF THE BOOK OF CHRONICLES

John W. Wright

Iain Provan has recently articulated his understanding of contemporary biblical scholarship in a most graphic way:

> It was one of the more interesting of the various punishments known to the ancients that a guilty party should be tied by arms and legs to two horses, which might then be sent off jointly at a gallop into the blue beyond. The consequences for the person thus attached to his equine companions were ultimately rather bloody, as each horse turned independently to seek pastures new. Those who care about the integrity of biblical narrative might well ask what it has done in recent times to deserve a similar ghastly fate. Why at this point in the history of our discipline are story and history found, in so much scholarship, to be heading at speed in opposite directions, torn apart with sometimes violent force?[1]

If such is Provan's concern, he need not worry about recent Chronicles scholarship. Here the 'guilty party' has remained closely tied to the thoroughbred of history; story remains unbridled in the pasture.

Such a situation is surprising. A narrative reading of Chronicles led Wilhelm deWette, the father of modern Chronicles scholarship, to question the historicity of the presentation of the history of Israel.[2] Even more so, Martin Noth's important study of Chronicles made redaction criticism the normative approach to the academic interpretation of Chronicles.[3] Yet while redaction criticism moved into narrative read-

---

1. I.W. Provan, 'Ideologies, Literary and Critical: Reflections on Recent Writing on the History of Israel', *JBL* 114 (1995), pp. 585-606 (585).

2. See J.W. Wright, 'From Center to Periphery: 1 Chronicles 23–27 and the Interpretation of Chronicles in the Nineteenth Century', in E.C. Ulrich *et al.* (eds.), *Priests, Prophets and Scribes: Essays on the Formation and Heritage of Second Temple Judaism in Honour of Joseph Blenkinsopp* (JSOTSup, 149; Sheffield: JSOT Press, 1992), pp. 20-42.

3. M. Noth, *The Chronicler's History* (JSOTSup, 50; Sheffield: JSOT Press, 1987), a translation of part of Noth's *Überlieferungsgeschichtliche Studien: Die*

ings—and beyond—in Gospel studies, Chronicles scholarship has largely remained content with questions of sources and editorial *Tendenz*. For instance, while Sara Japhet initially wrote a magisterial, redaction-based monograph on the ideology of Chr.,[4] her more recent commentary returned to questions of sources and history, rather than to the workings of the Chronicles narrative.[5] Japhet's research represents much of the work that has gone on in the field. Kent Richards's survey of recent Chronicles scholarship shows that the discussions that currently drive the field have not fundamentally changed since the discovery of the Samuel fragments from Qumran and the publication of Japhet's seminal article that challenged the authorial/editorial relationship between Chronicles and Ezra–Nehemiah.[6]

The avoidance of literary-critical questions in Chronicles study, however, seems unfortunate. Despite Provan's discomfiture, literary readings, even those that challenge a text's historicity, do not necessarily rend the text into a 'bloody corpse'. Narrative approaches may generate viable, interesting readings of the text. Nor does asking questions concerning structural relationships within the text compel one to an ahistorical end. 'On the contrary, to the extent that a careful analysis of narrative structure counters interpretations based on prejudice, convention or ideology, and the more precise such an analysis is, the better it helps to position the object within history.'[7] It may prove interesting to tie Chronicles to a narrative 'equine companion' and see in what condition we arrive in pastures new.

---

sammelnden und bearbeitenden Geschichtswerke im Alten Testament (Tübingen: Max Niemeyer, 1943). For a recent assessment of the entire work, see S.L. McKenzie and M.P. Graham (eds.), *The History of Israel's Traditions: The Heritage of Martin Noth* (JSOTSup, 182; Sheffield: Sheffield Academic Press, 1994).

4. See S. Japhet, *The Ideology of the Book of Chronicles and its Place in Biblical Thought* (BEATAJ, 9; Bern: Peter Lang, 1989).

5. See S. Japhet, *I & II Chronicles: A Commentary* (OTL; Louisville, KY: Westminster/John Knox Press, 1993).

6. K.H. Richards, 'Reshaping Chronicles and Ezra-Nehemiah Interpretation', in J.L. Mays, D.L. Petersen and K.H. Richards (eds.), *Old Testament Interpretation: Past, Present, and Future. Essays in Honor of Gene M. Tucker* (Nashville, TN: Abingdon Press, 1995), pp. 211-24; see also J.W. Kleinig, 'Recent Research in Chronicles', *CR:BS* 2 (1994), pp. 43-76.

7. M. Bal, 'The Point of Narratology', *Poetics Today* 11 (1990), p. 750.

Narratology as a Literary-Critical Approach to the Book of Chronicles

The discipline of narratology had a meteoric rise from its inception in the 1960s to its heights in the early 1980s. The discipline drew from fertile thought in several literary-critical traditions: Anglo-American 'New Criticism', Slavic formalism and French structuralism, with important contributions by Israeli scholars among others.[8] In those heady days, the field understood its task as nothing less than establishing a science of narrative: 'the analysis of the features and functions of all narrative'.[9] By abstracting formal literary relationships inherent within all narratives, it was believed that the field could discover the underlying structure of all narrative that would provide objective access to *the* meaning of the text. Narratology thus emerged as an expression of structuralism. It was therefore prone to the identical temptation of structuralism—to make claims that were 'fundamentally positivistic, holding out the promise of *the* right answer to problems, claiming a point of reference that gives it mastery over texts'.[10]

The 1980s were an unfortunate time to make such claims, and during this period deconstruction swept rapidly through literary criticism in the academy. Deconstruction, however, called into question the very possibility of a comprehensive system of structural relations, not merely as a method of analyzing a text, but also within a text itself:

> Every system is a construction, something that has been assembled, and construction entails exclusion. Every system excludes—is, in fact, a system of exclusions. Deconstruction seeks out those points within a system where it disguises the fact of its incompleteness, its failure to cohere as a self-contained whole. By locating these points and applying a kind of leverage to them, one deconstructs the system. This amounts neither to destroying nor dismantling the system in toto, but rather demonstrating how the (w)hole, through masking of its logical and rhetorical contradictions, maintains the illusion of completeness... To deconstruct is to identify points of failure in a system, points at which it is able to feign coherence only by excluding and forgetting that which it cannot assimilate, that which is 'other' to it.[11]

8. V.B. Leitch, *American Literary Criticism from the Thirties to the Eighties* (New York: Columbia University Press, 1988), pp. 247-48.

9. Leitch, *American Literary Criticism*, p. 247.

10. The Bible and Culture Collective, *The Postmodern Bible* (New Haven: Yale University Press, 1995), p. 99.

11. *Postmodern Bible*, p. 120.

Deconstruction's 'dismantling' of structures, therefore, undercuts not only the method of narratology, but its very agenda. So, narratology's rise was met with an even more precipitous fall.[12]

Ironically, the narratological study of the Hebrew Bible did not really gain widespread momentum until the end of the 1980s.

> Given the vigorous application of French structuralist theory to biblical texts in North America through the 1970's, it is surprising that biblical scholars did not then begin to draw upon the narratological tradition. It was only in the 1980's, with the decline of high biblical structuralism in North America, that narratological approaches became the preferred way of appropriating literary and cognate studies for biblical research.[13]

Narratological study of the Hebrew Bible, therefore, happily ascended, even as its narratological, theoretical foundation collapsed underneath it.

Meanwhile, Chronicles research seemed oblivious to the whole affair. Perhaps this was beneficial. Perhaps Chronicles interpretation thereby escaped narratological readings that sought a mathematical, formulaic 'objectivity' encoded in a technical language known only to the initiates. Given the absence of extremist, structuralist claims in Chronicles interpretation, perhaps the field need not react against such readings, but should rather be open to incongruities and inconsistencies within the text that arise within its structural relations.

Perhaps a narratological reading of Chronicles might emerge, and even flourish, by dropping its totalitarian aspirations of objectivity and universality. Rather than seeking a final domination over the text, narratology may be conceived instrumentally, 'as a set of tools, as a means to express and specify one's interpretative reactions to a text'.[14] In the

---

12. It is interesting that one of the main theorists of narratology, Gérard Genette, predicted this fall, even as he concluded his important theoretical and methodological work of narratology: 'This arsenal, like any other, will inevitably be out of date before many years have passed, and all the more quickly the more seriously it is taken, that is, debated, tested, and revised with time. One of the characteristics of what we can call *scientific effort* is that it knows itself to be essentially decaying and doomed to die out: a wholly negative trait, certainly, and one rather melancholy to reflect on for the "literary" mind, always inclined to count on some posthumous glory...' G. Genette, *Narrative Discourse: An Essay in Method* (Ithaca, NY: Cornell University Press, 1980), p. 263.

13. *Postmodern Bible*, p. 84.

14. M. Bal, *Narratology: Introduction to the Theory of Narrative* (trans. Christine van Boheemen; Toronto: University of Toronto Press, 1985), p. x; The Bible

words of Gérard Genette, a narratological reading of Chronicles 'is not an instrument of incarceration, of bringing to heel, or of pruning that in fact castrates: it is a procedure of discovery, and a way of describing'.[15]

Genette, and those who have followed him, may provide the theoretical foundations for such a narratological approach to the book of Chronicles. Fundamental to their work is the theoretical presupposition that we may distinguish between three structural layers within a text. These three layers are, depending on how one translates Genette's terminology, 'narration', the 'text' and the 'fabula'.[16] This distinction mirrors Chatman's distinction, popular in biblical studies, between 'discourse' and 'story', with the addition of the category 'narration'.[17] The 'fabula' 'designates the narrated events, abstracted from their disposition in the text and reconstructed in their chronological order, together with the participants in these events'.[18] The 'text' is 'what we read. In it, the events do not necessarily appear in chronological order, the characteristics of the participants are dispersed throughout, and all the items of the narrative contents are filtered through some prism or

and Culture Collective would seemingly concur with Bal: 'We should accomodate to structuralism as a philosophical option and a practical tool of the utmost importance, while disregarding its grandiose pretensions', *Postmodern Bible*, p. 104.

15. Genette, *Narrative Discourse*, p. 265.

16. These terms are taken from Christine van Boheemen's translation of Mieke Bal's *Narratology*, where Genette's terminology and method are developed into a narratological handbook. In the translation of Genette's work from French into English, however, Jan Lewin translates Genette's terminology as 'narrating', 'narrative' and 'story', thus leading to a confusing equivocation of 'story' between Bal's handbook and Genette's work (in English), from which Bal derived her basic terminology.

17. S.B. Chatman, *Story and Discourse: Narrative Structure in Fiction and Film* (Ithaca, NY: Cornell University Press, 1978).

18. S. Rimmon-Kenan, *Narrative Fiction: Contemporary Poetics* (London: Routledge, 1983), p. 3; see also Bal, *Narratology*, p. 5: 'A *narrative text* is a text in which an agent relates a narrative. A *story* is a fabula that is presented in a certain manner. A *fabula* is a series of logically and chronologically related events that are caused or experienced by actors.' Genette argues for the following: 'to use the word *story* for the signified or narrative content (even if this content turns out, in a given case, to be low in dramatic intensity or fullness of incident), to use the word *narrative* for the signfier, statement, discourse, or narrative text itself, and to use the word *narrating* for the producing narrative action and, by extension, the whole of the real or fictional situation in which that action takes place'. *Narrative Discourse*, p. 27.

perspective.'[19] The narration focuses on the abstraction called the narra-tor: 'Since the text is a spoken or written discourse, it implies someone who speaks and writes it.'[20]

Of these three structural levels, the reader may only directly access the second level, the 'text'; the other two levels are abstractions, logical constructs:

> Story [fabula] and narrating [narration] thus exist...only by means of the intermediary of the narrative [text]. But reciprocally that narrative [narration] can only be such to the extent that it tells a story, without which it would not be narrative... And to the extent that it is uttered by someone, without which... it would not be a discourse. As a narrative, it lives by its relationship to that story it recounts; as discourse, it lives by its relationship to the narrating that utters it.[21]

In other words, the 'what' of a narrative comes together with the 'how' of the narration within the concrete expression of the text itself. This relationship may be schematized as follows:

FABULA $\longrightarrow$ TEXT $\longleftarrow$ NARRATION

These distinctions provide an intellectual construct that permits an analysis of relationships between the basic elements of a narrative and its articulation within a specific text. Narratology, therefore, permits an analytic, disciplined means of accounting for the structural relationships that comprise a narrative text. While readers must constitute these rela-tionships themselves (rather than 'discover them' inherent within the text), narratological method permits the possibility of discussing and judging the reading in relation to the text itself. This public account-ability legitimates the use of the method.

For the purpose of this paper, I will seek to abstract the fabula of the book of Chronicles from the text. Inherent within the concept of a fabula is the concept of narrative change. Change itself, however, implies other concepts as well: agents that cause or experience change; time lapsed in order for change to occur; and a place where the change may occur. Mieke Bal defined 'fabula' as 'a series of logically and chronologically related events that are caused or experienced by actors'.[22] While a theoretician may analytically further dissect the four

19. Rimmon-Kenan, *Narrative Fiction*, p. 3.
20. Rimmon-Kenan, *Narrative Fiction*, p. 3.
21. Genette, *Narrative Discourse*, p. 29.
22. Bal, *Narratology*, p. 5.

basic elements of the fabula (often *ad nauseam*), these fundamental building blocks of the fabula provide us with sufficient background to turn finally to the text of Chronicles itself.

The Fabula of the Book of Chronicles

What narrative change does the book of Chronicles encode? This, of course, is the fundamental interpretive question, the whole that determines the meaning of its parts. Rodney Duke, in perhaps the most extensive, carefully done literary-rhetorical approach to Chronicles,[23] sees the fundamental change 'emplotted' through the establishment of a narrative 'paradigm':

> On the surface structure of the narrative, the Chronicler has selected and structured his account of Judah's history in order to present a certain story-line or emplotment. In this story, the reigns of David and Solomon serve as an ideal type. This ideal type then functions as a paradigm to which the successive reigns of the Davidic kings were compared, and by which they were evaluated.[24]

The event of Chronicles, the change in the narrative, therefore, is minor and repetitive, almost atemporal:

> When the story in Chronicles is viewed as a whole, one notices very little development of a main plot through such devices as tension and resolution. One might say that there is some movement in the overall story from the establishment of the official cultus and Davidic dynasty to their virtual demise at the end of the story. Still, there is very little development of an an [sic] overall story-line.[25]

According to Duke, the narrative thus accomplishes Chr.'s persuasive purpose: 'seeking Yahweh wholeheartedly through the proper cultic means would result in blessing for Israel, whereas failure to seek Yahweh would result in disaster'.[26] Chronicles does not so much chronologically unfold a plot as it asserts an achronological argument. Thus Duke's literary-rhetorical reading of Chronicles abstracts the

---

23. Duke writes, 'This study stands within the trend to approach Chronicles as a literary product without regard for the historical veracity of its materials', R.K. Duke, *The Persuasive Appeal of the Chronicler: A Rhetorical Analysis* (JSOTSup, 88; Bible and Literature Series, 25; Sheffield: Almond Press, 1990), p. 29.

24. Duke, *Persuasive Appeal*, p. 54.

25. Duke, *Persuasive Appeal*, p. 69.

26. Duke, *Persuasive Appeal*, p. 149.

narrative form of Chronicles into the Aristotelian category of an 'enthymeme': 'an inferential argument which states some conviction regarding human affairs and a reason why this conviction should be accepted'.[27] The overall narrative chronology of Chronicles becomes insignificant. Duke thereby uses a literary-rhetorical approach to develop the 'typological' approach to Chronicles, initiated by Rudolf Mosis, that currently dominates the interpretation of Chronicles.[28]

Sara Japhet, while not necessarily contradicting Duke's overall reading, argues for a much broader understanding of the event of Chronicles:

> Chronicles describes the history of Israel from beginning to 'beginning', that is, from the inception of human existence with Adam, through the destruction of the first commonwealth during the reign of Zedekiah, to the new commencement with the declaration of Cyrus.[29]

Japhet thereby emphasizes the narrative form of Chronicles—the narrative does, after all, begin with Adam in 1 Chron. 1.1 and concludes in 2 Chron. 36.22-23. By simultaneously abstracting the interpretive concept of 'beginning' from both the figure of Adam and Cyrus's proclamation, she ties the beginning to the end, thus generating out of her reading of the narrative event of the book its main import:

> Chronicles is a comprehensive expression of the perpetual need to renew and revitalize the religion of Israel. It makes an extremely important attempt to reaffirm the meaningfulness of contemporary life without severing ties between the present and the sources of the past; in fact, it strengthens the bond between past and present and proclaims the continuity of Israel's faith and history.[30]

Japhet's view here may subsume Duke's, but not vice versa. Japhet presents a wider narrative context for the book of Chronicles than Duke. Thus, while Japhet reads the genealogies of Chronicles as structurally significant within the series of events in Chronicles, for Duke, they are chiefly introductory, structurally insignificant, though possessing some rhetorical freight: 'My belief is that the genealogical section in Chronicles both leads the audience into the subject and thesis of the narrative and disposes the audience to a favorable reception of the speaker.'[31]

27. Duke, *Persuasive Appeal*, p. 82.
28. See R. Mosis, *Untersuchungen zur Theologie des chronistischen Geschichtswerkes* (FTS, 92; Freiburg: Herder, 1973).
29. Japhet, *I & II Chronicles*, p. 8.
30. Japhet, *I & II Chronicles*, p. 49; see also Japhet, *Ideology*, pp. 515-16.
31. Duke, *Persuasive Appeal*, p. 52.

Japhet's insight that the genealogies of 1 Chronicles 1–9 comprise an important component of the text's plot provides a starting point for my reading. Yet an analysis of the chronological structure of Chronicles suggests that Japhet's reading of Chronicles' series of events itself needs re-visioning, for Japhet mistakes the text's narrative order for the fabula's chronological structure. The narratological distinction between narrative order and chronology helps us discover the fabula of the book of Chronicles in its entirety in 1 Chronicles 1.1–9.38. This conclusion, as we will see, has wide-ranging implications for reading the book of Chronicles.

A Chronological Sequence of the Fabula of the Book of Chronicles

A fabula unfolds in a certain chronological and logical sequence: one event presupposes the occurrence of a previous event, that is, the birth of a child presupposes the prior birth of the child's parents. Yet a text may relate these events in a different narrative order: the text may tell of the child's birth first and return at a subsequent time to the parents' birth. This distinction between narrative order and the fabula's chronology provides one of the more fundamental distinctions between the fabula and its concrete expression within a particular text. To discover the order of events that constitutes a fabula, we must abstract the chronological sequence from the text. A narrative implies an underlying chronological sequence: an absolute chronology that exists within the duration of a narrative text.

The distinction between narrative order and chronological sequence becomes very significant when one turns to Chronicles. The text begins with Adam (1 Chron. 1.1), a chronological anchorage at the very origins of humanity. No chronological point exists in Chronicles prior to Adam. As mentioned above, the text ends in 2 Chron. 36.22-23 with Cyrus' decree for the return of the exiled Judeans to Jerusalem and the rebuilding of the temple. Yet though Cyrus's decree ends the narrative order of the text, it does not constitute the latest chronological point in the fabula of Chronicles. The chronology of Chronicles reaches beyond Cyrus' decree: 1 Chron. 9.2-34 records a list of the families living within the land following the exile.

The chronological markings of 1 Chron. 9.2-34 are complex and even contradictory. The chronology of the passage is vague, established as postexilic only by its placement following v. 1 and by the use of

הראשׁנים in v. 2: 'the first inhabitants in their possessions in their towns' (1 Chron. 9.2). Yet the chronology of the return remains ambiguous. The text depicts Jerusalem as repopulated (vv. 3-8). Several points require the assumption that the temple had been rebuilt. For instance, four chief gatekeepers are assigned to guard the temple properties (vv. 26-27) and singers live in temple rooms (v. 33). Yet, at other times, the text suggests a time before the rebuilding of the temple, a time that harkens back to a day even before the construction of Solomon's temple—the text speaks of a tent (אהל, vv. 16, 21), instead of a permanent building. To confuse matters more, v. 23 equates the temple and the tent: לבית־יהוה לבית אהל. The text seems to strain the chronology, blurring the distinction between the postexilic reconstruction of life in Yehud and the era before the first temple was built in Jerusalem.

The text's chronology strains even more. 1 Chronicles 9.2-34 substantially parallels Nehemiah 11. While its relative chronology is tied to the initial return from the exile (הראשׁנים; v. 2), the parallel to Nehemiah 11 ties its absolute chronology to the time of Nehemiah on the eve of the rededication of Jerusalem's walls. The text is, however, not only linked with the time of Nehemiah but also with pre-Solomonic Israel. The text refers anachronistically to the time of the wanderings in the wilderness through Phineas, son of Eleazar (v. 20), as well as in the references to the 'tent of meeting'. Additionally, the text has 'David and Samuel the seer establish them [the 212 gatekeepers?] in their trust' (v. 22b).

Are David and Samuel suddenly postexilic figures, or is the chronological setting of 1 Chron. 9.2-34 the Jerusalem of David's era? Does הראשׁנים mean 'first inhabitants' or 'former inhabitants'? How does the Davidic setting relate to the absolute chronology formed by Nehemiah 11?

1 Chronicles 9.2-34 implodes chronologically. The text points to a postexilic ending for the chronological sequence of Chronicles. Yet the resettlement of Jerusalem after the exile ends time as a linear sequence. The chronology of 1 Chron. 9.2-34 is non-specific, absorbing the late fifth century into the fourth century BCE. Like a black (w)hole, the chronology of the passage bends all time into itself, absorbing the time of David and Samuel into its chronological sequence. Pre-temple, first temple, pre-Second Temple and Second Temple eras all merge into one. Jerusalem, perpetually resettled, is Jerusalem initially settled.

The conclusion of the chronological sequence of the fabula of

Chronicles, therefore, differs markedly from its narrative order. While the chronology of Chronicles begins with time and moves through time, it ultimately ends time as a linear progression in history. The chronology of the fabula of Chronicles literally ends with the temporal merging of David and Samuel into the post- (or is it pre-?) exilic Jerusalem community.

It should come as no surprise, therefore, to find that the one other place in Chronicles that extends the chronological sequence of the fabula into an undesignated time following the exile involves the Davidic family. As is well known, 1 Chron. 3.10-24 extends the Davidic line through Solomon well into the Second Temple period. What is not generally recognized, however, is that in so doing, the text completes an uninterrupted chronological sequence (in contrast to narrative order) that began with Adam and ends sometime after the return from the exile with the Davidic family.

Chronicles constructs this chronological sequence by linking a series of genealogies together. Genealogical digressions interrupt the sequence, but always wrap back around to the central genealogical-chronological sequence. The sequence begins with 1 Chron. 1.1 and moves directly from Adam to Shem in v. 4. The central narrative picks up again in 1.24, with the repetition of Shem, and extends into v. 27, before continuing the movement from Abraham to Israel in 1.34. Following a digression, the narrative is rejoined in 2.1 with the repetition of Israel and the chronological extension into the next generation, Israel's twelve sons. The narrative continues through Judah and his descendants until the generation of David (2.3-16a). Following another narrative digression that fills out the generations of the other households within Judah, the central chronological sequence continues from David (3.1) through Solomon (whose name is repeated in 3.10, after its first appearance among the generation of David's children in 3.5) on through Jeconiah 'the captive' (3.17), Zerubbabel and his son, Hananiah, culminating in the seven sons of Elioenai (3.24). Here the chronological sequence of Chronicles reaches its latest point. The narrative progression begun in Adam ends in the seven sons of Elioenai, the son of Solomon, the son of David, the son of Judah, the son of Israel, the son of Shem, the son of Adam.

The chronology of the fabula of Chronicles, therefore, is established in the chronological progression encoded in 1.1-4a, 24-27, 34; 2.1-16a; 3.1-24. The chronology largely is a relative chronology: it develops internally without any specific chronological markers, rather than in relation to an event exterior to the narrative (genealogy). Two exceptions arise. First, the text specifies the exact number of years of David's reign in 1 Chron. 3.3: seven years and six months in Hebron, and 33 years in Jerusalem. Secondly, Jeconiah is designated as 'the captive' in 3.17. The relative chronology, therefore, is anchored in two events: David's reign and the Babylonian exile. Interestingly, the end of the chronological sequence has no absolute point, except as a time following the exile. The postexilic chronology becomes, strictly speaking, anachronistic, determined only by reference to what has gone on before.

Verses 21-23 reinforce this postexilic anachrony. While there is versional support for a textual emendation, perhaps it is best, as Williamson argues, to accept the MT reading. If so, 'there is no connection between these various groups, or between them and the grandsons of Zerubbabel in the first half of the verse. Consequently, it cannot be dated.'[32] When the chronological sequence enters the postexilic period, the sequence slips into temporal ambiguity. Read linearly, the chronology reaches 11 generations past Zerubbabel; non-linearly, four, all of whom could dwell within Zerubbabel's household.[33] In absolute chronological terms, the text melds the late sixth century with the late fifth or early fourth as a chronological (w)hole. Strictly speaking, the chronological end of the fabula of Chronicles ends chronology.

If so, the end of the chronological sequence within the genealogies corresponds to the chronological end re-presented in 1 Chron. 9.2-34. The story that begins with Adam dissolves into a post-exilic anachrony in the presence of Davidides. The beginning of time has moved to its end, the absorption of the past and future into an atemporal, continuous, Davidic past-present. The book of Chronicles does not reach from beginning to 'beginning'; it moves from beginning to end, not merely of the story, but of the very structure of time itself.

The Series of Events and Actors in the Fabula of Chronicles

If the above reading (de)limits the chronological boundaries of deep structure of the narrative of Chronicles, what series of events or

---

32. H.G.M. Williamson, *1 and 2 Chronicles* (NCB; Grand Rapids: Eerdmans, 1983), 58.

33. See S. Bendor, *The Social Structure in Ancient Israel* (JBS, 7; Jerusalem: Simor, 1996).

changes occurs within this chronology? To ask this question immediately raises the question of selection. As Mieke Bal writes:

> trying to establish which sentences in a text represent an event is often
> extremely difficult ... Such a selection, if it is at all feasible, ultimately
> results in an enormously large number of elements. It is impossible to
> work with so many elements; the relationships among the elements
> cannot be described if the collection is too large to survey.[34]

Thus it is necessary to limit arbitrarily the events that exhaust the
chronological extent of the fabula.

To solve this problem, narratological approaches commonly classify
events 'into two main kinds: those that advance the action by opening
an alternative ("kernels") and those that expand, amplify, maintain or
delay the form ("catalysts")'.[35] Yet this does not really solve the problem. At what point is the alternative advanced of essential significance
for the progression of the series of events? Ultimately, it seems that
such a selection depends upon an intuitive response to the text. As Bal
writes, 'The events selected can be related to one another in a variety of
ways. For this reason, one should not refer to *the* structure of a fabula,
but to *a* structure.'[36]

Still it is interesting to note that a certain formal pattern seems to
emerge in the development of the narrative of Chronicles. Again,
1 Chronicles 1–9 proves most instructive. The genealogical development of the fabula marks the significant turning points, the kernels, that
structure the series of events in Chronicles. Formal markings and
changes in the narrative pace draw attention to hinges that open the
fabula to development.

The central genealogical-chronological sequence in 1 Chron. 1.1-4a,
24-27, 34; 2.1-16a; 3.1-24 formally marks significant turning points,
kernels, by reducing the pace of the text, while, usually simultaneously,
inserting catalysts into the narrative. The narrative begins with single
names per generation for the first nine generations. The tenth generation
lists three: Shem, Japeth, Ham. The narrative digresses, covering the
families of these three, before resuming its march forward, repeating
Shem and moving into Arpachshad and beyond (1 Chron. 1.24). The
genealogies rush through single generations again until one reaches the

---

34. Bal, *Narratology*, p. 13.
35. Rimmon-Kenan, *Narrative Fiction*, p. 16.
36. Bal, *Narratology*, p. 23.

descendants of Abraham (1.24-27). The family of Esau (1.28-33) disrupts the chronological sequence following Israel, whose geneaology is further developed in 1.34. Here, though, the pace of the narrative slows through the listing of Israel's 12 sons. The text quickly moves to Judah (2.3) and then slows the pace through inclusion of broader family units until David, son of Jesse (2.15), is announced. A long catalyst fills in other descendants of the house of Judah before returning to David in 3.1. Again, the return is accompanied by a slower pace, as the children of David are listed, including Solomon (3.5). The genealogy returns to Solomon in 3.10 and accelerates until the sons of Josiah, the Judean/ Davidic line that leads to the Babylonian destruction of Jerusalem. The pace then slows with Zerubbabel and his immediate descendents (3.19-20). If the following lists are absorbed into the time of Zerubbabel, the pace quickly slows. If one reads the names linearly, the narrative then accelerates six generations until the final three generations of the list.

The text, therefore, uses genealogical digressions or catalysts to slow the narrative pace. Returns to previously mentioned figures emphasize significant generations at the same time that narrative alternatives— genealogical ways that the narrative might have gone but did not—are marked by alternative genealogical groups. These genealogies, however, provide false leads in the story—they progress only to end and return the reader to the central genealogical-chronological sequence.

The genealogies thereby signal several kernel events in the chronological sequence: the lives of Shem, Abraham, Isaac, Israel, Judah, David, Solomon, Josiah through the exile, Zerubbabel and descendants, immediate or distant. Later genealogies of other sons of Israel mentioned in 2.1-2 cover the same chronological ground, yet always remain chronologically exceeded by the line of Judah. Real narrative alternatives occur in the line of Shem, Abraham, Israel, Judah, David, Solomon and Zerubbabel. All other genealogies function as narrative catalysts, not kernels.

When one turns from this formal analysis of the genealogies to the structure of the remaining narrative, one cannot help but see the parallel between its structure and the kernel events marked in the genealogies. While the time of Shem receives relatively minor development in 1 Chronicles 1, the genealogies of 1 Chronicles 2–9 develop the narrative hinge of the era stretching from Abraham to Isaac to Israel to Judah. Each time the text introduces a new Israelite genealogy, it returns chronologically to this era. Simeon rejoined in 4.24; Reuben in

5.1; Levi in 6.1; Isaachar in 7.1; Naphtali in 7.13; and so on. The time of Israel and his sons represents a key narrative hinge, providing many alternatives for the development of the fabula, which, however, finds its fundamental progression in the line of Judah, David, Solomon, and so on.

Similarly, the genealogies mark the era of David and then Solomon as two kernel events. This corresponds well to the extensive narrative recapitulation given in 1 Chronicles 10–29 and 2 Chronicles 1–9 respectively. Josiah and his sons who bring on the exile also represent a fundamental narrative shift in the text, corresponding to their role in 2 Chronicles 34–36.

These kernels also help mark the fundamental actors in the fabula of the book of Chronicles. Shem, Israel, Judah, David, Solomon, Josiah and Zerubbabel all emerge as the central actors in the book, those whose actions determine the progression of the narrative to its end. One notices a certain narrowing of the scope of significant action here: from the father of a third of humanity, the actor becomes the father of a particular nation. Yet within this nation, one family stands out—Judah— and amid this family, one particular branch's actions bear a significance far exceeding any others: David and his royal descendants. A narratological analysis of the series of events, therefore, highlights what on a surface reading of the text is obvious, but so often not given sufficient interpretive weight: the major actants in Chronicles are kings. Chronicles is a thoroughly royalist document.

Only two surprises stand out when one looks at the kernels and actors marked in the genealogical narrative: (1) the relative unimportance of Hezekiah in the progression of the narrative in the geneaologies compared with the narrative of his reign in 2 Chronicles 29–32; and (2) the inclusion of Zerubbabel as an important actor. Perhaps the book of Chronicles skips the time of Zerubbabel in the repetition of its narrative in 1 Chron. 9.35–36.23, creating a fissure as the fabula of the text moves to its fulfillment; or perhaps the very structure of the fabula of Chronicles calls into question the current scholarly separation of the books of Ezra and Nehemiah from the book of Chronicles.

The series of events that constitutes the fabula of the book of Chronicles, therefore, moves from Adam to Shem to Abraham to Israel. As Japhet writes, 'Its aim is to delineate human history as the stage for the enacting of the history of Israel. It also expresses a unique concept of the election of Israel... as beginning with Adam.'[37] Yet the series of events continues to narrow. The progression of the narrative moves from Israel in general to Judah and his descendants in particular, and from Judah to David, and from David to Solomon. Father and son are related, yet distinct. Both represent narrative kernels, opening the narrative in new directions. The event moves through the descendants of David to Josiah, the exile and especially Zerubbabel. Narrowed to the family of David via Solomon, the series of events remains firmly embedded there. Ultimately the fabula ends with the implosion of time in postexilic Jerusalem with the line of David intact. Human history may be the stage for enacting the history of Israel in Chronicles; yet the history of Israel is also the stage for enacting the history of the Davidic family. In Chronicles the series of events ultimately progresses to focus on one set of actors: David and his descendants.

The Location of the Fabula of Book of Chronicles

Events, changes, do not merely occur: 'events always occur *somewhere*, be it a place that actually exists... or an imaginary place...'[38] Thus the analysis of the fabula of the book of Chronicles must include an analysis of place. In Chronicles as the series of events focuses on an increasingly particular set of actors, the location moves from 'no place' to a very particular place, Yahweh's temple in Jerusalem.

The events in Chronicles begin without any specific location. Names in 1 Chronicles 1 may represent geographical areas, yet they are presented as names, not locations. Indeed, whenever a concrete location is given ('the earth' in 1 Chron. 1.10, and the 'land of Edom' in 1.43), it appears outside the central genealogical-chronological structure. The fabula of Chronicles remains utopian through its initial series of events. Specific locations belong outside the real progression of events.

The fabula is given concrete localization for the first time in 1 Chron. 3.1, 3. The birth of David's first children and his initial reign occur in Hebron. Hebron, however, passes as David's reign—and children—are transferred to Jerusalem. From that point on, the direct genealogical structure remains centered in Jerusalem. While other locations are specified in 1 Chronicles 4–8, the central narrative remains localized in

---

37. Japhet, *I & II Chronicles*, p. 56.
38. Bal, *Narratology*, p. 7.

Jerusalem. In sum, the narrative location moves from no place to Hebron and then to Jerusalem.

It is thus with interest that one returns to the chronological end of the fabula in 1 Chronicles 9. Here, localization plays a much more significant role than in the central genealogical narrative. The location shifts to Babylon and back to the vague 'their possessions in their towns' (9.1-2). The location, however, quickly refocuses on Jerusalem (v. 3). But as 1 Chronicles 9 develops, the location quickly narrows to a place within Jerusalem: the temple-tent of meeting complex. Thus the final passage—before the chronology reverts to the line of Saul—identifies Jerusalem as the place of the temple:

> Now these are the singers, the heads of the ancestral houses of the Levites, living in the chambers of the temple free from other service, for they were on duty day and night. These were the heads of ancestral houses of the Levites, according to their generations; these leaders lived in Jerusalem' (vv. 32-33).

The fabula ends in Jerusalem, itself the location of the temple.

Again, one immediately recognizes the parallel between the location in the genealogies and the location in 1 Chron. 9.35–2 Chronicles 36. All Israel initially enthrones David in Hebron (1 Chron. 11.1-3), before moving quickly to Jerusalem (1 Chron. 11.4). Action will occasionally move away from Jerusalem, but will always return. Yet Jerusalem primarily becomes the place of the temple and its personnel. The narrative moves to its locative center in the temple within Jerusalem, where it remains until 2 Chron. 36.20, when the location shifts to Babylon. Yet here a difficulty arises. Again we are left with a quandary. Possibly the structure of the fabula locatively exceeds the limits of the text. The text merely presents a hopeful return to Jerusalem. The temple in 2 Chron. 36.22-23 remains a hope locatively placed in Babylon. Or, perhaps it may be that an analysis of the location of the fabula, found in 1 Chron. 1.1–9.34, again requires that we reconsider the relationship between the book of Chronicles and Ezra–Nehemiah.

The location of the fabula of Chronicles, therefore, shifts in the progression of the series of events. As the series of events progresses, its location becomes concrete, moving toward Jerusalem and the temple. It moves from no place (and therefore, every place?) through Hebron to Jerusalem and the temple, before briefly shifting to Babylon, and then back to Jerusalem and a (future?) temple in Jerusalem.

Conclusion: The Fabula of the Book of Chronicles

While I have analytically separated events, time, actors and location in this analysis of the fabula of Chronicles, it is obvious that none of these elements exists in isolation. Indeed, the structural relationships between these provide the analytical force of a narratological analysis. This analysis has argued that the fabula that the book of Chronicles encodes reaches from Adam to the postexilic period, where chronology literally ends. The actors narrow from persons who embrace all of humanity to a more and more specific family, ultimately arriving at David and his descendants, who both cause and experience the progression of events. Location, likewise, begins everywhere (or is it nowhere?) and progressively narrows to focus on a specific place—not merely Jerusalem, but the temple in Jerusalem. The fabula of the book of Chronicles, therefore, is constituted by inverse movements: as the events move the actors and location from the all-encompassing to the particular, events move the chronology from the particular to the all-encompassing. The result is a remarkable claim that the fabula seems to make: history has reached its end in a restored, postexilic Jerusalem temple in the presence of the ruling Davidic family.

The Narratology of the Book of Chronicles and Chronicles Studies

I began this article with Provan's concern that literary approaches to the Hebrew Bible have rent the field in two, resulting in a bloody ahistoricism. While not producing the type of history that Provan seems to want, a history behind the biblical text that may confer (coerce?) authority upon it, a narratological reading of Chronicles does not necessarily leave history nor historical-critical readings of Chronicles behind. Rather, I would argue that the above narratological reading interfaces with recent issues raised by historical-critical readings and provides important additional data for discussion.

First, after years of neglect, recent scholarship has begun to recognize the importance of 1 Chronicles 1–9 for the book of Chronicles.[39] This

---

39. See, e.g., M.D. Johnson, *The Purpose of Biblical Genealogies, with Special Reference to the Setting of the Genealogies of Jesus* (SNTSMS, 8; Cambridge: Cambridge University Press, 1969), pp. 37-76; S. Japhet, 'Conquest and Settlement in Chronicles', *JBL* 98 (1979), pp. 205-18; H.G.M. Williamson, 'Sources and

narratological reading would concur but extend the argument. The genealogies are not merely important for the book; in a structural sense, they *are* the book. Formally, what is usually called the 'narrative' of the book of Chronicles (1 Chron. 10–2 Chron. 36) is actually the slower paced repetition of what has already been narrated in 1 Chron. 1.1–9.34 itself. While details emerge in its retelling, 1 Chron. 1.1–9.34 narrates the fundamental structure of the book. Thus, to distinguish between the genealogies and the 'narrative' is not helpful. The basic structural division of the text occurs immediately following 1 Chron. 9.34. Verse 35 begins to recapitulate what has previously been narrated in a progressive chronological, narrative order that will extend through 2 Chronicles 36 into Ezra–Nehemiah.

A narratological reading of Chronicles, therefore, raises a second issue that has engaged much Chronicles scholarship—the relationship of the book of Chronicles to Ezra–Nehemiah. In the past 30 years, the critical consensus has shifted. Common authorship/editing has now been replaced by understanding Chronicles and Ezra–Nehemiah as distinct, separate works. Traditionally, this issue has been framed in terms of authorship. A narratological approach, however, shifts the question to whether the two belong within a common structure. The reading offered above suggests that the two indeed do share a narrative structure. If so, the intriguing problem becomes the formal significance of the absence of Davidic descendants in Ezra–Nehemiah. At the very least, an examination of the fabula of the book of Chronicles suggests that the field should not embrace this new consensus without additional data and discussion.

Finally, a narratological reading of Chronicles can contribute to an understanding of the ideology of the text in relationship to the historical context of its reception(s). The above analysis highlights the Davidic royalist ideology of the text expressed in the Davidic families' domination of the temple, its personnel and the nation. In the implosion of chronology at the fabula's end, this domination is naturalized and made relevant for all time. A narratological reading, therefore, exposes this claim and opens up questions about the relationship of Chronicles to

Redaction in the Chronicler's Genealogy of Judah', *JBL* 94 (1979), pp. 351-59; and more recently, M. Kartveit, *Motive und Schichten der Landtheologie in I Chronik 1–9* (ConBOT, 28; Stockholm: Almqvist & Wiksell, 1989); and M. Oeming, *Das wahre Israel: Die 'genealogische Vorhalle' 1 Chronik 1–9* (BWANT, 128; Stuttgart: W. Kohlhammer, 1990).

political struggles in postexilic Yehud, as well as the historical development of Second Temple eschatology and messianism. It can contribute to the placement of Chronicles within the wider social, historical and theological movements within Second Temple Judaism.

A narratological reading of the book of Chronicles is not a panacea. It will not provide a final, definitive reading of the text for all time and people. Yet it can provide a disciplined means of reading, which can promote responsible discussion, understanding and analysis of the text. If so, perhaps it is an endeavor worthy of our effort.

Part II

THEMES IN CHRONICLES

THE CHRONICLER AS AN INTERPRETER OF SCRIPTURE

William M. Schniedewind

The interpreter is both the heir to and the creator of tradition. Too often the latter role is emphasized while the former is neglected. In this article I will emphasize Chr. as a member of a community and the heir of a tradition. Interpretation is not simply an individual action; it bears the imprint of a community. It reflects a tradition of reading as well as charting the community's vision for the future. Already in the book of Chronicles some notion of authoritative literature—of Scripture develops. The very appearance of a sacred, and necessarily static, written text creates the need for the ever-developing customs and traditions of the community to revitalize this written Scripture through interpretation.

The title of this essay first begs the question, 'Who is Chr.?' I adhere to the near consensus that Chronicles and Ezra–Nehemiah were originally separate works.[1] With this said, I must confess that I have come— rather reluctantly—to the conclusion that Frank Moore Cross is largely correct in seeing stages in the composition of Chronicles and its attachment to Ezra–Nehemiah.[2] This conclusion largely reflects my understanding of Chronicles' purpose: to bolster the claims of both the Davidids and the rebuilt temple among the postexilic community. If the composition of Chronicles is placed in the late Persian period, then there should be little or no role for the Davidic covenant in Chr.'s work.[3] Additionally, there would be little need to legitimate the temple.

---

1. Following the well-known work of Japhet and Williamson, though more recently a forceful objection has been raised by J. Blenkinsopp, *Ezra–Nehemiah: A Commentary* (OTL; Philadelphia: Westminster Press, 1988).

2. F.M. Cross, 'A Reconstruction of the Judean Restoration', *JBL* 94 (1975), pp. 4-18 (= *Int* 29 [1975], pp. 187-203) and now pp. 151-72 in *From Epic to Canon: History and Literature in Ancient Israel* (Baltimore: The Johns Hopkins University Press, 1998).

3. S. Japhet points this out most recently in *I & II Chronicles: A Commentary* (OTL; Philadelphia: Westminster/John Knox Press, 1993) and comes to the surprising conclusion that the Davidic covenant is unimportant to Chronicles.

Fervent Davidic aspirations and the need to legitimate a rebuilt temple are properly located in the early Persian period. Since Williamson has argued persuasively that Chronicles has a royalist perspective and Braun that Chr. tries to rally the people around the temple, it is rather difficult to understand Chronicles as a late Persian work composed by the then firmly entrenched priestly circles. Riley actually suggests that this proves that there were fervent Davidic hopes among the priests in the late Persian period, but this hardly seems likely.[4]

If we judge by Ezra–Nehemiah or the later priestly work of Ben-Sirah, then there is little evidence to suggest that a politically entrenched priesthood developed fervent Davidic expectations. Why should they have? The more firmly entrenched priestly political leadership became, the more fervent Davidic aspirations threatened the position of the priests. Moreover, once the nexus between Chronicles and Ezra–Nehemiah is broken, it seems quite problematic to propose a late Persian date for the *initial* composition of the book. After all, it means the narrative ends almost two centuries before the time of the author of Chronicles. Would an author whose writing reflects a passion for his own postexilic community write a history so remote from his own time? Chr. is not an antiquarian. If the DtrH serves as a model, then we have authors who constantly bring history down to their own times. This is, in fact, the purpose of the shared ending of Chronicles and beginning of Ezra–Nehemiah. A late Persian author brings the book of Chronicles up-to-date by attaching it (somewhat awkwardly) to Ezra–Nehemiah. When I speak of 'Chr.' then, I am thinking of a late-sixth-century author of 1 Chronicles 10–2 Chronicles 36.

1. *The Idea of 'Scripture'*

The very notion that Chr. was an interpreter of 'Scripture', begs the question: what is 'Scripture'? And, to what extent is it anachronistic to label Chr. an interpreter of Scripture? These questions are often framed within a discussion of the history of canon. In other words, to what extent was the Torah complete and authoritative for the author of Chronicles? It is widely held that Ezra put the finishing touches to the Pentateuch in the late fifth century. This, however, is the final stage of Torah. The editorial activity of this final stage indicates it was a compi-

---

4. See W. Riley, *King and Cultus in Chronicles: Worship and the Reinterpretation of History* (JSOTSup, 160; Sheffield: JSOT Press, 1992).

lation of earlier written works. The compilation itself suggests that the
Torah had already passed into a textual form.

a. *Textuality and Scripture*
The very idea of 'Scripture' is dependent upon a textual culture. In an
oral culture the activities of composing, learning and transmitting blend
together. Tradition is constantly reinventing itself. Writing, on the other
hand, freezes tradition. As Plato so astutely observes in his speech to
Phaedrus, 'written words go on telling you just the same thing forever'.
Interpretation, however, gives a new voice to the paralysis resulting
from the written text.

Henri-Jean Martin observes that writing 'is not revolutionary, but it
appears every time that a revolution in communications prompts a
fusion into a larger whole. When this occurs it accelerates the changes
set in motion within that society.'[5] The first signs of literacy emerge
with the Josianic reformation, which is characterized by its obsession
with the 'book of the covenant' that is found in the temple and around
which the radical religious reformation seems to have taken shape (cf.
2 Kgs 23). Jack Goody has pointed out that literacy was a prerequisite
to the 'the orthodoxy of the book'.[6] The rising importance of writing in
ancient Israel responded to seminal changes in Jewish society and religion in the eighth to sixth centuries, but the new textuality also became
the catalyst for seminal change.

Biblical studies as a discipline has only begun to address the fundamental change from orality to textuality. In the classic work *Orality and
Literacy*, Walter Ong writes, 'Orality-literacy theorems challenge biblical study perhaps more than any other field of learning...'[7] Why?
Because much of biblical studies assumes a textual model without considering the differences between a primarily oral culture (and religion)
and a primarily textual culture. Perhaps the most obvious and pertinent
example is the now classical theory of the composition of the Pentateuch: the *Documentary* Hypothesis. A critical weakness of this theory,
whatever its explanatory power, is its reliance on a textual (or documen-

---

5. H.-J. Martin, *The History and Power of Writing* (Chicago: University of
Chicago Press, 1994), pp. 86-87.

6. J. Goody, *The Domestication of the Savage Mind* (Cambridge: Cambridge
University Press, 1977), p. 37.

7. W.J. Ong, *Orality and Literacy: The Technologizing of the Word* (London:
Methuen; Padstow, Cornwall: T.J. Press, 1982), p. 173.

tary) model.[8] Only recently have biblical scholars begun to rethink the paradigms of biblical studies with consideration of orality-literacy theory. To be sure, there were early forays into the problem of orality primarily inspired by the studies of Milman Parry and A.B. Lord in Greek literature. So, for example, the studies of Robert Culley explored the import of orality both in narratives like Genesis and in the poetry of Psalms.[9] A recent book by Susan Niditch, *Oral World and Written Word*,[10] is just one indication of a new direction in biblical studies. Chronicles reflects the transition to a religion of the book so that it is possible to characterize Chr. as 'an interpreter of Scripture'.

b. *Text in Chronicles*

A growing prominence of authoritative written texts is apparent through-out the book of Chronicles. For example, when the spirit of God comes upon Azariah (2 Chron. 15) he spouts a rambling, somewhat enigmatic, injunction to the people of Judah. Most interesting to the present concern is the statement: 'For a long time Israel was without the true God, and without a teaching priest, and without Torah (תורה)' (2 Chron. 15.3). The idea here of a 'teaching priest (כהן מורה)' apparently follows the absence of Torah, that is, a written tradition. Although the term 'Torah' (תורה) originally had the meaning of 'instruction' and hence originally had an oral context, this oral Torah or 'instruction' is trans-formed into the textual and written Torah in Chronicles (and other Second Temple literature). The transformation is implicit, for example, in 1 Chron. 16.40: 'according to all that is *written* in the Torah of YHWH which he *commanded* Israel (ולכל־הכתוב בתורת יהוה אשר צוה על־ישראל)'.[11] To begin with, the instruction was orally *commanded*, but

---

8. This is exactly where, e.g., R. Rendtorff attacks the theory in his work, *The Problem of the Process of Transmission in the Pentateuch* (JSOTSup, 89; Sheffield: JSOT Press, 1990).

9. R.C. Culley, *Studies in the Structure of Hebrew Narrative* (Semeia Supplements; Philadelphia: Fortress Press, 1976); Culley, *Oral Formulaic Language in the Biblical Psalms* (Near and Middle East Series, 4; Toronto: University of Toronto Press, 1967).

10. S. Niditch, *Oral World and Written Word: Ancient Israelite Literature* (Library of Ancient Israel; Philadelphia: Westminster/John Knox Press, 1996).

11. Also note 2 Chron. 23.18, 'according to that which was written in the Torah of Moses (ככתוב בתורת משה)'; 25.4 'according to that which was written in the Torah in the book of Moses (ככתוב בתורה בספר משה)'; 2 Chron. 31.3 and 35.6 'according to that which was written in the Torah of YHWH (ככתוב בתורת יהוה)'.

these things were consequently *written* down. Hence, the Torah that the priest teaches is now those commands that are written in a document as we learn in 2 Chron. 17.9:

> And [the priests] taught in Judah, having with them the *scroll of the Torah of YHWH*, and they went about among all the cities of Judah and taught the people (וילמדו ביהודה ועמהם ספר תורת יהוה ויסבו בכל־ערי יהודה וילמדו בעם).

Along these lines, it is worth comparing the few references to a scroll in the deuteronomic account of Josiah's reform with their reworking in Chronicles.

2 Kings 22	*2 Chronicles 34*
v. 11 'words of the scroll of the Torah'	v. 19 'words of the Torah'
v. 13 'words of this scroll'	v. 21 'the word of YHWH'
v. 16 'all the words of the scroll'	v. 24 'all the curses written in the scroll'

To these Chronicles independently adds (in its version of Josiah's reform) a reference to 'the scroll of the Torah of YHWH by the hand of Moses' (2 Chron. 34.33), and Chronicles omits the deuteronomic injunction put into the mouth of Josiah to celebrate the Passover 'as it is written in the scroll of this covenant' (2 Kgs 22.21). These differences are critical especially when one recognizes that Chr. follows much of the deuteronomic account quite closely, at times, word for word (cf. 2 Kgs 22.8–23.3 with 2 Chron. 34.15-32).[12] In particular, the substitution of 'the words of this scroll' (2 Kgs 22.13) with 'the word of YHWH' (2 Chron. 34.21) is critical because it belies a general textualization. Throughout biblical literature and particularly in the Former Prophets, the 'word of YHWH' refers to the oracular word of the prophets; hence, the well-known formula 'the word of YHWH came to the prophet'. There is no indication in biblical literature that this 'word of YHWH' was anything other than the divinely commissioned speech of the prophets—that is, apart from a few late references in Chronicles.[13] This points to Chronicles as a pivotal point in the textualization of ancient Israel's religion. In this respect it is probably not anachronistic to call Chr. an interpreter of Scripture.

---

12. For a convenient tool to compare these texts, see A. Bendavid's *Parallels in the Bible* (Jerusalem: Carta, 1972), p. 154.

13. See my book, *The Word of God in Transition: From Prophet to Exegete in the Second Temple Period* (JSOTSup, 197; Sheffield: Sheffield Academic Press, 1995), pp. 130-38.

2. *The Chronicler as Interpreter of History*

Chr.'s dependence on an interpretative tradition begins with the fact that the books of Chronicles rewrite the history of Israel known in Samuel–Kings.[14] This initial observation, however, is somewhat misleading. The book of Chronicles certainly parallels much of the material in 2 Samuel–2 Kings, but then only selectively and with many additions and omissions and much recasting. In the end the story is very different.

To begin with, Chronicles tells the story of Judah alone. It includes the northern kingdom of Israel only incidentally. Along these lines it also begins quite differently with nine chapters of genealogies that begin with Adam. In this respect the book of Chronicles parallels the entire 'Hexateuch' from Genesis–2 Kings, though admittedly opening genealogies allow only a rudimentary parallel. Still, it raises the question critical to this essay: Was the book of Chronicles intended to supplement or supplant Samuel–Kings? Since Chr.'s work stands complete in itself, it seems intended to supplant Samuel–Kings. It is important to recognize that Chronicles does not cite Samuel–Kings as authoritative (if it cites Samuel–Kings at all). The source citations of Chronicles probably are intended, at least in some cases, to refer to Samuel–Kings. However, these citations with the form 'Are not the rest of the acts of PN written in X?' do not necessarily or always imply that the cited source is canonical. Still, the frequent reference to prophets in Chr.'s source citations does confer a certain authority to those sources, and ultimately to Chr. who used the sources. It is only in this limited way then that we should think of Chr.'s use of historical sources as interpretation of Scripture.

a. *Editorial Rearrangement*
The most subtle means of revising and recasting the narratives of Samuel–Kings was the editorial selection and rearrangement of larger blocks of material. Selection is indeed a powerful interpretive tool.

---

14. A.G. Auld (*Kings without Privilege: David and Moses in the Story of the Bible's Kings* [Edinburgh: T. & T. Clark, 1994]) and S.L. McKenzie (*The Chronicler's Use of the Deuteronomistic History* [HSM, 33; Atlanta: Scholars Press, 1985]) have argued that Chr. had an earlier redaction or a different version of Samuel–Kings as its source. This point does not materially change my own argument, though it suggests one needs to be careful in evaluating the differences between the MT of Samuel–Kings and Chronicles.

There should be little doubt that Chr.'s omission of the Bathsheba narrative (2 Sam. 12) or the northern kings—to cite the most obvious examples—were part of a David-centric interpretation of Israel's history. Likewise, editorial rearrangement played a pivotal role in Chr.'s vision of the history of Israel. So, for example, Chr. placed all the narratives about David's military battles before his preparations for the temple. A couple of narratives are placed preceding David's unification of the kingdom and thereby give military justification for his acclamation as ruler of all Israel. Thus, narratives from Samuel (i.e. 2 Sam. 5.1-39; 1 Sam. 22.1-2; 2 Sam. 6.1-11; 5.11-25; 6.12-19) were carefully rearranged in 1 Chronicles 11–16. Many scholars have pointed out, for example, that Chr. rearranges the ark narrative so that it follows David's establishment in Jerusalem and the final defeat of the Philistines. The rearrangement of the ark narrative was undoubtedly part of Chr.'s broader interest in the temple. Perhaps Chr.'s most critical rearrangement involved the placement of David's census, which appeared in 2 Samuel as an appendix (ch. 24), but in Chronicles becomes a turning point in the narrative about the selection of the temple site (1 Chron. 21.1–22.1) and introduces David's preparations for the temple (1 Chron. 22–29). In sum, Chr.'s rearrangement of the narrative order of his sources was the first tool in his creative reinterpretation of the history of Israel, which highlighted the importance of the temple and the Davidic kings.

b. *Prophets as Interpreters*

Chr. himself employs the prophets as interpreters of the history of Israel.[15] Chr. uses prophets to comment upon and interpret past events. The role of the prophets is perhaps best summarized in 2 Chron. 20.20 by King Jehoshaphat, who implores the people with these words, 'Listen to me, O Judah and inhabitants of Jerusalem! Believe in the LORD your God and you will be established; believe his prophets and you shall succeed.' The prophets and their words are not so much interpreted in Chronicles as they are authoritative interpreters. In addition, the frequent citation of prophets in the source citations apportions them a role as interpreters of historical events, that is, as historians.

---

15. This is developed in much greater detail in my book, *Word of God in Transition*. Also see R. Micheel, *Die Seher- und Propheten-Überlieferungen in der Chronik* (BEATAJ, 18; Bern: Peter Lang, 1983).

c. *The Chronicler as Interpreter of Samuel–Kings*

Chr.'s many changes in the DtrH cannot be completely catalogued here.[16] For the present purposes it will suffice to illustrate a few changes in order to stress Chr.'s dependence upon an interpretive tradition.

Chr.'s dependence on an interpretive tradition may be illustrated by one verse from Chr.'s version of the dynastic oracle in 2 Samuel 7. Careful readers will notice two significant changes in Chr.'s version of the rhetorical question in 2 Sam. 7.5, 'Shall you build for me a house for my dwelling place? (האתה תבנה־לי בית לשבתי)'. First, Chronicles renders the rhetorical question, 'shall you? (האתה)', as a simple exclusion of David from temple building: 'It is not you who shall build for me a house to dwell in (לא אתה תבנה־לי הבית לשבת)' (1 Chron. 17.4). Chr. begins here to redirect attention on Solomon as the chosen temple builder.[17] H.G.M. Williamson points out that this change 'fits in with [Chr.'s] whole outlook which does not oppose temple building as such, but finds David himself to be unsuitable'.[18] In another small change—the addition of the definite article, 'the house (הבית)', as opposed to the indefinite 'a house (הבית)' in Samuel—Chr. most likely reflects an emphasis on the exclusivity of Jerusalem's claim. The addition of the definite article also changes the nuance of the statement, which now seems to assume that a house should be built—even if David was not chosen for the task. Braun emphasizes the difference by translating הבית as 'this house'.[19] While we must be careful not to overinterpret the

16. They are catalogued already by Isaac Kalimi, *Zur Geschichtsschreibung des Chronisten: Literarisch-historiographische Abweichungen der Chronik von ihren Paralleltexten in den Samuel- und Königsbüchern* (BZAW, 226; Berlin: W. de Gruyter, 1995); also see T. Willi, *Die Chronik als Auslegung: Untersuchungen zur literarischen Gestaltung der historischen Überlieferung Israels* (FRLANT, 106; Göttingen: Vandenhoeck & Ruprecht, 1972).

17. R.L. Braun develops this in a series of articles, 'The Message of Chronicles: Rally 'Round the Temple', *CTM* 42 (1971), pp. 502-14; Braun, 'Solomonic Apologetic in Chronicles', *JBL* 92 (1973), pp. 503-16; Braun, 'Solomon, The Chosen Temple Builder: The Significance of 1 Chronicles 22, 28, and 29 for the Theology of Chronicles', *JBL* 95 (1976), pp. 581-90. Also see R.B. Dillard, 'The Chronicler's Solomon', *WTJ* 43 (1980), pp. 289-300; and H.G.M. Williamson, 'The Accession of Solomon in the Books of Chronicles', *VT* 26 (1976), pp. 351-61.

18. H.G.M. Williamson, *1 and 2 Chronicles* (NCB; Grand Rapids: Eerdmans, 1982), p. 134.

19. See R.L. Braun, *1 Chronicles* (WBC, 14; Waco, TX: Word Books, 1986), pp. 195-99.

verse, we should also be careful not to minimize such changes or write them off as scribal errors or meaningless idiosyncrasies.

It is important to recognize that these exegetical maneuvers do not just reflect Chr.'s own creative exegesis. Rather, Chr. plows a furrow already broken by DtrH in his recontextualization of the dynastic oracle within Solomon's prayer, especially 1 Kgs 8.15-21. There, the DtrH reverses the apparent meaning of 2 Sam. 7.1-16. It acknowledges 2 Samuel 7 by using an explicit citation formula and then paraphrasing and rewriting the entire Nathan narrative. Of particular interest to us is v. 19, which reads, 'Only *you are not the one* that shall build *the* temple (רק אַתה לא הבנה הבית).' This clears up all the ambiguities from 2 Sam. 7.5. First, האתה תבנה becomes רק אתה לא הבנה; then, the indefinite בית becomes definite with the addition of the article (הבית). The wording is so close it must derive from 2 Sam. 7.5. The original meaning in the rhetorical question is clear in the following verses, which point out that YHWH had not asked for a temple. The problem was with the temple, not with the person who wanted to build it. This idea is subverted by Solomon's prayer, which suggests that the problem is simply that David was not the person *chosen* to build the temple. On the other hand, the addition of the definite article is critical, because it emphasizes that we are speaking not just of any temple—but of *the* temple (הבית). This addition is in keeping with what we might expect of a deuteronomic author for whom the centrality and exclusivity of Solomon's temple were paramount. Now, when we come back to Chronicles we must recognize that the author's changes are hardly original. Chr. is heir to a well-established interpretive tradition.

3. *The Chronicler as Interpreter of the Torah of Moses*

a. *Citations of Torah*
Chr. uses four formulae for his formal citations of Mosaic legislation. Occasionally Chr. employs either 'according to the commandments of Moses (כמצות משה)' (e.g. 2 Chron. 8.13), 'according to the Torah of Moses (כתורת משה)' (e.g. 2 Chron. 30.16), or 'according to the word of YHWH (כדבר יהוה)' (1 Chron. 15.15; 2 Chron. 35.6) to cite Mosaic legislation known in the Pentateuch.[20] The more common manner of

20. Another example of כדבר יהוה should probably be added by virtue of the emendation of בדבר יהוה in 2 Chron. 30.12 on the basis of some Hebrew manuscripts, the Peshitta and the Targums (cf. BHS apparatus). 1 Chron. 11.3, fol-

citing the Mosaic Law begins with 'as it is written (ככתוב)'. There is some variety in the construction of these 'as it is written' citations, including: (1) simply 'as it is written (ככתוב)' (2 Chron. 30.5, 18); (2) 'as it is written in the Torah of Moses (ככתוב בתורת משה)' (2 Chron. 23.18); (3) 'as it is written in the Torah of YHWH (ככתוב בתורת יהוה)' (2 Chron. 31.3; 35.26); (4) 'as it is written in the book of Moses (ככתוב בספר משה)' (2 Chron. 35.12); (5) 'as it is written in the Torah in the book of Moses (ככתוב בתורה בספר משה)' (2 Chron. 25.4).

The emphasis on citation of Mosaic tradition is more evident in Chronicles than in the DtrH. Even in the latter, particularly in what is usually ascribed to an exilic editor, we may observe an increasing importance in the *written* legislation of Moses. The motif is initiated in Deuteronomy 31, which explicitly states that 'Moses wrote down this Torah' and entrusted it to the priests (v. 9). The chapter concludes by repeating that Moses completed *writing* the words of the Torah in a scroll 'until their completion' (v. 24). This motif is taken up in isolated places in the DtrH (i.e. Josh. 1.8; 8.31-34; 23.6; 1 Kgs 2.3; 2 Kgs 14.6; 22.8-11). The motif culminates with the Josianic reforms, which are predicated upon the finding of a *book*. There is, however, no systematic or consistent development of the theme in the DtrH. The motif may be contrasted, for example, with the much more consistent development and use of the prophecy-fulfillment motif in the DtrH.[21] In Chronicles, on the other hand, the reference to the Mosaic legislation appears as a regular feature of the historian's presentation.

A variety of witnesses testify to the new emphasis that Chronicles, in contrast with the DtrH, placed on the written word as an authoritative basis of religion. Key to this process are the semantic shifts in vocabulary. For example, the term usually translated as 'Law (תורה)', which I have rendered as Torah, undergoes a transformation from a more nebulous and generic meaning, 'instruction', into its more restricted sense as a reference to the written Mosaic legislation (though probably not yet

---

lowing 2 Sam. 5.3, uses כדבר יהוה to refer to the prophetic word (as is more typical of biblical literature; see Schniedewind, *Word of God in Transition*, pp. 130-38). The formula כמצות מלך is used to refer to royal legislation (cf. 2 Chron. 8.15; 29.15; 30.6; 35.10, 16; also see כמצות דויד, in 2 Chron. 35.15).

21. See G. von Rad, *Studies in Deuteronomy* (SBT, 9; London: SCM Press; Chicago: Regnery, 1953), pp. 74-91; von Rad, 'The Deuteronomic Theology of History in I and II Kings', in *The Problem of the Hexateuch and Other Essays* (London: SCM Press, 1966), pp. 205-21.

the Pentateuch). The term 'to inquire (דרש)' begins its transition from
an oracular inquiry into interpretation of a written text.[22] Most importantly, the phrase 'the word of YHWH (דבר יהוה)' shifts from its previous exclusive use referring to oracular prophecy and now refers to
inspired written texts (both prophetic and Mosaic).[23] Joseph Blenkinsopp has characterized this as movement toward 'clerical' and 'scribal'
prophecy.[24] Ultimately, it is more than this, since prophecy itself
disappears (at least formally) in the wake of the transformation.[25]

b. *Indirect References to Torah*
Even where Torah is not cited explicitly, we find Mosaic legislation
cited. In the provisions of Joash's restoration of the temple (2 Chron.
24.4-14), the king instructs the Levites to collect a 'Mosaic tax
(משאת־משה)' (v. 6). Implicit in this term is Mosaic legislation that provides money for the temple. Most commentators understand this
Mosaic tax as extrapolated from the census tax (נשא ראש) in Exod.
30.11-16, whose funds were directed toward the tabernacle.[26] The connection, however, is at best loose. While Chr.'s apparent source (2 Kgs
12.4-16) seems more closely related to Exodus 30, Chr.'s appeal to a
tabernacle precedent has no close parallel in Exodus 30. Rather, it
seems to reflect developments in temple funding as found in Neh.
10.33, 'We placed ourselves under the obligation to give yearly one-
third shekel for the cultic work of the temple of our God'. The lack of a
direct reference to the Mosaic legislation is noteworthy here, especially
as it contrasts Chr.'s habit elsewhere. For this reason, it seems more
likely that the oblique reference to Mosaic tradition indicates an awareness that this 'Mosaic tax' has undergone a major exegetical transfor-

22. M. Fishbane, 'Torah', *Encyclopedia Miqra'it* (Jerusalem: Bialik, 1982),
VIII, cols. 469-83 [Hebrew].
23. See Schniedewind, *Word of God in Transition*, esp. pp. 130-38; also M.
Fishbane, *Biblical Interpretation in Ancient Israel* (Oxford: Oxford University
Press, 1985), pp. 493-524.
24. J. Blenkinsopp, *Prophecy and Canon* (Notre Dame, IN: University of Notre
Dame Press, 1977), pp. 128-38.
25. On the problem of the end of prophecy, see F. Greenspahn, 'Why Prophecy
Ceased', *JBL* 108 (1989), pp. 37-49; B. Sommer, 'Did Prophecy Cease? Evaluating
a Reevaluation', *JBL* 115 (1996), pp. 31-47.
26. J. Milgrom, *Studies in Levitical Terminology.* I. *The Encroacher and the
Levite. The Term 'Aboda* (Berkeley: University of California Press, 1970), p. 86;
Williamson, *1 and 2 Chronicles*, pp. 319-20; Japhet, *I & II Chronicles*, p. 844.

mation so that it hardly resembles the original legislation.

Another instructive example of indirect citation and revision appears in 1 Chronicles 23. This chapter is part of a larger complex that includes chs. 23–27, where many scholars found evidence of secondary editorial work because of apparent tensions within the chapters and in their editorial framework.[27] Adam Welch aptly poses the problem with 1 Chronicles 23:

> The want of unity in authorship appears in the opening chapter [ch. 23], for the same writer cannot be held responsible for the statement in v. 3 that the levites entered on office at 30 years of age, and for that in vv. 24 and 27 which gave the age as 20.[28]

As Sara Japhet has indicated throughout her commentary on Chronicles, Chr.'s attempt to combine divergent traditions can aptly explain these tensions. The viability of Japhet's approach can be illustrated in 1 Chronicles 23. Ultimately, I think the answer to this particular problem lies in the paradigm suggested by recent studies in inner-biblical exegesis and early Jewish interpretation. In this case, 1 Chron. 23.3 follows the lines of Numbers 4, where the levites begin their service in the house of God at age 30. 1 Chronicles 23.6-23 then lists the heads of the levitical clans. The last verses of 1 Chronicles 23 then lower the age requirement from 30 years (as in Num. 4) to 20 years, following the standard practice from the postexilic period (cf. 2 Chron. 31.17; Ezra 3.8). According to 1 Chron. 23.24-27:

---

27. See E.L Curtis and A.A. Madsen, *A Critical and Exegetical Commentary on the Books of Chronicles* (ICC; Edinburgh: T. & T. Clark, 1910), pp. 266-68; W. Rudolph, *Chronikbücher* (HAT, 21; Tübingen: J.C.B. Mohr [Paul Siebeck], 1955), pp. 156-58; F. Michaeli, *Les livres des Chroniques, d'Esdras et de Néhémie* (CAT, 16; Neuchatel: Delachaux & Niestle, 1967), pp. 120-21; Williamson, *1 and 2 Chronicles*, pp. 160-62; R.J. Coggins, *The First and Second Books of the Chronicles* (CBC; Cambridge: Cambridge University Press, 1976), pp. 118-20. Early on, the narrative repetition between 1 Chron. 23.1-2 and 28.1 led some scholars to attribute the intervening material to a secondary redactor. Source criticism employs repetition of this type to distinguish different traditions. However, repetition may also be used redactionally and authorially; see B.O. Long, 'Framing Repetitions in Biblical Historiography', *JBL* 106 (1987), pp. 385-99.

28. A.C. Welch, *The Work of the Chronicler: Its Purpose and its Date* (Schweich Lectures, 1938; London: Oxford University Press, 1939), p. 81.

> These are the levites according to their clan, the chiefs of the clans according to their divisions, in the list of names according to their enrollment, those who did the work for the service of the house of YHWH from twenty years old and above. For David said, 'YHWH the God of Israel has given rest to his people and he shall dwell in Jerusalem forever. And also, the levites no longer must carry the sanctuary and all the vessels for its service.' Thus, by the last words of David the levites were counted from twenty years old and above.

It should not be overlooked that Chr.'s exegetical maneuver here explicitly harmonizes the Pentateuchal regulation, expressed in Numbers 4 and recalled at the beginning of 1 Chronicles 23, with the postexilic practice attested in Ezra 3.8.

Verses 24-27 express a theology of rest beginning in the time of David as the reason for the changing of the levitical age. Elsewhere in Chronicles, this theology of rest explains why Solomon will be able to build the sanctuary. For example, in 1 Chron. 28.2 we read:

> Then King David rose to his feet and said: 'Hear me, my brothers and my people. I had planned to build a house of rest for the ark of the covenant of the LORD, for the footstool of our God; and I made preparations for building' (also see 1 Chron. 22.9).

In this respect, vv. 24 and 27 should be seen as the explanation offered for the change in levitical age, fitting with Chr.'s theology of rest about building of the temple. Chr. is saying that although in earlier times the Israelite census numbered the people from 20 years of age, the levites had an exemption since they had to carry the tabernacle (cf. Num. 1). According to Numbers 4, the levites are given the task of portage and are to be counted only when they become 30 years old because of their duties of temple service (cf. Num. 4.2-3, 21-22, 29-30; cf. Num. 1.47-53; Deut. 10.8). David's last words reinterpret this legislation. They reason that since the levites no longer had to carry (לשאת) the ark, they no longer had to be counted from 20 years old. Josiah's account of the Passover in 2 Chron. 35.3 reflects this same explanation:

> And (Josiah) said to the levites, who were teaching all Israel, who were consecrated to YHWH, 'Put the ark of holiness in the house which Solomon son of David king of Israel built; *you no longer must carry it upon your shoulders*, now serve YHWH your God and his people Israel.'

The language here echoes 1 Chron. 23.26. Chr. appeals to the levites who 'no longer must carry the ark on their shoulders'. This is an implicit reference to the revision of the levitical function in 1 Chronicles 23 (see esp. v. 26).[29] Finally, the interrelationship between the passages reflecting the revision in levitical age is another reason why it is difficult to posit 1 Chron. 23.24-27 as a scribal error (as Japhet),[30] or ascribe these verses to secondary editing (as Williamson),[31] or to attribute the complex of chs. 23–27 to a later redactional stage (as Welch).[32]

The revision in levitical age reflects a theology of YHWH's rest in temple building that is woven like a tapestry throughout Chr.'s work. This theology of rest contrasts with the deuteronomic theology of rest for the land and the people.[33] In Chronicles, the temple was 'the house of rest' for YHWH (e.g. 1 Chron. 28.2). In deuteronomic theology, the land is the place of rest for the people of Israel. For example, the centralization law in Deuteronomy emphasizes that centralization was not applicable to Israel because 'you have not yet come into the rest and the possession that the LORD your God is giving you' (Deut. 12.9). DtrH then picks up on this theme in several places, including the prayer of Solomon in 1 Kgs 8.56, which refers to YHWH, 'who has given rest (מנוחה) to his people Israel; not one word has failed of all his good promise, which he spoke through his servant Moses'. In keeping with this theological distinction, Chr. omits the notion that David gave rest to the land, an idea found in 2 Sam. 7.1, and Chr. rephrases 2 Sam. 7.11, 'I will give you rest (והנחתי) from all your enemies' to read ' I will subdue all your enemies (והכנעתי)' (1 Chron. 17.10; also cf. 1 Chron. 17.1 with 2 Sam. 7.1). Chr. had to omit or rephrase passages in DtrH that associated rest with the land and the people, since he associated rest with the construction of the temple, not the conquest of the land.[34] Consequently, 1 Chron. 22.9 associates the notion of rest with Solo-

29. See Fishbane, *Biblical Interpretation*, pp. 134-38, 154-59.

30. Japhet, *1 & 2 Chronicles*, p. 412.

31. Williamson, *1 and 2 Chronicles*, pp. 161-62.

32. Cf. Welch, *The Work of the Chronicler*, pp. 81-96.

33. Williamson (*1 and 2 Chronicles*, p. 162) argued that these verses reflect 'a different outlook from that of the Chronicler himself' since 1 Chron. 17.1 omits the notion of rest in its *Vorlage* (cf. 2 Sam. 7.1) and 1 Chron. 22.9 associates the notion of rest with Solomon.

34. R. Micheel draws a similar conclusion, arguing that Chr. considered David a 'man of war' (1 Chron. 22.8; 28.3) and Solomon was the 'man of peace'. This explanation would also account for the editing of 2 Sam. 7 without suggesting that there were two redactors. Micheel, *Die Seher- und Propheten-Überlieferungen*, p. 15.

mon, who is called 'the man of rest'. This association undoubtedly arises because Solomon was the temple builder (cf. 22.10). It is worthwhile digressing here to point out that it is this interweaving of themes like 'rest' in the book of Chronicles that makes it difficult to pull out threads from the tapestry of Chronicles without unraveling the entire work. While there are decorative touches added to the fringes—and here I am thinking of the genealogies and the stitching in of Ezra–Nehemiah—it is difficult to disassemble the work itself. No doubt Chr. wove together threads of different colors into his work, but there is no wholesale editing or redaction that went on in 1 Chronicles 10–2 Chronicles 36.

The aforementioned examples illustrate an emerging problem between the written body of Mosaic legislation and either non-Mosaic traditions or elaborations of the written tradition. The frequent use of 'as it is written (כתוב)' highlights the growing authority of the written Torah. Alongside the process of canonization that this implies, there also follows a growing problem between the written text and actual practice. Certainly, the beauty of the oral tradition was its flexibility and adaptability. The written tradition with all its attendant authority presented a critical problem to the viability of the tradition within a living community. The need to address this new reality of a written authority—that is, Scripture—by textually revising, reinterpreting and circumventing it is one of the fundamental signs that the canonical process had begun.

c. *According to the Interpretive Tradition (כמשפט)*

The problem that the canonization of a *written* text presented is tripartite. First, there is the difficulty of apparent contradictions within the Mosaic legislation. Thus, a process of harmonization can be seen in the tradition (e.g. 2 Chron. 35.13). Secondly, the natural development of social and cultic institutions inevitably creates incongruity with the older traditions. This process can readily be seen in Deuteronomy (e.g. the centralization of the cult) and can also be witnessed in Chronicles (e.g. 1 Chron. 23.24-27).[35] Thirdly, there arose a need for those institutions and customs not legislated in the Torah to receive some legitimation. The maintenance, organization and building of the temple is the most significant omission in the Torah and would subsequently find a

---

35. On revision in Deuteronomy, see B.M. Levinson, *Deuteronomy and the Hermeneutics of Legal Innovation* (Oxford: Oxford University Press, 1997).

variety of alternative methods of legitimation. One critical term used in justifying harmonization, elaboration and creative interpretation of Torah was כמשפט ('according to tradition/*mishpaṭ*').

The 24 priestly courses, which were well known in the later Second Temple period (cf. *m. Suk.* 5.6-8; Josephus, *Ant.* 7.14.7), are not set forth in the Torah, but only in Chronicles. 1 Chronicles 24.1-19 describes the division of the priestly courses that concludes in v. 19 as follows:

> These were their offices for their cultic service when they came to the temple according to the tradition/*mishpat* (כמשפט) given through Aaron their father, just as YHWH, God of Israel, commanded him (כאשר ... צוהו).

This remarkable appeal to an Aaronic legislation for the priestly courses using a citation formula (כאשר ... צוהו) can only vaguely be connected with any Pentateuchal tradition. Numbers 18 is one of the two places in the Torah where God speaks to Aaron directly.[36] There God puts the responsibility for priestly and levitical duties into Aaron's charge; however, no textual link can be found between Numbers 18 and 1 Chronicles 24. It is nevertheless noteworthy that Numbers 18 plays a role in postexilic exegesis. In Neh. 10.35-40, the citation formula 'as it is written in the Torah' undoubtedly refers to Numbers 18.[37] In other words, Numbers 18 was part of the literary horizon of the early postexilic community.[38] The use of the term 'according to the tradition/*mishpaṭ* (כמשפט)' to refer to this tradition is a critical departure from the frequent, explicit citations of the *written* Mosaic legislation and bears further investigation.

The term 'according to the tradition (כמשפט)' is employed exclusively with reference to the temple cult. It is well known that the temple is one of the central concerns of Chronicles. As mentioned before, the temple and its services were one area not prescribed in the Pentateuch.

36. The other place is Lev. 10.8. See the *Mek.* 1.1-15 for rabbinic traditions on why God spoke to Moses rather than Aaron.

37. See Fishbane, *Biblical Interpretation*, pp. 214-16.

38. The concept of the 'literary horizon' draws upon reception theory as articulated by H.R. Jauss. See his essay, 'Literary History as a Challenge to Literary Theory', *New Literary History* 2 (1970), pp. 7-37. For a further development of reception theory as applied to biblical studies, see my book, *Society and the Promise to David: A Reception History of 2 Samuel 7.1-17* (Oxford: Oxford University Press, 1999).

To be sure, the tabernacle prefigures the temple and many of its prescriptions could be transferred to the temple. Such transference, however, is an innovation predicated upon interpretation.

Michael Fishbane has argued that 'according to the tradition
(כמשפט)' functions as a 'shorthand cross-reference' to ritual specifi-
cations that are given in detail elsewhere.[39] This description is perhaps
apt for the inter-Pentateuchal use of כמשפטם in Numbers 29, where vv.
6 and 33 refer back to prescriptions mentioned earlier. Thus, in Num.
29.33 the expression במספרם כמשפטם should be understood to mean
that sacrifices were to be made 'in the number prescribed'. This, however, hardly fits the use of כמשפט in Lev. 5.10, which seems to be a
further extrapolation, rather than an explicit citation, of Lev. 4.3-17. A
critical difference between the two is the use of the suffix pronoun in
Num. 29.6 and 33, which points to an antecedent tradition. The lack of
the suffix pronoun in Lev. 5.10 suggests that this *mishpaṭ* has no
antecedent.[40] Rather, it is according to an interpretative *judgment* or a
customary practice. The ambiguity of the term *mishpaṭ*, which can
mean both 'regulation, ordinance' and 'judgment, custom', is critical.
The semantic range of *mishpaṭ* includes both the *written* law and the
judgment made on the basis of an *interpretation* of the law. It can mean
both a legal regulation and a social custom. As a result, *mishpaṭ* can
refer to both the legal ordinance and the ongoing concern to correlate
the written legislation to new situations, institutions and contexts.

In the DtrH the expression 'according to the tradition (כמשפט)' has
more the sense of 'that which is customary'. So, for example, we find
the expressions 'according to the custom of the Sidonians (כמשפט
צדנים)' and 'according to the custom of the nations (כמשפט גוים)'
(2 Kgs 17.33). These references are certainly not to written legislation,
but rather to conventions or traditions. Likewise, these examples may
be employed to elucidate 'according to the custom (כמשפט)' in 2 Kgs
11.14. In this case, the priest Jehoiada arranges to have Joash crowned,
and Joash is made to stand 'in the temple by the pillar, as was the
custom (כמשפט)'. Evidently, this was part of the traditional coronation

---

39. Fishbane, *Biblical Interpretation*, pp. 209-10.

40. The same distinction holds in Neh. 8.18, where the innovative addition of an
eighth day to Sukkot is 'according to the tradition (כמשפט)'. Contrast the use of
'according to the prescription of it (כמשפטו)' in Exod. 26.30 and Num. 9.14 with
'according to this prescription (כמשפט הזה)' in Josh. 6.15, which follow explicit
legislation.

ceremony.[41] Similarly, in 1 Sam. 8.11 the prophet Samuel uses the expression 'according to the custom of the king (כמשפט המלך)' to refer to a set of commonly known conventions about how kings acted. It is with such references in mind that we must consider Chr.'s use of the expression 'according to the tradition (כמשפט)'.

Perhaps the best known among the examples of *mishpaṭ* in Chronicles is in the harmonization of the regulations about preparing the Passover animal. In Chronicles we find the odd sentence, 'And they boiled (ויבשלו) the Passover animal in fire (באש) according to the *mishpaṭ* (כמשפט)' (2 Chron. 35.13). This incongruent mix of boiling and roasting was obviously intended to resolve the conflicting laws in Exod. 12.9, where the Israelites are explicitly commanded not to eat the meat raw or boiled (מבשל) but roasted in fire (צלי באש), and Deut. 16.7, where the meat is supposed to be boiled (ובאשת). The force of כמשפט in this context can only be to rationalize and ultimately justify the harmonization.[42] The basis for this addition may be Chr.'s own ingenious exegetical innovation, but it seems more likely that the *mishpaṭ* was to emphasize that the innovation was 'according to the interpretive tradition'.

Chr.'s description of the temple furnishings has ten lampstands as opposed to the Pentateuchal prescription for one six-branched lampstand for the tabernacle (cf. 2 Chron. 4.7, 20; Exod. 25.32; 37. 17-23). In reworking 1 Kgs 7.49, which describes the temple furnishings including the ten lampstands, Chronicles adds that these furnishings were 'according to tradition (כמשפט)' (2 Chron. 4.20). Chr.'s addition of כמשפט here, though it is quite minor, obviously responds to some perceived problem. Undoubtedly Chr. was aware that the tabernacle prescriptions provided for only one lampstand; hence, the ten lampstands were an extrapolation from this. Still, the lampstands were made from gold as prescribed (כמשפטם, 2 Chron. 4.7). One lampstand might have been sufficient for a desert tabernacle or small royal shrine; one would certainly not have been sufficient for the Solomonic temple.

The precise rituals of temple sacrifice, especially as they pertained to the role of the levites, are also not prescribed in the Pentateuch. A curious blend of an appeal to Mosaic legislation and tradition in the account of Hezekiah's reform undoubtedly results from this omission.

41. See G. von Rad's essay, 'The Royal Ritual in Judah', in *The Problem of the Hexateuch and Other Essays* (London: SCM Press, 1966), pp. 222-31.

42. See Fishbane, *Biblical Interpretation*, pp. 134-36.

In 2 Chron. 30.16 we read, 'They took their stations, as was their custom according to the Torah of Moses (כמשפטם כתורת משה), man of God. The priests dashed the blood which they received from the levites.' The priests' sprinkling of blood upon the altar is certainly according to the Torah of Moses (e.g. Lev. 17.6), but as Michael Fishbane has pointed out, there is no prescription of the priests receiving the blood from the levites in the Pentateuch.[43] This addition of what must have been the traditional levitical role undoubtedly accounts for the addition of כמשפט. A clever blending of the Torah of Moses and the cultic ritual tradition is then reflected by the apposition of כמשפט 'according to custom' and כתורת משה 'according to the Law of Moses'. Ultimately, the non-Mosaic cultic tradition receives further legitimation by its association with the written Mosaic legislation.[44]

Another temple-related concern of Chronicles is the ark tradition. Chr.'s transformation of this tradition reflects a number of interpretive revisions of his source (cf. 1 Chron. 13-15 with 2 Sam. 5-6).[45] Among those revisions, Chr.'s use of כמשפט in 1 Chron. 15.13-15 is of particular interest to this study:

> Because you were not there the first time, YHWH our God burst out against us, for we did not seek him according to tradition (כמשפט). The priests and levites sanctified themselves (התקדשׁו) in order to bring up the Ark of YHWH, God of Israel. The levites carried the Ark of God by means of poles on their shoulders (וישׂאו ... בכתפם במטות), as Moses had commanded according to the word of YHWH (כאשר צוה משה כדבר יהוה).

Chr.'s reference to the 'word of YHWH' draws upon Num. 4.10, where the work of bearing the holy things with poles is first mentioned, as well as Num. 7.9: 'He did not give any [cart or oxen] to the Kohathites since they were charged with the holy things (עבדת הקדשׁ) which were to be carried on the shoulders (בכתף ישׂאו).' Chr.'s use of key terms (במוטות, בכתפם, וישׂאו) in conjunction with the citation of Mosaic authority (כאשר צוה משה) is sufficient to prove that Chr. was referring to Mosaic legislation. In particular, it is clear that v. 15 reflects explicitly what is according to the command of Moses, namely levitical portage. This requirement clearly contrasts with the way that the ark

---

43. Fishbane, *Biblical Interpretation*, p. 533.

44. Contrast the Josianic reform, where there is an appeal to royal and prophetic authority (2 Chron. 35.10, 15) to justify the stations of the levites beside the priests during the cultic service.

45. See the discussion by Japhet, *I & II Chronicles*, pp. 271-308.

was transported, as described in 2 Samuel 6. On the other hand, the explicit statement in 2 Sam. 6.3 that a 'new cart' was used alongside the apparent arbitrariness of the striking down of Uzza (2 Sam. 6.6-10) suggests that the (proto-)deuteronomistic historian was unaware of any violation of Mosaic regulations. By the time of Chr.'s composition, however, Chr. was well aware of the infringement. It is easy enough to explain 1 Chron. 15.15 in this light.

However, how should we understand vv. 13-14 and especially the enigmatic statement, 'We did not seek him according to tradition (כמשפט)'? Verses 13b-14 appear to be Chr.'s own addition, which arises from the semantic shift of עבודה from 'physical labor', as in Priestly literature, to 'cultic service', as it appears in Chronicles and other late literature.[46] Once עבדת קדש is understood in a cultic sense as worship, Chr.'s narrative begins to make more sense. The statement that the levites and priests 'sanctified themselves (התקדשׁו)' becomes pivotal since it uses the same root (קדשׁ) to play on the idea of 'holy service (עבדת קדשׁ)'. The expanded semantic meaning of עבודה is, in fact, already suggested by Chr. earlier in the narrative where David commands that 'no one but the levites were to carry the ark of God, for YHWH had chosen them to carry the ark of YHWH (לשׁאת את־ארון יהוה) and to serve him forever (עד־עולם)' (1 Chron. 15.2). The first part of this statement corresponds with the regular Priestly meaning of עבודה, namely physical service, whereas the second part of this statement reflects the expanded semantic meaning of cultic service. The expression 'to seek him according to the tradition' likely means that they did not seek out the cultic requirements. Chr.'s use of 'according to the tradition (כמשפט)' in 2 Chron. 15.13 apparently reflects the expanded role of the levites, which turns on the meaning of עבודה in the narrative (as well as generally in Chronicles).

This interpretation of *mishpaṭ* as referring to authoritative tradition as opposed to the written Mosaic Torah gains further support from the only completely unambiguous reference in 1 Chron. 8.14. This text is part of a passage (vv. 12-15) about Solomon establishing the duties of the priests and levites in the newly built temple 'according the tradition established by David his father (כמשפט דויד אביו)'. This refers to 1 Chronicles 23–26, where David establishes the duties and organi-

---

46. See Milgrom's discussion of עבודה, especially his observations about the reuse of עבודה in Chronicles and Nehemiah (*Studies in Levitical Terminology*, pp. 60-87).

zation of the priests and levites for the planned temple. The appeal to *mishpaṭ* makes a cross-reference to the Davidic prescriptions. It is important to recognize that these prescriptions are, on the one hand, non-Mosaic, and yet, on the other hand, considered to be an elaboration of Mosaic legislation.

The reference to *mishpaṭ* is not simply a tendentious appeal to a non-existent authority. Rather, it appeals to the tradition of the community. Sometimes this tradition finds its basis in Davidic commandments; other times it appears to be an elaboration or revision of Mosaic legislation. David is the main source of non-Mosaic authorization, although Aaron also plays a role. Ambiguous appeals to a *mishpaṭ* are unlikely to have been the invention of Chr. with no basis in the tradition of the community. Although Chr. undoubtedly has done much creative reinterpretation in his history, the appeal in these cases to a *mishpaṭ* suggests that he was not merely giving his own creative harmonization but that these interpretations had some basis within the community of tradents. At least, this is the impression Chr. wishes to make!

d. *Text and Canon*

Chr.'s citation and use of tradition—both written and oral—certainly raises questions about the development of the Pentateuchal traditions. Those who wish to see a very late codification of the Pentateuch will have to take some pause at this. Over a decade ago Michael Fishbane's book, *Biblical Interpretation in Ancient Israel*, ably detailed the long history of legal interpretation in ancient Israel. More recent studies such as those by Bernard Levinson, *Deuteronomy and the Hermeneutics of Legal Innovation*, and James Kugel, *The Bible as it Was*,[47] further establish this long, deep and rich web of interpretation. By Chr.'s time, Pentateuchal traditions were not only known and considered authoritative, but legal reflection and precedents had already grown up within the Pentateuch and outside of it. To put it differently, not only was the basic outline of Pentateuchal law known, but a significant body of oral traditions and legal precedents had already developed. Specifics of Chr.'s use of Pentateuchal traditions are detailed in Judson Shaver's book, *Torah and the Chronicler's History Work*.[48] However, Shaver's

---

47. J.L. Kugel, *The Bible as it Was* (Cambridge, MA: Belknap Press of Harvard University Press, 1997).

48. J.R. Shaver, *Torah and the Chronicler's History Work: An Inquiry into the*

conclusion, namely that the fluidity between Chronicles and the Penta-teuch indicates that the Pentateuch was not codified, is hardly convinc-ing.[49] After all, few would argue that the Temple Scroll or Rabbinic Halakah proves that the Torah was not codified. As I have just pointed out, the expression כמשפט also indicates not fluidity, but rather, the development of legal precedents and interpretive traditions. It was iron-ically the written codification of Torah that necessitated its reinterpreta-tion and sometimes even its apparent subversion!

At this point we may return to that problematic term 'Scripture'. Is it right to think of Chr. as an interpreter of Scripture? To my mind, if Scripture is defined loosely as 'sacred and authoritative writings', then there can be no doubt that Chr. was an interpreter of Scripture. Cer-tainly, the Mosaic Code was considered authoritative, and a body of oral law—based on the legal precedents that had grown up around the Mosaic Code—had arisen. In a word, a Mosaic Code was 'Scripture' to Chr. To a much lesser extent, the DtrH was also 'Scripture' to Chr. That is, it was apparently attributed to prophets and required inspired and authoritative figures to interpret and recontextualize it for the postexilic community. The written text of the DtrH, however, did not have the same status as the Mosaic Torah.

4. *The Chronicler's Focus on the Postexilic Community*

Interpretation is the activity of both an individual and a community. Chr. is an interpreter within a community. This realization that reading is contextualized by a community, its traditions and its needs, should inform our paradigms of historical criticism. Interpretation is an ongo-ing process in society. With each generation, within each new social and historical context, the community tries to relate itself to its past through the hermeneutic process. Chr. has to be seen as one who com-bines, harmonizes and interprets divergent traditions.

From a different perspective, we should see in the book of Chronicles one stage in the continuing reinterpretation of the history of Israel. These stages include at least two (and I would say three) redactions of

Chronicler's References to Laws, Festivals, and Cultic Institutions in Relationship to Pentateuchal Legislation (BJS, 196; Atlanta: Scholars Press, 1989).

49. See E. Ben Zvi's review of Shaver's, *Torah and the Chronicler's History Work* in *JBL* 110 (1991), pp. 718-20.

the DtrH. They also include at least two stages of the book of Chronicles. In each successive generation, the community relates itself to its past through the hermeneutical process. This process is framed by well-established constraints of the community, but it also breaks free through individual creativity. In this paper, I have emphasized the former, namely that Chr. first of all inherited and transmitted a well developed interpretive tradition. And, his application of the interpretive tradition served the community. I have deliberately chosen to put aside Chr.'s own individual creativity in order to highlight what I consider a neglected aspect of Chr.'s work as interpreter. This aspect of Chronicles should put to rest once and for all the idea that Chr. was working with very few sources, as well as the exaggerated claim that Chr. was an inventor of fiction. Not at all. Not only did Chr. have sources beyond the DtrH, but Chr. also was not so much an inventor of history as he was a purveyor of tradition.

Treasures Won and Lost: Royal (Mis)Appropriations in Kings and Chronicles

Gary N. Knoppers

Introduction

Among the imperial archives of the Neo-Assyrian palaces at Nineveh are detailed records documenting the receipt, inventory and disbursement of precious metals and semi-precious stones.[1] That the range of items on these lists is rather limited reflects the fact that precious metals and stones served as the 'regular currency of elite exchange' between the royal palace and its clients both inside and outside the country.[2] The meticulous records—kept by scribes and perhaps under direct royal supervision—of silver, gold and semi-precious stones indicate the great value that these objects held for the crown. Aside from palaces, the other major repositories of wealth in ancient Nineveh were temples. Indeed, some Neo-Assyrian palace records register disbursements of a variety of gold and silver objects to 'the gods'.[3]

In serving as great storehouses of wealth, the palaces and temples of Nineveh were, of course, not unique. In the ancient Near East, palace and temple complexes served as the homes for some of the nation's most valuable treasures. In this respect, ancient temples were important not only as places of worship, but also as banks. Considering the high value of the precious items located in ancient Near Eastern sanctuaries and palaces, it comes as no great surprise that these same structures attracted the attention of foreign invaders. The authors of ancient Near Eastern royal inscriptions often take delight in detailing the plunder gained through the defeat and plunder of their nation's foes. For

---

1. F.M. Fales and J.N. Postgate, *Imperial Administrative Records. I. Palace and Temple Administration* (SAA, 7; Helsinki: Helsinki University Press, 1992).
2. Fales and Postgate, *Imperial Administrative Records*, p. xxiv.
3. Fales and Postgate, *Imperial Administrative Records*, §§ 62, 81.

example, in the third campaign of Šamšī-Adad V against Nairi and the Medes, Šamšī-Adad claims to have captured the fortified city of Uraš:

> I surrounded that city, captured it, [and] with the blood of their warriors I dyed their city red like red wool. I massacred 6,000 of them. I captured Pirišāti their king, together with 1,200 of his fighting men. I carried off from them countless quantities of booty, possessions, property, oxen, sheep, horses, utensils of silver [and gold], [and] pieces of bronze.[4]

But not all plunder was taken by sheer force. On some occasions kings surrendered their wealth voluntarily. Confronted with the prospect of an invasion by a powerful foreign king, a minor ruler might choose to empty his treasuries and dispatch their contents in the hope that his tribute would convince the invader to desist from launching a hostile takeover of the country. Or, if a lesser monarch were faced with a foreign invasion, he might appeal to a third party to deliver him. In this scenario, the minor king would be expected to surrender tribute to the third party and become his client.[5] Hence, when Niqmaddu II of Ugarit was confronted with an attack by hostile neighbors, he journeyed to Šuppiluliuma of Ḥatti, prostrated himself before the Great King, and agreed to pay tribute.[6]

The ancient Near Eastern interest in how national wealth is gained, managed and lost sheds light on why the history of the treasuries (אוצרות), whether of temple or palace, is a consistent concern of the Deuteronomists[7] and Chr.[8] These biblical writers take an interest in how

4.   A.K. Grayson, *Assyrian Rulers of the Early First Millennium BC, I (858–745 BC)* (Royal Inscriptions of Mesopotamia: Assyrian Rulers, 3; Toronto: University of Toronto Press, 1996), 1 p. 185 (A.O.103.1.iii.11-15).

5.   This assumes, of course, that the lesser monarch was not already a client to the king. If this were not the case, the client would have been submitting tribute regularly. Hence, in the El Amarna letters, Lab'ayu defends himself to his Egyptian patron: 'I am a loyal servant of the king. I am not a rebel or negligent (*lā arnāku u lā ḫaṭāku*). Neither do I withhold my tribute' (*u lā akalli bilātiya*; *EA* 254.10-13). See further W.L. Moran, *The El Amarna Letters* (Baltimore: The Johns Hopkins University Press, 1992), pp. 306-307.

6.   *RS* 12.227.13-16, 44-46; 17.340.20-24a, rev. 13-14; *KTU* 3.1.10-12; G.N. Knoppers, 'Treaty, Tribute List, or Diplomatic Letter? *KTU* 3.1 Re-examined', *BASOR* 289 (1993), pp. 81-94.

7.   1 Kgs 7.51; 14.26; 15.18-20; 2 Kgs 12.18-19; 14.14; 16.8-9; 18.14-16; 20.13-15; 24.13; 25.8-10, 13-17. By the Deuteronomists, I mean the Josianic Deuteronomist (Dtr1) and the exilic Deuteronomist (Dtr2). For the purposes of this essay, which mainly deals with the work of Chr., I am concentrating on the final

monarchs amass wealth or lose it. Both works chart the history of the treasuries during the heyday of the united kingdom, the repeated despoliations in the era of the dual monarchies and the disaster of the Babylonian exile. What is particularly revealing in comparing these two historical works is the extent to which Chr.'s portrait of the treasuries—their distribution and history—diverges from that of the Deuteronomists. Employing literary techniques such as omission, addition, revision and recontextualization, Chr. generates a substantially different presentation from that of Samuel–Kings.[9] Much more so than the Deuteronomists,

edition of DtrH. The actual history of composition of this extensive work is likely to have been rather involved. See my *Two Nations under God: The Deuteronomistic History of Solomon and the Dual Monarchies. I. The Reign of Solomon and the Rise of Jeroboam* (HSM, 52; Atlanta: Scholars Press, 1993), pp. 17-56; and more recently, the extensive treatment of T. Römer and A. de Pury, 'L'historiographie deutéronomiste (HD): Histoire de la recherche et enjeux du débat', in A. de Pury, T. Römer and J.-D. Macchi (eds.), *Israël construit son histoire: L'historiographie deutéronomiste à la lumière des recherches récentes* (Le monde de la Bible, 34; Geneva: Labor et Fides, 1996), pp. 9-120.

8. 1 Chron. 9.26; 26.20-26; 27.25-28; 28.12; 29.8; 2 Chron. 5.1; 8.15; 11.11; 12.9; 16.2, 4; 25.24; 32.27-29; 36.7, 10, 17-19. For the purposes of this study, I am using 'Chr.' ('the Chronicler') to refer to the author of 1 and 2 Chronicles and 'chronistic' to refer to a text or feature within the broader corpus of Chronicles, Ezra and Nehemiah. I agree with D.N. Freedman ('The Chronicler's Purpose', *CBQ* 23 [1961], pp. 432-42); S. Japhet ('The Supposed Common Authorship of Chronicles and Ezra–Nehemiah Investigated Anew', *VT* 18 [1968], pp. 330-71; Japhet, 'The Relationship between Chronicles and Ezra–Nehemiah', in J.A. Emerton (ed.), *Congress Volume: Leuven, 1989* [VTSup, 43; Leiden: E.J. Brill, 1991], pp. 298-313); F.M. Cross ('A Reconstruction of the Judean Restoration', *JBL* 94 [1974], pp. 4-18 [= *Int* 29 (1975), pp. 187-203]); and H.G.M. Williamson (*Israel in the Books of Chronicles* [Cambridge: Cambridge University Press, 1977], pp. 5-70; Williamson, 'The Composition of Ezra i–vi', *JTS* 34 [1983], pp. 1-30) that one author is not responsible for Chronicles, Ezra and Nehemiah. I disagree, however, with Japhet and Williamson in making too sharp a distinction between the perspective of the author of Chronicles and the perspective(s) of the author(s) of Ezra–Nehemiah. In my judgment, these authors live at different times, but belong to a single tradition or school. Hence, I see both continuity and discontinuity between Chronicles and Ezra–Nehemiah. For a survey of opinion, see R.L. Braun, 'Chronicles, Ezra and Nehemiah: Theology and Literary History', in J.A. Emerton (ed.), *Studies in the Historical Books of the Old Testament* (VTSup, 30; Leiden: E.J. Brill, 1979), pp. 52-64.

9. I. Kalimi's recent book contains an extensive discussion of Chr.'s various compositional techniques, *Zur Geschichtsschreibung des Chronisten: Literarisch-*

Chr. closely integrates royal actions toward the treasuries into his presentation and evaluation of particular periods and reigns. This achievement is all the more remarkable in that Chr.'s work is heavily indebted to DtrH for much of the information he includes about endowments, tribute payments and disbursements. But the interest of this essay is not limited either to a comparison between Samuel–Kings and Chronicles or to an examination of how Chr. employs certain modes of composition. This essay is also interested in how the fate of the nation's wealth is tied to larger themes in Chr.'s work.

1. *The Deuteronomistic History*

In Samuel–Kings David has little or no role to play vis-à-vis the national treasuries. To be sure, Solomon's endowment of the temple is made possible, in part, by David's beneficence (2 Sam. 8.10-13), but the Deuteronomists' treatment of David does not contain any explicit reference to endowments for the national treasuries. In Samuel–Kings, the reign of Solomon, and not that of David, features unrivaled prosperity. There is, however, a marked contrast between the reign of Solomon and the period of the dual monarchies. The former is portrayed as a time of unprecedented prosperity, peace and glory, while the latter is largely portrayed as a time of decline.[10] In the former, wealth is accumulated at a dizzying pace and tribute flows into Jerusalem. In the latter, wealth in the form of tribute leaves Jerusalem for other lands. This process of decline continues until the temple itself is ransacked and destroyed in the Babylonian exile.

a. *Solomon*
In the first period of Solomon's reign, the temple and palace are built (1 Kgs 6–7), the temple is dedicated (1 Kgs 8), and various potentates

---

historiographische Abweichungen der Chronik von ihren Paralleltexten in den Samuel- und Königsbüchern (BZAW, 226; Berlin: W. de Gruyter, 1995). See also the earlier treatment of T. Willi, *Die Chronik als Auslegung: Untersuchungen zur literarischen Gestaltung der historischen Überlieferung Israels* (FRLANT, 106; Göttingen: Vandenhoeck & Ruprecht, 1972), pp. 111-75.

10. My focus in this essay is on wealth and the national treasuries. Attention to other considerations, such as the regnal evaluations of certain kings, such as Asa, Jehoshaphat, Joash, Amaziah and Hezekiah, yields a more temperate view of the history of Judah during the divided monarchy.

send their tribute to Jerusalem (1 Kgs 10.1-29). Solomon appears as an extraordinarily wealthy king. From Hiram of Tyre, Solomon accepts 120 talents of gold as his tribute (1 Kgs 9.14). From the queen of Sheba, Solomon receives 120 talents of gold, as well as large quantities of spices and precious stones (1 Kgs 10.10). In dispatching tribute to Israel's king, Hiram and the queen of Sheba are by no means alone: 'All the kings of the earth sought the face of Solomon...each bringing his tribute—vessels of silver, vessels of gold, robes, weapons, spices, horses and mules—according to the amount due each year.'[11]

Successful trade practices contribute to Solomon's affluence. Hiram and Solomon's joint expedition nets the Israelite monarch the enormous sum of 420 talents of gold from Ophir (1 Kgs 9.26-28).[12] Aside from the wealth derived through trade with other nations, Solomon receives 666 talents of gold annually (1 Kgs 10.14). When the bullion gained through trade is coupled with the income gained through tribute, the result is a period of untrammeled prosperity. In Solomon's fabled reign, 'All of the king's drinking cups were gold and all the vessels in the Lebanon Forest Palace were of pure gold. Silver did not count for anything in the days of Solomon.'[13] Fabulous wealth, in turn, enables Solomon to furnish the new palace and temple lavishly. Golden shields and bucklers are deposited into the Lebanon Forest house (1 Kgs 10.15-16). An incomparable ivory throne, overlaid with gold, is successfully made for Solomon's use (1 Kgs 10.18-19).

This age of endowments, tribute and riches is unique in DtrH. No other time in Israel's history even approximates the affluence experienced in the first phase of Solomon's reign.[14] Nor is this splendor an accidental motif in the presentation of Solomon's reign. His peerless

11. 1 Kgs 10.24-25. In 1 Kgs 10.24, I read כל מלכי הארץ with the LXX, the Syriac and MT 2 Chron. 9.23 (*lectio facilior*). The MT has כל־הארץ. In 1 Kgs 10.25, I read with the MT, כלי כסף וכלי זהב. The LXX assumes a Hebrew text reading כלי זהב, having omitted וכלי כסף through haplography (*homoioteleuton*).

12. The LXX[B] presents a figure of 120, while the MT 2 Chron. 8.18 presents a figure of 450. I read with the MT (maximum variation). The reading of the LXX[B] assimilates to the figure in 1 Kgs 9.14 and 10.10.

13. At the beginning of 1 Kgs 10.21, I read with the LXX. The MT reads שלמה after המלך (an explicating plus) and omits by haplography (*homoioteleuton*) וכירות זהב following זהב. Later in 1 Kgs 10.21, I am reading with MT 2 Chron. 9.20 (אין כסף נחשב...) over against the corrupt MT (אין כסף לא נחשב...).

14. 1 Kgs 3.4-14; 10.23-24; G.N. Knoppers, '"There Was None Like Him": Incomparability in the Books of Kings', *CBQ* 54 (1992), pp. 411-17.

status, confirmed in the summary of 1 Kgs 10.23, 'and King Solomon was greater than all the other kings of the earth in riches and in wisdom' (ויגדל המלך שלמה מכל לעשר סלכי הארץ ולחכמה), marks the realization of the divine promise of matchless wisdom, wealth and glory given to Solomon at Gibeon (1 Kgs 3.4-14).[15]

b. *The Dual Monarchies*

Israel's time of bounty comes to an abrupt end with the advent of the divided monarchy (1 Kgs 11.1–12.20).[16] In his narration of the history of Judah, the DtrH mentions a series of temple and palace plunderings by a variety of monarchs.[17] If, economically speaking, Solomon's reign marks a time of unparalleled wealth and glory, the period of the divided monarchy marks a time of repeated ravishings of the temple and palace treasuries.[18] The raids are carried out by foreign, Israelite and domestic kings. The first foreign monarch to plunder the treasuries is Shishak, who exploits the palace and temple storehouses during the reign of Rehoboam (1 Kgs 14.26). He 'took everything; he also took all of the golden shields, which Solomon had made' (1 Kgs 14.26).[19] In addition to this raid by a foreign monarch, there is one incident of an Israelite king, Jehoash, plundering the Jerusalem treasuries during the reign of Amaziah (2 Kgs 14.14). As with Shishak's invasion, this pillaging occurs in the context of an invasion of Judah.

The authors of Kings also describe how some Judahite kings plunder their own storehouses to ward off real or potential foreign attacks. Asa does this by sending booty gained by seizing 'all the silver and the gold remaining in the treasuries of the house of Yahweh and the treasuries of the royal palace' and dispatching them to Ben-hadad of Damascus to induce the Syrian king to counter an attack against Judah led by King

15. Knoppers, *Two Nations under God*, I, pp. 118-34.

16. Knoppers, *Two Nations under God*, I, pp. 135-223.

17. M. Delcor, 'Le trésor de la maison de Yahweh des origines à l'exil', *VT* 12 (1962), pp. 353-77; S. Meier, 'Temple Plundering in the Book of Kings' (unpublished paper, 1984); E.T. Mullen, 'Crime and Punishment: The Sins of the King and the Despoliation of the Treasuries', *CBQ* 54 (1992), pp. 231-48; N. Na'aman, 'The Deuteronomist and Voluntary Servitude to Foreign Powers', *JSOT* 65 (1995), pp. 37-53.

18. All of the treasury raids in Kings (and Chronicles) have to do with Jerusalem. There are no accounts of raids on the treasuries of the northern capitals.

19. Mullen, 'Crime and Punishment', pp. 236-37.

Baasha of Israel (1 Kgs 15.18).[20] Joash takes a more direct approach. He seizes all the dedicated gifts of his predecessors—Jehoshaphat, Jehoram and Ahaziah—along with the gold found in the palace and temple treasuries and sends them to Hazael of Syria to convince Hazael not to launch a campaign against Jerusalem (2 Kgs 12.18-19). Ahaz employs a similar strategy to that successfully used by Asa. He sends the silver and gold from the palace and temple repositories to Tiglath-pileser of Assyria as a bribe (שֹׁחַד) to ward off a joint attack by Rezin of Syria and Pekah of Israel (2 Kgs 16.8).

King Hezekiah of Judah also exploits the temple and palace treasuries as part of a larger defensive strategy. Faced with an Assyrian invasion that devastated all of Judah's fortified towns, Hezekiah sends Sennacherib 300,000 talents of silver and 30 talents of gold (2 Kgs 18.13-14). He also delivers all the silver found in the temple and palace storehouses to Sennacherib (2 Kgs 18.15). Finally, Hezekiah's tribute includes bullion gained by stripping the temple doors and posts, which Hezekiah himself had plated (2 Kgs 18.16). There is one other incident that involves the national coffers. Hezekiah is faulted for showing off his treasuries to the Babylonian embassies of Merodoch-baladan (2 Kgs 20.13-15).[21] In DtrH this is an event that carries the stigma of being linked to a future Babylonian deportation (2 Kgs 20.14-18).[22]

The period of the dual monarchies can be characterized as a time in which tribute, in the form of silver and gold, leaves Jerusalem for other lands. Rather than attracting wealth from monarchs in other lands to enhance their own positions, Judah's kings dispatch their nation's wealth to ward off invasions and potential threats. Of all the kings of Judah mentioned in DtrH, only two institute major temple renovations: Joash (2 Kgs 12.5-17) and Josiah (2 Kgs 22.3-8).[23] Of all the kings of

---

20. Such appeals for military intervention were not uncommon in the ancient Near East. See S.B. Parker, *Stories in Scripture and Inscriptions: Comparative Studies on Narratives in Northwest Semitic Inscriptions and the Hebrew Bible* (New York: Oxford University Press, 1997), pp. 76-104, esp. 89-94.

21. H. Tadmor and M. Cogan, *II Kings* (AB, 11; New York: Doubleday, 1988), pp. 258-63.

22. Since this article is focused on the final edition of DtrH, the much-debated composition of this oracle need not detain us.

23. For secondary references, see my *Two Nations under God: The Deuteronomistic History of Solomon and the Dual Monarchies. II. The Reign of Jeroboam, the Fall of Israel, and the Reign of Josiah* (HSM, 53; Atlanta: Scholars Press, 1994), pp. 125-35.

Judah only one, Asa, actually makes a donation of dedicated gifts (those of his fathers) to the temple, presumably to the temple treasuries (1 Kgs 15.15).[24] But this same king soon takes 'all of the silver and gold left in the temple and palace treasuries' and dispatches them to Ben-hadad as a treaty inducement (1 Kgs 15.18).

There is some scholarly debate as to what to make of this pattern of Judahite kings dispatching tribute to other kings. According to some commentators, royal raids on the national treasuries are an integral element in the evaluation of a king's reign. Dispatching tribute to a foreign king is purportedly a sin deserving of divine retribution.[25] But there is some reason to doubt the validity of this proposition.[26] If raids on the storehouses were an essential component of assessing the royal conduct in DtrH, the verdict would have to tilt toward the positive. Four out of six kings associated with treasury raids are rated positively—Asa (1 Kgs 15.11-14), Joash (2 Kgs 12.3-4), Amaziah (2 Kgs 14.3-4) and Hezekiah (2 Kgs 18.3-6).[27] Moreover, the one king—Hezekiah—who is associated with two negative treasury incidents happens to be one of the most highly esteemed kings in DtrH (2 Kgs 18.3-6). These facts lead to two possible conclusions: either the Deuteronomist was inclined to view treasury raids as a positive factor in rating kings or such raids did not inform his regnal evaluations. There is, in my judgment, much to be said for the second conclusion. The deuteronomistic judgments of northern and southern kings center on whether kings support the centralization of the Yahwistic cultus in Jerusalem (*Kultuseinheit*) and whether they eliminate other cults (*Kultusreinheit*).[28] One could argue,

---

24. The author also mentions that Rehoboam replaced Solomon's golden shields, which were delivered as booty to Shishak, with bronze shields (1 Kgs 14.27).

25. So Mullen, 'Crime and Punishment', p. 235.

26. E. Würthwein, *Die Bücher der Könige* (ATD, 11; Göttingen: Vandenhoeck & Ruprecht, 1984), pp. 87-89; Parker, *Stories in Scripture*, pp. 89-99.

27. Although hardly any writers in the ancient world would look upon raids on their national treasuries as a welcome development, some recognized that in times of national crisis, drastic measures needed to be taken to bolster the position of their armed forces and national leaders. One is reminded of the comment by Thucydides (in reference to the preparations of Pericles) that the considerable sums of money in the temples could be used to support the war effort and that even the gold on the statue of Athena in the Parthenon, weighing 40 talents, could be easily removed in the event of a national emergency. Thucydides, *History of the Peloponnesian War* (Penguin Classics; New York: Penguin, 1954), 2.13.5.

28. H-.D. Hoffmann, *Reform und Reformen: Untersuchungen zu einem Grund-*

however, with some legitimacy that the larger pattern of treasury onslaughts contributes to a sense of doom in the deuteronomistic narration of the Judahite monarchy. After the glorious age of Solomon, good news about the welfare of the palace and temple coffers is hard to come by. Nevertheless, whether a given monarch raided the treasuries is not a productive theological concern in evaluating the record of that monarch.

c. *The Babylonian Exiles*

In his narration of Judah's final years, the exilic editor (Dtr2) draws a number of parallels between the age of Solomon and that of Judah's final decline. Whereas 1 Kings 6–7 devotes considerable coverage to the construction and fixtures of the temple, 2 Kings 24–25 devotes considerable coverage to their destruction. While it is true that the pre-exilic Deuteronomist (Dtr1) mentions both foreign and domestic kings despoiling the temple treasuries, the exilic Dtr2 consistently highlights the connection with Solomon.[29]

A bleak fate for Judah, Jerusalem and the central sanctuary is forecast in the deuteronomistically phrased divine speech, which appears as an epilogue to Josiah's reign.[30] In blaming Manasseh for the Babylonian exile, the exilic author of 2 Kgs 23.26-27 quotes Yahweh as saying:

> I shall even turn my face away from Judah as I turned away from Israel.
> And I shall reject (וּמָאַסְתִּי) this city, Jerusalem, which I chose (בָּחַרְתִּי),
> and the house of which I said, 'my name shall be there (יִהְיֶה שְׁמִי שָׁם)'
> (2 Kgs 23.27).[31]

---

thema der deuteronomistischen Geschichtsschreibung (ATANT, 66; Zürich: Theologischer Verlag, 1980); B. Halpern, *The First Historians: The Hebrew Bible and History* (San Francisco: Harper & Row, 1988), pp. 207-40; Knoppers, *Two Nations*, II, pp. 232-54.

29. 1 Kgs 6–7; 2 Kgs 24.13; 25.8-10, 13-17. See also the more general discussions of Delcor, 'Le trésor de la maison', pp. 358-77; Meier, 'Temple Plundering', p. 20; Mullen, 'Crime and Punishment', pp. 247-48.

30. Huldah's first oracle (2 Kgs 22.16-17) also mentions Yahweh's bringing evil against 'this place (הַמָּקוֹם הַזֶּה)'. Scholars disagree about whether this refers to the temple in particular or to Jerusalem in general. Knoppers, *Two Nations under God*, II, pp. 140-57. On the sins of Manasseh, see most recently B. Halpern, 'Why Manasseh Is Blamed for the Babylonian Exile: The Evolution of a Biblical Tradition', *VT* 48 (1998), pp. 473-514.

31. Conspicuously absent from this series of rejections is an explicit rejection of the Davidic house itself.

This intriguing judgment oracle alludes to a number of earlier passages, among which is Solomon's first temple blessing (1 Kgs 8.16).[32] Yahweh's speech recalls the traditum announcing the choice of Jerusalem for the presence of Yahweh's name (ואבחר בירושלם להיות שמי שם, 1 Kgs 8.16), but only to rescind it.[33]

The final humiliations of Judah, Jerusalem and the temple begin with Jehoiachin's surrender to Nebuchadnezzar II in 598 BCE (2 Kgs 24.12). In his judgment oracle to Hezekiah, Isaiah had predicted that everything in the royal palace would be carried off to Babylon (2 Kgs 20.17-18).[34] Nebuchadnezzar's spoils are, however, even more extensive than Isaiah forecast.[35] The Babylonian king not only removes treasures (אוצרות) from the palace, but also removes all of the treasures (אוצרות) from the temple and strips all of the golden vessels that King Solomon of Israel made in the temple (היכל) of Yahweh.[36]

The long history of despoliations ends with the destruction of the

32. 1 Kgs 8.16 (// 2 Chron. 6.5) and 29 (cf. 2 Chron. 7.16) are the only other texts in DtrH featuring a combination of the verb היה and the name (שם) applied to the temple. 2 Chron. 6.6 and 33.4 refer to Jerusalem. T.N.D. Mettinger, *The Dethronement of Sebaoth: Studies in the Shem and Kabod Theologies* (ConBOT, 18; Lund: C.W.K. Gleerup, 1982), p. 39.

33. MT 1 Kgs 8.16 has suffered a textual disturbance. The reading of 2 Chron. 6.5-6, partially attested by LXX 1 Kgs 8.16, is shared by 4QKgs[a]. MT 1 Kgs 8.16 lacks ולא־בחרתי בעיר מכל שבטי ישראל לבנות בית להיות שמי שם because of haplography (*homoioteleuton* from להיות שמי שם to שם שמי להיות). See further J.C. Trebolle Barrera, '4QKgs', in *Qumran Cave 4: Deuteronomy, Joshua, Judges, Kings*, IX (DJD, 14; Oxford: Clarendon Press, 1995), p. 177. Other texts in Kings referring to the divine election of Jerusalem include 1 Kgs 8.44, 48; 11.13, 32, 36 [MT]; 14.21; 2 Kgs 21.7.

34. R.E. Clements convincingly argues that Isaiah's speech refers not to the Babylonian exile of 586 BCE, but to the spoliation of Jerusalem and the exile of some Davidids in 598–587 BCE. R.E. Clements, *Isaiah and the Deliverance of Jerusalem: A Study of the Interpretation of Prophecy in the Old Testament* (JSOTSup, 13; Sheffield: JSOT Press, 1980), pp. 64-69. For a similar argument, see H. Tadmor and M. Cogan, 'Hezekiah's Fourteenth Year: The King's Illness and the Babylonian Embassy', in B.A. Levine *et al.* (eds.), *Harry M. Orlinsky Volume* (*EsIsr*, 16; Jerusalem: Israel Exploration Society, 1982), pp. 198-201.

35. According to the Babylonian version of this event, Nebuchadnezzar simply carried off 'vast tribute' (*bilassa kabittu*), A.K. Grayson, *Assyrian and Babylonian Chronicles* (Texts from Cuneiform Sources, 5; Locust Valley, NY: J.J. Augustin, 1975), p. 102.

36. 2 Kgs 24.13. The last assertion conflicts with 1 Kgs 14.25-26.

temple itself during the reign of Zedekiah. Nebuzaradan, chief guard of Nebuchadnezzar, burns and destroys the temple (2 Kgs 25.8-10). Both the invasion during the reigns of Jehoiakim and Jehoiachin and the invasion during the reign of Zedekiah are associated with a series of deportations that result in an empty and devastated land.[37] This pattern of destruction lends a sense of finality to the coverage of the national treasuries. The exilic editor's concern is typological. Solomon carefully prepares and implements the construction of the temple. In the Babylonian invasion of 598 BCE the process of destruction begins. All that Solomon built is dismantled, pilfered or destroyed in the exiles of 598 and 586 BCE. The studied parallel with the age of temple construction is also evident in the description of the temple's doom (2 Kgs 25.9, 13-17). García López points to an 'undeniable' parallel between 1 Kgs 3.1 and 2 Kgs 25.9a, 10.[38] In the description of Solomon's reign, the author refers to Solomon's construction of his palace (ביתו), the temple (בית יהוה) and the wall surrounding Jerusalem (חומת ירושלם סביב). Aside from a reference to Solomon's corvée to build them (1 Kgs 9.15), these three public works projects are not mentioned together again until the narration of their destruction. Nebuzaradan burns the temple (בית־יהוה), the palace (בית המלך), all the houses of Jerusalem and every great house, while the entire Chaldean army tears down the wall surrounding Jerusalem (חומת ירושלם סביב).

This parallel between the period of Solomon and the period of destruction is followed by another dealing with temple paraphernalia (2 Kgs 25.13-17) corresponding to 1 Kgs 7.15-26. The writer documents how the Chaldeans break up the bronze columns, the bronze stands and the bronze tank, which Solomon made for the temple.[39] In

---

37. 2 Kgs 24.10-12, 14-17; 25.1-7, 11-12, 18-21. The book of Kings mentions one exile to Egypt (2 Kgs 25.22-26), which is also connected to the theme of divine judgment. This exile to Egypt is associated with the realization of a deuteronomic curse. R.E. Friedman, 'From Egypt to Egypt: Dtr1 and Dtr2', in B. Halpern and J.D. Levenson (eds.), *Traditions in Transformation: Turning Points in Biblical Faith. Essays Presented to Frank Moore Cross, Jr.* (Winona Lake, IN: Eisenbrauns, 1981), pp. 167-92.

38. F. García López, 'Construction et destruction de Jérusalem: Histoire et prophétie dans les cadres rédactionnels des livres des rois', *RB* 94 (1987), pp. 226-32.

39. 1 Kgs 7.15-26. J. Van Seters believes that this information about temple plunder may have been derived from records of temple income and disbursements.

other words, Kings portrays the actual destruction of certain temple furnishings.[40] The plunder, stripping and destruction of *realia* in the Babylonian exile of 586 BCE, like their manufacture in the time of Solomon, is definitive. Having rifled the bronze from various temple artefacts, the Chaldeans transport this bullion to Babylon (2 Kgs 25.13, 16-17).[41] The Chaldeans also plunder sundry bronze vessels (2 Kgs 25.14), while the chief of the guards takes 'whatever was of gold and whatever was of silver' (2 Kgs 25.16). The fall of the temple is complete (cf. 1 Kgs 9.4-9).

The portrayal of the palace and temple treasuries in the final years of Judahite independence contributes to larger deuteronomistic themes in the narration of the united and the divided monarchies. The correspondences that Dtr2 develops between the formative age of temple construction (1 Kgs 3.1; 6.1–9.9) and the disgrace of temple destruction lend closure to his treatment of Judahite history. The glories of the Solomonic age are definitively reversed in the age of the Babylonian exiles. Dtr2 exposes the once-exalted institutions of palace and temple as vulnerable and fallible institutions.

2. *The Chronicler's History*

As a lover of Jerusalem and an avid supporter of the (second) temple, Chr. would have been disturbed by a number of features in the deuteronomistic presentation. First, the pattern of domestic and foreign kings plundering the Jerusalem treasuries would not set an inspiring example for his audience. Certainly, the ransacking and razing of the Jewish temple at Elephantine was the cause of great distress for the Jewish community situated there.[42] Not only was the temple itself

---

In Search of History: Historiography in the Ancient World and the Origins of Biblical History (New Haven: Yale University Press, 1983), pp. 300-301.

40. The situation is different in Jeremiah (cf. 2 Kgs 24.13-14 with Jer. 27.19-22; and 2 Kgs 25.13-17 with Jer. 52.17-23).

41. The reference is to 1 Kgs 7.15-26, but the parallels are not always exact. The reason for the discrepancies is unclear, because the relationships among the textual witnesses to 1 Kgs 7 and 2 Kgs 25 are complex. J.C. Trebolle Barrera, *Salomón y Jeroboán: Historia de la recensión y redacción de 1 Reyes 2–12, 14* (Bibliotheca Salmanticensis, Dissertationes 3; Salamanca/Jerusalem: Universidad Pontificia/Instituto español biblico y argueologico, 1980), pp. 307-20.

42. The story of the sanctuary's demise is related in letters petitioning the Jerusalem and Samarian authorities for their help in reconstruction. B. Porten and

destroyed, but 'as for the gold and silver basins and the other t[h]ings [which were in that sanctuary—everything they took and made their own]' (ומזרקי הזהב והכסף ודנ[ב]רים [אשר היו במקדש ההוא את הכל] [לקחו לשלהם).[43] It is bad enough for an adversary to pillage one's national institutions, but it is even more disconcerting for domestic monarchs repeatedly to do the same.

Secondly, the deuteronomistic pattern is almost uniformly negative. There is only one counter-example of new dedications being made to the temple (Asa), and there are no examples of new wealth flowing in to Jerusalem. It may have been difficult to gather support for the second temple, given the unhappy record of the first. The temple built by Zerubbabel and Jeshua certainly had its defenders. The prophet Haggai urges his listeners to support the temple rebuilding project headed by Zerubbabel and Jeshua by forecasting that in a little while 'the precious things of all the nations shall come' (2.7). Silver and gold both belong to Yahweh, the prophet declares (Hag. 2.8). The authors of Ezra take note of the benefactions made to the Jerusalem temple at various stages of postexilic history.[44] But if, judging by the pattern of pre-exilic (deuteronomistic) history, the fate of such benevolence is ultimately to enrich the coffers of foreign potentates, what incentive would there be to make dedications at all?

Thirdly, the fact that some of Judah's better kings indulge in this activity complicates the attempt to argue that such a strategy is reprehensible. It is one thing for a series of bad kings to plunder their treasuries, but it is another for a series of good kings to do so. In Kings four out of six monarchs associated with the ransacking of the temple are evaluated positively. To complicate matters further, the one king who is associated with two treasury incidents happens to be one of the two most highly rated kings in Judahite history. Fourthly, in every case the domestic pillaging achieves the desired effect. In the international world of *Realpolitik*, the royal exploitation of the treasuries relieves pressure on Judah and its capital (e.g. 2 Kgs 12.19). If the ploy works every time, there is something to be said for it.

Finally, the picture of unmitigated destruction that attends the closing

---

J.C. Greenfield, *Jews of Elephantine and Arameans of Syene: Aramaic Texts With Translation* (Jerusalem: Hebrew University Press, 1984), pp. 91-101.

43. Porten and Greenfield, *Jews of Elephantine*, p. 97 (= A.E. Cowley, *Aramaic Papyri of the Fifth Century B.C.* [Oxford: Clarendon Press, 1923], § 31.11).

44. Ezra 1.6; 2.68-69 (cf. Neh. 7.69-71); 6.4; 7.15-22; 8.24-30, 33-34.

years of the Judahite monarchy in Kings would pose problems for postexilic writers, such as the authors of Chronicles, Ezra and Nehemiah, who wished to emphasize continuity between the First and Second Temple eras. With the exception of those temple treasures that were sent to Babylon with King Jehoiachin (2 Kgs 24.13), everything else in the palace and temple treasuries is purloined, cut apart or destroyed in the invasions of 598 and 586 BCE. The bleak presentation of Kings offers few grounds for hope based on the fate of the temple, the palace and their associated contents.

The testimony of Chronicles is at once more complex and more hopeful than that of DtrH. The differences between the two works are of both a theological and a historical nature. Each of Chr.'s compositional techniques—additions, omissions, revisions and recontextualization—contributes to the process of defining his unique perspective on the history of the national treasures. Chr. does not deny that spoils repeatedly left Jerusalem for destinations in other lands during the Judahite monarchy, but his glowing presentation of the united kingdom, his reconsideration of certain treasury incidents, his balancing of declines with recoveries, his positive contributions to Judahite history, his particular way of exalting Hezekiah and his temperate view of the Babylonian exiles all succeed in generating an alternative portrait to the history of decline offered by Samuel–Kings.

a. *The United Monarchy*
Chr. dwells on the establishment and endowment of the treasuries in the united monarchy, most notably in the reign of David. DtrH first raises the issue of the temple treasuries in his presentation of Solomon's reign (1 Kgs 7.51). In contrast, Chr.'s treatment of David contains a series of extended references to the treasuries in particular and to Israel's wealth in general. In his coverage of David's string of military victories, Chr., unlike DtrH, overtly connects David's war dedications (1 Chron. 18.7-8a, 9-11 // 2 Sam. 8.7-11) with Solomon's temple. The bronze that David captures from Hadadezer is employed by Solomon to construct 'the bronze sea, the columns and the bronze vessels' (1 Chron. 18.8b). The emphasis on the complementarity of David and Solomon's reigns is, of course, a hallmark of Chr.'s presentation of the united monarchy.[45]

45. R.L. Braun, 'Solomonic Apologetic in Chronicles', *JBL* 92 (1973), pp. 503-16; Braun, 'Solomon, the Chosen Temple Builder: The Significance of 1 Chronicles 22, 28 and 29 for the Theology of Chronicles', *JBL* 95 (1976), pp. 581-90; H.G.M.

As soon as the site of the future temple is selected (1 Chron. 22.1), David begins preparations for its eventual construction. David sets aside (כון) enormous quantities of gold, silver and bronze for the use of his son and successor (1 Chron. 22.2-4, 14). Because 'the house that is to be built for Yahweh must be exceedingly great' (להגדיל למעלה; 1 Chron. 22.5), the head of state secures unbelievable quantities of materials for the temple project.[46]

Chr.'s David does much more to ensure the success of his son and temple builder.[47] In preparation for the transition to Solomon's reign, an aging but still lucid David establishes a national administration (1 Chron. 23.1–27.34).[48] Part of this planning involves the appointment of levitical supervisors for the treasuries of the temple and for the treasuries of the dedicated gifts (1 Chron. 26.20-26).[49] The Gershonites are put in charge of the former, while the Qohathites are put in charge of the latter. David not only anticipates various needs of the promised temple and its associated treasuries, but he also—through the aegis of God's spirit—presents a design for these structures. In his second speech to Solomon, David delivers the pattern (תבנית) for the entire temple complex, including the temple courts, chambers, furniture and utensils (1 Chron. 28.11-19). Much like the inspired Moses before him (Exod. 25.9, 40), who produces a plan (תבנית) for the tabernacle, David bequeaths a plan for the temple to his son. The grand architectural

Williamson, 'The Accession of Solomon in the Books of Chronicles', *VT* 26 (1976), pp. 351-61.

46. The fabulous numbers—'100,000 talents of gold and 1,000,000 talents of silver, as well as iron and bronze beyond weighing'—have occasioned much discussion. R.W. Klein provides an overview, 'How Many in a Thousand?', in M.P. Graham, K.G. Hoglund and S.L. McKenzie (eds.), *The Chronicler as Historian* (JSOTSup, 238; Sheffield: Sheffield Academic Press, 1997), pp. 270-82.

47. 1 Chron. 22.3, 4, 5, 8, 14, 15; cf. 29.2, 21.

48. J.W. Wright, 'The Legacy of David in Chronicles: The Narrative Function of 1 Chronicles 23–27', *JBL* 110 (1991), pp. 229-42.

49. I view most of 1 Chron. 23-27 as an integral part of Chr.'s work; see S. Japhet, *The Ideology of the Book of Chronicles and its Place in Biblical Thought* (BEATAJ, 9; Bern: Peter Lang, 1989); J.W. Wright, 'From Center to Periphery: 1 Chronicles 23–27 and the Interpretation of Chronicles in the Nineteenth Century', in E.C. Ulrich *et al.* (eds.), *Priests, Prophets, and Scribes: Essays on the Formation and Heritage of Second Temple Judaism in Honour of Joseph Blenkinsopp* (JSOTSup, 149; Sheffield: JSOT Press, 1992), pp. 20-42; W.M. Schniedewind, *The Word of God in Transition: From Prophet to Exegete in the Second Temple Period* (JSOTSup, 197; Sheffield: Sheffield Academic Press, 1995), pp. 165-70.

design includes a scheme for 'the treasuries of the house of God and of the treasuries of the dedicated gifts' (1 Chron. 28.12).[50]

A related part of David's strategic planning involves endowments. The contributions do not simply focus on David. According to 1 Chron. 26.26, the treasury of the dedicated gifts housed donations made by David, the clan chiefs and the commanders of thousands and hundreds. War spoils are used to strengthen the house of Yahweh (1 Chron. 26.27). Those benefactors whose dedications make their way to the treasury include Samuel the seer, Saul son of Kish, Abner son of Ner and Joab son of Zeruiah (1 Chron. 26.28). It seems that in Chronicles any Israelite leader who ever waged war during the reigns of Saul and David makes a dedicatory gift.[51] In his speech to the entire assembly (1 Chron. 29.1-5), David makes much the same point publicly. He speaks of his personal generosity toward the temple project, including setting aside his own considerable supply (סגלה) of gold and silver, but he also beckons those gathered to make their own freewill offerings. The assembly (קהל) does not disappoint. The military, clan and tribal leaders all make extravagant donations to the work of the temple involving thousands of talents of gold, darics, silver, bronze and iron (1 Chron. 29.6-7). The plentiful gifts for the temple provided by these leaders include (precious) stones to the treasury of the temple (1 Chron. 29.8). Israel under David enjoys extensive wealth but dedicates it to a higher purpose.

The endowments provided by David are put to good use by Solomon. In Chr.'s account of Solomon's reign, which is heavily dependent on DtrH, Solomon brings David's dedicatory gifts, the silver, the gold and all of the vessels into the treasuries of the temple (2 Chron. 5.1). Solomon studs the house of Yahweh with precious stones and overlays

---

50. In addition to the appointments made for the temple treasuries, appointments are made for the royal treasuries and for the treasuries in the country, towns and citadels (1 Chron. 27.25). Here again, Chr.'s presentation differs from that of the DtrH. While the Deuteronomists' treasuries consist of the palace and temple storehouses, Chr.'s treasuries include regional storehouses as well. Following the disaster of Israel's secession, Rehoboam recovers and oversees a number of reforms (2 Chron. 11.5-23), which include strengthening fortified towns and provisioning them with storehouses (אצרות) of food, wine and oil (2 Chron. 11.11-12). In tending to the provincial storehouses, Rehoboam renews a pattern set by his grandfather David (1 Chron. 27.25).

51. E.L. Curtis and A.A. Madsen, *A Critical and Exegetical Commentary on the the Books of Chronicles* (ICC; Edinburgh: T. & T. Clark, 1910), p. 287.

its interior with gold (2 Chron. 3.4-9). Similarly, Solomon plates many of the temple furnishings with gold (2 Chron. 3.10-13; 4.8, 19–22). David's provisions for the levitical supervisors are also implemented. In Solomon's reign there was no departure from 'the command of the king concerning the priests and the levites in any matter, including the treasuries' (2 Chron. 8.15). As in Kings, Solomon's reign is a time of heightened prosperity (2 Chron. 1.15; 9.22, 27). Trade with other lands enhances the nation's coffers (2 Chron. 1.16-17; 8.17-18; 9.21, 28) and tribute flows in from the nations (2 Chron. 9.1-14, 23–24). As in Kings, Solomon furnishes the Lebanon Forest house with golden shields, golden bucklers and assorted golden vessels (2 Chron. 9.15-16, 20). Similarly, he fashions an incomparable ivory throne, overlaid with gold, for his palace (2 Chron. 9.17-19; cf. 1 Kgs 10.18-19).

Together with the material in David's reign, the references in Solomon's reign create a highly positive image of the way in which the united monarchy generates an enduring legacy for subsequent generations. Unlike the Deuteronomists' David, Chr.'s David has a formative role to play in establishing this legacy. Solomon's wealth becomes, in part, a Davidic bequest. Chr.'s portrayal of David's relation to Solomon generates a picture of the united monarchy that is, however, more than a time of sustained wealth. Much of the wealth that David acquires he dedicates to future generations. Both as the head of state and as a private citizen, David contributes enormous quantities of precious metals to the cause of Israel's national institutions. In Chronicles, self-sacrificial giving has its long-term rewards. The self-denial practiced by David and by Israel's leaders is validated by Solomon's achievements. The lavish furnishings of the temple are made possible, in part, by earlier endowments. In Chronicles the people also have an active role to play. The temple is not simply a royal chapel planned by one Davidic king and built by another, but also the patrimony of all the people.[52] Similarly, the very success of Israel's national institutions results from a consistent pattern of royal and popular largess. Over against the disparate presentations of David and Solomon in DtrH, the presentation of David, Solomon and Israel in Chr.'s history establishes an intergenerational argument for supporting and enhancing the temple.

52. H.G.M. Williamson, 'The Temple in the Books of Chronicles', in W. Horbury (ed.), *Templum Amicitae: Essays on the Second Temple Presented to Ernst Bammel* (JSNTSup, 48: Sheffield: JSOT Press, 1991), pp. 15-31.

b. *The Judahite Monarchy*
In Chr.'s history, the planning and endowments of David are properly exploited by Solomon. But the era of the dual monarchies is not such a success. In his narration of Judahite history, Chr. follows the DtrH in recording a series of Jerusalem temple despoliations by domestic and foreign kings (2 Chron. 12.9; 16.2; 25.24). In agreement with the testimony of Kings, Chr. records raids on the temple or palace treasuries during the reigns of Rehoboam (1 Kgs 14.26 // 2 Chron. 12.9), Asa (1 Kgs 15.18 // 2 Chron. 16.2), Amaziah (2 Kgs 14.14 // 2 Chron. 25.24) and Ahaz (2 Kgs 16.8 // 2 Chron. 28.21). But these parallels suggest more congruence between the two works than actually exists. Chr.'s versions of the despoliations vary from that of the Deuteronomists in a number of important ways.

To begin with, Chr. recontextualizes his *Vorlagen* in new settings. In the case of Asa, whom he evaluates positively (2 Chron. 14.1-3), he situates his contributions to the treasury in the productive period of Asa's reign, while he consigns the raid on the treasuries to the regressive period of his reign.[53] Chr. distances the two incidents from each other by placing them within two distinct phases of Asa's reign, one long and progressive (2 Chron. 14.1–15.19) and the other short and regressive (2 Chron. 16.10). Similarly, in the case of Amaziah, whom Chr. also evaluates positively, Chr. contextualizes the raid of Joash of Israel to a regressive period in Amaziah's reign (2 Chron. 25.14-28).[54] In this way, Chr. can present Asa and Amaziah as good kings without commending their exploitation of the national treasuries. On the contrary, Chr.'s commentary on both episodes is negative. Asa's pact with Ben-hadad is criticized by Hanani the seer as foolish reliance upon Syria (2 Chron. 16.7-9). In Chr.'s version of Asa's tenure, the appeal to Ben-hadad is also ultimately ineffective.[55] Because he did not rely on

53. R.B. Dillard, 'The Reign of Asa (2 Chr. 14-16): An Example of the Chronicler's Theological Method', *JETS* 23 (1980), pp. 207-18.

54. The reign of Amaziah in Chronicles is artfully arranged. M.P. Graham, 'Aspects of the Structure and Rhetoric of 2 Chronicles 25', in M.P. Graham, W.P. Brown and J.K. Kuan (eds.), *History and Interpretation: Essays in Honour of John H. Hayes* (JSOTSup, 173; Sheffield: JSOT Press, 1993), pp. 78-89.

55. The author of Chronicles recasts and supplements virtually all of the international covenants of Samuel–Kings to demonstrate that they incurred divine wrath and actually failed to achieve their desired effects. Chr. reworks pacts in his *Vorlage* to show what he deems to be their deleterious effects on Judah. G.N. Knoppers,

Yahweh, Asa is continually beset by wars (2 Chron. 16.9).

In the case of Rehoboam, whom Chr. evaluates negatively (2 Chron. 12.14), the same principle holds. The author consigns Shishak's raid on the treasuries to a regressive phase of Rehoboam's reign (2 Chron. 12.1-9), while he contextualizes Rehoboam's construction of provincial fortified towns in one of the reform periods of his reign (2 Chron. 11.1-23).[56] Shishak's raid appears as divine punishment for the backsliding of Rehoboam and Judah (2 Chron. 12.5). Chr. also disputes the inference from Kings that Rehoboam's actions spared Jerusalem from Shishak's assault.[57] Judah's capital survives the campaign of the Egyptian king because of Yahweh's compassion upon Judah's leaders and king after they had humbled themselves before him (2 Chron. 12.6-7). In this manner Chr. does more than offer a variant picture from that of Kings. He creates a larger sense of coherence within his narration by integrating royal actions toward the treasuries into his larger presentation and evaluation of a king's reign.

If recontextualization is one literary technique the author employs to create a different history of the treasures from that of Kings, rewriting is another. The reign of Joash (Jehoash in Chronicles) serves as the first example. In Chr.'s revision of Joash's tenure, a Syrian army invades Judah and takes booty from Judah (2 Chron. 24.23) during a regressive phase in the Judahite king's reign (2 Chron. 24.17-24). Chr. nowhere mentions the palace and temple treasuries in discussing this incident.[58] Nor is the gain of booty on the Arameans' part the result of a conscious choice on Joash's part. In DtrH, the strategic decision of the Judahite king saves Jerusalem from a direct Aramean assault (2 Kgs 12.18-19). But in Chronicles the success of the Syrians has nothing to do with

'"Yahweh is not with Israel": Alliances as a *Topos* in Chronicles', *CBQ* 58 (1996), pp. 601-26.

56. Rehoboam's reign encompasses several distinct segments. Chr. attributes the inconsistency in Rehoboam's actions to a lack of resolve on his part: 'He did what was evil, because he had not set his heart to seek Yahweh' (2 Chron. 12.14). See further, my 'Rehoboam in Chronicles: Villain or Victim?', *JBL* 109 (1990), pp. 423-40.

57. Shishak comes up against Jerusalem and takes tribute (1 Kgs 14.25-26), but the text does not speak of an actual siege or invasion of Jerusalem. The implication seems to be that Rehoboam used the palace and treasury contents to accommodate the Egyptian king.

58. The treatment of Joash (2 Chron. 24.1-27) also makes no mention of King Hazael of Syria (2 Kgs 12.18-19).

superior strength or military strategy. On the contrary, 'the Syrian army
came with just a few men', but Yahweh delivered the larger Judahite
army into their hands, because 'they [the people of Judah] abandoned
Yahweh, the God of their fathers' (2 Chron. 24.24).[59] Chr.'s reworking
of this episode in Joash's reign has a number of complementary effects.
By leaving the fate of Jerusalem out of the equation, Chr. refuses to
concede the point of Kings. He severs the link between Joash's actions
in dealing with the Syrians from the difficult world of *Realpolitik*. In
Chronicles the negative results of the invasion are totally unnecessary.
The Syrian victory is subordinated to the perfidy of Joash and Judah's
leaders, which elicited divine wrath (2 Chron. 24.17-18).

Another good example of revision is the reign of Ahaz. In Chronicles, the record of Ahaz is one of unmitigated decline (2 Chron. 27.9–
28.27).[60] In the aftermath of a series of successful foreign invasions
Ahaz does not reverse course, but petitions the kings of Assyria 'to help
(לעזר) him' (2 Chron. 28.16).[61] But in Chronicles the appeal for an
alliance with Tiglath-pileser does not work.[62] The Assyrian monarch
comes not to save Ahaz, but to oppress him (2 Chron. 28.20).[63] In Chr.'s
rendition, it is at this point that Ahaz plunders temple and palace so as
to pay the king of Assyria. But, whereas in DtrH, the plunder of the
Jerusalem temple treasuries successfully extricates Ahaz from the threat
posed by the Syro-Ephraimite coalition (2 Kgs 16.5-10), in Chronicles
it comprises a futile attempt to relieve Judah from Assyrian oppression.

59. Consistent with his reappropriation of holy war ideology, Chr. does not see
large numbers as the key to military success. If anything, the size of Judah's armies
in victories (e.g. 2 Chron. 13.13-21; 14.7-14) bears an inverse proportion to the size
of those involved in defeat (e.g. 2 Chron. 24.23-24; 28.6; 32.8).

60. Ahaz doggedly refuses to reform after repeatedly going astray. E. Ben Zvi,
'A Gateway to the Chronicler's Teaching: The Account of the Reign of Ahaz in
2 Chron. 28, 1-27', *SJOT* 7 (1993), pp. 216-49.

61. I follow the MT's מלכי אשור, rather than the text assumed by the LXX's
מלך אשור (*lectio difficilior*). Note also the use of מלכי־ארם in 2 Chron. 28.23.

62. Chr.'s reworking of his *Vorlage* is rather complex. Ben Zvi, 'Gateway',
pp. 227-30; M.E.W. Thompson, *Situation and Theology: Old Testament Interpretations of the Syro-Ephraimite War* (Sheffield: Almond Press, 1982), pp. 79-124;
Knoppers, 'Alliances as a *Topos*', pp. 608-11.

63. The addition of the MT ולא חזקו, 'and he did not strengthen him' or 'and he
did not overtake him' (S. Japhet, *I & II Chronicles: A Commentary* [OTL;
Louisville, KY: Westminster/John Knox Press, 1993], p. 907), may be an expansion. I read with the LXX (*lectio brevior*).

Punning on the root עזר ('to help'), Chr. remarks that Ahaz's expro-priation of the treasuries 'was of no help to him' (ולא לעזר לו) 2 Chron. 28.21).[64] Ahaz's petition to Tiglath-pileser is an abject failure.

Chr.'s thorough reworking of his *Vorlage* sheds light on his larger handling of treasury despoliations. Chr. does not deny that there were such despoliations by Ahaz and other Judahite monarchs. Like the authors of Kings, Chr. concedes that a series of kings surrendered spoils to other monarchs either by force of invasion or by voluntary conces-sion. But this negative pattern is not determinative for those living in Chr.'s own time. Things could have been otherwise. Chr. revises his *Vorlage* to undermine, if not reverse, its force. Exploitation of the treasuries is a sign of abject weakness and moral turpitude, rather than a defensive strategy in the context of international diplomacy. Moreover, Chr. neither endorses nor admits to an ineluctable linkage between despoliation and the alleviation of foreign bondage. In Rehoboam's time Jerusalem is saved by divine mercy and not by expropriation of Solomon's treasuries. In the reign of Asa, the Judahite king's pact with Ben-hadad leads to further wars. In the case of Ahaz, the strategem of voluntary tribute clearly fails.

A third compositional technique that Chr. employs to generate a dis-tinctive history of the national treasuries is omission. Chr. does not mention all of the despoliations recorded in DtrH.[65] Chr.'s many changes to the deuteronomistic account of Hezekiah's reign include Hezekiah's relationship to the temple and palace treasuries. There is no report of Hezekiah's looting of 'all of the silver found in the temple of Yahweh and in the treasuries of the royal palace' as a tribute payment to King Sennacherib (2 Kgs 18.15). Nor does Chr. mention that Hezekiah stripped the temple doors and posts to augment his shipment

---

64. H.G.M. Williamson, *1 and 2 Chronicles* (NCB; Grand Rapids: Eerdmans, 1982), p. 348.

65. My assumption is that Chr. had access to most, if not all, of the treasury incidents in Kings (1 Kgs 14.26; 15.18; 2 Kgs 12.18; 14.14; 16.8; 18.15; 20.13-15; 24.13; 25.8-10, 13-17). It is possible that Chr.'s *Vorlage* of Kings did not contain all of these references. On this matter, see the proposal of S.L. McKenzie, *The Chronicler's Use of the Deuteronomistic History* (HSM, 33; Atlanta: Scholars Press, 1985), pp. 181-88, and the more radical theory of A.G. Auld, *Kings without Privilege: David and Moses in the Story of the Bible's Kings* (Edinburgh: T. & T. Clark, 1994). I am not convinced, however, that Chr. and the Deuteronomists drew from a common source. See my review of Auld's book in *ATJ* 27 (1995), pp. 118-21.

of spoils to the Assyrian king (2 Kgs 18.16). In short, the entire tribute episode in Kings (2 Kgs 18.13-15) is missing from Chronicles. Quite to the contrary, Chr.'s Hezekiah builds treasuries and endows them.

The other treasury incident in Hezekiah's reign—his reception of the Babylonian envoys of Merodoch-baladan, in which he showed them his entire storehouse, the silver, gold, spices and fine oil—'all that was found in his treasuries' (2 Kgs 20.12-13)—is also largely omitted from Chronicles. The whole matter of the Babylonian envoys is obliquely mentioned at the conclusion of Hezekiah's reign as a divine examination of his character: 'and so in the [matter] of the envoys of the Babylonian officials, those sent to him to inquire about the sign which occurred in the land, God abandoned him to test him, to know all what was in his heart' (2 Chron. 32.31). The implication seems to be that Hezekiah passed this divinely administered test, but the matter is shrouded in some ambiguity.[66] In any event, the circumstances surrounding the foreign visit have to do with the sign that Hezekiah received from Isaiah (2 Kgs 20.8-11). In Chr.'s version, the diplomatic visit has nothing at all to do with the national treasuries. Nor is any connection made between this particular incident and a future Babylonian exile.

The two omissions directly affect Chr.'s larger history of Judah, substantially reducing the number of negative treasury incidents and altering the larger pattern of treasury raids found in Kings. One of the Judahite kings whom both DtrH and Chr. evaluate most positively does not employ spoils to ward off foreign kings in Chronicles. Two negative treasury episodes in Kings are replaced by one positive episode in Chronicles. In this manner, Chr. both reduces the number of good kings who despoil the treasuries and succeeds in presenting a much more temperate account of the Judahite monarchy than that found in Kings.

The fourth literary strategy employed by Chr. is his addition of new material. Chr. depicts times of economic renewal for Jerusalem and

---

66. R.B. Dillard, *2 Chronicles* (WBC, 15; Waco, TX: Word Books, 1987), pp. 259-60; H.G.M. Williamson, *1 and 2 Chronicles*, pp. 387-88; P.R. Ackroyd, 'The Biblical Interpretation of the Reigns of Ahaz and Hezekiah', in W.B. Barrick and J.R. Spencer (eds.), *In the Shelter of Elyon: Essays on Ancient Palestinian Life and Literature in Honor of G.W. Ahlström* (JSOTSup, 31; Sheffield: JSOT Press, 1984), pp. 247-59; Japhet, *I & II Chronicles*, pp. 995-96. For a different view, see A. Shinan and Y. Zakovitch, 'Midrash on Scripture and Midrash within Scripture', *ScrHier* 31 (1986), pp. 268-69.

Judah, most of which are unparalleled in DtrH. The first such reformer is the one king of Judah in Kings who also makes significant temple dedications. King Asa institutes a series of positive measures (2 Chron. 14.4-6; 15.8-18). These include the consecration of silver, gold and a number of items to the temple (2 Chron. 15.18). But, as in DtrH, Asa's legacy vis-à-vis the treasuries is mixed. He subsequently empties the temple and royal treasuries to induce Ben-hadad to attack an invading Baasha of Israel (2 Chron. 16.2). The short period of decline at the end of Asa's reign is reversed by one of recovery, which attends the beginning of the reign of his successor Jehoshaphat.[67] In the first phase of his reign, unparalleled in Kings, Jehoshaphat rebuilds his kingdom by implementing reforms, deploying troops and fortifying cities (1 Chron. 17.1-2).[68] In so doing, Jehoshaphat grows stronger and becomes more widely respected. All of Judah brings tribute (מנחה) to the new king, who, like Solomon, experiences 'riches and honor in abundance' (2 Chron. 17.5).[69] Some of Judah's neighbors send great tribute (מנחה) and silver to Jehoshaphat (1 Chron. 17.11). Jehoshaphat, in turn, builds fortresses and store-cities (ערי מסכנית) in Judah (2 Chron. 17.12-13a). To be sure, Jehoshaphat's recovery is not explicitly linked to new contributions for the Jerusalem treasuries, but the larger picture is clear. Chr.'s record balances the despoliations by some kings with the reconstructions and amassing of wealth by others.

The positive contributions made by one reformer—Jehoshaphat—are renewed by another—Hezekiah (2 Chron. 32.27-29). Following the disaster of Ahaz's reign, Hezekiah begins a period of recovery. His first priority is rebuilding the temple. Hence, unlike DtrH, Chr.'s history lists three kings: Joash (2 Chron. 24.4-14), Hezekiah (2 Chron. 29.3-36) and Josiah (2 Chron. 34.8-17), as initiating temple repairs. Hezekiah also builds himself treasuries (אצרות) to house silver, gold, precious

67. K. Strübind, *Tradition als Interpretation in der Chronik: König Josaphat als Paradigma chronistischer Hermeneutik und Theologie* (BZAW, 201; Berlin: W. de Gruyter, 1991); G.N. Knoppers, 'Reform and Regression: The Chronicler's Presentation of Jehoshaphat', *Bib* 72 (1991), pp. 500-24.

68. Jehoshaphat's reforms—a major feature of Chr.'s account of his reign—have been used in a variety of ways for historical reconstruction, not all of them convincing, G.N. Knoppers, 'Jehoshaphat's Judiciary and the Scroll of YHWH's Torah', *JBL* 114 (1994), pp. 59-80.

69. In Chronicles, popular support, riches and tribute all suggest divine favor. See Japhet, *Ideology*, pp. 150-76; and R.B. Dillard, 'Reward and Punishment in Chronicles: The Theology of Immediate Retribution', *WTJ* 46 (1984), pp. 164-72.

stones, shields and a variety of expensive utensils (2 Chron. 32.27).[70] This is but one indication of the great prosperity that attends the latter portion of his reign (2 Chron. 32.28-30). That Chr. has King Hezekiah build and endow treasuries marks a complete reversal of the picture in Kings. There, as we have seen, Hezekiah despoils the temple store-houses to ward off an invading Sennacherib (2 Kgs 18.13-15). In Kings the end of Hezekiah's reign is marred by the spectre of a future Baby-lonian exile, but in Chronicles the end of Hezekiah's reign is largely a story of economic success. In constructing and supporting national treasuries, Hezekiah's reign recalls some of the glories of the united monarchy.[71]

The point in discussing the accomplishments and wealth of Judah's kings is not that Chr. portrays the divided monarchy as a glorious age. He clearly does not. While the time of David and Solomon is presented as the high point of Israelite history, Chr. presents the later history of Judah's economic fortunes as mixed—a record of both declines and improvements.[72] The combination of omissions and additions creates a sense of balance.[73] Virtually every regression is followed by a recovery. Chr.'s record is, in fact, so consistent on this matter that his treatment of the palace and temple treasuries could be considered to be one of the many *topoi* found in his writing. In speaking of *topoi* in Chr.'s work, recent commentators have cogently argued that the material in Chroni-cles falls into repeated patterns.[74] Through his use of *topoi*, Chr. struc-

---

70. Their location is, however, unspecified. G.N. Knoppers, 'History and Histo-riography: The Royal Reforms', in Graham, Hoglund and McKenzie (eds.), *The Chronicler as Historian*, pp. 192-97.

71. R. Mosis interprets Hezekiah as a second David (*Untersuchungen zur The-ologie des chronistischen Geschichtswerkes* [FTS, 92; Freiburg: Herder, 1973], pp. 164-69), but Williamson sees Chr.'s Hezekiah as a second Solomon (*Israel in the Books of Chronicles*, pp. 119-25). It is doubtful whether Chr. had such a rigid demarcation in mind. In his actions Hezekiah resembles both David and Solomon. See the discussion by M.A. Throntveit, 'Hezekiah in the Books of Chronicles', in D.J. Lull (ed.), *Society of Biblical Literature 1988 Seminar Papers* (SBLSPS, 27; Atlanta: Scholars Press, 1988), pp. 302-11.

72. R.H. Lowery, *The Reforming Kings: Cult and Society in First Temple Judah* (JSOTSup, 120; Sheffield: JSOT Press, 1991), pp. 62-209; Knoppers, 'History and Historiography', pp. 187-203.

73. See also E. Ben Zvi, 'A Sense of Proportion: An Aspect of the Theology of the Chronicler', *SJOT* 9 (1995), pp. 37-51.

74. P. Welten (*Geschichte und Geschichtsdarstellung in den Chronikbüchern*

tures, interprets and unifies history. Chr.'s patterning of the past lends an exemplary status to his writing.[75] The author's treatment of the treasuries in the united and divided monarchies presents both an ideal of construction, devotion and endowments, which contributes to the nation's well-being, and a pattern of destruction, failure and plunder, which contributes to the nation's decline. In this manner, Chr. communicates a larger message to his audience. Chr. accepts the fact that history includes regressions, but he insists that leaders and the community at large can also progress and make new contributions to their nation's legacy. Whereas Chr. relegates despoliations to negative phases in royal careers, he promotes dedications as illustrative of loyal conduct. Each monarch has the wherewithal to reverse the course set by his ancestors and, indeed, to reverse his own course.[76] In this, Chr.'s history departs markedly from the pattern evident in the final edition of DtrH, a work that has been described as 'a history of destruction'.[77] Chr. provides his audience with positive examples to follow. The ravishing of the palace or temple treasuries by some kings is offset by the prosperity and dedications of others.

c. *The Babylonian Exiles*

Chr.'s distinctive perspective on Judahite history is, perhaps, nowhere so much in evidence as in his depiction of Judah's final years. Chr.'s portrayal of the events leading up to the Babylonian exile, which draws upon both Kings and Jeremiah, is less severe and more temperate than that of DtrH. Whereas the final chapters of Kings depict a series of devastating exiles and temple lootings, Chr. briefly depicts three plun-

[WMANT, 42; Neukirchen–Vluyn: Neukirchener Verlag, 1973]) discusses the *topoi* of war reports, descriptions of military techniques and records of military fortifications. Mosis (*Untersuchungen zur Theologie*, pp. 17-43) contends that the Chronicler's portrayal of Saul is indicative in its vocabulary and imagery of an exilic situation that consistently reappears in Chronicles. In my judgment, alliances constitute one of Chr.'s *topoi*. Knoppers, 'Yhwh Is Not with Israel', pp. 601-26.

75. P.R. Ackroyd, 'History and Theology in the Writings of the Chronicler', *CTM* 38 (1967), pp. 501-15; Ackroyd, 'The Chronicler as Exegete', *JSOT* 2 (1977), pp. 2-32; Willi, *Chronik als Auslegung*, pp. 160-69; R.K. Duke, *The Persuasive Appeal of the Chronicler: A Rhetorical Analysis* (JSOTSup, 88; Bible and Literature Series, 25; Sheffield: Almond Press, 1990), pp. 143-44.

76. G. von Rad, *Old Testament Theology* (2 vols.; New York: Harper & Row, 1962), I, pp. 349-50.

77. Japhet, *Ideology*, p. 364.

derings: one by Nebuchadnezzar during the reign of Jehoiakim, which sends some temple vessels (מכלי בית יהוה) to Babylon (2 Chron. 36.7);[78] another during the reign of Jehoiachin, in which the precious vessels of the temple (כלי חמדת בית־יהוה) accompany Jehoiachin into exile (2 Chron. 36.10); and a third during the reign of King Zedekiah that dispatches all of the temple vessels, whether great or small (כל כלי בית האלהים הגדלים והקטנים), to Babylon (2 Chron. 36.18). This last deportation is definitive. In this respect, the influence of Jeremiah (Jer. 27.19-22*; 28.6), over against Kings, is evident.[79] The temple treasures, the royal treasures and those of the officials leave Jerusalem; 'everything' is brought intact to Babylon (2 Chron. 36.18). Unlike the detailed contrasts developed in Kings between the age of temple construction and the age of temple destruction, the overthrow of the temple and its contents is described in only three verses.[80]

Chr.'s version of the temple plunder and destruction has two complementary effects. It plays down the devastation wrought by the Babylonian invasions in Kings,[81] and it creates an open-ended future for the temple artifacts.[82] Whereas DtrH presents two temple lootings, the first of which results in the deportation of the temple and palace treasures (2 Kgs 24.13) and the second of which results in the destruction of the temple and all that was in it (2 Kgs 25.9, 13-17), Chr.'s history consistently portrays a Babylonian destination for both the temple vessels (2 Chron. 36.7, 10) and the temple and palace treasures (2 Chron. 36.18). The author's presentation of Judah's final years offers

78. In this context, see also Dan. 1.1-2; 5.2-3, 23.

79. As J.G. Janzen (*Studies in the Text of Jeremiah* [HSM, 6; Cambridge, MA: Harvard University Press, 1973], pp. 46-47, 69-75) and W.L. Holladay (*Jeremiah 2: A Commentary on the Book of the Prophet Jeremiah, Chapters 26–52* [Hermeneia; Minneapolis: Fortress Press, 1989], pp. 114, 123) observe, the LXX of Jer. 27.19-22 is to be preferred (*lectio brevior*) over against the MT. On Chr.'s use of Jeremiah, see further I. Kalimi and J.D. Purvis, 'King Jehoiachin and the Vessels of the Lord's House in Biblical Literature', *CBQ* 56 (1994), pp. 452-56.

80. 2 Chron. 36.17-19; cf. 2 Kgs 25.9, 13-17. The attention given to all of the post-Josianic kings in Chronicles is substantially reduced when compared with the presentation in Kings. Kalimi and Purvis, 'King Jehoiachin and the Vessels', pp. 449-52.

81. See Japhet, *Ideology*, 364-73, although I do not agree with all of her conclusions.

82. P.R. Ackroyd, *Studies in the Religious Tradition of the Old Testament* (London: SCM Press, 1987), pp. 46-60.

his readers grounds for hope, based on the fate of the temple and palace artifacts. The Davidic-Solomonic temple is razed, but the Davidic-Solomonic legacy does not end with the destruction of this shrine. It continues in the deported temple vessels and furnishings.

In Ezra and Nehemiah there is a consistent emphasis on the return and reuse of temple artifacts.[83] The temple vessels have been called, in fact, 'a continuity theme' in the chronistic history (Chronicles, Ezra and Nehemiah).[84] Given this and other evidence, one can say that in the chronistic history there is a clear line of continuity between the pre-exilic and postexilic Jerusalem communities. As in Chr.'s depiction of the Judahite monarchy, a period of decline is followed by a period of recovery. But the positive fate for the temple vessels in Ezra and Nehemiah is adumbrated in Chronicles itself.

This brings us to another way in which Chr.'s handling of the national treasuries differs from that of the Deuteronomist. The genealogical introduction to Chr.'s history (1 Chron. 1–9) contains an account of the reestablishment of services for the (second) temple (1 Chron. 9.23-33).[85] This passage notes that four chief gatekeepers (גבורי השערים) are placed in charge of the temple chambers and treasuries (1 Chron.

---

83. Ezra 1.7-11; 5.13-15; 6.5; 7.19-20; 8.26-28, 33-34; Neh. 10.40; 13.5-9. W. Rudolph, *Esra und Nehemia samt 3. Esra* (HAT, 20; Tübingen: J.C.B. Mohr [Paul Siebeck], 1949); J. Blenkinsopp, *Ezra–Nehemiah: A Commentary* (OTL; Philadelphia: Westminster Press, 1988). So also 1 Esdr. 1.43, 45, 54; 2.10-15; 4.44, 57; 8.17, 55; Jdt 4.3.

84. Ackroyd, *Studies*, pp. 56-59. Conversely, some early Jewish and Samaritan interpreters thought that the temple vessels were hidden and would not be revealed until some point in the future when cultic services would be restored. See I. Kalimi and J.D. Purvis, 'The Hiding of the Temple Vessels in Jewish and Samaritan Literature', *CBQ* 56 (1994), pp. 679-85.

85. Along with a number of commentators, I view much of the genealogical material in 1 Chron. 1–9 as integral to Chr.'s work. See S. Japhet, 'Conquest and Settlement in Chronicles', *JBL* 98 (1979), pp. 205-18; Japhet, *I & II Chronicles*, pp. 1-10; H.G.M. Williamson, *1 and 2 Chronicles*, pp. 37-40; M. Kartveit, *Motive und Schichten der Landtheologie in I Chronik 1-9* (ConBOT, 28; Stockholm: Almqvist & Wiksell, 1989). For a different view, see A.C. Welch, *The Work of the Chronicler: Its Purpose and its Date* (Schweich Lectures, 1938; London: Oxford University Press, 1939); M. Noth, *Überlieferungsgeschichtliche Studien: Die sammelnden und bearbeitenden Geschichtswerke im Alten Testament* (Tübingen: Max Niemeyer, 2nd edn, 1957 [1943]), pp. 110-31; W. Rudolph, *Chronikbücher* (HAT, 21; Tübingen: J.C.B. Mohr [Paul Siebeck], 1955), pp. 6-91.

9.26).[86] The pattern of disruption and recovery that characterizes the history of the Judahite monarchy, is also present here. Although the history of Israel's development in the land ends with the Babylonian deportations (1 Chron. 2.1–9.1), it resumes in the postexilic period (1 Chron. 9.2-44). In Chronicles the exile itself becomes only an interruption, albeit a major interruption, in the ongoing story of Israel and its national institutions.

The theme of continuity in spite of upheaval is also present at the end of Chr.'s history. Although Chronicles retells the disaster of the Babylonian exile, along with the destruction of the temple, the book ends with the summons of King Cyrus of Persia to rebuild the Jerusalem temple (2 Chron. 36.22-23). In this respect, Chr.'s treatment of the fate of the temple is a good example of his generally optimistic view of history. By mentioning the decree of Cyrus authorizing the reconstruction of the temple, Chr.'s history ends by pointing back, however allusively, toward the foundations first laid by David and Solomon centuries earlier.

---

86. R.L. Braun, *1 Chronicles* (WBC, 14; Waco, TX: Word Books, 1986), pp. 141-44.

WHEN THE FOREIGN MONARCH SPEAKS

Ehud Ben Zvi

Introduction

Several works have examined the royal speeches in the book of Chronicles, typically focusing on the speeches of the Judahite and Israelite kings.[1] This tendency is not surprising since (1) the overwhelming majority of royal speeches in Chronicles are set in the mouths of these kings;[2] (2) Israel (or Judah) and Jerusalem are at the center of the book;[3] and (3) foreign monarchs are mentioned only insofar as they interact with Israel or Judah and never in terms of their own importance.[4]

---

1. See, e.g., M.A. Throntveit, *When Kings Speak: Royal Speech and Prayer in Chronicles* (SBLDS, 93; Atlanta: Scholars Press, 1987); Throntveit, 'The Chronicler's Speeches and Historical Reconstruction', M.P. Graham, K.G. Hoglund and S.L. McKenzie (eds.), *The Chronicler as Historian* (JSOTSup, 238; Sheffield: Sheffield Academic Press, 1997), pp. 225-45, esp. 227-32.

2. Comprehensive lists of the speeches in Chronicles, each organized according to a particular category, are presented by R.K. Duke in *The Persuasive Appeal of the Chronicler: A Rhetorical Analysis* (JSOTSup, 88; Bible and Literature, 25; Sheffield: Almond Press, 1990), pp. 155-76. Only five instances of speeches presented in the direct mode are attributed to foreign monarchs; see below, pp. 215-24.

3. By 'Israel' I mean here the theological construct designated by this name in the Jerusalemite-centered discourse of the Achaemenid period. From the perspective of the book of Chronicles, the people of the northern kingdom of Israel (despite their unlawful polity) are to be included in that Israel. On these issues, see H.G.M. Williamson, *Israel in the Book of Chronicles* (Cambridge: Cambridge University Press, 1977), pp. 87-140; Williamson, *1 and 2 Chronicles* (NCB; Grand Rapids: Eerdmans, 1982), pp. 24-26; S. Japhet, *The Ideology of the Book of Chronicles and its Place in Biblical Thought* (BEATAJ, 9; Bern: Peter Lang, 1989; 2nd edn, 1997), pp. 308-34; cf. G.N. Knoppers, ' "Yhwh Is Not with Israel": Alliances as a *Topos* in Chronicles', *CBQ* 58 (1996), pp. 601-26. From the perspective of Chronicles, however, the only polity consistent with the will of YHWH in the monarchic period was that polity formed around a Davidic king and Jerusalem.

4. This is not to deny that other issues—perhaps related to the background of

The present article, however, deals with the speech of non-Israelite monarchs. In five cases the narrator in Chronicles presents the narratee with the (subjective) perspective of a foreign monarch as expressed in the monarch's own words, be this in oral or written form. In other words, five times in the book of Chronicles the narrator directly transmits the speech of a foreign monarch or quotes a document written by a foreign ruler.[5] These direct quotations serve as strong indicators of the character of the person quoted.[6] As such, the quotations shed considerable light on the world of knowledge and worldview held by the foreign monarchs, as well as on their use of language as characters within the world of the book.[7] Significantly, the information so provided

Hebrew Bible scholarship—may have contributed to that tendency as well. This matter is, of course, beyond the scope of this article.

5.   The narrator's quotation from a written source (such as a letter from Huram, king of Tyre, to Solomon; see 2 Chron. 2.10) cited here should be differentiated from the (unacknowledged) use of written sources such as the books of Samuel and Kings (or closely related precursors) by the (historical) author(s) of the book of Chronicles.

6.   These are typical examples of an indirect presentation of a character. On these issues see, e.g., S. Rimmon-Kenan, *Narrative Fiction: Contemporary Poetics* (London: Methuen, 1983), pp. 63-65.

7.   This world does not necessarily reflect the 'actual world' from the perspective of the historical personages outside the 'world of the book', whose names are mentioned in that world (e.g. Neco). In fact, it is highly unlikely that the worldview and choice of language of these historical personages would be like those advanced in Chronicles. Yet neither (1) the narratee in the world of the book nor (2) a rereadership of the book of Chronicles that accepts the reliability of the narrator are informed by, nor relate in any way to the most likely viewpoint held by historical figures such Necho, Sennacherib or a king of Tyre who ruled many centuries before the compostion of the book of the Chronicles. This narratee and this rereadership are informed of and interact with the viewpoints of *textual* characters who populate the universe of the book of Chronicles (i.e. Chr.'s Necho, Chr's. Sennacherib and the like).

I use the term 'rereadership' rather than 'readership' (and 'rereader' instead of 'reader') to draw attention to the fact that it is likely that the book was read more than once by any individual. This is certainly the case, if the book was supposed to be studied (cf. Josh. 1.8; Hos. 14.10). On the importance of rereading I have written elsewhere: *A Historical-Critical Study of the Book of Obadiah* (BZAW, 242; Berlin: W. de Gruyter, 1996), pp. 4-5, 18-19, 25, 89-90, 260-66; 'Micah 1.2-16:

has clear bearing on the ideology or theology that is reflected and shaped by the relevant pericopes in the book of Chronicles and by the book as a whole.

Thus, this work is a contribution to the study of a larger topic, namely the characterization of foreign monarchs (and indirectly, or at the connoted level, the theological construction of foreign nations and of the 'other' in general)[8] in the book of Chronicles. Since this larger topic is not feasible within the limits of a single article, the present study focuses on a particular subset of characterizations of foreign monarchs, namely those communicated by direct speech. This subset has been chosen because of particular features associated with the direct representation of these 'foreign' characters in the book, from their own subjective perspective and through their own words, thoughts and feelings.[9] Recourse to direct speech in the narrative serves to communicate a sense of immediacy (and a related sense of authenticity) to both the narratee and the intended rereadership of the book. The communicated senses carry affective claims. In fact, the direct representation mentioned is most likely to contribute to a positive identification of the original rereaders of the book of Chronicles with the characters in the book, provided these characters share the theological position and ideals of the omniscient and reliable narrator present in the text, as was likely understood by the communities of rereaders for whom it was written (in which case they serve the rhetorical goals of the narrator well). Alternatively, they may evoke a strong sense of distance between the character and themselves, when the character's speech is crafted so

Observations and its Possible Implications', *JSOT* 77 (1998), pp. 103-20; and *Micah* (FOTL; Grand Rapids: Eerdmans, in press).

8. References to foreign monarchs are likely to carry a connoted sense of representation of the larger group; within Chronicles itself see, e.g., 1 Chron. 19.9 (cf. 2 Sam. 9.8) and 2 Chron. 9.22 (cf. 1 Kgs 10.24). This is consistent with the tendency to identify representatives and represented, which in some cases may take the form of an identification of ruler/king and people. This being so, characterizations of foreign monarchs may serve (if used with appropriate caution) as a potential window on the characterization of 'foreign people', or, more precisely, of foreign people who live in 'their own countries' and do not belong to the 'community of Israel'. On 'foreigners and aliens' living in and among Israel, see Japhet, *Ideology*, pp. 334-51.

9. Within the world of the book as shaped by the narrator, the words of these characters are consistent with their thoughts and feelings; their speech is truthful and reliable. See n. 10 below.

as to condemn the speaker in the most unequivocal terms (from the viewpoint of the narrator and anyone who accepts the worldview advocated by the narrator).[10] Finally, recourse to direct speech in the narrative serves to enhance credibility, which in the case of a work such as the book of Chronicles may suggest that substantial issues are at stake.

By way of concluding this introductory section, it must be noticed that in some instances in which the narrator in Chronicles presents the direct speech of a foreign monarch, the text is strongly influenced by parallel texts in DtrH.[11] So it is true that some of the considerations and conclusions advanced here may resonate in future studies that address similar issues in DtrH. In fact, for reasons that will be discussed below in section three, this situation is not entirely unexpected. Yet given that this is a study of a subset of characters who exist in the book of Chronicles, the analysis must proceed within the world of Chronicles. In this regard, the following considerations should be underscored: (1) neither the narrator nor the narratee (nor the quotee) in the world of the book is aware of parallel texts in Samuel, Kings, Ezra or elsewhere; (2) the intended rereaders of the book of Chronicles are neither asked to skip

10. On these issues as they appear in Chronicles, see Duke, *Persuasive Appeal*, esp. pp. 119, 146; on biblical narrative more generally, see Y. Amit, '"The Glory of Israel Does Not Deceive or Change his Mind": On the Reliability of Narrator and Speakers in Biblical Narrative', *Prooftexts* 12 (1992), pp. 201-12; cf. also the summary in J. Sanders, 'Perspective in Narrative Discourse' (Proefschrift Katholieke Universitetit Brabant, Tilburg, 1994), pp. 203-204, and the bibliography cited there; for a broader, narrative perspective and for a comprehensive discussion on 'quotation', see M. Sternberg, 'Proteus in Quotation-Land: Mimesis and the Forms of Reported Discourse', *Poetics Today* 3 (1982), pp. 107-56. On general issues associated with 'focalization' (or 'perspective')—including ideological facets—see, e.g., Rimmon-Kennan, *Narrative Fiction*, pp. 71-85.

As in any other case of direct quotation, of course, the question of the reliability (from the perspective of the narrator or one who identifies with the narrator) of the transcribed or cited speech must be taken into account. Moreover, as in cases of characterization by a particular action or speech, the question of whether the indicated character of the personage in the book is temporal or a constant feature in the narrative must also be addressed. See Y. Amit, 'The Glory'; Rimmon-Kennan, *Narrative Fiction*, pp. 61-67.

11. See (1) the letter of Huram to Solomon in 2 Chron. 2.10-15 (cf. 1 Kgs 5.21 + 7.13-14 + 5.22); (2) the words of the queen of Sheba to Solomon in 2 Chron. 9.5-8 (cf. 1 Kgs 10.6-9); and (3) Sennacherib's words to the Judahites in 2 Chron. 32.10-15 (cf. 2 Kgs 18.19-35 and Isa. 36.4–37.15).

these texts nor consider them less integrally part of the book of Chronicles than any 'non-parallel' section; and (3) if the world of knowledge of the rereadership for whom the book of Chronicles was composed included an awareness of parallel accounts in other literary works within their repertoire—as is usually assumed, and with good reason—then it is much more likely that the memory of another similar and clearly congruent story would strengthen rather than weaken the message conveyed by the story in Chronicles. Likewise, the redaction-critical question of whether some of the texts discussed here, or even any of them, are to be attributed (originally) to 'the Chronicler' (hereafter, 'Chr.')[12] or to a different source[13] carries no real weight for the purpose of the present study, because the narrator in the book certainly does not know of the existence of Chr., nor is the narratee addressed by Chr. Moreover, neither the intended nor the original rereadership of the book of Chronicles is addressed by Chr. but by the implied author of the book of Chronicles. This author included in the text both the material that is often attributed to Chr. in modern research and material that is associated with Chr.'s sources.

12. 'Chr.' (the Chronicler) as used here refers to a reconstruction of the historical persona of an individual who (1) was responsible for the composition of the original book of Chronicles (which is identical to the present book except for later additions whose existence and scope are a source of debate), and (2) to whom are attributed (a) the texts (or most of the texts) in Chronicles that are believed to have no parallel in any source available to 'Chr.' and (b) instances of rewording of the original sources at his disposal. It is to be stressed that part (2) of this definition in particular creates an inherent differentiation and a most significant distance between 'Chr.' and the implied author of the book of Chronicles that is much larger in scope than the usual one between an 'actual' and an 'implied' author, because the texts assigned by this definition to 'Chr.' are substantially different from those associated with the implied author of the book.

13. Leaving aside the clear cases of deuteronomistic sources, there has been a substantial debate on whether Neco's words to Josiah in 2 Chron. 35.21 came from Chr. See, e.g., H.G.M. Williamson, 'The Death of Josiah and the Continuing Development of the Deuteronomistic History', *VT* 32 (1982), pp. 242-47; C.T. Begg, 'The Death of Josiah in Chronicles: Another View', *VT* 37 (1987), pp. 2-8; H.G.M. Williamson, 'Reliving the Death of Josiah', *VT* 37 (1987), pp. 9-15. The proclamation of Cyrus in 2 Chron. 36 appears also in Ezra 1.2-3a. There is a tendency not to attribute it to Chr. See, e.g., Williamson, *1 & 2 Chronicles*, p. 419, and see section 2.5 below.

2. Gathering the Data: The Five Instances of Direct Speech
in which the Speaker is a Foreign Monarch

2.1 Huram's letter to Solomon (2 Chronicles 2.10-15)

Huram's words are a written response to Solomon's previous message
to him (2 Chron. 2.2-9).[14] Solomon's message advances a request for an
artisan (v. 6) and timber (vv. 7-8), and it specifies a certain compensa-
tion (v. 9). The request itself is prefaced by a relatively long introduction (vv. 2-4), whose role in the world of the text is to persuade Huram
to fulfill Solomon's request. Following the quotation of Solomon's
speech, the narrator cites the written response sent by Huram, to which
the narrator, significantly, claims to have access. The text cited begins
with praise of YHWH, David, Solomon and Israel (vv. 10-11) and then
moves to Huram's acceptance of the request and finally to some of the
details involved in the operation (vv. 12-15).[15]

For the purposes of this article several aspects of the exchange
between Huram and Solomon are noteworthy. First, Solomon is
described as attempting to persuade Huram to help him build a great
(גדול) house for the name of YHWH (vv. 3-4) by stressing that גדול
אלהינו מכל־האלהים ('our God is greater than all other gods'). This is a
quotation from Exod. 18.11, with the difference that the term 'YHWH'
is replaced with 'our God'. From the point of view of the book of
Chronicles, this change seems to call attention to and reinforce the
message about the incomparability of 'our God' to 'all other gods', by
referring to both with the same noun. Significantly, the text seems
explicitly to exclude Huram as non-Israelite. Solomon's message conveys to him that the incomparable god is 'our [i.e. Israel's] God', not
yours (i.e. Tyre's) god. The fact that the character Solomon is described
as having this belief about YHWH is certainly expected, but this quotation from Solomon's speech already points to his perception of Huram.
After all, he is attempting to persuade Huram (an ally, not a vassal, nor
anyone who may potentially be counted as an Israelite within the world
of the book of Chronicles)[16] to help him in his religious endeavors by

---

14. Chronicles often refers to written texts (e.g., 1 Chron. 4.41; 28.19; 29.29;
2 Chron. 21.12; 30.1; 32.7).

15. For an analysis of the structure of the pericope, see S.J. De Vries, *1 and 2
Chronicles* (FOTL, 11; Grand Rapids: Eerdmans, 1989), pp. 241-42.

16. Solomon does not refer to Huram as a vassal. In Chronicles, Huram's
speech may connote a subjective perspective (i.e. Huram's) that he is not an equal

stating YHWH is (1) our god and not yours; and (2) a god far superior to any divine being, including your own gods. Was the Solomon of Chronicles correct in his understanding of the character of Huram of Chronicles? Huram's response, as we will see, answers that question in the affirmative.

In addition, as far as Solomon's perception of Huram within the world of Chronicles is concerned, it is worth noting that Solomon considers Huram a worthy partner for theological reflection about the reasonability of building a house for one who cannot be contained even by the 'highest heavens'[17] or for reflection about Solomon's own role in the building project (2 Chron. 2.5 MT). Significantly, Solomon is presented as a wise and reliable character in this narrative.

Huram opens his response by stating that Solomon's kingship is the result of an expression of אהבת יהוה את־עמו (YHWH's love of his people; v. 10). It should be stressed already at this point in the discussion that (1) within the world of the book of Chronicles the queen of Sheba, who most likely never read Huram's missive to Solomon, repeated almost verbatim Huram's written words (2 Chron. 9.8); and (2) YHWH's love for Israel is explicitly mentioned only twice in Chronicles. In both instances those who mentioned YHWH's love for Israel are foreign monarchs who speak from their own perspectives.[18] Huram's reference to YHWH's love for Israel explains why Solomon is worthy of building the house for the name of YHWH. It also communicates an important feature in the Tyrian king's perspective: he fully accepts the fact that YHWH has a particular relationship with Israel (and not with Tyre or any other nation). But who is YHWH according to Huram?

After the opening of the letter in v. 10 (just discussed), the narrator reappears and repeats that the speaker is Huram. This 'unnecessary' second intervention of the narrator serves to focus attention on the

---

to Solomon—because of the use of deferential language in vv. 13-14. In a way, it is expected that Huram would see himself inferior (or at a subordinate level from a theological perspective) to Solomon because of Huram's understanding of the relations linking YHWH, Israel and the house for the name of YHWH to be built by Solomon (see below in section three), but this does not mean vassalage. Cf. S. Japhet, *I & II Chronicles: A Commentary* (OTL; Louisville, KY: Westminster/John Knox Press, 1993), pp. 545-46.

17. Cf. Deut. 10.14; 1 Kgs 8.27; 2 Chron. 6.18.

18. Cf. Japhet, *Ideology*, pp. 94-96.

identity of the quotee, his non-Israelite status and his royal position. Yet it is Huram, the king of Tyre, who writes to Solomon ברוך יהוה אלהי ישראל אשר עשה את־השמים ואת־הארץ ('blessed be YHWH, the God of Israel who made heaven and earth'). Thus, the king of Tyre reaffirms (1) the unique status of YHWH, by pointing to creation theology (a point not explicitly advanced by Solomon in his original message); and (2) YHWH's unique relation to Israel. Moreover, Huram's writing style is reminiscent of Pss. 115.15; 121.2; 124.4; 134.3; 146.6.

Huram's reference to Solomon as the expected son of David in v. 11b does not actually follow Solomon's words in vv. 2-9, nor may the knowledge suggested by this reference be derived from them. Huram's words are, however, reminiscent of Nathan's oracle and of David's retelling of that oracle to Solomon (see, in particular, 1 Chron. 17.11-12; 22.10,12; notice that the pair בינה and שכל [NRSV, 'discretion' and 'understanding'] occurs in 1 Chron 22.12 and 2 Chron. 2.11 but nowhere else in Chronicles, or the Hebrew Bible for that matter).[19] Thus Huram is construed in the world of the text as one who is aware of and fully convinced of the validity and worthiness of that oracle, just as an Israelite should have been according to Chronicles.

Although Solomon requires a skilled artisan he does not advance any requirements regarding his 'ethnic' background. Huram, however, cares to provide one whose mother is a Danite[20] and father is a Tyrian. Since, within the world of Chronicles, Huram rules over Tyrians and not Israelites during Solomon's days, he cannot send an Israelite. So he sends a person who is the closest to an Israelite that a Tyrian could be.[21]

The literary (or rhetorical) effect created by Huram's decision (as expressed in this letter) to send a skilled artisan bearing the same name is difficult to miss. This sharing of the name 'Huram' enhances the

19. The references to YHWH's Torah, and to statues and ordinances given by YHWH to Moses in 1 Chron. 22.12-13 are not followed in Huram's speech. The lack of a potential reference, however, is not a solid basis for an argument about the characterization of Huram. Arguments in this article are built upon the *presence* of clear indications of the character of foreign monarchs.

20. Cf. Exod. 35.34, where the artisan Oholiab from the tribe of Dan is mentioned. See below, pp. 224-25.

21. Here the child follows the father's line, because of patrilocality and according to the tendency for wives to be integrated into the household and kin of their husbands. Yet, it must be stressed that had this artisan not been a Tyrian resident, but someone who lived in and among Israel, according to Chronicles, he would have been an Israelite. See Japhet, *Ideology*, pp. 346-50.

association of the king and his representative in Solomon's project.[22] From the viewpoint of the narratee and the rereaders of the book of Chronicles, later references to Huram, the artisan, in 2 Chron. 4.11, 16 likely evoke the image of both the artisan and the person whom he represents.

Huram's speech in vv. 13-14 echoes Exod. 35.31-35, a point made by Japhet in her recent discussion of the verses. She is most likely correct when she proposes that Chr. was influenced by Exod. 31.31-35.[23] But one must keep in mind that the words in vv. 13-14 are presented to the rereader as coming from Huram, and accordingly, they contribute strongly to his characterization. In other words, the rereaders of the book of Chronicles are presented with a king of Tyre whose voice echoes the Torah, or at the very least an authoritative text such as Exodus.

In sum, Huram emerges as a foreign monarch who accepts the Israelite view of YHWH as creator, preeminent above all gods (including the Tyrian gods) and one who 'loves' Israel. He also holds that Israel (as opposed to any other people, include Tyrians) is 'YHWH's people'. Huram is also as fully convinced of a divinely ordained role for Solomon, and is most eager to associate himself with him in the building of a great house for YHWH. Finally, Huram's language also resonates with authoritative (later to be 'biblical') texts extant within the putative world of his day. So Huram presents himself in this pericope as someone who seems aware of these texts, their language and even their status among the Israelites, as well as one who is convinced of their theological validity.

Since in principle the words of a character may or may not be presented as reliable in a narrative,[24] one has to ask whether the narrator (and the intended audience) considered Huram's characterization of himself in this letter to be reliable. The general context of his speech in the book of Chronicles strongly suggests that he was truthful in his letter. If so, he is a foreign monarch whose foreignness is, on the one the hand, stressed (he is the king of Tyre), but at the same time substantially blurred by his speech. His theological viewpoint, thoughts

22. Yet, of course, the king and the artisan cannot be one; Huram the artisan is called חירם in 2 Chron. 4.11 (twice) but חורם אבי in 2 Chron. 2.12 and 4.16.

23. Japhet, *I & II Chronicles*, pp. 544-45.

24. The usual exception is YHWH, whose words (from the viewpoint of the narrator and the original audiences of biblical texts) were considered reliable. See Y. Amit, 'The Glory', pp. 201-12, esp. p. 205.

and language are characteristic of pious Israelites in the world of Chronicles. He is a liminal figure, a Tyrian in whom the worldview and words of a 'pious Israelite theologian' (similar to the implied author of Chronicles) seem to reverberate.[25]

2.2 *The Speech of the Queen of Sheba (2 Chronicles 9.5-8)*

In one of the pericopes of the extended narrative about Solomon in Chronicles, the queen of Sheba is the main character, along with Solomon of course.[26] Yet from the perspective of a general overview of Solomon's narrative, she is a secondary character who comes to the forefront, interacts with Solomon and then disappears as soon as her literary role is fulfilled—namely, once her interaction with Solomon reinforces the characterization of the latter as a great, wise king, and conveys the message that YHWH is the one to whom Israel should be thankful for such a great king. In this case, the narrator allows her to advance her own perspective on the king (this is a typical case of focalization), so as to reinforce the narrator's characterization of Solomon. Her astonishment at Solomon's wisdom, court foods and temple service, as well as the precious presents that she gives to him all serve this purpose.

Yet by acknowledging the supreme wisdom of Solomon, she is characterized too. She stands side by side with the narrator and with any ancient Israelite rereader of the text who accepts the reliability of the narrator or the greatness of Solomon and who associates this greatness with YHWH's blessing over Israel. In fact, the narrator, the queen of Sheba and the rereaders all share a common appreciation of Solomon, his wisdom and the order he created (see v. 4). The fact that the narrator and the original rereadership of the book of Chronicles identify with her evaluation of the Israelite king (and of YHWH) strongly suggests a positive characterization of the queen of Sheba in the text. Additional indicators reinforce this positive characterization. For instance, the words of (such a worthy character as) Huram to Solomon reverberate in her speech (see v. 8). It is not only that both speeches propose a divine role

25. Cf. the sailors in the book of Jonah, who also behave and speak as 'pious Israelites' are expected.

26. On this particular pericope and its co-texts in the book of Chronicles, see (among others) W. Johnstone, *1 & 2 Chronicles. I. 1 Chronicles 1–2 Chronicles 9: Israel's Place among the Nations* (JSOTSup, 253; Sheffield: Sheffield Academic Press, 1997), pp. 368-74.

in the selection of Solomon as king over Israel, but also that these are the only two occasions in which one finds a clear and explicit statement of YHWH's love (אהבה) for Israel in the book of Chronicles. It is also worth noting that, from the perspective of the queen of Sheba, YHWH made Solomon king so that he might execute משפט וצדקה ('justice and righteousness'). Moreover, she also blesses YHWH for establishing Israel for ever (להעמידו עולם, v. 8; cf. 1 Kgs 15.4 and 1 Chron. 17.4). All this taken into account and given that the narrator presents the speech of the queen of Sheba as reliable and truthful,[27] there can be no reasonable doubt that her perspective is affirmed by the narrator and the intended rereadership.

In sum, the queen of Sheba is presented in the same way as Huram: a foreign monarch whose perspective and speech are similar to those of a pious Israelite in the world of Chronicles. Her foreignness is, of course, an essential attribute: she comes from afar, hears in her own country of Solomon's fame (vv. 1, 5) and affirms his legitimacy to that fame as a superior monarch (note her extravagant gifts to him, a feature that carries at least some connotation of hierarchy [v. 9] and their asymmetric exchange of gifts). Yet, just as in the case of Huram, her foreignness is blurred, because her theological viewpoint, thoughts and language are characteristic of pious Israelites in the world of Chronicles. She is another liminal figure, a Shebaite with whom a 'pious Israelite theologian' seems to resonate.

2.3 *Sennacherib's Speech (2 Chronicles 32.10-15)*

Unlike all other foreign monarchs whose words are presented as direct speech in Chronicles, Sennacherib is a villain in the story, and his speech leads to his defeat and death. The speech attributed to him and the narrator's subsequent account in vv. 16-19 reinforce each other and explain what sort of villain Sennacherib is—or better, what stands for villainy. In this case, the main issue is the acceptance and promotion of a theological position that holds YHWH, the god of Israel, to be in the same conceptual category as the gods of other nations (see vv. 14, 17, 19; and contrast, e.g., with the 'conversation' between Huram and Solomon discussed in 2.1). Within the world of Chronicles, such villains do not succeed.

Sennacherib also seems to believe that he and the previous Assyrian

27. If this had not been the case, then her speech would not have served the purpose of expressing the greatness of Solomon.

kings—rather than the Assyrian gods—have achieved victories over (non-Assyrian) gods and will surely overcome YHWH's opposition (because YHWH is just another 'national' god). There is more than a hint of the long ancient Near Eastern tradition of describing the enemy as a hubristic king or a person who challenges the will of the gods and against all reason thinks that they can be successful in their endeavor.[28] Of course, the *topos* is well known, and when readers find it, they have the clear expectation that the offending character will be punished and their endeavor fail. This expectation is fulfilled in the narrative, but it is worth stressing that here Hezekiah and Isaiah have to pray before the villain meets his fate. Thus the issue is not only what stands for villainy, but also how to confront villainy, especially that embodied in a ruler who commands powerful forces.

Sennacherib's address is a typical case of direct speech in the service of the characterization and condemnation of a (negative) character, 'with their own words' as it were. Here direct speech does not lead to the identification of the rereaders with the speaker but is meant to create a strong sense of distance and rejection of the speaker and his perspective.[29] In fact, the strongly ironic (from the perspective of the narrator) speech of Sennacherib elicits an inversion of identification: the intended rereaders are likely to identify with an 'anti-Sennacherib', that is with one who thinks exactly the opposite to Sennacherib.

It is important to note that Sennacherib's speech serves not only to characterize Sennacherib and to shape an 'anti-Sennacherib', but also to characterize Hezekiah in a way similar to that anti-Sennacherib figure. Hezekiah is explicitly presented in Sennacherib's speech as one who (1) trusts in YHWH (and not in his own military power, vv. 10-11); (2) centralizes the cult (vv. 12-13), which is a most positive feature from the viewpoint of the narrator and the intended rereadership of the book of Chronicles; and (3) certainly does not think that YHWH is like other gods (vv. 14-15). Thus Sennacherib's words serve to confirm and reinforce the narrator's explicit characterization of Hezekiah elsewhere in 2 Chronicles 29–32 and to elicit further identification with the character

28. Cf. the characterization of Naram-Sin in the Cuthaean Legend of Naram-Sin and the Curse of Agade (see T. Longman III, *Fictional Akkadian Autobiography* [Winona Lake, IN: Eisenbrauns, 1991], pp. 103-17, 228-31); also B. Oded, *War, Peace and Empire: Justifications for War in Assyrian Royal Inscriptions* (Wiesbaden: L. Reichert Verlag, 1992), pp. 121-24.

29. Cf. Sternberg, 'Proteus in Quotation-Land', pp. 117-19.

of this pious king of Judah, one of the main heroes of the book of Chronicles.[30]

Finally, it is worth noting that although Sennacherib's speech is surely ironic, it is obvious that it is not presented as deceitful from the perspective of the speaker. In this regard, the intended rereadership is provided by a reliable narrator with a trustworthy speech. In fact, this reliability is a necessary condition for the condemnation of Sennacherib, the glorification of Hezekiah and the communication of the theological import of the text.

2.4 Neco's Words to Josiah (2 Chronicles 35.21)

In the case of Neco, the king of Egypt,[31] it is he who admonishes Josiah, the king of Judah, not to oppose God (אלהים). But as the narrator explains in the next verse, Josiah would not listen to the words of Neco, which are now explicitly presented by the reliable narrator of Chronicles as מפי אלהים ('from the mouth of God'; cf. 2 Chron. 36.12 and Jer. 23.16).[32] Thus the narrator not only certifies the reliability of Neco's words, but also characterizes him as a person who (1) conveys God's words, namely, a person who fulfills the role of a prophet, as some kings of Judah did;[33] and (2) is fully aware that the word of God must be obeyed. Further, according to Neco's words—characterized as from the mouth of God—God *is* with Neco. In Chronicles this expression and the status that it conveys are usually associated with pious kings of Judah or Israel (see 1 Chron. 17.2; 22.20; 2 Chron. 1.1; 15.9).

In sum, the foreignness of King Neco is explicitly mentioned (and perhaps subtly connoted by the consistent use of the word אלהים rather

30 'The space that the Chronicler has devoted to Hezekiah's story is one way of affirming that Hezekiah is the greatest Judaean monarch after David and Solomon.' Japhet, *I & II Chronicles*, p. 912.

31. The book of Chronicles consistently avoids the term 'pharaoh', which was certainly known to the intended rereadership and appears many times in DtrH, including 'parallel accounts'. The only instance in which the word 'pharaoh' appears is in reference to a 'daughter of pharaoh', who married and was controlled by Israelites (see 1 Chron. 4.18; 2 Chron. 8.11; MT 2 Chron. 4.18 is often included in English translations within v. 17 [for this transposition, see Johnstone, *1 & 2 Chronicles*, I, p. 63]). On this verse, see also Japhet, *I & II Chronicles*, pp. 114-15.

32. Needless to say, as expected from the literary/theological *topos*, Josiah meets his fate.

33. See Y. Amit, 'The Role of Prophecy and the Prophets in the Teaching of Chronicles', *BethM* 28 (1982/83), pp. 113-33, esp. pp. 121-22 (Hebrew).

than YHWH[34]), but it is also blurred by the narrative, because his role and words are similar to those of a pious Israelite in the world of Chronicles. Significantly, both of the last two 'godly' addresses in Chronicles are placed in the mouths of foreign monarchs: one in that of Neco, king of Egypt, here in 2 Chron. 35.31, and the other in that of Cyrus, king of Persia, in 2 Chron. 36.23.[35] Significantly, Persia and Egypt are the two most important foreign powers from the perspective of Achaemenid Yehud.

2.5 *Cyrus's Edict (2 Chronicles 36. 23)*

The fifth and last instance in which the text presents the perspective of a foreign king by means of direct speech consists of a version of the well-known and much discussed decree of Cyrus.[36] A few observations are in order. First, the figure quoted (Cyrus) is presented as someone who refers to YHWH as 'God of heaven' (אלהי השמים). Although this expression is found nowhere else in the book of Chronicles, it is certain that Achaemenid-period Judahites, with whom one must associate the re-readership for which Chronicles was composed, would have accepted such an identification (see Gen. 24.3, 7; Jonah 1.9; Ezra 1.2 [// 2 Chron.

---

34. Cf. R. Mason, *Preaching the Tradition* (Cambridge: Cambridge University Press, 1990), pp. 117-18. Caution is necessary here, though, because in Chronicles as a whole there seems to be no real semantic difference between אלהים and יהוה. In fact, the former term tends to replace the latter. For a 'classical' discussion of the issue, see Japhet, *Ideology*, pp. 30-37.

35. 'It is, perhaps, surprising that the last two addresses are put in the mouths of foreign kings. However, this one from Neco shows that the Davidic line was not necessarily permanent, while that of Cyrus shows that the real goal of God's purposes was the temple.' Mason, *Preaching the Tradition*, p. 118.

36. Given the focus of this paper on characterization within the world of Chronicles, issues such as the existence and identification of the original source of this decree (to be differentiated from the claim in the text) and its historical reliability (in contemporaneous terms) are not central to the discussion advanced here, unless it is proven that the intended and the actual ancient rereaders of Chronicles reread the book in a mode governed by contemporaneous redaction-critical or historiographical concerns, but this is highly unlikely. For works addressing these concerns see, e.g., E.J. Bickerman, 'The Edict of Cyrus in Ezra 1', in *Studies in Jewish and Christian History* (3 vols.; Leiden: E.J. Brill, 1976), I, pp. 72-108; H.G.M. Williamson, *Ezra, Nehemiah* (WBC, 16; Waco, TX: Word Books, 1985), pp. 3-14; Williamson, *1 & 2 Chronicles*, p. 419; L.L. Grabbe, *Judaism from Cyrus to Hadrian*, I (Minneapolis: Augsburg/Fortress Press, 1991), pp. 32-36, and the bibliography mentioned in these works.

36.23]; Neh. 1.4, 5; 2.4, 20). In addition, the foreign king attributes to YHWH the royal victories over 'all the kingdoms of the earth' (כל־ממלכות הארץ; for the expression, see, e.g., Deut. 28.25; Isa. 23.17; cf. 1 Chron. 29.30; 2 Chron. 17.10; 20.6, 29). This position and the worldview that it suggests are consistent with the sentiment expressed, for instance, in 2 Kgs 19.15 (// Isa. 37.16) and with what the figure of Isaiah—as it was understood by the community of rereaders—would have expected Cyrus (i.e. YHWH's anointed) to acknowledge (see Isa. 45.1-3).[37] In addition, this foreign monarch claims that YHWH has commanded him to build a house for YHWH in Jerusalem (cf. 1 Chron. 22.6; and within the larger discourse of a community of rereaders aware of the book of Isaiah, see Isa. 44.28).

To be sure, Cyrus is explicitly and emphatically presented as a foreigner, as a Persian monarch. His reference to 'Jerusalem, which is in Judah' reinforces this characterization,[38] which is itself, of course, consistent with historical memories. In addition, though, it also serves to shape the figure of the distant king who acknowledges the validity of the theology of the Jerusalemite center. Although Cyrus is unequivocally presented as a non-Judahite, his otherness is consistently blurred, because he understands (1) YHWH as the high god;[39] (2) his good fortune as the result of YHWH's will and (3) that he is supposed to do what YHWH has commanded him to do (which, in fact, he does).[40] As a divinely chosen builder of the temple, his image reflects some of the luster of the glorious reigns of David and Solomon, and in any case, in this role as temple builder, he takes upon himself with the narrator's (and the intended audience's) full approval one of the most important roles ever allocated to the Davidic dynasty.

37. Cf. Bickerman, 'Edict', pp. 80, 95-97.

38. Perhaps the more so, if this wording represents or imitates 'bureaucratic style'. Cf. Bickerman, 'Edict', p. 80.

39. It is also worth noting that whereas Cyrus's choice of words in the parallel text in Ezra 1.3 (אלהיו עמו ויעל מי בכם מכל־עמו יהי), which may be understood as 'anyone of you of all his [YHWH's] people, his god be with him and go up') might suggest a lack of acknowledgment of YHWH as 'the God', the wording in 2 Chron. 36.23 (עמו ויעל מי־בכם מכל־עמו יהוה אלהיו), 'anyone of you of all his [YHWH's] people, may YHWH his god be with him and go up') clearly does not, because this is a blessing formula. On these issues, see Bickerman, 'Edict', pp. 81-82.

40. Cf. the situation in the encounter between Neco and Josiah discussed above in 2.4.

3. *Synthesis and General Conclusions*

Although the instances discussed in this article represent only some of the characterizations of foreign kings in the book of Chronicles, they are important. First, these are the only characterizations of foreign monarchs that are shaped through direct speech. As mentioned above, the direct representation of these biblical characters from their own subjective perspectives and through their own words, thoughts and feelings carries a sense of immediacy to both the narratee and the intended rereadership of the book. Moreover, when the characters are presented as sharing the theological position and ideals of the omniscient and reliable narrator, as *is* the case in four of the five instances discussed above, the presence of direct speech contributes to rereaders' positive identification with the characters and enhances the credibility of the text.

This being so, one may ask about the purpose achieved by these characterizations, and especially so, given that the primary aim of Chronicles (and its narrator) is to convey certain theological messages and to shape a memory of the past that serves to advance them. In other words, one may ask, 'Why would the authorial voice be construed so as to elicit this sense of positive identification and enhanced credibility among the intended rereadership in these particular cases of foreign monarchs?'

One may begin to answer this question by noting that this article clearly shows that in all these instances the quoted speech of the foreign monarch reinforces the rhetorical appeal of the relevant texts. In addition, the speech supports the theological message of the narrator and of the authorial voice.

Given the research goals and parameters of this article, it is worth stressing that all the relevant texts characterize foreign monarchs in a reliable manner, within the world of the book.[41] Once one turns to the main features of these reliable characterizations, it becomes evident that they reflect a tension between (1) a foreignness that is essential to the characters (otherwise they will not be foreign monarchs at all); and (2) a clear tendency to 'Israelize' their subjective viewpoint and to convey a sense of 'sameness' in the human world populated by Israelites and

41. Significantly, all the speeches discussed here are presented as reliable from the perspective of the individual speaker and the narrator of the book of Chronicles.

foreigners. It is not only that these alien monarchs all speak 'typical' Hebrew,[42] but, even more significantly, that their words include allusions to biblical Hebrew texts and expressions—a fact that seems to imply that the quotees were imagined as aware of the latter and of their 'authority' within the Israel of their times. Moreover, four of the five uphold positions (and behaviors) that are expected of 'pious' Israelites.[43]

Of course, a tendency to 'Israelize' or 'appropriate' the foreigner is only to be expected in a book written in Achaemenid Yehud dealing with Israel and Israelite theology that 'contains no reference to the nations in their own right'[44] and was written within and for a Yehudite and mostly Jerusalemite rereadership. Nevertheless, it is clear that such foreign monarchs may be appropriated in positive, negative or neutrally valued ways, and appropriated characters may or may not be assigned important roles in the narrative.

This article has revealed several things. First, four out of five of the aforementioned foreign kings are construed for the rereadership as positive characters and so are unequivocally supported by an authoritative, reliable narrator. Secondly, as often occurs in theological presentations of interaction between 'insiders' and 'outsiders', the value of the latter from the viewpoint of the former depends on the degree to which the other or foreigner resembles the insider. In the cases discussed in this paper, all good foreign monarchs must remain 'foreigners' to some extent, but at the same time, they are 'Israelized' in a substantial manner (see above, section 2). Yet the characterization of these monarchs as (partially) 'Israelized' figures is itself a significant feature. Thirdly, these characters never evolve into stereotypical, flat figures of

---

42. The foreign origin of speakers may be conveyed by the association of their speech with (actual or 'fictional') ethnolects. See, for instance, M. Cheney, *Dust, Wind and Agony: Character, Speech and Genre in Job* (ConBOT, 36; Lund: Almqvist & Wiksell, 1994), pp. 203-75. See also Isa. 21.11-12 and I. Young, 'The Diphthong *ay* in Edomite', *JSS* 37 (1992), pp. 27-30.

43. The exceptional case is that of Sennacherib. Within the world of Chronicles it would have been impossible to present a positive speech by Sennacherib during his siege of Jerusalem in the days of Hezekiah and Isaiah. Yet his speech clearly serves positive goals from the perspective advanced by the narrator (and the authorial voice), as shown above in 2.3.

44. Japhet, *Ideology*, p. 53. Japhet's position about Chronicles' lack of interest in the religious status of the nations should be rephrased, however, if the conclusions of this article are accepted and if 'religion' implies some form of 'theological worldview'.

a 'type' (namely, the 'foreign monarch'). The opposite is true as well: each character develops his or her own clearly distinctive voice and is located in an individual setting (within the world of the book) that is not shared by the other foreign monarchs. Fourthly, although the characters themselves serve supportive roles in the characterization of Israelites (e.g. Solomon) or corroborate the narrator's presentation and point of view, significant roles are allocated to them in the narrative itself and in the explicit communication of theological messages. One may mention, for instance, (1) the only two references in Chronicles to the widely accepted idea in postmonarchic communities that YHWH loves Israel are conveyed by two of these foreign monarchs; (2) the last two godly messages conveyed to Israel or to its proper king are assigned to two kings, each of whom represents one of the two main powers dealing with the Jerusalemite/Yehudite community in the Achaemenid period; and (3) one of these foreign monarchs (the Persian) is directly associated with the building of the temple.

Even if, for the sake of the argument, one were to assert that all the features just summarized are coincidental, resulting from the inclusion of material from diverse written sources in Chronicles and, consequently, that no message was meant to be communicated by Chr., it would still be impossible to maintain this with regard to the implied author (or narrator) of the book of Chronicles (as opposed to Chr.). Moreover, if one accepts that 'the meanings' of a text are negotiated through the interaction of the readers (in this case, rereaders) and the text,[45] then one must accept that 'the meanings' of Chronicles for a community of rereaders in Achaemenid Jerusalem[46] included the con-

---

45. For general theoretical issues associated with these matters, see H. de Berg, 'Reception Theory or Preception Theory?', in S. Tötösy de Zepetnek and I. Sywenky (eds.), *The Systemic and Empirical Approach to Literature and Culture as Theory and Application* (Edmonton: Research Institute for Comparative Literature and Cross-Cultural Studies, University of Alberta; Siegen: Institute for Empirical Literature and Media Research, Siegen University, 1997), pp. 23-30.

46. If 'the meanings' are negotiated between the community of readers and the text, then different communities of readers may arrive at different meanings, i.e., 'meanings' are contingent on historical (in its larger sense) circumstances. See, e.g., L.K. Handy, 'One Problem Involved in Translating to Meaning: An Example of Acknowledging Time and Tradition', *SJOT* 10 (1996), pp. 16-27. If the 'meaning(s)' of a text, or better 'reception texts', which are the only ones that participate in the communicative process, are contingent on historical circumstances, then references to 'the meaning(s)' of the text must be marked in relation to the reading/

struction of a theologically construed world in which the aforementioned characterizations played a role.

If those rereaders identified themselves with that world, as one would expect, then they assumed that foreign monarchs (and by implication, foreigners generally) have at least the potential for piety. From these accounts, the rereadership learns that foreign monarchs (and by implication all people) have at least the potential to acknowledge and recognize the supreme deity of YHWH along with the elevated status of Israel/Judah/Jerusalem vis-à-vis 'the nations' (see the words of Huram and the queen of Sheba, and perhaps those of Cyrus, too)—to be partially Israelized and, accordingly, to be able to play a positive role in YHWH's economy.

These positions are consistent with the views regarding a future in which the nations will come to acknowledge YHWH and the role of Zion/Jerusalem and Israel (cf., e.g., Isa. 2.2-3; Mic. 4.2-3;[47] Zech. 8.21-22).[48] This feature is associated with a hope for a reversal of the present situation of these communities. Moreover, it also reflects a certain need to bring 'the other' to affirm one's position, a feature that is common in literary works that deal with the construction of social identities.

A final observation: the construction of positive images of foreign kings generally and particularly those of Egypt and Persia towards the end of the book, along with the explicit association of the building of the temple with a Persian king (rather than a Davidid) in the last verse of the book, cannot but reflect political perspectives within the postmonarchic community(ies) for which and within which the book of Chronicles was composed. It is worth noting in this regard that within the perspective of such (a) community(ies), the meanings conveyed by the texts discussed here are clearly consistent with the idea that the principal kings of the area are not necessarily evil, nor do they necessar-

---

reception community, from whose perspective the proposed 'meaning(s)' may or may not have validity.

47. On Mic. 4.2-3, see my forthcoming commentary, *Micah* (FOTL; Grand Rapids: Eerdmans).

48. As in other texts reflecting the same views, foreigners are in need of interaction with either YHWH or Israel (or its representatives) or both to bring forward their perspectives. Of course, this is a result of the Israel-centered character of the text, but this fact does not detract from the field of the interaction between the nations/foreigners, Israel and YHWH within the discourse of the postmonarchic Jerusalemite elite.

ily oppose the will of YHWH (i.e. just as Davidic kings varied in their piety). In particular, the concluding reference to Cyrus suggests not only that the rule of foreign kings over Jerusalem is not necessarily a bad thing, but, in fact, it seems to raise the possibility that YHWH's kingship over Jerusalem may be executed by Cyrus.[49] This possibility is consistent with references to Cyrus as YHWH's anointed and as YHWH's shepherd (both royal attributes) in Isa. 44.28; 45.1.[50]

Moreover, these meanings are also consistent with and seem to reflect a particular aspect of the conceptual world of the community. In this respect, a bright future is one in which foreigners will recognize YHWH and the role of Israel in the divine economy.[51] From the theological perspective of the postmonarchic community, this amounts to the partial (but substantial) 'Israelization' of the world, which in turn reflects the broad sweep of the will of YHWH—not that foreign powers be overthrown, but that non-Israelites accept the will and instruction of YHWH (see 2 Chron. 2.10-15; 9.5-8; 35.21; 36.23) and that Israel cooperate with them under those circumstances.[52]

---

49. This is consistent with the tendency among Achaemenid kings to 'adopt the title and status' of some of the local monarchs of the past. See, e.g., C. Tuplin, 'The Administration of the Achaemenid Empire', in I. Carradice (ed.), *Coinage and Administration in the Athenian and Persian Empires* (BAR International Series, 343; Oxford: BAR, 1987), pp. 111-12. The point here, of course, is that this tendency appears in a document that was written within and for a Yehudite/Israelite community of *literati*.

50. Yet it should be stressed that within the discourse of Chronicles, 'worthy' foreign monarchs (whether they rule over their own countries in monarchic times or over an empire that includes postmonarchic Judah) are the only rulers who are presented as substantially Israelized (see characterizations above in section 2).

51. See, in particular, the characterizations of Huram and the queen of Sheba.

52. The observations advanced in the last two paragraphs remind me, for one, of Bickerman's sharp words of more than 30 years ago: 'The whole conception of the Chronicler shows that he wrote when Persian rule seemed destined for eternity and the union between the altar in Jerusalem and the throne in Susa seemed natural and indestructible... Accordingly, the tendency of his work is to recommend a kind of political quietism which should please the court of Susa as well as the High Priest's mansion in Jerusalem... The idea of a Messianic age which was destined to come after the overthrow of the Persian world power, finds no place in the work of the Chronicler' (Bickerman, *From Ezra to the Last of the Maccabees* [New York: Schocken Books, 1962], p. 30). See also my previous 'excursus' in 'A Gateway to the Chronicler's Teaching', *SJOT* 7 (1993), pp. 247-48.

FOREIGNERS, WARFARE AND JUDAHITE IDENTITY IN CHRONICLES

Armin Siedlecki

The historiography of 1 and 2 Chronicles has often been noted for its 'theologizing' tendencies. While both histories of the Hebrew Bible (1 Samuel–2 Kings and 1 Chronicles–Nehemiah) record Judah's and Israel's past within the context of a theological framework, the Chronicler's[1] concerns with the temple, the significance of the levites in Judah's religious system and the idealization of David and the Davidic dynasty indicate that his history elevates the significance of religious practice in Judah over more political elements. This tendency is understandable in light of Judah's position as a province in the late Persian (or possibly early Ptolemaic) empire without political independence. While 1 Samuel–2 Kings views Judah as a politico-religious community within national boundaries, the secondary history understands Judah as an ethnic-religious community without such clearly definable geographic borders.

The question of Judahite identity is necessarily a precarious one in this situation. As Davies puts it:

> ethnicity and cultic affiliation are gradually being merged as the biblical 'Israel' becomes more closely defined ideologically and practically. Here is a society still anxious about its identity, its ethnic boundaries under real or potential threat, perhaps still seeking to define itself around a cult, an ancestor, an ancient promise, a body of law, a single deity.[2]

---

1. The use of the term 'Chronicler' (hereafter, 'Chr.') should not imply that the two books of Chronicles were composed by a single author. Any singular designation of the text's author is merely a conventional referent to indicate that for the purpose of this study, 1–2 Chronicles will be viewed as a textual unit. While source-critical questions are undoubtedly important for a full interpretation of Chronicles, this article will not focus on questions of composition and editing.

2. P.R. Davies, 'Defending the Boundaries of Israel in the Second Temple Period: 2 Chronicles 20 and the Salvation Army', in E.C. Ulrich *et al.* (eds.), *Priests, Prophets and Scribes: Essays on the Formation and Heritage of Second*

One way of thinking about communal identity is to define oneself negatively over against other groups. A Judahite is a Judahite is not an Edomite. In other words, Judah's self-understanding in 1–2 Chronicles is in part reflected in how non-Judahite groups are portrayed. However, since the secondary history is rather parochial in its scope, foreign groups are presented primarily within the context of political or, often, military encounters. This fact is in itself rather striking if one considers the otherwise theologizing tenor of the text. If Chronicles views Judah as a ethnic-religious community, why does Chr.'s work include such a vast amount of political-historical information? Furthermore, religion is rarely the issue in Judah's relations with other groups. Therefore, one must ask, 'Why does Chr. write about political warfare, victories and defeat at a time when Judah had no military autonomy, let alone a functioning army?'

A 'national history' is, by definition, primarily concerned with the events that shaped the nation whose past is being described. Hence, it is only natural to expect that Chr.'s history is almost exclusively focused on the affairs of Israel and Judah.[3] This focus is blurred in instances where Judah's affairs intersect with the actions of other nations. Thus, military encounters between Judah and its neighbors could be seen as a threat to Judah's national identity in and of itself. In other words, the history of Judah ceases to be the exclusive history of Judah at precisely those points where the text is forced to include reports about other nations. It is no surprise, therefore, that Chr. should regard peace as the ultimate divine blessing.[4] Peace allows Judah to be itself, to exist in textual autonomy without the infringement of the other upon its literary self-representation.

On the other hand, if we follow Van Seters in adopting Huizinga's

Temple Judaism in Honour of Joseph Blenkinsopp (JSOTSup, 149; Sheffield: JSOT Press, 1992), p. 54.

3.   While the term 'Israel' is used in an inclusive sense throughout the reigns of David and Solomon, referring to all 12 tribes of Israel, it is often employed in a restricted sense after the split of the northern kingdom under Jeroboam. (On the use of 'Israel' by Chr., see H.G.M. Williamson, *Israel in the Books of Chronicles* [Cambridge: Cambridge University Press, 1977].) Unlike the primary history, Chr. includes the history of the northern kingdom of Israel only in cases where it coincides with the affairs of the kingdom of Judah.

4.   Cf. I. Gabriel, *Friede über Israel: Eine Untersuchung zur Friedenstheologie in Chronik I 10–II 36* (ÖBS, 10; Klosterneuburg: Östereichisches Katholisches Bibelwerk, 1990), pp. 199-204.

definition of history as 'the intellectual form in which a civilization renders account to itself of its past',[5] we must ask whether such an exclusive rendering is possible and sustainable. Literary forms are not isolated structures, and their constitutive components can be effective only if presented in a relational framework. Likewise, the subject Judah can only appear as meaningful in the genre of historiography if it stands in relation to what is not Judah. The text of 1–2 Chronicles thus needs to mediate the implicit tension between Judah's self-representation and Judah's presentation in relation to the other.

In this article I shall attempt to answer some of these questions. What can we say about Judah's relationship to other peoples in Chronicles? What does the portrayal of other nations reveal about Chr.'s concept of Judah as a distinct ethnic-religious community? Is the distinction between Judahites and non-Judahites always clearly defined, or is there ambiguity in the ideological boundaries that delineate and define the people of Judah? What, finally, is the role of warfare in Judah's rela-tionships with other groups? To limit the scope of this project, I shall deal only with Judah's immediate neighbors, Edom, Moab, Ammon, Aram and the Philistines. This choice is primarily motivated by a desire to keep this study at a manageable level, but also by the notion that Judah's identity with regard to the nations is perhaps best explored at the geographical margins of Judah. The approach taken to address these issues will be primarily literary-rhetorical. I shall not attempt to recon-struct historical events on the basis of Chr.'s work. I will, however, take seriously the genre of historiography as the characteristic form of 1–2 Chronicles. In other words, while I shall not attempt to determine 'what actually happened', I shall proceed from the assumption that the books of Chronicles are a genuine presentation of Judah's past as understood from its author's/compiler's position. As such, the text of 1–2 Chronicles reflects the concerns of Chr.'s time and place.[6]

---

5.   J. Van Seters, *In Search of History: Historiography in the Ancient World and the Origins of Biblical History* (New Haven: Yale University Press, 1983), p. 1.

6.   Similarly, J.W. Wright has argued in a recent study ('The Fight for Peace: Narrative and History in the Battle Accounts in Chronicles', in M.P. Graham, K.G. Hoglund and S.L. McKenzie [eds.], *The Chronicler as Historian* [JSOTSup, 238; Sheffield: Sheffield Academic Press, 1997], pp. 150-77) that the battle accounts contained in Chronicles differ in part substantially from the same battle reports in DtrH, but that these divergences generally point towards a more or less coherent, programmatic ideology: 'Battle accounts in Chronicles may provide significant

Some Preliminary Considerations

The second half of the twentieth century has witnessed the greatest displacement of people in recorded history.[7] The removal and relocation of people from their place of birth to a new country has erased many of the imagined (and commonly accepted) boundaries that existed before World War II. Furthermore, the rise of multinational corporations and the expansion of a 'global economy' has created new parameters of signification for the question of national identity. These developments have given rise to much discussion about the inner dynamics of human communities in the post-colonial, postmodern era. This discourse has focused on two primary areas of research: (1) the heterogeneous make-up of larger communities, such as states or nations; and (2) the parameters and boundaries that constitute more-or-less homogeneous subgroups within such larger communities. The latter may be of particular interest to students and scholars in the field of postexilic biblical literature, since the question of identity is generally held to be of crucial importance for the formation and stabilization of the Judahite/ Jewish community during the Persian and Hellenistic periods.

In particular, the anthropologists Frederick Barth[8] and Bernhard Siegel[9] have tried to develop comprehensive theories to deal with ethnic subgroups within larger communities. Their work is primarily concerned with the maintenance of 'boundaries' that distinguish one particular ethnic community from another. One of the conclusions that has emerged from this line of inquiry is the observation that certain forms of social organization or practice are

---

material for understanding the historical/ideological matrix that produced the Maccabean/Hasmonean theology of warfare, texts from Qumran (especially texts such as the War Scroll), and images of war in Jewish apocalyptic literature. This is an entirely different project just beginning to be pursued, yet perhaps is more promising than looking for continuities between Chronicles and pre-exilic history buried in "historical kernels" behind the narrative of Chronicles' (pp. 176-77).

7. Cf. A. Bammer, 'Introduction', in A. Bammer (ed.), *Displacements: Cultural Identities in Question* (Theories of Contemporary Culture, 15; Bloomington: Indiana University Press, 1994), pp. xi-xx (xi).

8. F. Barth, *Ethnic Groups and Boundaries: The Social Organization of Cultural Difference* (Scandinavian University Books; Oslo: Universitetsforlaget, 1969).

9. B. Siegel, 'Defense Structuring and Environmental Stress', *AJS* 76 (1970–71), pp. 11-32.

the result, not of a desperate attempt to cling to pointless and antiquated traditions from a previous era or homeland, but rather a creative construction of a 'culture of resistance' that preserves group solidarity and cultural identity.[10]

A similar argument has been advanced by Mary Douglas,[11] who has suggested that the biblical purity rules should be viewed as positive mechanisms through which a society structures its normative worldview. These theories have contributed immensely to our understanding of the sociological realities behind biblical texts from the Persian or Hellenistic periods. Thus, with regard to Ezra 9–10 Daniel Smith has proposed that Ezra's breaking up of mixed marriages is not nearly as odd as it seems, but that it should be viewed as a basic survival mechanism for the precarious identity of the early postexilic community.[12] Hence, another troubling passage of Scripture has been adequately dealt with, explained on scientific terms, and should therefore no longer trouble us.

Or should it? Since my research focuses on the work of Chr. rather than on Ezra–Nehemiah, I will not speculate whether the postexilic Judahite community really needed such a survival mechanism when they seemed to be surviving just fine before the arrival of Ezra, albeit possibly with a slightly different national ideology than the one envisioned by the Persian-Jewish community. I do, however, want to address the problems inherent in such an approach when it is carried out without adequate attention to the relationships involved in 'boundary maintenance'. To be sure, boundary lines preserve the inner integrity of any entity they circumscribe. By definition they 'include' and 'protect', but they also exclude. Furthermore, by describing the separation between 'within' and 'without' they not only exclude the other, but also define it. In other words, the question of Judahite identity in the Second Temple period must be viewed in a relational framework, since the ideological boundaries described by the literature of the time not only serve to ensure the survival of 'group insiders' but also to define the outside, the other, the very things that are said to threaten the integrity of the inside.

---

10. D.L. Smith, 'The Politics of Ezra: Sociological Indicators of Postexilic Judaean Society', in P.R. Davies (ed.), *Second Temple Studies*. I. *Persian Period* (JSOTSup, 117; Sheffield: JSOT Press, 1991), pp. 73-97 (84).

11. M. Douglas, *Purity and Danger: An Analysis of Concepts of Pollution and Taboo* (New York: Praeger; London: Routledge, 1966).

12. Smith, 'Politics of Ezra', pp. 83-84.

Michel Foucault has coined the term 'heterotopia' to describe a countersite, in which other sites of a particular culture are simultaneously represented, contested and inverted.[13]

> A heterotopia is like the image in a mirror. The mirror is a real place ...
> [b]ut the image in the mirror exists in a sort of virtual space that causes
> the observers simultaneously to see themselves over there where they are
> actually not, and from that vantage point to reconstitute themselves here
> where they actually are.[14]

Thus, the creation and maintenance of ideological boundaries by Chr. implies not only a revulsion at the other, a rejection of what is not Israelite in order to ensure the survival of the group, but also a dependence on the other. Israel/Judah requires the other in order to define its own position as a distinct subgroup within the larger Persian empire.

The Genealogies

The genealogies of 1 Chronicles 1–9 are generally viewed as one of the more tedious parts of the secondary history. These opening chapters lack the didactic elements of wisdom literature or the poetic value of the psalms, and any dynamic narrative elements that might contribute to anything even remotely resembling a plot are kept to an absolute minimum. At first glance, one-third of 1 Chronicles may well appear to have more in common with a phone book than with a literary classic. Nonetheless, even phone books are not without their value. Surely, anyone intending to move a piano would rather turn to the Yellow Pages than to the book of Proverbs. Likewise, we can assume that there is a rather specific purpose for the inclusion of the lengthy genealogies at the beginning of the secondary history—strange as this block of material may appear to the modern Western reader. A story about a dis-

---

13. M. Foucault, *The Order of Things: An Archaeology of the Human Sciences* (repr.; New York: Vintage Books, 1973), p. xviii.

14. F.V. Greifenhagen, 'Egypt in the Symbolic Geography of the Pentateuch', a paper presented at the 1996 meeting of the SBL in New Orleans, 1996, pp. 13-14. An interesting example of heterotopic construction is provided by a world map drawn by Richard Nixon when he was 17 years old, 'on which a solid wall separates Europe from Asia, and on which Vietnam constitutes a prominent peninsula attached to the United States in the place of Florida. From such a map one learns very little about the actual Vietnam, but one learns a lot about Richard Nixon!' (p. 3).

cussion between a Jewish and a Gentile university student related by
Kraft illustrates this point quite well:

> The Gentile asked the Jewish student what his favorite passage of
> Scripture was. His immediate response was, 'The first eight chapters of
> First Chronicles'. These are Hebrew genealogies. From my (Gentile)
> point of view I have often wondered why God allowed so much space in
> his Word to be 'wasted' on such trivia. But to a Hebrew (and to many
> other kinship oriented societies around the world) genealogical lists of
> this nature demonstrate in the deepest way the specificity of God's love
> and concern that lies at the heart of Gospel.[15]

Even though Kraft's choice of the word 'Gospel' to illustrate his
point is perhaps somewhat unfortunate, the little episode does demonstrate quite nicely how genealogical lists can be meaningful to an
ancient as well as to a modern reader. Robert Wilson's study of
genealogies in the Hebrew Bible has demonstrated convincingly that
such lists have indeed a very specific social function. His research has
identified two different types of genealogies: (1) linear genealogies,
which usually aim to underscore the legitimacy of a particular person of
social group (priests, kings, etc.); and (2) segmented genealogies, which
describe the interrelationship of specific groups to each other. Furthermore, Wilson has argued that it is possible for different (and possibly
even conflicting) genealogies to exist side by side, depending on their
intended function.[16] Since the lists of 1 Chronicles transcend the usual
scope of socially significant genealogies, and since they include elements of both linear and segmented genealogies, we should treat them
as complex compositions that signify several socially and theologically
relevant points. The most comprehensive study in this respect has been
produced by Oeming, who has argued that 1 Chronicles 1–9 reflects the
same basic themes that are significant for all of 1–2 Chronicles.[17] He

---

15. C.H. Kraft, *Christianity in Culture: A Study in Dynamic Biblical Theologizing in Cross-Cultural Perspective* (Maryknoll, NY: Orbis Books, 1979), p. 229.

16. R.R. Wilson, 'The Old Testament Genealogies in Recent Research', *JBL* 94
(1975), pp. 169-89.

17. M. Oeming, *Das wahre Israel: Die 'genealogische Vorhalle' 1 Chronik 1–9*
(BWANT, 128; Stuttgart: W. Kohlhammer, 1990). The thematic points outlined by
Oeming (p. 216) are as follows: (1) David ([1.49-54]; 3; 4.30; 7.2; 9.22); (2)
Jerusalem (5.41; 8.28, 31; 9); (3) Temple (4.23; 5.36; 6.16-17, 33-34; 9.10ff); (4)
Levites (6.16, 33ff, 9.18-34); (5) Judah (4.9-10, 27; 5.1, 41); (6) Sin (2.7; 5.18-26;
9.1); (7) the history of the state from its inception to its fall (1.10, 12, 19, 43-54;

suggests that the genealogies do not merely summarize the prehistory of
Israel and Judah before the establishment of the monarchy, and the
temple system before David, but that the lists are a carefully crafted
composition attempting to delineate the true Israel as understood by the
author(s) of 1–2 Chronicles, as organized in concentric circles represented by the following spheres: World–Israel–Jerusalem–Temple.[18]
Thus, the genealogies of Chronicles address the question of identity in a
very immediate way. Since the lists represent a 'mixed style', consisting of linear as well as segmented genealogies, 1 Chronicles 1–9 is
trying to describe the 'origin' of Israel as well as its relation to other
peoples. For the purpose of this article I shall be mainly concerned
about how these two aspects contribute to the separation between
Oeming's first and second circle, between the world and Israel.[19]

Since the list extends back to Adam, the ancestor of all peoples, the
first question to be addressed is, 'At what point in time does Israel
emerge as a genealogical signifier?' Clearly, one cannot speak of Ham
or Japhet as foreigners in relation to Israel before the existence of Israel
as a people. Abraham emerges as a possible candidate for the founding
father of the nation. Certainly in the Pentateuch, Israel's history begins
with the call of Abraham and YHWH's promise that a great nation will
descend from him. Likewise, the Pentateuchal designation 'God of
Abraham, Isaac and Jacob' seems to indicate Abraham's primary position in this regard. The genealogies of Chronicles, however, present a
slightly different picture. Williamson has observed that the genealogies
in Chronicles draw attention to Jacob rather than Abraham. This
becomes obvious if one compares the structure of presentation for
genealogies that precede Jacob with those that follow him. The lists

5.6, 41; 8.6-7; 9.1-2); (8) war reports/territorial expansions (2.22-23; 4.38-43; 5.9-
10, 18-25; 8.6-7, 13); (9) building reports (4.23; 5.36; 6.17; 8.12).

18. Interestingly, the same concentric arrangement is characteristic of the Mish-
nah and provides the structural logic behind many purity rules within the tannaitic
corpus of literature.

19. The term 'Israel' here refers to both Israel and Judah. In this study I shall
follow Williamson's argument (*Israel in the Books of Chronicles*) that 1–
2 Chronicles does not give expression to an anti-Samarian bias, and that the northern kingdom is not considered a foreign nation, even though its separation from
Judah and the Davidic dynasty is certainly condemned. Chronicles thus uses the
term 'Israel' to designate both the northern and the southern kingdom, and my own
use of the term will reflect this inclusive position. Any differences between the two
kingdoms, as well as the military conflicts between them will be addressed later.

before Jacob treat the secondary lines of descent first, before proceeding to the line that eventually gave rise to the people of Israel. Thus, for example, the families of Ishmael (1 Chron. 1.29-31) as well as Abraham's descendants through Keturah (1 Chron. 1.32-33) precede the line of Isaac (1 Chron. 1.34). A switch occurs with the descendants of Jacob. Here, the text inverts the preceding order of placing the secondary lines first and places the most important tribe at the beginning (Judah; 1 Chron. 2.3; 4).[20] In this respect it is also noteworthy that there are no non-Israelite lines of descent represented after Jacob. Any genealogical line after 1 Chronicles 1 is an Israelite line. Hence, it is the figure of Jacob who signifies the emergence of Israel as a people distinct from other peoples.[21]

Where does this leave Jacob himself? He marks the boundary between Israel and the other. His name itself is Israel, and yet, strictly speaking, he cannot be called an Israelite, a בֶּן־יִשְׂרָאֵל. Still, it would be wrong to include Jacob among the foreign nations, since he himself is the common denominator for all Israelite tribes. The person of Jacob may be of central significance for the genealogy of Chronicles, but it is precisely because of this centrality that the figure of Jacob remains a marginal signifier in the line of descent. Representing the demarcation between Israel and the nations, he belongs at the same time to both and to neither. Hence, the most fundamental boundary effected by the genealogies of Chronicles is characterized by an inherent ambiguity and ambivalence, separating Israel from the other, while at the same time connecting the two.

There is yet another element that complicates the emergence of Israel as a distinct nation in the genealogies. Esau is listed alongside Jacob as the son of Isaac. Chronicles makes no attempt to explain why Jacob should be the favored one of the twins, and any narrative elements about Jacob's trickery at the expense of his older brother, as found in

---

20. Cf. H.G.M. Williamson, *1 and 2 Chronicles* (NCB; Grand Rapids: Eerdmans, 1982), pp. 44-45. This inversion is also significant, since it alters the order presented in the book of Genesis. Although Chronicles does not present Judah as Jacob's firstborn, Judah's textual primacy in the genealogies undoubtedly gives expression to his prominence among the tribal ancestors.

21. It is also noteworthy that Jacob is always called 'Israel' in Chronicles. Hence, Israel as a nation has its origin with Israel the person. My use of the name 'Jacob', rather than 'Israel' is for purely practical reasons, in order to avoid confusion between Israel the people and Israel the individual.

the Genesis account, are absent in the secondary history. Still, the text gives expression to the primacy of Jacob by listing the descendants of Esau before proceeding to enumerate the tribes of Israel. As mentioned earlier, the structural shift from presenting the secondary (non- or rather pre-Israelite) lines first to giving textual primacy to the most important (Israelite) lines of descent occurs with Jacob, so that Esau, as Jacob's older brother, should be the last non-Israelite to be contained in Chr.'s genealogy. This is not in itself surprising; it is, however, unusual that the text abandons its otherwise terse, summarizing style to elaborate on the genealogy of Israel's neighbor Edom. The text not only lists the children of Seir (1 Chron. 1.38-42),[22] but even provides the names of the kings who reigned over Edom 'before any king ruled over the Israelites' (1 Chron. 1.43-51a).[23] Esau's/Edom's genealogy then concludes with a list of Edomite clans (1 Chron. 1.51b-53).

This attention to detail with regard to a non-Israelite people is indeed unusual and surprising. Williamson is correct to note that there is no apparent reason for this elaborate inclusion, but that the problem arising from this inclusion is even more acute for those who regard 1 Chron. 1.38-53 as secondary.[24] Ackroyd's suggestion that Chr. is reminding his readers that 'physical descent is not everything, and also that their neighbors are not unrelated to them'[25] is only partially helpful. Why would the author of Chronicles want to caution against the relative value of lines of descent before proceeding to provide another eight chapters of genealogical data? Clearly, such an objection would invalidate the entire genealogical component of the composition. In other

22. J.R. Bartlett has argued compellingly that Seir and Edom were initially distinct groups, the former having its origin west of the Arabah in the highland south of Beer Sheba and the latter being located in southern Transjordan. J.R. Bartlett, 'The Land of Seir and the Brotherhood of Edom', *JTS* 20 (1969), pp. 1-20; cf. also Bartlett, *Edom and the Edomites* (JSOTSup, 77; Sheffield: JSOT Press, 1989). By the time Chronicles had been composed, however, the people of Edom inhabited the region south of Judah, rather than the traditional homeland of the Edomites. In other words, Edom may have simply supplanted the people of Seir during the Persian period (and possibly even somewhat earlier). In any case, it seems clear that Chronicles understands 'Seir' and 'Edom' as synonymous designations for the same people.

23. All translations are mine unless otherwise noted.

24. Williamson, *1 and 2 Chronicles*, p. 44.

25. P.R. Ackroyd, *I & II Chronicles, Ezra, Nehemiah* (TBC; London: SCM Press, 1973), p. 32.

words, if physical descent is not that important, why waste valuable time compiling nine full chapters of genealogies? On the other hand, his suggestion—that the relatively elaborate inclusion of Edom immediately before a complete list of the tribes of Israel may serve to illustrate the relation between Israel and Edom—points to an important function of the genealogy in general. As mentioned earlier, segmented genealogies often serve to illustrate the relationships of particular groups to each other. While this function can be a positive one, specifying the responsibilities or obligations of one group to another, it can also be negative, in that it serves to define the two groups as clearly distinct entities. The concept of relationality is based on the assumption that the two (or more) elements that are to be correlated are, in fact, separate entities. In other words, A can only be related to B if B is not identical to A.

The inclusion of Edom immediately before the list of Israel's tribal genealogies may, therefore, serve to establish a negative correlation between the two peoples. Being an Israelite means (among other things) *not* being an Edomite. Thus, while Esau is presented as Jacob's brother, and as such stands in close genealogical proximity to Israel, Edom also represents the other, the foreign nation, that threatens the identity of Israel. Perhaps Esau's genealogy is described with such relative detail precisely because Edom is more closely related to Israel than any other nation. I shall return to this point later, as it is of particular relevance for several of the narrative portions of Chronicles.

Moving on to the portrayal of other peoples in Chr.'s genealogies, 1 Chron. 4.22 contains a curious reference to some descendants of Judah, '…Jokim and the men of Cozeba, and Joash and Saraph', who had an association with Moab (אשר־בעלו למואב וישבי לחם …). This reference is highly ambiguous in several respects, and the text itself seems to acknowledge its problematic nature by adding the explanation והדברים עתיקים ('now these records are ancient'). In other words, either the ancient records (should they be an authentic source for Chr.) are corrupt, or the author/compiler of the genealogies was himself unsure about how to understand this reference. This appeal to the antiquity of the record is somewhat reminiscent of the notation found in modern Bible translations, 'meaning of Hebrew uncertain'. It is unclear who is, in fact, referred to in this particular notation. Since the governing word (בעלו) is plural, the corresponding subjects could be Saraph and Joash, but it might refer to the men of Cozeba and even Jokim as well. Be that as it may, a more problematic component of the verse is the verb itself. Most commentators have translated it 'ruled over' (Moab),[26] which is certainly a possibility. A somewhat different translation is suggested by the NRSV, which reads 'who married into' (Moab).[27] Semantically, both solutions are possible, and since 1 Chron. 4.22 is the only occurrence of the verb בעל in conjunction with the preposition ל, it is impossible to resolve this ambiguity.

Having established that the subject as well as the denotative significance of the verb of this verse are quite uncertain, it is perhaps not surprising that the object of the sentence is not altogether unproblematic either. The MT reads that the relationship of some of Judah's descendants pertains to Moab and Jashubi-lahem, while most translations follow the Vulgate and Targum in reading 'and returned to Lehem' (i.e. positing a corruption of וישבו to וישבי). The LXX is particularly vague, reading 'they changed (ἀπέστρεψεν) [their names?] to Abederin and Athukiim'. If one accepts that וישבי (MT) represents a corruption of וישבו, one must ask further why these Judahites returned after having married into, or possibly ruled over Moab? Did they marry Moabite women and return to Judah with their foreign wives, or did they gain control of the region of Moab and eventually get driven out by the local population? If one adopts the Greek alternative, one must wonder what might have prompted these Judahites to change their names? Unfortunately, the text simply does not provide enough information to make a conclusive judgment on these matters. Thus, given the ambiguity of all the components listed within this record, it may be best to follow Chr. in his assessment that these records are ancient and not especially helpful in trying to reconstruct the exact relationship between a particular group of Judahites with Moab.

The next reference to Moab in the genealogical portion of Chronicles is perhaps grammatically less problematic, but 1 Chron. 8.8 exhibits the same vagueness and ambiguity regarding Hebrew–Moabite relations. Shaharaim, a descendant of Benjamin is said to have had children

26. So RSV. Cf. also S. Japhet, *1 & 2 Chronicles: A Commentary* (OTL; Louisville, KY: Westminster/John Knox Press, 1993), p. 117, who reads 'mastered'. Williamson, *1 and 2 Chronicles*, p. 61, suggests that בעלו should perhaps be understood as a corruption or even as a regional dialectical form of פעלו 'worked for' (Moab).

27. This translation is reflected in the Targum. The LXX is not helpful in this instance, reading κατῴκησαν 'who settled in' (Moab).

(הוֹלִיד) in the land of Moab after he had sent away his wives Hushim and Baara. It is unclear whether his new wife (Hodesh, v. 9) was, in fact, Moabite or Israelite. The name itself contains no clue and may simply mean 'new' (חדש, although one would expect a feminine form of the adjective). Again, the record is too brief and cursory to allow even for a probable answer to this question. There is no indication as to why he sent away his first two wives, of whom at least Hushim had also born him sons (1 Chron. 8.11), or what Shaharaim was doing in Moab in the first place. Williamson has argued that the reference to Moab betrays the antiquity of the source used by the author/compiler, 'for such conditions, paralleled for instance by 1 Sam. 22.3-4 and Ruth 1, would have been unlikely after Moab regained its independence from Israel'.[28] Japhet goes a bit further and suggests that this brief reference reveals 'an ethnic-sociological reality'.[29] Since Benjamin was a warrior tribe confined to a relatively small territory between Judah and Ephraim, the reference to Moab may indicate the need of some Benjaminites to expand westward into Transjordan. Even though there is no further evidence to substantiate such a reconstruction, Japhet's explanation is at least not implausible. However, expansion into non-Israelite territory not only involves settlement in a new region, but also contact with the local population there. Since the text does not mention any military actions undertaken to claim Moabite land for Benjamin, one may posit that the author/compiler understands Shaharaim's move into Transjordan as a peaceful affair, either through intermarriage with a local Moabite woman or through otherwise amicable relations between the two groups. 1 Chronicles 8.8 thus presents an implicitly positive picture of Moabite–Israelite interactions, even if these relations are not well defined or described.

There are two references to Aram in the genealogical portion of Chronicles, both of which pertain to the region of Gilead. In 1 Chron. 2.23, Aram (together with Geshur) takes a number of villages from Jair, a descendant of both Judah and Manasseh. While the territorial claim on Gilead among the tribes of Israel is, therefore, itself somewhat ambiguous,[30] the mention of a successful Aramean campaign in the

28. Williamson, *1 and 2 Chronicles*, p. 84.
29. Japhet, *1 & 2 Chronicles*, p. 193.
30. Japhet (*1 & 2 Chronicles*, p. 80) has argued convincingly that the ethnic connection between Judah and Manasseh through Hezron (a Judahite) and an unnamed daughter of Machir (a Manasseite) serves the primary function of legitimating a

region serves to underscore the marginal position of Gilead as an ethnic and territorial component of Israel, claimed by Hebrew as well as Aramean groups. This ambiguity is further expressed in 1 Chron. 7.14, which states that Machir was the offspring of Manasseh and his Aramean concubine. The text is essentially neutral in its report of Machir's mixed parentage. There is no implicit condemnation of this interethnic association, as for example in Ezra–Nehemiah (e.g. Neh. 13.23-27). The only conclusion that can be drawn from these two references is that Israel's ethnic and territorial boundaries in northern Transjordan are presented as rather permeable in the genealogies of Chronicles.

Outside the list of the descendants of Esau (1 Chron. 1.38-42) and the list of Edomite kings and clans (1 Chron. 1.43-54), there is only one indirect reference to Edom or rather to Mt Seir in the genealogical portion of Chronicles. 1 Chronicles 4.42 reports that a group of five hundred Simeonites went to Mt Seir, not to battle Edom but to destroy a remnant of the Amalekites. Japhet has argued that we are dealing here not merely with a military expedition, but rather with a massive migration of a Simeonite group into Transjordanian territory.[31] Her attempt to explain the rather high number of Simeonites mentioned here is quite plausible, but her localization of the event east of the Jordan may not be correct. As mentioned earlier, Bartlett has suggested that the original location of Mt Seir was south of Judah in the Negev and that it only later became associated with the territory of Edom in Transjordan.[32] Chr. uses 'Edom' and 'Mt Seir' completely interchangeably but may have understood the territory of the Edomites to be located south-west of the Jordan, which corresponds to the historical location of Edom in the late Persian/early Hellenistic period.[33] In any case, the Simeonites are battling Amalekites rather than Edomites, who are otherwise presented neutrally in 1 Chronicles 1–9.

Before concluding the discussion of the genealogical portion, it should be mentioned that 1 Chron. 2.3 is the only specific reference to

Judahite claim on large parts of Gilead, generally associated with Manasseh.

31. Japhet, *1 & 2 Chronicles*, p. 126.

32. Bartlett, 'The Land of Seir and the Brotherhood of Edom', pp. 1-20.

33. Cf., e.g., D.V. Edelman, 'Edom: A Historical Geography', in D.V. Edelman (ed.), *You Shall Not Abhor an Edomite for He Is your Brother: Edom and Seir in History and Tradition* (Atlanta: Scholars Press, 1995), pp. 1-11.

the land of Canaan or the Canaanites in the two books of Chronicles.[34] Judah's three oldest sons, Er, Onan and Shelah are born to him by a Canaanite woman, the daughter of Shua (בת־שוע הכענית). Although Er is identified as 'evil in the eyes of YHWH' (v. 3), and Judah's line is continued through his daughter-in-law Tamar, most likely also a Canaanite, rather than through the daughter of Shuah, Judah's marriage to a Canaanite woman is not in itself condemned. Moreover, the fact that there are no further references to any interaction between Israelites and Canaanites indicates that the latter did not present much of a problem for Chr. Judah's marriage to a Canaanite woman clearly does not jeopardize the ethnic integrity of the people of Judah, most likely because the Canaanites had vanished from the scene by the time of Chr.

The Reign of David

Chr. idealizes David. His reign and his involvement in the founding of Jerusalem's religious institutions (temple, priesthood, etc.) are presented as paradigms for the perfect Israelite king. David is successful in all of his military undertakings, and any blemishes of his administration reported in 1 Samuel, such as the Bathsheba incident (1 Sam. 11–12) or the revolt and temporary reign of Absalom (1 Sam. 15-18) are simply not included in the secondary history. In short, according to 1 Chronicles, David can do no wrong. Hence, David's relations with non-Israelite peoples might also be seen as expressive of Chr.'s perception of an 'ideal foreign policy'.[35]

The narrative portion of Chronicles opens with Saul's death at the hand of the Philistines. While 1 Samuel speaks at length of the 'Philistine threat' and Saul's inability to deliver the Israelites from the Philistines, Chr. provides no such background information. 1 Chronicles 10.1 merely states that the Philistines were at war with Israel (ופלשתים נלחמו בישראל). This condition remains unresolved for a while, and 1 Chronicles 11 first reports the capture of Jerusalem and provides a list of David's warriors before the Philistines again resurface in the text in

---

34. There are general references in the royal speeches of Chronicles to the nations driven out of the land before the Israelites, but they are never identified by name.

35. For a summary of Chr.'s treatment of David, see S. Japhet, *The Ideology of the Book of Chronicles and its Place in Biblical Thought* (BEATAJ, 9; Bern: Peter Lang, 1989), pp. 467-78.

1 Chron. 12.19. Here a group of Manassites is reported to have joined David's forces earlier when he had come with the Philistines to battle against Saul. This reference presumably relates to David's support of the king of Gath, related by 1 Samuel 27–29 but omitted by the Chronicler, being somewhat of an embarrassment, because it presents the perfect king David in allegiance with non-Israelites against his own people. Thus, the brief note is immediately followed by an explanation that David did not, in fact, help the Philistines fight his compatriots, due to suspicion by the Philistines that he would ultimately support Saul rather than the king of Gath (cf. 1 Sam. 29.4). Williamson notes that this '*caveat* itself was of importance for the Chronicler, because in his presentation for Israel to help Gentiles or be helped by them 'would mean that they themselves were no longer helped by God'.[36] While this observation is true, one must wonder why Chr. included the reference, since he had other problematic episodes from the life of David. Furthermore, since the episode of David's service to the king of Gath is not found in Chronicles, why was this short and cryptic note not left out as well, especially since even Chr. realized that it required some sort of disclaimer. Thus, the Philistines are initially portrayed in an ambivalent light at the beginning of David's reign.

This situation changes somewhat in 1 Chronicles 14. David is now actively battling the Philistines after they have made a raid in the valley of the Rephaim. Two elements in this story are noteworthy: (1) David inquires of YHWH whether he would be victorious against the Philistines (14.10); and (2) after a successful battle David burns the Philistine gods abandoned at Baal-Perazim (14.12). The former is significant in that it gives expression to God's active role in Israelite warfare, which is further underscored in the second battle of David against the Philistines immediately following 1 Chron. 14.8-12, where God even instructs David in military strategy ('surround them and come to them from opposite the balsam trees', 14.14). The second element, David's destruction of the Philistine gods differs from its synoptic parallel in 2 Sam. 5.21, where David and his men simply carry the idols away. Japhet views this discrepancy as an example of midrashic exegesis by Chr., in an attempt to make David's actions conform to the laws of warfare in Deuteronomy.[37]

36. Williamson, *1 and 2 Chronicles*, p. 109.
37. Cf. Japhet, *1 & 2 Chronicles*, p. 289. There has been some debate whether this change was in fact an innovation by Chr., or whether it was already found in

1 Chronicles 14 concludes with the observation that on account of David's victories against the Philistines, his fame went out into all the lands and instilled fear of him in all the nations (v. 17). The story then proceeds with the detailed description of how the ark is installed in Jerusalem (1 Chron. 15–17) before reporting David's military exploits against the Arameans and Ammonites. Again, Chr.'s account differs from 2 Samuel in not including the Bathsheba incident. Hence, the turning point in David's fortunes, which is an essential structural element in the DtrH's portrayal of David, is omitted from Chronicles. The story simply relates the military success of David against the Moabites (1 Chron. 18.2), the Aramean king Hadadezer of Zobah (18.3-8), the Edomites (18.12-13) and the Ammonites (1 Chron. 19), concluding with the capture of Rabbah (1 Chron. 20.1-3; without reporting the death of Uriah the Hittite, who is nonetheless mentioned as one of David's warriors in 1 Chron. 11.41). David's wars are then concluded with one further victory against the Philistines.

Rather than analyzing the details of David's wars, I would like to focus for a moment on the compositional structure of 1 Chronicles 11–20. David's military adventures began with a rather ambivalent portrayal of the Philistines but conclude with the latter's defeat by Israel. David's relationship with the Philistines is highly ambiguous in chs. 11–12, so much so, that the Philistines themselves do not seem to know what to do with David, as they send him away rather than let him fight in their battle against Saul (12.19). Israel's independence is gradually asserted through a number of military victories, first against the Jebusites in Jerusalem (11.4-9) and then against the Philistines in ch. 14, thereby confirming David's (and Israel's) relationship with the Philistines as clearly oppositional. David's military success story continues with victories against the people of Transjordan, the Edomites, Moabites, Ammonites and the Arameans. At the center of these reports is the story of the installation of the ark in Jerusalem, followed by God's covenant with David, which confirms YHWH's support for the house of David. The compositional structure of 1 Chronicles 10–20 can therefore be represented in the following way:

Chr.'s *Vorlage* (cf. esp. W.E. Lemke, 'The Synoptic Problem in the Chronicler's History', *HTR* 58 [1965], pp. 349-63). However, Williamson (*1 and 2 Chronicles*, p. 119) is correct in pointing out that the exact date of origin of this midrashic emendation cannot be determined nor is it of particular relevance for understanding Chr.'s purpose.

A Initial situation: ambivalent relationship with the Philistines (1 Chron. 10)
   B David's wars: capture of Jerusalem (11.4-9), wars with the Philistines
      (14.8-17)
     C Installation of the ark: (chs. 15–16)
     C´ God's covenant with David, David's Prayer (ch. 17)
   B´ David's wars: against the Edomites, Moabites, Ammonites, Arameans
      and the Philistines (18.1–20.8)
A´ Final situation: ark installed, well-defined (oppositional) relationship with
    Israel's neighbors

The war reports thus provide a textual frame for Chr.'s ark narrative, defining not only Israel's geographic borders, but also describing the ideological boundaries of David's kingdom around the central signifier of YHWH's blessing of the Davidic dynasty, the presence of the ark in David's newly established capital city—Jerusalem. In a sense, the story of David's wars constitutes a 'hedge around the ark', keeping the other at bay and distinct from the installation of the ark, the first step in the establishment of the temple cult, which is generally seen as the ideological center of the secondary history. Both form and content of 1 Chronicles 10–20 thus give expression to Chr.'s understanding of Israel's identity with regard to its center as well as its borders.

Nonetheless, even this well-constructed ideological edifice is not without its loose ends. Two elements are of particular significance here: (1) the list of David's warriors (11.26-46); and (2) the obscure identity of Obed-Edom with regard to the ark (13.13-14) and the organization of the temple service (15.18, 21). Since David's wars against the Philistines, Arameans and Ammonites have served to define Israel's identity and relationship to its neighbors, one would expect that Israel's army should not contain foreign mercenaries. There are, however, a number of non-Israelites listed among the mighty men of David, such as Zelek the Ammonite (11.39), Uriah the Hittite (11.41) and Ithmah the Moabite (11.46). Braun has suggested that this list serves to underscore the fact that '*all Israel* was enthusiastic in its support of David's kingship, which was of course according to God's plan ... So God's leaders and those who support them in every age are bound together as one to accomplish his will.'[38] While a 'star-studded list' of mighty men would undoubtedly give expression to a strong base of support for David, the list not only encompasses 'all Israel', but also Ammonites, Hittites and Moabites. In other words, even in its attempt to define itself in

---

38. R.L. Braun, *1 Chronicles* (WBC, 14; Waco, TX: Word Books,1986), p. 162.

contradistinction to other nations through battles and wars, David's Israel includes members of the very nations that Israel engages in war. This is particularly true for the Ammonites (one wonders if David had the same misgivings about Zelek [11.39] before besieging Rabbah that the Philistines had about David before battling Saul), but also for the Moabites, who are listed among the peoples from whom David had carried off gold (i.e. whom he had subdued; 1 Chron. 18.11). Thus, the other is present within Israel, even in Israel's attempt to keep the other at bay. Once again, the boundaries between Israel and the nations are more ambiguous than one might suspect, especially in matters of warfare.

Another element should be mentioned with regard to the list of David's warriors. While the first part of this list (11.26-41a) has its synoptic parallel in 2 Sam. 23.24-39, the latter half (41b-47) is unique to Chronicles. Williamson, who suggests that it is unlikely that the second part is a postexilic fabrication, points out that all the place names in this section that can be identified are located in Transjordan.[39] The historicity of the list will not be addressed at this point, although it may be pointed out that it is unlikely that Chr. would draw up a list that does not otherwise contribute to the development or coherence of the text. It is, however, noteworthy that the list has been included at all, especially since it is missing from the account in 2 Samuel. The place names in Transjordan represent another marginal element in the warrior list, placing the origin of some of David's mighty men in a region that was at the fringe of Israel's territory and that was at times disputed and claimed by other peoples. Certainly at the time of the composition of Chronicles, it is unlikely that any territory east of the Jordan was considered part of Yehud. The inclusion of warriors from Transjordan may, therefore, be an attempt by Chr. to lay a historical claim on such territories. On the other hand, the mention of place names from this marginal region at the same time obscures the clear-cut boundaries between Israel and its neighbors east of the Jordan. The fact that Israelites are listed alongside non-Israelites (Ithmah the Moabite; 11.46) further contributes to this ambiguity.

The second problematic element to be considered here is the mention of Obed-Edom among the levites associated with the installation of the

---

39. Reuben (42), Ashtaroth and Aroer (44), Moab (46) and possibly Mahanaim (46; 'the Mahavite') and Zoba (47; 'the Mezobaite'). Williamson, *1 & 2 Chronicles*, p. 104.

ark and the system of cultic worship set up by David. 1 Chronicles
13.13-14 reports that the ark was kept at the house of Obed-Edom for
three months before being transferred to Jerusalem, and 1 Chronicles 15
includes Obed-Edom among the levites involved in the transportation
of the ark.[40] His name itself (עבד אדם) is perhaps somewhat surprising,
since it is the only personal name to appear in Chronicles that includes
the name of a non-Israelite people (Edom). Taking the first part of the
name as a participial form of עבד*, Obed-Edom could be translated
either as 'servant Edom' or 'servant of Edom'. However, both options
are somewhat puzzling. Why should a levite's name give expression to
Edom's subordination, and whose servant should Edom be (YHWH's,
Israel's, David's, etc.)? Or, why should a levite be called a 'servant of
Edom'? Surely, one of the functions of the levitical gatekeepers is to
keep Edomites away from the sacred precincts, not to serve them. It
seems that the ambivalent relationship between Jacob and Esau from
1 Chronicles 1 (see above, pp. 238-39) is carried over into the narrative
portion of the book and is preserved in the name of one of the temple
servants.

Perhaps even more surprising than Obed-Edom's name is his identification as a Gittite (הגתי; 1 Chron. 13.13), which would make him a
Philistine. This is also the conclusion of Japhet, who admits that such
an identification 'makes his choice rather problematic'.[41] It should be
noted that the Obed-Edom tradition has its synoptic parallel in 2 Sam.
6.10-11. Since Chr.'s version is almost identical to the other account,[42]
one can assume that the inclusion of Obed-Edom is, in fact, based on an
older source, which is simply repeated here. Nonetheless, even Chr.
must have perceived the problematic nature of David's choice, since
Obed-Edom is supplied with a levitical pedigree in 1 Chron. 26.4-8.[43]
This explanation provides additional information, making his role in the
Jerusalem cult somewhat more palatable, but it does not explain his

---

40. Verse 18 lists him as one of the gatekeepers (השערים) and v. 21 associates
him with those who play the lyre.

41. Japhet, *1 & 2 Chronicles*, p. 281.

42. 2 Sam. 6.10 stated that David was not willing to take the ark into his care
(ולא־אבה דוד להסיר...), while 1 Chron. merely notes that David did not take the
ark into his care (ולא־הסיר דויד...).

43. This genealogical supplement, which is lacking in 2 Sam., but which is
accepted by Josephus (*Ant.* 7.4), is generally agreed to be based on Chr.'s own
interpretation (cf. Japhet, *1 & 2 Chronicles*, p. 281).

earlier designation as Gittite. Could he have been a man from Gath, known to David from his earlier service to the king of that city, who was later made an Israelite through some creative genealogical restructuring? The text is ambiguous and open-ended here, leaving the implicit tension unresolved. In any case, Chr.'s attempt to explain this possible inconsistency neither resolves nor conceals this problem, but merely heightens the degree of ambiguity that characterizes Israel's relationship with the Philistines. The presence of Obed-Edom among the levites remains a textual aporia.

The Reign of Solomon

While Chr.'s description of the reign of David contains a fair number of battles and war reports, Solomon's kingship over Israel is characterized as a time of peace and commerce.[44] Hence, Israel's relations with non-Israelites are characterized by economic rather than military factors. The peaceful nature of Solomon's reign is already indicated in David's charge to Solomon to build a temple in Jerusalem, in which David refers to an earlier word of YHWH that his son and successor will be a man of peace (אִישׁ מְנוּחָה; 1 Chron. 22.9): 'His name will be Solomon (שְׁלֹמֹה) and I shall give peace (שָׁלוֹם) and quiet to all Israel in his days.' In other words, Israel's existence as a people is not threatened by the infringement of other peoples upon Israel's territory. The lines of separation are clearly drawn, and there is no dispute about what is Israelite and what is not. The entire people exist, so to speak, in a perfect state.

The political boundaries of this ideal state are described most directly in 2 Chron. 9.26, 'And he ruled over all the kingdoms from the river to the land of the Philistines and to the boundary of Egypt'. The river as the first boundary mark is generally understood to be the Euphrates. Thus Solomon's kingdom basically reflects the territory conquered and held by David (including Edom, Moab, Ammon and Aram). It is perhaps noteworthy that Solomon's domain extends to the land of the Philistines. David is reported to have beaten the Philistines in at least three battles (1 Chron. 14.8-12, 13-16; 20.4-8). Furthermore, the Philistines are listed among the peoples from whom David had carried off silver and gold (1 Chron. 18.11), i.e. had exacted tribute. According to these reports, Philistia should therefore be included in David's king-

---

44. For a summary of Chr.'s treatment of Solomon, see Japhet, *Ideology*, pp. 478-89.

dom, and hence implicitly in Solomon's. However, 2 Chron. 9.26 is a
bit vague on the matter. If the land of the Philistines was indeed part of
his general sphere of authority it would have been sufficient for the text
to state that he ruled all the kingdoms to the boundary of Egypt, as this
would have included the coastal strip of Philistine settlement. The
designation עד־ארץ פלשתים can be taken to mean 'up to and including
the land of the Philistines' or 'stopping short of the land of the
Philistines'. As this verse is the only reference to the Philistines with
regard to Solomon's reign, it may be impossible to settle this question.
Nonetheless, the textual ambiguity may perhaps reinforce the idea
noted earlier that Israel's relationship to the Philistines was not as
clearly defined as one would perhaps initially assume (see above).

Among the kingdoms with which Solomon was conducting his economic ventures, Aram is the only region that falls within the boundaries
of his administration. Solomon is reported to have exported Egyptian
chariots and horses to the kings of the Hittites and the kings of Aram
(2 Chron. 1.17). At the same time, however, he is said to have built
storage facilities in Hamath, well within Aramean territory (2 Chron.
8.4).[45] The two statements appear to contradict each other, since Solomon could not have exported horses to Aram, if Aram fell within his
own administrative jurisdiction. The text offers no attempt to reconcile
the two ideas, thus it is likely that Solomon's building activities in
Hamath represent an ideal within Chr.'s conception of Solomon's reign,
while his trade with the Aramean kings (and the implicit recognition of
their political independence from Israel) may reflect the historical
reality.

None of the other nations subdued by David are identified as trading
partners of Israel. Edom is mentioned only once in relation to
Solomon's maritime ventures in the Red Sea: 'Then Solomon went to
Ezion-Geber and to Eloth on the sea-coast in the land of Edom'
(2 Chron. 8.17). The economic nature of Solomon's presence in these
two towns indicates quite clearly that the scenario described here does
not entail a military conflict with the Edomites. Ezion-Geber and Eloth
(Elath) provided access to the sea and, hence, to maritime transports.

---

45. The same verse mentions that Solomon built Tadmor in the wilderness. This
reference may be a scribal error, since the synoptic parallel in 1 Kgs 9.18 reads
'Tamar' instead of 'Tadmor' (modern Palmyra). On the other hand, it is possible
that Chr. did have Tadmor in mind in order to emphasize that Solomon's authority
extended well into Aramean territory.

Solomon was able to utilize this access, because the land of Edom, according to Chr.'s conception, was within the boundaries of his kingdom.

Among the regions not included in David's/Solomon's empire, Phoenicia seems to have special status. As is the case in 1 Kings, Chronicles portrays Huram of Tyre (Hiram in 1 Kgs) as the chief architect of Solomon's temple and as one of his primary economic associates. Besides Tyre, Egypt and Kue are identified as major trading partners and exporters of horses to Israel (2 Chron. 1.14-17). This account is almost identical to 1 Kgs 10.26-29 and seems to reflect a long-standing tradition about Solomon's commercial activities with Egypt. The same is true for Solomon's marriage to an Egyptian Pharaoh's daughter, which contributes to the impression that Solomon was indeed a 'major player' in international politics. Although this marital alliance is mentioned four times in 1 Kings (3.1; 7.8; 9.16; 11.1), it occurs only once in Chronicles: 2 Chron. 8.11, which describes the housing arrangement made for Pharaoh's daughter.

> And Solomon brought up the daughter of Pharaoh from the city of David to the house which he had built for her, for he said: 'My wife shall not live in the house of David, king of Israel, for the places to which the ark of YHWH has come are holy.'

This explanation, which is not found in 1 Kings seems to confirm the idea that foreigners are to be kept away from the ark of the covenant, already noted above in relation to David's wars with the nations surrounding Israel.[46] On the other hand, Dillard and Japhet have argued that the decisive issue in this verse is not the fact that Solomon's wife is a foreigner, but rather her identity as a woman.[47] Dillard bases his reading on the phrase 'no wife of mine' (לי אשה...לא), which emphasizes gender rather than ethnic background. Unfortunately, the text provides no other examples as to what arrangements Solomon made for any of his other wives. Japhet admits as much and points out that although the idea that women should be kept apart from the ark is not expressed elsewhere in the Bible, 'a similar concept is found in the instructions of the sectarian (Essene) literature of which this verse may

---

46. This verse is somewhat problematic, since the house of David is never associated with the tent of the ark. The LXX offers a slightly different version, reading 'city of David' (ἐν πόλει Δαυιδ) rather than 'house of David'.

47. R.B. Dillard, *2 Chronicles* (WBC, 15; Waco, TX: Word Books, 1987), p. 65; Japhet, *1 & 2 Chronicles*, p. 626.

be regarded as an early precursor'.[48] While this suggestion is provoca-
tive, it is not altogether convincing, since it is highly conjectural that
this verse may have served as an inspiration to the community of
Qumran several centuries later. Thus, while we have no biblical
evidence to support the idea that gender rather than ethnicity was the
main issue in 2 Chron. 8.11, there are examples that foreigners are to be
kept apart from what has been consecrated to God, both in Chronicles
(see above) and elsewhere in the Bible (cf. Ezek. 44.9). Furthermore,
the account in 1 Kgs 11.1-8, which speaks of Solomon being led astray
by his foreign wives, clearly blames the king's apostasy on the fact that
his wives were foreigners, rather than on the fact that they were women.
Thus, even though Egypt is generally portrayed in Chronicles as being
on good terms with Israel, the removal of Solomon's Egyptian wife
may have more to do with her being a foreigner than with her gender.

There are two passages in Chronicles dealing with Solomon's treatment of non-Israelites living within the boundaries of his kingdom: the
census of aliens living in Solomon's kingdom, and the conscription of
local non-Israelites for forced labor:

> And Solomon counted all the men who were sojourning in the land of
> Israel, after the census that his father David had taken, and he found
> 153,600. He assigned 70,000 of them as laborers, 80,000 as stone cutters
> in the hill country, and 3,600 as overseers to put the people to work.
> (2 Chron. 2.16-17)

> All the people who were left of the Hittites, the Amorites, the Perizites,
> the Hivites and the Jebusites who were not of Israel, from their descen-
> dants, who were left after them, whom the Israelites had not completely
> destroyed, these Solomon conscripted for forced labor until this day. But
> of the people of Israel, Solomon did not take any as servants for his
> work. (2 Chron. 8.7-9a)

Both passages affirm that there are, in fact, non-Israelites living within
the borders of Israel, but that they are clearly separated from the people
of Israel on account of their economic function. Although the first passage does not list the national origin of the aliens sojourning in Israel, it
is unlikely that the text is referring to those people who had been conquered earlier by David. Since both passages mention organized, forced
labor, the unidentified sojourners are probably the same group that is
identified in the second passage in a classic deuteronomistic list of the
indigenous inhabitants of the promised land. Both passages have their

48.   Japhet, *1 & 2 Chronicles*, p. 626.

synoptic parallels in 1 Kings,[49] although there are a few minor differences in both cases. 2 Chronicles 8.8 reports that the Israelites 'did not completely destroy (לא־כלום)' the local population, while 1 Kgs 9.21 specifies that 'they *could* not exterminate' (לא־יכלו...להחרימם)' the populace, thereby avoiding the potentially embarrassing implication that Israel's enemies were in fact stronger than Chr.'s own people.

The second difference between the two accounts is perhaps more significant. Chronicles omits the reference in 1 Kgs 9.13 to the fact that Solomon conscripted forced labor out of all Israel. This reference in 1 Kings is in direct conflict with 1 Kgs 9.22, which states (as in 2 Chron. 8.9a) that Solomon did not use Israelites as servants. This tension is not present in Chr.'s account. Here the economic distinction between Israelites and non-Israelites appears quite simple: all 153,600 non-Israelites living in the land are subjugated to forced labor, while no Israelite is employed in such a function. Thus, Chronicles has again harmonized and idealized the account found in 1 Kings.

Israel's relations with its neighbors during the time of Solomon are presented as relatively unproblematic in Chronicles. There are no battle reports, and the land enjoyed peace and quiet, along with economic prosperity. Solomon's non-Israelite trading partners are primarily Phoenicia and Egypt (along with Kue), that is, nations whose territory is not disputed or claimed by Israel. An exception occurs in the case of the kings of Aram, to whom Solomon exports Egyptian horses. Likewise, Israel's border with Philistia is somewhat unclear in Chr.'s account. Besides these two uncertainties, the ideological boundaries between Israelites and non-Israelites are clearly defined (and in some cases harmonized) by Chr. Israel's relationship to the other is characterized by superiority, not in the military sense, as was the case during the time of David, but rather in socio-economic terms. Hence, peace and prosperity go hand-in-hand during Solomon's reign.

The Divided Kingdom

Israel's history after the reign of Solomon is, properly speaking, the history of Judah. After the separation of the ten northern tribes from Judah and Benjamin under Jeroboam, the northern kingdom is only mentioned in instances where its history coincides with that of the kingdom of Judah. Until relatively recently, this exclusion has led most

49. 2 Chron. 2.16-17 // 1 Kgs 5.13-18; 2 Chron. 8.7-9a // 1 Kgs 9.20-21.

scholars to suppose that the history of Chr. is characterized by a strong anti-northern polemic. The common consensus was that for Chr., the only true Israel was Judah, not the northern kingdom. The books of Chronicles were, therefore, primarily construed as propaganda against the postexilic Samaritan community in the North.[50] The scope of this article does not permit a thorough investigation of this question. Suffice it to say, that this view has since been called into question, especially since Williamson's study of the use of the term 'Israel' by Chr., in which he has compellingly argued that, while Chronicles considers the northern kingdom to be in apostasy after the rebellion of Jeroboam, the ten northern tribes are, nonetheless, considered part of the people of Israel.[51] In other words, while the Davidic king in Judah constitutes the true ruler over Israel, the people of the northern kingdom are not seen as foreigners, but rather as fellow Israelites, ruled by an illegitimate government.

Nonetheless, the separation of the two kingdoms raises a number of problematic issues. While the genealogies as well as the respective reigns of David and Solomon represent Israel as a people consisting of 12 tribes rather than two, the existence of two separate royal administrations indicates that we are, in fact, dealing with distinct political entities. Furthermore, the fact that Judah and Israel face each other as opponents in war on more than one occasion (cf., e.g., 2 Chron. 13.13-22; 25.17-24) seems to confirm this separation. Thus, the relationship between Judah and the northern kingdom is characterized by a high degree of ambiguity. While the North is considered Israelite, it is at the same time also located outside the ideological boundaries of Israel as understood by Chr. In other words, Judah and Israel are both similar and dissimilar. This tension is perhaps at work even in the question of whether Chronicles is characterized by an anti-northern polemic. Even von Rad, who otherwise argues that the North is excluded from the true

---

50. Cf., e.g., W. Rudolph, *Chronikbücher* (HAT, 21; Tübingen: J.C.B. Mohr [Paul Siebeck], 1955); M. Noth, *Überlieferungsgeschichtliche Studien: Die sammelnden und bearbeitenden Geschichtswerke im Alten Testament* (Tübingen: Max Niemeyer, 2nd edn, 1957). This view was based primarily on two considerations, (1) the common authorship of Chronicles and Ezra–Nehemiah; (2) a date of composition within the Hellenistic period, i.e. following the establishment of the Samaritan sanctuary at Mt Gerizim. Both presuppositions have been challenged by Williamson (*Israel in the Books of Chronicles*) and S. Japhet (*Ideology*).

51. Williamson, *Israel in the Books of Chronicles*.

Israel, admits,[52] in light of Abijah's speech to the people of Israel, that the northerners constitute a *Brudervolk* with respect to Judah.[53]

Von Rad's use of the term *Brudervolk* is interesting, since it captures some of the ambivalence of the relationship between North and South. Of course, in the genealogies of Chronicles 1–9 another brother of Israel is mentioned, namely Esau, the ancestor of the Edomites. The consanguinity between Israel and Esau does not, however, prevent antagonism between the two brothers. Thus, while Esau is portrayed in a neutral fashion in the genealogies, his descendants, the Edomites, are the recipients of some of the most severe violence by the people of Judah (cf. esp. 2 Chron. 25; see below). Likewise, the northern kingdom serves as a 'brother' to Judah, being closely related and dissimilar at the same time. It is, so to speak, the result of Israel's self-alienation, having its origin inside Israel, while also belonging to the realm of the other. The resulting tension—between Chr.'s desire to incorporate the northern kingdom in its inclusive understanding of Israel and to define Judah as the legitimate kingdom governed by the house of David—characterizes the portrayal of the North in Chronicles and the puzzlement of modern scholars wrestling with this ambivalent portrayal.

With the separation of the ten northern tribes from the southern kingdom, Israel becomes Judah's 'monstrous double' to use Girardian terminology, and as is often the case with the 'monstrous double', violence serves as a mediating mechanism, expelling the double fully into the realm of the other, thereby preserving the integrity of the community.[54] This mechanism is perhaps best captured in Abijah's speech to and subsequent battle against the North. As king of Judah, Abijah addresses 'Jeroboam and all Israel' (2 Chron. 13.4), pointing out the illegitimate nature of Jeroboam's government, culminating in the appeal: 'Children of Israel, do not wage war against YHWH, the God of your ancestors, for you shall not prevail' (2 Chron. 13.12b). Abijah considers the rebellion of the North a direct attack on YHWH, who is nonetheless identified as the God, not only of Judah, but also of the rebellious northerners themselves (אלהי־אבתיכם). Appropriately, it is also YHWH who defeats the northern kingdom in the battle that follows

52. Japhet calls it 'changing horses in midstream' (*Ideology*, p. 323).

53. G. von Rad, *Das Geschichtsbild des chronistischen Werkes* (BWANT, 54; Stuttgart: W. Kohlhammer, 1930), p. 33.

54. R. Girard, *Violence and the Sacred* (Baltimore: The Johns Hopkins University Press, 1977).

Abijah's speech: 'And God defeated Jeroboam and all Israel before Abijah and Judah' (2 Chron. 13.15). The tension appears resolved, at least for the time being. Israel and Judah are distinct entities in 2 Chron. 13.15, both grammatically and ideologically. Hence, it is through the battle itself that Israel ceases to be Judah's 'monstrous double' and is expelled from the community.

It is interesting to note that 1 Kgs 15.1-8, which deals with the reign of Abijah (Abijam in 1 Kgs) in Judah, does not report this victory over the North. Regarding any military conflicts between the two kingdoms, the text is content to observe that 'there was war between Abijah and Jeroboam' (1 Kgs 15.7). Thus, while the text of 1 Kings is willing to let the tension between the two kingdoms persist, Chr. attempts to resolve Judah's identity crisis. Of course, the problem is not resolved once and for all, since the northern kingdom persists as a separate political entity. Furthermore, in Chr.'s account, the towns taken by Abijah in the aftermath of the battle (Bethel, Ephron [Ophrah] and Jeshanah; 2 Chron. 13.19) are not deep inside the territory of the northern kingdom but in the Bethel hills, between Benjamin and Ephraim. Japhet remarks that '[r]ather than a full scale war, aiming to return the Israelites to obedience to Davidic rule, v. 19 describes the occupation of limited Benjaminite territory on the border of Ephraim'.[55] Thus, the primary issue seems to be the definition of the boundary rather than conquest, expulsion of the other rather than its incorporation.

Turning to the portrayal of non-Israelite peoples during the time of the divided monarchy, Judah's relationship with its immediate neighbors is significantly more complicated than it was during the time of David and Solomon. Most significant here is the fact that Judah is not always victorious in battle. Daniel Gard has shown convincingly that Judah's military success is directly dependent on the ruling king's fidelity to YHWH and to the Jerusalem cult.[56] Thus, for example, Jotham, who is judged positively by Chr. (ויעש הישר בעיני יהוה ['and he did what was right in the eyes of YHWH']; 2 Chron. 27.2), is victorious against the Ammonites, while Ahaziah, who is judged negatively (ויעש הרע בעיני יהוה ['and he did what was evil in the eyes of YHWH']; 2 Chron. 22.4), is defeated by the Arameans. Furthermore, all kings who receive a negative evaluation are, in fact, punished with military

55. Japhet, *1 & 2 Chronicles*, p. 697.
56. D.L. Gard, 'Warfare in Chronicles' (PhD dissertation, University of Notre Dame, 1991), pp. 323-31.

defeat.[57] Thus, peace and/or military victory on the one hand, and war and defeat on the other, are clearly shown to be the means of divine retribution for Judah's government within Chr.'s understanding of history. A similar conclusion was reached by Gabriel, who had argued that the absence of war is seen as the ultimate divine blessing in the book of Chronicles.[58] This conclusion is congruent with Gard's analysis as well as with my earlier observations about the reign of Solomon. Ruffing has gone further and argued that Chr.'s understanding of history comprises a theologized understanding of war, in which battle reports serve the primary function of encouraging fidelity to and dependence on YHWH alone:

> war is a situation of extreme danger, in which the people of Yahweh are completely at the mercy of the enemy's military potential. At the same time, however, war is a situation in which Yahweh is accessible to his people in a particular way through his saving intercession.[59]

The studies by Gard, Gabriel and Ruffing have contributed immensely to our understanding of the perception of warfare in general in the book of Chronicles. Given Chr.'s theologizing tendency, the idea that peace or military success and failure are directly tied to the religious faithfulness of Judah's king to YHWH and to YHWH's cult should come as no surprise. The other is kept at bay only as long as the monarch, as the center of society, remains loyal to Judah's god, the guarantor of both peace and victory and the ultimate religious signifier of Judah's identity. However, while these studies have focused in depth on the ideological center of Chr.'s view of history, they have yet to consider the boundaries, the impact of warfare on the identity of Judah as a people. Since the idea of divine retribution through military success or failure gives expression to an interrelationship between the theological center of society and its boundaries (which are either preserved or threatened), a study of warfare in Chronicles should not only consider

57. For a convenient listing of Judah's kings, their evaluation by Chr. and their military activities, see Gard, 'Warfare in Chronicles', pp. 329-31.

58. See Gabriel's summary in *Friede über Israel*, pp. 199-204.

59. '...ist der Krieg jeweils Ort extremer Gefährdung, ein Ort, an dem das Jahwevolk völlig hilflos der gewaltigen militärischen Potenz der feindlichen Mächte ausgeliefert ist. Zugleich jedoch ist der Krieg der Ort, an dem Jahwe in besonderer Weise durch sein rettendes Eingreifen für sein Volk erfahrbar wird.' A. Ruffing, *Jahwekrieg als Weltmetapher: Studien zu Jahwekriegstexten des chronistischen Sondergutes* (SBB, 24; Stuttgart: Katholisches Bibelwerk, 1992), p. 362.

the causal relationship between the behavior of Judah's king and his military performance, but also the implications of the infringement of foreigners on Judah's borders. In other words, while Chr.'s war reports affirm the need to remain faithful to YHWH, at the same time they preserve stories about specific battles in which Judahites fought a non-Israelite people. The intention of these reports may be of a theological nature, but the stories of battles against specific enemies also contribute to the national consciousness of the intended readers of the text. Thus, while Gabriel's conclusion that YHWH acts as an all-powerful defender of Israel against the nations is indeed insightful, the remark that 'the nations (*Völkerwelt*) as such are of no interest [to Chr.]' does not capture the complexity of the problem of war in Chronicles.[60]

A recent study by Knoppers has taken a closer look at the depiction of Judah's alliances with foreign nations and with the northern kingdom of Israel.[61] Analyzing Asa's treaty with Ben-hadad and Ahaz's treaty with Tiglath-pileser, he concludes that both alliances are criticized by Chr. and that in both cases Judah's national security is threatened rather than preserved. The case of Asa is particularly interesting, since his reign is initially judged favorably in Chronicles (2 Chron. 14–15), as is indicated by the phrase 'his heart was true (שלם) all his days' (15.17) and by the fact that there are no war reports for the first 35 years of Asa's reign ('and there was no war until the thirty-fifth year of the reign of Asa'; 15.19). The turning point occurs when Asa enters into an alliance with the Arameans, which is openly condemned by the prophet Hanani (16.7-9). He announces that as a result of Asa's foreign policy he will henceforth be plagued by constant wars (מעתה יש עמך מלחמות; 16.9). The synoptic account in 1 Kings 15, however, states that 'there was war between Asa and King Baasha of Israel all their days' (v. 16), even before Asa enters into alliance with Ben-hadad. Chr. has thus inverted the causal relationship between the threat of war and Asa's foreign alliance.[62] The treaty with Ben-hadad thus had the exact opposite effect of what it was designed to achieve. Rather than securing the borders of Judah, Judah's national security is now continually threatened.

Turning to Judah's alliances with the northern kingdom of Israel,

60. Gabriel, *Friede über Israel*, p. 202.

61. G.N. Knoppers, ' "Yhwh Is Not with Israel": Alliances as a *Topos* in Chronicles', *CBQ* 58 (1996), pp. 601-26.

62. Knoppers, 'Yhwh Is Not with Israel', p. 608.

Knoppers remarks that such pacts are viewed as negatively by Chr. as any treaties with non-Israelites. Knoppers addresses the joint expedition of Ahab and Jehoshaphat to Ramoth-Gilead (2 Chron. 18), the naval alliance of Jehoshaphat and Ahaziah (2 Chron. 20.35-37), and the story of Amaziah and the Ephraimite mercenaries (2 Chron. 25). All three of these accounts are met with prophetic rebuke. Jehu, the son of Hanani, condemns Jehoshaphat for 'helping the wicked and loving those who hate YHWH' (19.2), and the prophet Eliezer announces that YHWH would thwart the royal plan to go to Tarshish, because Jehoshaphat had joined forces with Ahaziah of Israel. Amaziah is criticized by an unnamed man of God for relying on the military strength of the northern kingdom rather than on YHWH (25.7-8).[63] Furthermore, all three joint ventures result in failure. The battle at Ramoth-Gilead proves to be disastrous for the Judahite–Israelite coalition and Ahab of Israel is killed (18.28-34); the fleet built by Jehoshaphat and Ahaziah is shipwrecked at Ezion-Geber; and the mercenaries dismissed by Amaziah after the prophetic rebuke return to Judah with a vengeance, defeating the army of the southern kingdom (2 Chron. 25.17-24).

While all these examples demonstrate that Chr. does not place faith in numbers and that it is faith in YHWH—rather than military strength through political alliances—that is decisive in Judah's wars, they also show that alliances per se are a threat to Judah's national integrity. As Knoppers rightly points out, 'For Judah to enter a pact with Israel would violate the norms of its own existence'.[64] Hence, the fidelity to Judah's national god emphasized by Gard, Gabriel and Ruffing is not only based on theological considerations but also on the idea that foreign alliances (even alliances with the northern kingdom) are in themselves a threat to the identity of Judah. Joint ventures with other kings could not possibly strengthen Judah's power, since such pacts blur the ideological boundaries that describe and define the people of Judah. The results are always the same, failure and military defeat—an infringement on political borders of the kingdom.

This notion also holds true even for foreign alliances that attack Judah. 2 Chronicles 20.1-23 tells the story of an invasion by the combined forces of the Moabites, Ammonites and the people of Seir.

---

63. The defeat of Amaziah by the Ephraimites is, however, primarily based on the king's apostasy of worshiping the gods of the Edomites, whom he had just defeated (25.5-16). This story is analyzed below (pp. 264-65) in more detail.

64. Knoppers, 'Yhwh Is Not with Israel', p. 612.

Besides these, the exact composition of the anti-Judean coalition is somewhat uncertain. The MT lists the Ammonites twice in 20.1 (once as בני עמון, and once as העמונים), while the LXX reads Μιναίων for the second occurrence. Most Bible translations follow the Greek version in this case and read 'Meunites', rather than 'Ammonites' as the third party in this coalition.[65] However, the Meunites are not mentioned in the text after this initial introduction. Instead, the coalition is elsewhere said to consist of Ammonites, Moabites and Edomites (20.22-23). The enemy's identity is therefore somewhat uncertain from the very beginning. Furthermore, the text is not clear about the coalition's point of origin. The MT as well as the LXX has them marching from Aram, which is not possible, since this identification is immediately followed by the remark that 'they are already at Hazazon-Tamar (En-Gedi)'. If the enemy was attacking from the North, En-Gedi would not be en route to Jerusalem. Hence, most modern translations follow the Vulgate in reading 'Edom', rather than 'Aram'. This emendation is congruent with the identification of Mt Seir as the third coalition partner, but the reliability of the Latin version for this reading is questionable.

The story has no parallel in 2 Kings, which gives a much briefer account of the reign of Jehoshaphat in general. The victory of Judah over this coalition is overwhelming, so much so that the text concludes: And the fear of YHWH came over all the kingdoms of the countries when they heard that YHWH had battled with the enemies of Israel. And the realm of Jehoshaphat was quiet, and his God gave him rest all around (2 Chron. 20.29-30).

The theological overtones of this battle are obvious. It was YHWH who had defeated the enemies of Jehoshaphat. In fact, the text does not actually report any military activity by Jehoshaphat and his army, but is rather characterized by liturgical performances (praying, singing, etc.), followed by YHWH's intervention and the enemies' destruction of each other:

> As they began to sing and praise, YHWH made an ambush against the Ammonites, Moab and Mount Seir, who had come out against Judah and they were routed. For the Ammonites and Moab attacked Mt Seir, so as to annihilate and destroy them completely. And when they had finished off the people of Seir, they all helped to destroy each other. (2 Chron. 20.22-23)

---

65. The Meunites were an Arab people, located at the southern border of Judah. Cf. Williamson, *1 and 2 Chronicles*, pp. 293-94.

Davies succinctly summarizes the moral of the story:

> If your cause is just and you are faithful to your deity (and if that deity is YHWH), you will not need an army to protect you. Spend your defense budget on hymnbooks and musical training for your brass band! The only army you need is a Salvation Army.[66]

This theological point is not disputed, but Davies rightly points out that there is a more fundamental issue at stake here, pertaining not only to religious belief, but also to political and ideological questions regarding territories and boundaries. He notes that if we accept that the anti-Judean coalition consisted of Ammonites, Moabites and Edomites, the text of 2 Chronicles 20 presents us with an interesting intertextual dilemma, since these three peoples, according to Deuteronomy 2, are said to have been given their territory by YHWH.

> Of course, Jehoshaphat makes it clear that the gift to Israel is superior, and it is Israel who are the true chosen descendants of Abraham—by virtue (v. 8) of their having not only occupied the land of Israel, but also having built the sanctuary, on the basis of which they will be saved by YHWH from their enemies![67]

Davies' conclusion is intriguing and would fit well the idea that the battle reports in Chronicles not only make a theological point but also a political-historical one, dealing with questions of communal identity in juxtaposition with other ethnic or national groups. There are, however, a number of textual uncertainties requiring the reader to accept that we are, in fact, dealing with Edomites rather than Meunites as discussed, which make it difficult to accept Davies's point as more than a suggested reading. On the other hand, the same textual uncertainties may reveal another important point to the story. Judah's coalitions are by definition unholy, since they blur the ideological boundaries that separate the people of Judah from other nations (cf. above pp. 258-59. However, the same principle may also apply to coalitions formed by other peoples. Hence, the precarious nature of the anti-Judean coalition in 2 Chronicles 20 is already expressed through the ambiguous identification of its members. It is not clear exactly who belongs to the enemy army or, for that matter, where they are coming from (Aram or Edom). Small wonder then that the Ammonites and Moabites turn against the people from Mt Seir and subsequently proceed to destroy each other.

---

66. Davies, 'Defending the Boundaries', p. 45.
67. Davies, 'Defending the Boundaries', p. 52.

The political-military union of these peoples has invalidated their
existence as a distinct group and has obscured their identity as well as
their place of origin.

Before leaving this episode, it should be noted that although Jehoshaphat's victory (or rather YHWH's victory on behalf of Jehoshaphat) is
overwhelming, it is textually framed by two episodes in which Jehoshaphat is portrayed as less than perfect. These two stories, which were
discussed earlier, report Jehoshaphat's entanglements in foreign
alliances—for which he was judged unfavorably. Thus, even though
Judah prevails over its neighbors in 2 Chronicles 20, the textual boundaries surrounding this victory indicate that Chr. views Judah's autonomy and identity under Jehoshaphat as more precarious than this
success would imply.[68]

The period following the reign of Jehoshaphat is marked by even
stronger political instability. For Chr. as well as for 2 Kings, this
instability is tied directly to the marital alliance of the house of David in
Judah with the house of Ahab in Israel through Jehoram's marriage
with Athaliah, as is indicated by the statement, 'He walked in the way
of the kings of Israel' (21.6), which describes the reign of Jehoram, as
well as Chronicles' judgment on Ahaziah, 'He too walked in the ways
of the house of Ahab' (22.3). This unacceptable situation is further
underscored by an Edomite rebellion at the beginning of Jehoram's
reign. Again, the blurring of ideological boundaries (the marriage
between the houses of David and Ahab) coincides with a weakening of
Judah's geo-political borders. Furthermore, Jehoram is unable to gain
control over the rebellious Edomites, since the text states that 'Edom
has been in revolt against the rule of Judah to this day' (21.10). The
political instability culminates with the reign of Athaliah, the only ruler
over Judah who was not a descendant of David. A partial rehabilitation
of Judah is achieved, according to Chr., through a violent overthrow of
Athaliah's regime and the coronation of Joash.

Joash, like Asa, is a king whose reign is judged positively at the
beginning, but negatively toward the end of his rule. The turning point
is described in 24.18, which states that Joash served the asherim and the
idols. Significant for this study is the report of his death. Both 2 Chron.

---

68. For an extensive analysis of Chr.'s treatment of Jehoshaphat's reign, see K.
Strübind, *Tradition als Interpretation in der Chronik: König Josaphat als
Paradigma chronistischer Hermeneutik und Theologie* (BZAW, 201; Berlin: W. de
Gruyter, 1991).

24.23-27 and 2 Kgs 12.18-23 relate essentially the same story. Joash is attacked by the Arameans, severely wounded in battle and eventually slain by his own servants. However, while the version in 2 Kings only supplies the names of the two servants who conspired against Joash (Shimeath and Jehozabad), 2 Chron. 24.26 further identifies the two as an Ammonite and a Moabite. Japhet has suggested that it is unlikely that Chr. would have invented this information, that it must therefore have been found in his source and that it was only subsequently omitted in Kings.[69] While this is certainly possible, it is not entirely true that Chr. had no motive for making the conspirators foreigners. If political instability and religious infidelity are in fact interdependent with the precariousness of Judah's national boundaries and the presence of the other within Judean society, the identification of the two murderers as foreigners would fit Chr.'s understanding of history rather well.[70]

After this incident, Moab is not mentioned again in 2 Chronicles, while Ammon appears on two other occasions. In both instances the Ammonites are portrayed as subordinate to Judah, as they pay tribute to Uzziah (26.8) and are defeated by Jotham (27.5). Somewhat more problematic is the portrayal of the Philistines and the Edomites during the time of the divided monarchy. Both nations are at times depicted as powerful enemies of Judah, and at others as subordinate to the Davidic king. In 2 Chron. 17.11, some Philistines are said to bring tribute to (the mostly good king) Jehoshaphat. As mentioned earlier, the reign of Jehoram opens with a revolt of Edom against the authority of the Davidic king. In 21.16-17, also during the reign of Jehoram, the Philistines (along with some Arabs) follow suit, invade Judah and carry away the possessions of the king. The situation appears to be brought under control by Uzziah, who is judged positively in Chronicles and who successfully attacks the Philistines. This situation does not last, however, since the Philistines return to make raids on Judean cities in the Shephelah and in the Negev during the reign of Ahaz (28.18).

---

69. Japhet, *1 & 2 Chronicles*, p. 854.

70. A similar suggestion has been made by Ackroyd, who writes that 'when king (or people) turn to alien gods, their judgement will be at the hands of alien instruments of divine wrath'. (*I & II Chronicles, Ezra, Nehemiah*, p. 161. Cf. also Williamson, *1 and 2 Chronicles*, p. 326; C.C. Torrey, 'The Chronicler as Editor and as Independent Narrator', in *Ezra Studies* (Chicago: University of Chicago Press, 1910), pp. 212-13; M.P. Graham, 'A Connection Proposed Between II Chr 24, 26 and Ezra 9–10', *ZAW* 97 (1985), pp. 256-58.

It is striking that the Philistines returned immediately after Ahaz appealed to Assyria for help against the Edomites, who had again invaded Judean territory. Knoppers argues that 'in Chronicles Ahaz is arguably Judah's worst king'.[71] In any case, Ahaz's attempt to ally himself with Assyria is doomed to failure, and once again it coincides with the invasion of Judah by foreigners. The causal relationship between the attempted alliance and the foreign invasions is not entirely clear. Of course, it would make sense for Judah to appeal for Assyrian help as a result of local foreign invasions. Nonetheless, given Chr.'s view of foreign alliance in general, one should at least regard Ahaz's appeal to Assyria and the breach of Judah's borders as interrelated. Reliance on foreign powers and the influx of foreign elements go hand in hand.

The most elaborate text (and possibly the most disturbing) dealing with Edom is found in 2 Chron. 25.5-16, which describes the slaughter of the Edomites. This passage is substantially longer than the synoptic parallel in 2 Kings 14, where only a single verse is devoted to the incident: 'He (Amaziah) defeated Edom in the Valley of Salt, he took Selah in battle and called it Jokthel, its name to this day' (v. 7). Chr.'s version describes Amaziah's preparation for the battle as well as the immediate consequences of this encounter. The story begins with Amaziah's hiring of 100,000 mercenaries from Ephraim (v. 6) and their subsequent dismissal on account of a prophetic critique of this alliance (vv. 7-9). Having separated himself from the northern kingdom, Amaziah and the army of Judah defeat the Edomites in the Valley of Salt, killing ten thousand of them in battle (v. 11) and capturing and executing another ten thousand (v. 12). The story then takes a surprising turn, since Amaziah proceeds to worship the gods of Edom, presumably statues that were captured in battle. Having successfully expelled the other from the boundaries of Judah (figuratively as well as literally) he imports their sacred guardians (the representations of the deities that were meant to ensure the survival of the Edomites!) into Judahite territory (again, figuratively as well as literally). Clearly, we are not dealing with a simple case of 'boundary maintenance' here. In fact, the boundaries appear to be drawn and erased at the same time, obscuring the identity of Amaziah's Judah, rather than defining it. The resulting punishment for Amaziah's action is a military defeat by Israel, Judah's highly ambiguous 'alter-ego'.

71. Knoppers, 'Yhwh Is Not with Israel', p. 608.

One more thing should be mentioned with regard to this episode. 2 Chronicles 25.24 describes the looting of the Jerusalemite temple by the northern army, which carries off all the vessels 'which were with Obed-Edom (עבד־עם אדום)'. The ambiguous identity of Obed-Edom has already been discussed, and, although it appears obvious that we are not dealing with the same person here, it is possible that the text has in mind the family of Obed-Edom, or even a particular group of levites commissioned by David's Obed-Edom. The reference in 25.24 is too brief and cryptic to allow for any meaningful conclusions. Suffice it to say that it is highly ironic that the northern army, as a punishment for Amaziah's worship of Edomite gods, carries off those vessels from the temple that were in the care of a person (or office) whose name means 'servant of Edom'.[72] The text of 2 Chronicles 25 is thus full of ambiguities, including the dismissal and return of soldiers from the North, the expulsion and inclusion of the other through the defeat of the Edomites and the subsequent worship of their gods, and finally the resurfacing of a levite with a very unusual name and a somewhat controversial pedigree.

Conclusions

Chr.'s view of the relationship between Judah and its neighbors is characterized by a constant mediation of tensions. While the text attempts to give expression to the distinctiveness of the people of Judah with regard to non-Judahites, the boundary lines between Judah and the other is more often blurred than not. The emergence of Israel as a people in the genealogies is marked by numerous ambiguities regarding the status of Jacob's identity and the relationship between Jacob and Esau. The beginning of David's reign displays an even greater precariousness with regard to Israel's identity. David's relationship with the Philistines is especially suspect. There is, however, a gradual expulsion of the other during the reign of David, primarily through a number of successful battles against the peoples surrounding Judah, that confirm the (geographical and ideological) boundaries of his kingdom. Yet, even in David's victorious wars, there are some loose ends, as some of

72. Cf. M.P. Graham, 'Aspects of the Structure and Rhetoric of 2 Chronicles 25', in M.P. Graham, W.P. Brown and J.K. Kuan (eds.), *History and Interpretation: Essays in Honour of John H. Hayes* (JSOTSup, 173; Sheffield: JSOT Press, 1993), pp. 85-89.

David's wariors are identified as foreigners. In other words, the other is present even in David's attempt to expel it.

David's wars also provide a textual frame for the ark narrative. Hence, the cultic center of Judah's society is protected by a literary hedge, setting it apart from foreign influence. This is noteworthy, since the interrelationship between Judah's cult and its boundaries is a major focus of the history after David. The war reports of this period display a direct correlation between the fidelity of Judah's king to YHWH and to YHWH's temple and his success in warfare. Only Solomon's reign is blessed with continual peace, so that his relationships with foreigners are located exclusively in the economic rather than military realm. The kings following him on the throne of Judah are characterized by various degrees of religious faithfulness and corresponding success in the battles they wage against their neighbors. The other is never fully absent from Judah: it may be temporarily expelled, but it returns, erasing the boundaries that separate Judah from the nations.

Edom and the northern kingdom of Israel receive somewhat more attention than other neighbors of Judah during the divided monarchy. In the case of Israel, this may be explained by the problematic status of the northern kingdom, being at the same time similar and dissimilar to Judah. The northern kingdom represents Judah's 'alter-ego', the externalization of its own alienation from itself. Likewise, Edom is portrayed as Israel's brother in the genealogies. Thus, there exists a heightened degree of similarity between Judah and Edom or Israel, and hence a stronger need for Judah to define itself as separate from either one. As elsewhere in the text, this separation is achieved through the inclusion of war reports, which in the case of the slaughter of the Edomites in 2 Chronicles 25 can be particularly vicious (20,000 Edomites are killed). Chr.'s underlying logic is that Judah must be different from Edom, since it has fought the Edomites in the Valley of Salt. The remembrance of such battles thus contributes the ethnic-ideological distinction drawn by Chr. between Judah and its neighbors, even at a time when Judah had no national independence or functioning army. However, in light of the ambiguity that characterizes Chronicles' portrayal of Edom and the northern kingdom of Israel, it is perhaps worthwhile to note that Idumea and Samaria were the two regions into which Judah expanded when it did have a functioning army under the Hasmoneans, not too long after the books of Chronicles were written.

WHAT CHRONICLES HAS TO SAY ABOUT PSALMS

Howard N. Wallace

The books of Chronicles stand in a unique position within the Hebrew
Bible. It is widely acknowledged that various parts of the Bible have
been used as source material in the writing and editing of other parts.[1]
However, the extent to which this has happened in Chronicles and the
way in which it has happened grants these books that unique position.
Thus, Chronicles can act not only as a source for the study of history
and theology in the postexilic period, but as a window into how biblical
works were viewed and used, at least by one section of Judean society,
during the long process leading to widespread canonization.

The books of Samuel and Kings are the main extant sources for the
work of Chr.[2] However, psalm texts have also been employed to a
significant, even if much lesser, extent. These have been used in three
ways: in direct quotation of biblical psalms (1 Chron. 16.8-36 quoting
Pss. 105.1-15; 96.1-13 and 106.1, 47-48; and 2 Chron. 6.41-42 quoting
Ps. 132.8-10); by allusion to psalm texts within the Chronicles narrative
(1 Chron. 29.15; cf. Ps. 39.12 [Ps. 39.13][3]); or by use of psalm texts as
a refrain within the narrative (1 Chron. 16.41; 2 Chron. 5.13; 7.3, 6 and
20.21; cf. Ps. 136.1 etc.).

Study of the psalm texts within Chronicles has never really been vig-
orous. Until the 1970s the psalm portions in Chronicles were virtually

---

1.   See D.A. Carson and H.G.M. Williamson, *It Is Written: Scripture Citing
Scripture. Essays in Honour of Barnabas Lindars, SSF* (Cambridge: Cambridge
University Press, 1988) for a broad treatment of this topic.

2.   I will use the term 'Chronicles' to refer to the two books of Chronicles
together, and 'Chr.' ('Chronicler') to refer to the author(s) of the books. The term
'psalms' will be used to refer to psalms generically, and 'Psalms' to refer to the
book of Psalms.

3.   All biblical references are to the English versification. Where the MT
versification differs from the English, it will be given in square brackets.

neglected as part of the text. There seems to have been two reasons for
this. First, there was the virtual dismissal of Chr. as a literary artist.
This can be seen clearly, for example, in Wellhausen's discussion on
Chronicles in his *Prolegomena*. He either used or concurred with the
use of words such as 'distortion', 'mutilation', 'contradiction', 'rude'
(and so on) in relation to Chr.'s work. He followed de Wette closely in
this treatment.[4] Secondly, where attention was given to Chr.'s literary
sources, the discussion was almost exclusively in terms of the books of
Samuel and Kings.[5] What discussion was to be found on the psalm portions was sometimes confined to text-critical remarks, specifically an
examination of variants in the texts of the relevant psalms between the
book of Psalms and Chronicles.[6]

Only in the last two or three decades have a few scholars given attention to a wider range of questions concerning these psalm texts.[7] In
their studies they have attempted to illumine the various ways in which

4. J. Wellhausen, *Prolegomena to the History of Ancient Israel* (ET; New
York: Meridian, 1957), pp. 171-227. On De Wette's influence on Wellhausen's
understanding of Chronicles, see most recently K. Peltonen, *History Debated: The
Historical Reliability of Chronicles in Pre-Critical and Critical Research* (2 vols.;
Publications of the Finnish Exegetical Society, 64; Helsinki: Finnish Exegetical
Society; Göttingen: Vandenhoeck & Ruprecht, 1996), I, pp. 233-45. Note also the
several studies referred to by E.L. Curtis and A.A. Madsen, *A Critical and Exegetical Commentary on the Books of Chronicles* (ICC; Edinburgh: T. & T. Clark,
1910), pp. 24-26, in which it was the assumption that Chr. was 'essentially a mere
copyist'.

5. M. Noth, *The Chronicler's History* (JSOTSup, 50; Sheffield: JSOT Press,
1987), pp. 51-67 (German original 1943), is an extreme case here, but also cf. the
notes of Curtis and Madsen, *Chronicles*, pp. 17-26.

6. E.g. J.M. Myers, *1 Chronicles* (AB, 12; New York: Doubleday, 1965),
p. 121.

7. J.A. Loader, 'Redaction and Function of the Chronistic "Psalm of David"',
OTWSA 19 (1976), pp. 69-75; T.C. Butler, 'A Forgotten Passage from a Forgotten
Era', *VT* 28 (1978), pp. 142-50; H.G.M. Williamson, *1 and 2 Chronicles* (NCB;
Grand Rapids: Eerdmans, 1982), pp. 128-30; A.E. Hill, 'Patchwork Poetry or Rea-
soned Verse? Connective Structure in 1 Chronicles XVI', *VT* 33 (1983), pp. 97-
101; R.M. Shipp, '"Remember his Covenant Forever": A Study of the Chronicler's
Use of the Psalms', *ResQ* 35 (1992), pp. 29-39; J.W. Kleinig, *The Lord's Song: The
Basis, Function and Significance of Choral Music in Chronicles* (JSOTSup, 156;
Sheffield: JSOT Press, 1993), pp. 133-48, 157-80; S. Japhet, *I & II Chronicles: A
Commentary* (OTL; Louisville, KY: Westminster/John Knox Press, 1993), pp. 316-
20.

Chr. has used psalm sources to construct his own psalm texts, the placement of these texts within the larger work of Chronicles and their theological significance. No longer should it be possible to dismiss these passages by referring to the appropriate sections in commentaries on the Psalter or by seeing them simply as examples of liturgical practice in the time of David as understood by Chr.[8] The psalm texts must be addressed as integral parts of the larger, sophisticated, literary and theological work of Chr.

Since the inappropriate separation of the psalm texts from their broader context in Chronicles has been redressed to a great degree, now might be an appropriate time to take another look at the general direction of those earlier studies. In other words, can we ask whether and how the study of these psalm texts within their Chronicles context might inform psalm studies in general? This article will begin to address that question in a modest way by looking at three issues: the text of the psalms used in Chronicles, general implications for psalm studies of how the psalms have been used in Chronicles and the role of David in relation to the psalm texts in Chronicles.

The Text of the Psalms

It might seem odd that a paper on the general topic of Chronicles as literature should begin with observations in the area of textual criticism. However, in this case, if not also in others, it is important. The various Hebrew and Greek versions of the texts in which we are interested not only reveal a history of the transmission of the texts, but also witness to the history of interpretation and literary shaping of those texts. Indeed the two cannot always be separated, and a study of variants can reveal as much about the literature itself as it does about the accidents of scribal art.

Many studies of the psalm texts in Chronicles have compared the texts in MT Chronicles with the texts of the relevant psalms within MT book of Psalms.[9] A number of the more important variants would seem to indicate intentional editing of the psalms in 1 Chron. 16.8-38. First, the use of the name 'Israel' in 1 Chron. 16.13 stands in contrast to 'Abraham' in Ps. 105.6. Chr. frequently uses the name 'Israel' for Jacob. Moreover, there is a widespread focus in Chr. on Jacob as the

---

8. Myers, *1 Chronicles*, p. 121.
9. Even recently in Kleinig, *The Lord's Song*, pp. 139-41.

patriarch from whom later Israel is to be traced. It would appear then that the text of the psalm has been emended to focus attention on Jacob/ Israel rather than simply maintain the poetic parallel between Abraham and Jacob as two of the patriarchs.[10]

Secondly, the use of the imperative זכרו in 1 Chron. 16.15, compared to the Qal perfect זכר in Ps. 105.8, calls the people to a remembrance of the covenant with God rather than declaring God's own faithfulness to it. This change is consistent with the rest of the psalm[11] and creates a text in which both the audience presumed by the text (i.e. in David's time) and that in Chr.'s own time can be addressed. Thirdly, Ps. 96.10a has been displaced from its expected position in 1 Chron. 16.30 to v. 31 and has been altered from 'Say among the nations, "The Lord is king!"' to 'Let them say among the nations, "The Lord is king!"' Some scholars attribute this to an omission and later correction.[12] However, the text makes sense as it stands in 1 Chronicles 16, where the nations are called to worship the Lord, and in v. 31 the heavens and earth are called to proclaim the majesty of the Lord. If Chr.'s audience is indeed struggling under a foreign power, then it might be more appropriate to hope for some manifestation of the Lord's sovereignty in nature than to see the people themselves declaring it convincingly before their political and military masters.[13] The changes could well have been made with this in mind. Finally, other emendations such as the use of the second person בהיותכם in 1 Chron. 16.19 for בהיותם in Ps. 105.12, the occurrence of וחדוה במקמו in 1 Chron. 16.27 for ותפארת במקדשו in Ps. 96.6, and of לפניו in 1 Chron. 16.29 for לחצרותיו in Ps. 96.8, again either address the audience specifically or seem to be there to bring the psalm into line with the context created by Chr.[14]

Several other variants between 1 Chron. 16.8-36 and Psalms 105, 96 and 106 can be noted. They involve variations in spelling, suffixes, number or prepositions; the inclusion or omission of particles, especially את; and even the omission of semi-colons. Unlike the variants

---

10. Williamson, *1 and 2 Chronicles*, pp. 40-44.

11. Williamson, *1 and 2 Chronicles*, p. 129. Cf. also Butler, 'A Forgotten Passage', pp. 149-50; Japhet, *I & II Chronicles*, p. 317.

12. E.g. Williamson, *1 and 2 Chronicles*, p. 130; and Japhet, *I & II Chronicles*, p. 318.

13. Fire from heaven is seen in 1 Chron. 21.26 and 2 Chron. 7.1 as the sign of divine approval.

14. Cf. Japhet, *I & II Chronicles*, pp. 317-18.

discussed above, these do not greatly affect the overall interpretation of the psalm in Chronicles, compared with the psalms as they appear in the book of Psalms.

A similar situation exists with the inclusion of Ps. 132.8-10 in 2 Chron 6.41-42 at the conclusion of Solomon's prayer at the dedication of the temple. There is a greater density of variants in this short passage than in the longer psalm text in 1 Chron 16.8-36. These variants involve the inclusion or completion of the longer divine epithet אלהים יהוה on three occasions and changes in vocabulary on three occasions. Once again the changes in vocabulary do not affect the overall direction of the passage.[15] However, the inclusion of the divine epithet does change the tone of the psalm, focusing attention much more on the Lord.

A major change in 2 Chron. 6.41-42 is at the end of the psalm portion, where the words, 'On account of your servant David' (Ps. 132.10a), have been replaced by 'Remember the steadfast love for your servant David'[16] and situated following the request for the Lord not to turn away the face of his anointed. This, in conjunction with the three-fold repetition of the divine epithet, serves to end the prayer with the emphasis on the Lord's fulfillment of his promise to the Davidic dynasty.[17]

It would appear then that most major variants between Chr.'s psalm texts and the texts as we find them in the book of Psalms arise out of editorial interests. However, the number of variants that do not seem to be attributable to editorial concern suggests that the Hebrew text of Psalms employed by Chr. for 1 Chron. 16.8-36 and 2 Chron. 6.41-42 belonged to a different textual tradition than the one witnessed in the

15. The presence of the word 'salvation' in 2 Chron 6.41c may have been influenced by Ps. 132.16.

16. The interpretation of לחסדי דויד as either a subjective genitive, 'steadfast love *of* David' (so, e.g., R.B. Dillard, *2 Chronicles* [WBC, 15; Waco, TX: Word Books, 1987], pp. 51-52; Japhet, *I & II Chronicles*, pp. 604-605), or an objective genitive, 'steadfast love *for* David' (so, e.g., Williamson, *1 and 2 Chronicles*, pp. 220-21), has been vigorously debated. In my opinion the arguments of Williamson, based on the context within Chronicles with the possible allusion to Isa. 55.3, almost certainly an objective genitive, are the most convincing for the present case.

17. This emphasis is present in Ps. 132 also but is largely evident in the verses following the quotation in 2 Chron. 6.41-42 (i.e. Ps. 132.11-12). The change in Chr.'s version makes the issue more explicit within the quotation.

MT of Psalms 105, 96, 106 and 132 in the book of Psalms.[18] While it is possible that the 'editorial changes' could have already been present in Chr.'s psalms source, the fact that some of these changes are consistent with the views of Chr. expressed elsewhere suggests that they have indeed been made by Chr.

A look at the LXX for 1 Para. 16.8-36 and 2 Para. 6.41-42, as well as for LXX Psalms 104, 95 and 105,[19] reveals that in both cases the LXX follows the respective MT texts closely in the major as well as some minor variants.[20] In cases where one or both LXX texts differ from their respective MT texts, this is usually the result of a clear addition within the LXX text tradition or a misreading of the Hebrew *Vorlage(n)*.[21] It can also be noted that in many places where the Hebrew texts are identical, the Greek translators have varied in their choice of vocabulary or grammatical formation. From this it would seem that each of the Greek translations of MT Psalms 105, 96 and 106 and of 1 Chron 16.3-36 and 2 Chron. 6.41-42 has been undertaken without influence from the other. Each bears a strong witness to the text tradition evinced in its Hebrew *Vorlage*. There are apparently no major variations between the Greek Psalms manuscripts at the points of difference between the MT of 1 Chron. 16.8-36 and 2 Chron. 6.41-42 and the MT of Psalms 105, 96, 106 and 132 in the book of Psalms.

With regard to psalm texts available in the Dead Sea Scrolls, only a the few verses from the psalms in the Chronicles texts under consideration are extant, namely Ps. 96.1-2 (1QPs[a] and 4QPs[b]), Ps. 105.1-11 (11QPs[a] and 4QPs[e]) and Ps. 132.8-10 (11QPs[a]). Of these the only variants from the MT to be found are in Ps. 105.3-11. In nearly all these cases the reading found in 11QPs[a] is unique among extant witnesses, with the MT psalms text agreeing with the relevant LXX psalms text.

Some tentative observations can be made in light of this discussion. It

18. Cf. the conclusion reached by P.R. Ackroyd, *I & II Chronicles, Ezra, Nehemiah* (TBC; London: SCM Press, 1973), pp. 64-65, 113.

19. These are equivalent to MT Pss. 105, 96 and 106. The LXX Psalms text used is that in A. Rahlfs, *Psalmi cum Odis* (Göttingen: Vandenhoeck & Ruprecht, 3rd edn, 1979). It is noted that the preparation of a new edition of the Septuagint Psalter has been mooted (see P.W Flint, *The Dead Sea Psalms Scrolls & the Book of Psalms* [STDJ, 17; Leiden: E.J. Brill, 1997], p. 229).

20. E.g. in MT 1 Chron. 16.13 with the name of the patriarch, and in v. 27.

21. E.g. in MT 1 Chron. 16.9, 10, 11, 13 (עבדו), 26 and 29-30. The main exception is v. 19, where MT Chron. בהיותכם stands alone against LXX 1 Para. 16.19, MT Ps. 105.12 and LXX Ps. 104.12.

should be borne in mind, however, that they relate to only a small amount of text. First, I suggested above that the Hebrew text of Psalms employed by Chr. belonged to a different textual tradition to the one witnessed in the MT book of Psalms. It also seems that the Greek translations of both the book of Psalms and the psalms in Chronicles have been done independently and follow their respective Hebrew *Vorlagen* fairly closely. The text of the relevant psalms in 11QPs[a] appears to represent a third textual tradition. A. Pietersma has noted the greater frequency of copying Greek psalms texts due to the fact that they were used widely within the liturgy of the early church. This leads him to conclude that 'we might anticipate thick layers of traditional material in the Greek Psalms'.[22] The conclusion that we have three possible Hebrew textual traditions witnessed within this small corpus of psalms could suggest that 'thick layers of traditional material' existed also in the Hebrew Psalms by virtue of the frequent copying associated with synagogue worship.

Secondly, in a study of the relationship between 11QPs[a] and the LXX Psalms, J. Cook recognized that, from a broad perspective, the relationship is rather complicated. However, he noted, among other things, that: 'In many instances the LXX actually agreed with MT as opposed to 11QPs[a]';[23] although he also conceded that 'there is a great measure of agreement between (LXX and 11QPs[a])'.[24] While this article is limited in its corpus, it does confirm these points.

Thirdly, while Chr.'s psalms source comes from a different textual tradition to that witnessed in the MT book of Psalms, a study of the variants between the two suggests that it is not unreasonable to presume that Chr. has used some of the same principles in operating with this source that he does in using the narrative from the books of Samuel and

22. A. Pietersma, 'Ra 2110 (P. Bodmer XXIV) and the Text of the Greek Psalter', in D. Fraenkel *et al.* (eds.), *Studien zur Septuaginta: Robert Hanhart zu ehren aus Anlass seines 65. Geburtstages* (Abhandlungen der Akademie der Wissenschaften in Göttingen, Philologisch-Historische Klasse, 190; Göttingen: Vandenhoeck & Ruprecht, 1990), p. 263.

23. J. Cook, 'On the Relationship between 11QPs[a] and the Septuagint on the Basis of the Computerized Data Base (CAQP)', in G.J. Brooke and B. Lindars (eds.), *Septuagint, Scrolls and Cognate Writings: Papers Presented to the International Symposium on the Septuagint and its Relations to the Dead Sea Scrolls and Other Writings, Manchester, 1990* (SBLSCS, 33; Atlanta: Scholars Press, 1992), p. 127.

24. Cook, 'On the Relationship between 11QPs[a] and the Septuagint', p. 128.

Kings. That is, Chr. has stayed fairly close to his source, with the more significant variants appearing to be the result of Chr.'s theological *Tendenz*.[25] This *Tendenz* involves a particular stance toward the notion of a united Israel, a focus on the temple and a focus on the Lord's covenant with the Davidic dynasty in close association with the temple. Thus, Chr.'s use of his psalm sources is quite sophisticated. Chr. has given new meaning to the text within a new context through relatively small changes. He has also modified the function of the psalm, again through relatively small changes. This raises questions about the *Gattung* of the psalm texts in Chronicles. We will return to this in the next section.

The Way the Psalms Are Employed

Japhet describes Chr.'s attitude toward biblical sources as:

> an interesting combination of servitude and freedom: on the one hand a basic adherence to his source text on all the levels of literary expression, and on the other a skilful blend of omissions, additions and changes along the way, which transforms the final composition into a story which is not only divergent, but sometimes contrasting.[26]

While she is referring to Chr.'s use of a broad array of sources from biblical works, her comment is no less relevant for the use of psalms in Chronicles. As we have already noted from the text-critical point of view, Chr.'s attitude toward his psalms source is complex. This is no less the case in other areas and several points should be noted.

I remarked above that some scholars in the past have seen the use of the psalms in Chronicles strictly in terms of liturgical issues.[27] In the light of more recent studies it is clear that theological and literary issues are also involved. While these three issues interact in the text, it will serve the purpose of this study best to treat them independently at first. Their interrelatedness can be seen in that context.

First, in theological terms it has been recognized by many that the historical context of Chr. has been determinative in the choice and use of the psalms. In 1 Chron. 16.8-36, where the literary context is that of

---

25. For a discussion of these, see S.L. McKenzie, *The Chronicler's Use of the Deuteronomistic History* (HSM, 33; Atlanta: Scholars Press, 1984).

26. Japhet, *I & II Chronicles*, p. 15.

27. See n. 8 above.

the transfer of the ark of the Lord to Jerusalem prior to the construction of the temple, two themes stand out. These are Israel among the nations and the idea of YHWH's sovereignty over the other gods and nations.

De Vries has argued that in 1 Chronicles 16 Chr. has taken three psalm excerpts, with some internal changes, and arranged them around the first theme noted above, namely 'Israel among the nations'. The quotation of Psalm 105 is curtailed at an appropriate point and Psalm 96 used as the heart of the section. The central point concerns Israel as the chosen people whom the nations will one day recognize as such. De Vries concludes:

> Political conditions had made the strident nationalism of the psalms a practical impossibility, hence ChrH arranges and adapts the preexilic [sic] poems as vehicles for bolstering the people's faith that some day they may yet become what the psalms say they are.[28]

Such remarks could also be made about the quotation of Ps. 132.8-10 in 2 Chron. 6.41-42.

A similar view is expressed by Butler when dating the editing of the psalm portion in 1 Chronicles 16 to c. 300 BCE. He sees a strong possibility that the editor of the psalm and of Chr. is identical.[29] He argues:

> By simply omitting the remainder of ps. cv, the editor has transformed the meaning of the old material to speak to a new generation, few in number, wandering between world powers, but armed with God's eternal covenant and his warning to the nations not to harm his designated leaders.[30]

Psalm 96 functions in a similar way but, with the focus on the sovereignty of YHWH, it gives Israel grounds for confidence in life among the nations. The concluding verses from Psalm 106 add a plea for deliverance, indicating that thanksgiving is not yet complete.[31]

In the context of seeking to bolster the faith of the people, Chr. adapts the psalms used in 1 Chronicles 16 in such a way that the audience is directly addressed. We have already noted the effect of the textual variants in v. 15, where the Qal perfect זכר has been replaced by a plural

---

28. S.J. De Vries, *1 and 2 Chronicles* (FOTL, 11; Grand Rapids: Eerdmans, 1989), p. 151. See also Williamson, *1 and 2 Chronicles*, pp. 128-29.

29. Butler, 'A Forgotten Passage', p. 149.

30. Butler, 'A Forgotten Passage', p. 144. Cf. also R.L. Braun, *1 Chronicles* (WBC, 14; Waco, TX: Word Books, 1986), p. 192.

31. Butler, 'A Forgotten Passage', pp. 144-45.

imperative זכרו, and in v. 19, where I have read בהיותכם ('when you were') rather than בהיותם ('when they were'). As I have argued, these changes have the effect of making the whole psalm one that is addressed to the people rather than partially to the Lord. In essence the psalm is addressed to the worshipers of David's day, but the use of material familiar to Chr.'s own time suggests that the message of the book is relevant to a later period.[32] The inclusion of the plea for continued deliverance at the end of the psalm also engenders an open-ended sense to the thanksgiving and praise earlier in the psalm.

Secondly, while the psalm texts in Chronicles have certain theological and ultimately 'pastoral' functions, they also have various liturgical functions. Earlier I criticized Myers's opinion that in 1 Chron. 16.8-36 Chr. illustrates the origin and practice of psalm singing in temple worship. There is no doubt some validity to his statement, but overall it is too limited.

In a recent work Kleinig has attempted to outline Chr.'s understanding of the theological role of sacred song within the sacrificial ritual by an exegesis of texts from Chronicles.[33] He argues that in the Chronicles narrative the climax is not on the institution of sacrificial worship in Jerusalem but rather on that of the choral service. In fact, he states that within Chronicles David transfers the ark to Jerusalem precisely to inaugurate choral liturgy there.[34] Thus, the function of the levitical choir is elevated to a position equal to that of the sacrificial priests.[35] In 1 Chron 16.4-6, 37-42 Chr. spells out how, when, where and by whom the Lord is to be proclaimed, thanked and praised in the choral liturgy. It is only in the psalm that the reason why is given, namely to proclaim the Lord's name, and hence his presence with his people, and to present the congregation's petitions to the Lord.[36]

Even if one does not accept all of Kleinig's argument about the purpose of Chr. in relation to choral music, he does show the complexity of the authenticating role of the psalms in Chronicles. Just as the psalms have a theological function within Chronicles, so they say more about the liturgy of the temple worship than simply illustrating its origin and practice. There is an element of authentication in Chr.'s use of psalm

---

32. Cf. Williamson, *1 and 2 Chronicles*, p. 128.
33. Kleinig, *The Lord's Song*, p. 29.
34. Kleinig, *The Lord's Song*, p. 144.
35. Kleinig, *The Lord's Song*, p. 31.
36. Kleinig, *The Lord's Song*, pp. 145-48.

texts. The repetition of the word תָּמִיד ('always') before and after the psalm, as well as within it (vv. 6, 11, 37, 39), affirms this. The close connection of prayer, psalms and singing is clearly illustrated.[37] However, the use of the psalms also gives theological substance to the practice.

Thirdly, we must note that the psalms quoted by Chr. form part of the larger work of 1 and 2 Chronicles and thus also fulfill a clear literary role. 1 Chronicles 16 is associated with David bringing the ark to Jerusalem. Singers, musicians and instruments are appointed in preparation for the event, and 1 Chron. 16.8-36 records the praises sung on the occasion. Thus, the psalm is incorporated into the immediate narrative sequence. But this sequence also belongs to a larger structuring of the text. At the end of David's reign he blesses the Lord (1 Chron. 29.10-19) using, in part, words (v. 15) that possibly allude to Ps. 39.12 [Ps. 39.13] and Job 8.9. Moreover, the themes within the prayer echo those of 1 Chron 16.8-36, namely the sovereignty of the Lord over all the earth (29.11-12), the combination of thanks and praise (v. 13), the wandering, landless and vulnerable state of their ancestors (v. 15), ending with a final petition (vv. 18-19).[38] David's final prayer in 1 Chron. 29.10-19 and the psalms sung by the levitical singers in 1 Chron 16.8-36 form a framework around the preparations by David for the building of the temple.[39]

Other quotations of psalms or psalmic refrains fit into this larger structure. The quotation of Ps. 132.8-10 in 2 Chron. 6.41-42 picks up the two major themes of Psalm 132, the transfer of the ark and the promises to David. The former recalls the occasion of 1 Chron. 16.8-36, while the latter recalls 1 Chronicles 17 (// 2 Sam. 7).[40] The use of the psalmic refrains is also associated with the major psalm quotations in all but one instance. They occur in 1 Chron. 16.41 after reference to

---

37. Japhet, *I & II Chronicles*, p. 601.

38. Note also on this Williamson, *1 and 2 Chronicles*, p. 185.

39. Williamson, *1 and 2 Chronicles*, p. 185. We should also note in this context M.A. Throntveit's argument that David's prayer in 1 Chron. 29.10-19 'is thoroughly consistent with the form and content of the Chronicler's other royal prayers and should be retained in a discussion of the Chronicler's structure and theology'. M.A. Throntveit, *When Kings Speak: Royal Speech and Royal Prayer in Chronicles* (SBLDS, 93; Atlanta: Scholars Press, 1987), p. 96.

40. The theme of humility, evident in David's prayer in 1 Chron. 17.16, is also echoed in David's last prayer (1 Chron. 29.14).

those expressly charged to give thanks to the Lord and in a cluster
around the occasion of the completion of the temple (2 Chron. 5.13;
7.3, 6). The exception is in 2 Chron. 20.21, where the army goes to
battle under Jehoshaphat. The association of the majority of these
psalmic refrains with the transfer of the ark to Jerusalem and the completion of the temple would seem to be intended by Chr.

Shipp suggests, drawing on similar refrains in Akkadian incantations
associated with the installation of statues in temples, that the psalmic
refrains in Chronicles were initially connected with temple worship,
possibly in temple dedications or cultic installations or even at times of
crisis, and that the refrain:

> called upon the community and the Lord to remember the everlasting
> nature of the Covenant commitment of the Lord to Israel, to remind God
> of his promise to deliver Israel in light of the present distress, and to
> remind them that they could rely on God for covenant faithfulness
> because he is good.[41]

The context of the temple dedication fits well with the context of the
refrains within the narrative. However, the suggestion that Chr. writes
to a contemporary audience struggling under the weight of a foreign
power could also fit well with the use of the refrains in times of crisis.
Two possible contexts, one associated with the time frame within the
narrative and one with the time frame of the writer and his immediate
audience, could be interrelated in the text.

Literary questions are involved not only at the level of the structure
of Chr.'s total work but also at the level of the internal structure of the
psalm in 1 Chron. 16.8-36. This aspect of Chr.'s psalm text has been
studied carefully by Hill,[42] Butler[43] and—building on these earlier
studies—by Shipp.[44] I do not wish to repeat their findings here but to
note the recognition of internal coherence and structuring that points
toward sophisticated, literary artistry on the part of Chr.

We can see from this discussion of theological, liturgical and literary
aspects that Chr.'s treatment of his psalm sources in terms of content is
complex, just as the textual treatment was, in its own way. There is an
intermingling of the three aspects. It was noted above that several

41. Shipp, 'Remember his Covenant Forever', p. 31.
42. Hill, 'Patchwork Poetry or Reasoned Verse?', pp. 97-101.
43. Butler, 'A Forgotten Passage', pp. 143-45.
44. Shipp, 'Remember his Covenant Forever', pp. 33-37.

scholars have made the point that Chr. is using and adapting the psalms in an effort to bolster the faith of a community struggling under a foreign power. Others have argued that there is here an effort to shape the liturgical life of the people. Thus literary, liturgical and theological issues need to be addressed in relation in an effort to understand the psalms in Chronicles. This is the case both in their individual structure and in their employment within the life of the faith community. We cannot simply treat the psalms in Chronicles as poems, or as isolated literary units, divorced from issues of faith and ritual. The employment of a variety of critical approaches is required in their study.

While this article deals with a particular situation in Chronicles, it has implications for broader Psalms study, especially in the area of form criticism. First, it is relevant to the matter of the classification of psalms and especially the relation of *Gattung* to *Sitz im Leben*. For Gunkel, a 'common situation in life' together with the sharing of 'a great number of thoughts and moods' and 'a literary form [*Formensprache*]' allowed the various types of 'Cult Songs' to be distinguished. The first of these features played an important role. Literary types were not the inventions of individuals but developed within the community over generations. However, over time they decayed:

> Mixtures or inner transformations occur with great frequency when the literature we are discussing becomes old, especially when the original setting of the literary types has been forgotten or is no longer clear.[45]

Gunkel's student, Mowinckel, shared some common principles with him, while having quite a different view regarding the place of the cult in the psalms:

> The study of the formal criteria of the different stylistic 'types' shows the way to the different situations in life from which they have sprung. To each of the main psalm types corresponds a definite situation; they have all their definite setting or place in life.[46]

While Gunkel and Mowinckel differed in identifying that 'setting' or 'place in life', they both assumed that the situation in life associated with the psalm was 'definite'. That is to say, a certain type of psalm was developed in relation to a certain situation. Mowinckel acknowledged

---

45. H. Gunkel, *The Psalms: A Form-Critical Introduction* (ET; Philadelphia: Fortress Press, 1967 [1930]), p. 36.
46. S. Mowinckel, *The Psalms in Israel's Worship* (2 vols; Nashville: Abingdon Press, 1962), I, p. 28.

that the situation 'also determined form'[47] but still the situation was fixed.

Westermann goes beyond this in his work on the praise of God in the psalms. For him the categories of the psalms are not primarily literary or cultic. The essential element in them is that 'They designate the basic modes of that which occurs when man turns to God with words: plea and praise'. He continues:

> As these two basic modes of 'prayer' change and expand, the categories also change and expand. They can travel great distances from this original occurrence, but their origin in it can be recognized in all the branchings of the Psalm categories.[48]

Westermann only accepts to a limited extent Gunkel's thesis that the cult is the *Sitz im Leben* of the psalms. He goes beyond the cult 'to the basic occurrence which transpires in "cult" when men speak to God: the polarity of speaking to God as plea and as praise'.[49] This is the real *Sitz im Leben* for the psalms according to Westermann:

> As an occurrence from man to God each Psalm is a unit. Thus its structure can be recognized, the structure of a live occurrence. It is a unit, whose members show that they belong to the whole. Never however does this whole become an external scheme, into which a living content is pressed.[50]

While Westermann takes the issue of *Sitz im Leben* a step beyond that proposed variously by Gunkel and Mowinckel, we should note that he still speaks of *Sitz im Leben* in terms of a singular, originating situation. However, his understanding of *Sitz im Leben* has a degree of flexibility about it and lends itself to a variety of contexts, although Westermann himself does not pursue this.

The recognition that psalms can be used in a variety of contexts has been made by many scholars from Gunkel onward. However, in most instances the *Sitz im Leben* of particular psalm types are considered as fixed in some way.[51] We have already noted Gunkel's view on this.

---

47. Mowinckel, *The Psalms in Israel's Worship*, I, p. 28.

48. C. Westermann, *The Praise of God in the Psalms* (Richmond, VA: John Knox Press, 1965), p. 153.

49. Westermann, *The Praise of God in the Psalms*, p. 154.

50. Westermann, *The Praise of God in the Psalms*, pp. 154-55.

51. There are some exceptions to this: e.g. W.G. Williams, 'Liturgical Aspects in Enthronement Psalms', *JBR* 25 (1957), pp. 118-22.

Writing generally about the transmission of literary types to new 'settings in life', K. Koch notes 'that no literary type remains in existence for long after it has been entirely severed from its point of origin'.[52] J. Barton points out that to a form critic the psalms are 'public, official and anonymous examples of a genre',[53] having defined a genre or *Gattung* in terms of a 'conventional pattern, recognizable by certain formal criteria... used in a particular society in social contexts which are governed by certain formal conventions'.[54] He acknowledges the use of psalms as 'vehicles of intensely personal prayer and faith' but sees this as part of the study of the history of biblical interpretation rather than as part of Psalms study itself.[55]

The study of the psalms in Chronicles suggests a much more complex situation in the relation of *Gattung* to *Sitz im Leben* than many have assumed to date. In general it would support Gunkel's point that the 'situation in life' was one of the characteristics that marked a particular type of psalm. In other words, *Sitz im Leben* is important for the determination of *Gattung*. However, it raises the question of whether a change in situation[56] influences or changes our understanding of *Gattung* for a particular psalm. Those who see *Sitz im Leben* as a fixed, originating situation would see a psalm's *Gattung* as relatively fixed, given a stability of form and content. The notion of *Sitz im Leben* embodies within it a sense in which situation precedes form or, at most, form arises in response to situation. But where an established *Gattung* is used in a new context the psalm now clearly precedes the situation. In this event, one might expect that the new situation would affect how the *Gattung* is understood, and the *Gattung*, in turn, would have some effect on how the situation is faced. Thus, in cases where psalms or portions of psalms are employed in new contexts, a more complex relationship between *Gattung* and situation seems to exist. It is one in which situations can change in relation to *Gattung*, and *Gattung* can be

---

52. K. Koch, *The Growth of the Biblical Tradition: The Form-Critical Approach* (London: A. & C. Black, 1969), p. 36.

53. J. Barton, *Reading the Old Testament: Method in Biblical Study* (Louisville, KY: Westminster/John Knox Press, rev. edn, 1996 [1984]), p. 39.

54. Barton, *Reading the Old Testament*, p. 32.

55. Barton, *Reading the Old Testament*, p. 39.

56. I refrain from using the German expression *Sitz im Leben* at this point, because it carries with it Gunkel's understanding of an 'original' situation.

modified in relation to situation, while the actual form might remain the same or be varied slightly.

The situation in Chronicles clearly suggests a certain freedom in the use of psalm texts with either parts of psalms being used in specific contexts or whole or parts of psalms being combined.[57] In the case of 1 Chron 16.8-36, Psalms 105 and 96 have been used to form the bulk of the 'new' psalm. Psalm 105 has been variously categorized by scholars. Some have focused on vv. 1-6 of the psalm and emphasized its hymnic aspects.[58] Others, or sometimes even the same scholars, have concentrated on the bulk of the psalm, emphasizing its review of Israel's history.[59] Variously, its *Sitz im Leben* 'may have been the ceremony of the renewal of the Covenant'[60] or possibly the autumn festival and its tradition of the *Heilsgeschichte*.[61] Psalm 96, on the other hand, has been widely recognized as having to do with the celebration of the kingship or enthronement of YHWH and has variously been described as one of the 'Enthronement Psalms...a sub-division of the Hymns'[62] or as a 'Yahweh as King hymn'.[63] There is widespread agreement that it is one of a number of hymns associated with the Feast of Tabernacles, the New Year festival.[64]

The setting of the psalm in 1 Chron. 16.8-36 varies from those envisaged by commentators for Psalms 105 and 96. There are undoubtedly elements that allow the two psalms to live in their new context, especially the hymnic nature of each. However, the shift from possible covenant renewal ceremonies or New Year celebrations to one of bringing the ark to Jerusalem is considerable. In the process the *Gattung* has

---

57. Ps. 132, which most scholars associate with the bringing of the ark to Jerusalem, is quoted in part in Chronicles in the context of Solomon's prayer of dedication for the temple.

58. E.g. A.A. Anderson, *The Book of Psalms* (2 vols.; NCB; Grand Rapids: Eerdmans, 1972), II, p. 725; A. Weiser, *The Psalms: A Commentary* (OTL; Philadelphia: Westminster Press, 1962), p. 673.

59. Thus Anderson, *Psalms*, II, p. 725; H.-J. Kraus, *Psalms 60–150: A Commentary* (Minneapolis: Augsburg Press, 1989), p. 308; L.C. Allen, *Psalms 101–150* (WBC, 21; Waco, TX: Word Books, 1983), p. 40.

60. Anderson, *Psalms*, II, p. 726.

61. Anderson, *Psalms*, II, p. 679.

62. Anderson, *Psalms*, II, p. 680; Weiser, *Psalms*, p. 628.

63. Kraus, *Psalms 60-150*, p. 251.

64. Anderson, *Psalms*, II p. 681; Weiser, *The Psalms*, p. 628; Kraus, *Psalms 60–150*, p. 251.

changed to one of thanksgiving, drawing on the early verses of Psalm 105. The kingship of YHWH is now seen in his faithfulness to his promise to his people in the presence of other nations in a particular situation. On the strength of these shifts it seems difficult to follow Barton's separation of psalm study from history of interpretation, wherein all uses of a *Gattung* in situations other than its originating situation are assigned to the latter. If the *Gattung* of a psalm can be affected by a new situation, as seems to be the case in 1 Chron. 16.8-36, then that is legitimate material for Psalms study itself. Psalms study ought not to be confined to an interest in matters of stylistics or the mostly hypothetical reconstruction of original contexts. The ongoing presence of these psalm texts within the life of a community is their continued use in formal and informal liturgies in a variety of contexts. Perhaps one of the starting points for their study ought to be in those examples where we see reasonably clear evidence of their employment.

Psalms of so called 'mixed' *Gattung* might well be an important part in this work. They have been handled in a variety of ways, sometimes by dividing them, and sometimes by stressing points of coherence.[65] Psalms or psalm portions of reasonably identifiable *Gattung* have usually been treated in isolation. This has enriched our knowledge of the psalms to a degree. However, the work of Chr., albeit a limited piece of evidence, suggests that attention to the mixed *Gattung* itself is important. As well as the possible mutual relationship between *Gattung* and *Sitz im Leben* noted above, it should also be realized that the combination of *Gattungen* could create a new *Gattung*. Further analysis of those psalms we know to be 'mixed', both from within the canonical collection and from the Qumran manuscripts, might aid us in understanding more about the procedures used in producing new psalms from old stock. This study will be limited by the fact that it is only in Chronicles and a few other places in the Hebrew Bible that we have examples of psalms set in any liturgical or literary contexts.

One final point we might note at this juncture is Westermann's idea of defining *Sitz im Leben* in terms of human dialogue with God. While he does still speak of *Sitz im Leben* in singular, originating terms, we noted above a certain flexibility in his definition that was not found with Gunkel, Mowinckel and some others. It is also interesting that his understanding of *Sitz im Leben* allows him to move on to define the

65. E.g. Pss. 19, 27, 40, 66 and 108.

Gattung for the two primary psalms used in 1 Chron. 16.8-36 as psalms of descriptive praise.[66] He describes Psalm 106, of which only vv. 1 and 47-48 are quoted, as a psalm of declarative praise.[67] Westermann's approach to *Sitz im Leben* and his subsequent categories of psalms seem to lend themselves more readily to analyzing the situation in 1 Chron. 16.8-36.[68]

David and Psalms

Another area in which the study of the psalm texts in Chronicles has a contribution to make is that of the association of the psalms with David. This association is something that developed over time. There is an increase in the number of the psalms connected with David in the LXX over the MT, according to the superscriptions.[69] This trend seems to continue to a limited extent in some of the Qumran scrolls.[70] The Qumran psalms manuscript 11QPs[a] credits David, in a summary statement, with the composition of 3,600 psalms and other songs to a total of 4,050 compositions. The end of this manuscript clearly makes a claim for the Davidic authorship of the Psalter as represented by the scroll.[71] In the New Testament this tendency to connect the psalms with David continues, as we see the attribution to him of further psalms not directly associated with him in the MT (e.g. in Acts 4.25-26 and Heb. 4.7). Within early Jewish tradition the attribution of psalms to David was also widespread.[72] In the Babylonian Talmud, a statement attributed

---

66. Westermann, *The Praise of God in the Psalms*, pp. 122, 148.

67. Westermann, *The Praise of God in the Psalms*, pp. 114-15.

68. D.J.A. Clines's indirect suggestion that Westermann's thesis deserves more attention might still bear heeding. D.J.A. Clines, 'Psalm Research Since 1955. II. The Literary Genre', *TynBul* 20 (1969), pp. 105-25, esp. 112.

69. A. Pietersma, 'David in the Greek Psalms', *VT* 30 (1980), pp. 213-26, notes that the divergence between the Old Greek and MT in the superscriptions to the Psalms may not be as great as Rahlfs reckoned (p. 225). He also notes, however, that 'within the Greek textual traditions the Davidic Psalter was expanding, probably in a similar fashion to what had occurred at the pre-Greek stage' (p. 218).

70. See the synopsis of the psalm superscriptions in Flint, *The Dead Sea Psalms Scrolls*, pp. 118-34, and particularly Pss. 33, 91 and 104.

71. J.A. Sanders, *The Psalms Scroll of Qumran Cave 11 (11QPsa)* (DJD, 4; Oxford: Clarendon Press, 1965), p. 92. For further discussion of the Davidic emphasis in 11QPs[a], see Flint, *The Dead Sea Psalms Scrolls*, pp. 193-94.

72. Even as early as the second century BCE, David would seem to be regarded

to Rabbi Meir, a disciple of Rabbi Akiba, claims:

> All the praises which are expressed in the book of Psalms, David uttered
> them all ... concerning himself or concerning the people. '*Ledawid
> mizmôr*' means that the Presence descended upon him, and afterwards he
> composed poetry (*B. Pes.* 117a).[73]

Thus there would seem to be a growing tradition in which David is not
only connected with the psalms but is seen increasingly as the author of
them all.

The general topic of the association of David with the psalms has
been the subject of a few recent studies. The question has been raised
whether this growing attribution was simply a historical claim or
whether more was involved in the process. Some scholars have proposed that the latter is the case. On the basis of the evidence outlined
briefly above, Cooper has concluded, 'The Davidic attribution of
Psalms ... is best understood as a productive interpretive strategy rather
than as an historical claim'.[74] J.L. Mays has similarly stated in relation
to the overall biblical portrayal of David and the Psalms, 'the David of
Psalms is an intra-textual reality ... and its function and effect is
hermeneutic; its usefulness has to do with the interpretation of the text
as Scripture and in liturgy'.[75] That is, the attribution does not simply
indicate a belief by earlier editors of Davidic authorship, although I
would argue that must have been part of the case, especially in the cases
of those psalms where some event in David's life is mentioned in the
heading. What is more important, as Mays sees it, is that the mention of
David stamps the psalm with authority and provides a context within
which the psalm is to be interpreted by later generations.

Study of the psalms in Chronicles opens up the question of how far
back this tradition of Davidic association might be traced. Some
scholars would see the basis for the association in the biblical tradition
connecting David with music and poetry as found in 1 Sam. 16.14-23;

---

as *the* psalmist, if that is how we are to read Ecclus. 47.8-10.

73. Quoted from A.M. Cooper, 'The Life and Times of King David According
to the Book of Psalms', in R.E. Friedman (ed.), *The Poet and the Historian: Essays
in Literary and Historical Biblical Criticism* (HSS, 26; Chico, CA: Scholars Press,
1983), pp. 117-31, esp. 117. Cooper cites many other traditions along this line (see
pp. 117-18).

74. Cooper, 'Life and Times of King David', p. 125.

75. J.L. Mays, 'The David of the Psalms', *Int* 40 (1986), pp. 143-55, esp. 154.

2 Sam. 1.19-27 and Amos 6.5.[76] However, Cooper warns against too ready an identification of the three separate traditions of David as musician, David as poet and David as psalmist.[77] With his caution in mind, a look at the tradition in Chronicles might still offer some useful reflection in the area and especially on whether the association of the psalms with David involves more than a matter of authorship.

The focus on David in Chronicles is generally recognized in terms of giving authorization to the ritual practice and personnel associated with temple worship in Chr.'s own generation. In part this is done by portraying David as a cult founder, both equal in status to Moses and in the same tradition.[78] But the authorization did not just lie with David. It extended to Solomon and the line of his successors. We noted above that the quotation of Ps. 132.8-10 in 2 Chron. 6.41-42 not only picked up the two major themes of Psalm 132 but also the occasion and content of 1 Chronicles 15–17. Williamson sees the use of Psalm 132 at the end of Solomon's prayer at the dedication of the temple as a way of returning to the major themes of Chr.'s account of David, namely bringing the ark to Jerusalem and the temple site. A powerful link is thus forged between David and Solomon and their work is to be seen as a unity.[79]

This link, however, goes beyond Solomon. Throntveit's argument that in Chronicles Hezekiah is seen as a new David *and* a new Solomon is convincing and signals a further unity between the later period of a reunited monarchy and the earlier period under David and Solomon.[80] It is Hezekiah who ultimately defines the contents of the choral music associated with temple rites. He does this in 2 Chron. 29.25-30, as he

---

76. E.g. J.A. Soggin, *Introduction to the Old Testament* (OTL; London: SCM Press, 3rd edn, 1989), p. 427; and Mays, 'The David of the Psalms', pp. 146-51.

77. Cooper, 'The Life and Times of King David', pp. 127-30.

78. See Kleinig, *The Lord's Song*, pp. 28-29; S.J. De Vries, 'Moses and David as Cult Founders in Chronicles', *JBL* 107 (1988), pp. 619-39; and H.G.M. Williamson, 'The Accession of Solomon in the Books of Chronicles', *VT* 26 (1976), pp. 351-61, who argues for a parallel between the Deuteronomy–Joshua transition from Moses to Joshua and the transition from David to Solomon in Chronicles.

79. Williamson, 'The Accession of Solomon', p. 359.

80. Throntveit, *When Kings Speak*, p. 124, in response to arguments by R. Mosis, (*Untersuchungen zur Theologie des chronistischen Geschichtswerkes* [FTS, 92; Freiburg: Herder, 1973]), H.G.M. Williamson (*Israel in the Books of Chronicles* [Cambridge: Cambridge University Press, 1977], pp. 119-25) and P.R. Ackroyd (*I & II Chronicles*, pp. 179-89).

restores temple worship after its corruption during the reign of Ahaz.
He stations the levites with their instruments, and orders the making of
the burnt offering, which was to be accompanied by singing. Both
Hezekiah and all present worshiped. We are told that Hezekiah did this
according to the command of David which, in turn, had come from the
Lord through his two prophets Gad and Nathan (v. 25). Twice more we
are reminded that the instruments played by the levites are those
assigned by David (vv. 26-27). Finally, in v. 30 we are told that Hezekiah and the officials instruct the levites to praise the Lord with 'the
words of David and of the seer Asaph'. In this process 'some psalms
were selected for use in divine worship. They were thus given canonical
status and authority as "the song of the LORD" (29.27) by virtue of their
reputed origin and liturgical use.' [81]

Hezekiah's authority in this reform and designation of the psalms as
the appropriate choral music to accompany the sacrifices clearly goes
back to David and is ultimately grounded in divine revelation.[82] The
fact that v. 30 parallels David's own instruction in appointing singers
for the temple rites (cf. 1 Chron. 15.16) underscores this as does the fact
that v. 30 bears a faint similarity to David's own establishment of the
singing of praises at the transfer of the ark to Jerusalem (cf. 1 Chron.
16.7). This latter act of praise consists of singing psalms (1 Chron.
16.8-36), which is in turn consistent with Hezekiah's instruction later.
There is a unity of action and authority in all this.

The sense of authority in matters of temple worship and the use of the
psalms is not only one that is of historical interest, but also one that is
consciously applied to Chr.'s own generation. This is done specifically
through the psalm quotations and the alterations to them. We saw above
the changes to Psalm 105 in 1 Chron. 16.15 and 19, which made the
psalm a consistent address to the audience, and the changes to Psalm 96
in 1 Chron. 16.27 and 29, which brought the psalm into line with the
postexilic situation.

Several other points about the psalm text in 1 Chronicles 16 also
indicate that it has been shaped to speak specifically to Chr.'s own
community. The break in the quotation of Psalm 105 at v. 15 not only

---

81. See Kleinig, *The Lord's Song*, pp. 61-62.

82. As J.W. Kleinig notes ('The Divine Institution of the Lord's Song in
Chronicles', *JSOT* 55 [1992], pp. 75-83), this was also consistent with Mosaic tradition, fulfilling the divine commands in Num. 10.10; Deut. 10.8 and 18.5, as well as
the injunction in Deuteronomy for the people to rejoice in the Lord's presence.

removes the accounts of Israel's stay in Egypt and of the Exodus, themes not taken up in Chronicles, but serves to emphasize two other points. First, it stresses the insignificance of Israel, its landless status and the Lord's protection of Israel among the nations (Ps. 105.12-15 [= 1 Chron. 16.19-22]). This fits well with the declaration of the Lord's sovereignty over the nations and their gods stressed in Psalm 96 (= 1 Chron. 16.23-33). Secondly, it links the audience closely with the ancestral period, the covenant with the patriarchs and the promise of the land (Ps. 105.7-11 [= 1 Chron. 16.14-18]). The quotation of Ps. 106.47 in 1 Chron. 16.35 concludes the psalm text in 1 Chronicles with a plea for deliverance. This plea is in place at the end of Psalm 106 but—as with some of the other points noted above—seems out of place in the context within which Chr. has placed his mixed psalm text, namely at the conclusion of David's wars and at the point where he starts to plan and build those elements that (according to Chr.) are at the heart of his peaceful and stable empire. The psalm in 1 Chron. 16.8-36 speaks to a community much more vulnerable in a world ruled by powerful foreign nations. It seems to speak to a community uncertain of its homeland and its future. We have also noted the same themes present in David's final prayer in 1 Chron. 29.10-19.[83]

Thus, one gets the impression that the psalm text has been constructed to address the audience of Chr.'s day but set in the context of David's bringing the ark to Jerusalem and organizing temple worship. This brings the authority of David more immediately to bear on the worship and life of the postexilic community. This community, as much as the people of the times of David and Hezekiah, stands under the command of David, and hence under divine command, regarding its worship and the place of the psalms in that. Japhet has suggested that this point is even made by the use of symmetry in the construction of 1 Chronicles 16. Chr. has used a 'sophisticated literary technique, which endeavours to combine two matters: the permanent arrangements for the ark and the psalm which was sung before the ark of God "on that day"'. She notes the specific connection between v. 7 and vv. 37-38, where there is reference to 'Asaph and his brothers' being instructed to sing respectively 'on that day' and 'regularly'. The pattern for subsequent times is set in 1 Chronicles 16.[84]

83. Cf. Williamson, *1 and 2 Chronicles*, p. 185; Japhet, *I & II Chronicles*, p. 317; Butler, 'A Forgotten Passage', pp. 143-45.
84. Japhet, *I & II Chronicles*, p. 312.

For Chr. the authority of David no doubt played a significant role in the establishment of worship in the Second Temple. This authority was even extended to the establishment of psalm singing in the temple liturgies. While we are not certain of all Chr. intended in writing his history, it would not seem unreasonable to suppose that the portrayal of David's authority in relation to psalms in this context was either illustrative of, or perhaps even influenced, a growing association of David with the psalms. In part, this manifests itself in the growing attribution of psalms to David by means of the superscriptions and headings in the book of Psalms. Even if Chronicles comes from more limited temple circles, as some have argued,[85] its illustrative and influential nature need not be diminished. Cooper recognizes that the strong emphasis in Chronicles on David organizing levitical singers could be due to some groups of levites trying to establish the legitimacy of their role—vis-à-vis that of the priests—in the liturgy of the Second Temple. But this interpretation of David as organizer of liturgy could then spill back into the book of Psalms, where the heading is attached to some psalms, thus designating David as their author. The same approach continued in the LXX, Qumran and elsewhere, as more and more psalms were attributed to David.[86]

While this remains a hypothesis, given the paucity of hard evidence, it is nonetheless plausible. On the basis of the arguments above, the tradition associating David with the psalms could well have had ancient origins. In Chronicles this tradition was not confined to the matter of authorship, although that was an element. In Hezekiah's instruction to the levites regarding the singing of praises to the Lord, he certainly includes psalms attributed to David but also those attributed to Asaph. The corpus of psalmody surely included more than just those directly attributed to David, and even the psalms combined in 1 Chronicles 16 are 'non-Davidic' in the MT (though Ps. 96 is attributed to David in LXX). But Chronicles also provides a context within which the psalms are to be used. At one level this context is the worship of the temple. With due liturgical attention and in proper order the psalms are to be used in the context of corporate worship associated with the burnt offer-

85. P.D. Hanson, '1 Chronicles 15–16 and the Chronicler's Views on the Levites', in M. Fishbane and E. Tov (eds.), *'Sha'arei Talmon': Studies in the Bible, Qumran, and the Ancient Near East Presented to Shemaryahu Talmon* (Winona Lake, IN: Eisenbrauns, 1992), pp. 69-78.

86. Cooper, 'The Life and Times of King David', pp. 127-30.

ing and other rites. At another level, the context within which Chr. sets
the singing of psalms is one of national uncertainty and vulnerability.
These two levels are brought together in 1 Chronicles 15–17 under the
authority of David. He sets the pattern for Israel's worship, which can
include both its thanksgiving and its pleas for deliverance. But the
association with David is even more complex than this. Within Chronicles David is portrayed as a warrior king whose authority stands over
all that follows. His instruction sets the proper liturgical context within
which praises and pleas need to be offered, and his victories give
confidence to those who offer them. We have here a picture of the king,
David, who guides by his decree, shapes the lives of his people by his
authority in office and encourages them by his victories.

David's role in Chronicles in relation to the psalms is very much tied
to his office and position. He is not shown uttering the psalms as an
individual in prayer, nor is it suggested that his psalms were expressions of personal piety. What patterns of prayer he personally passes on
are only taken up by kings. But while this is predominantly the case,
some qualification must be made. First, although most of the 'negative'
aspects of David's character and reign that are portrayed in the books of
Samuel are not recorded in Chronicles, some qualifications are made to
his character in the latter. Bailey and Knoppers have shown that in
Chronicles David is not entirely innocent of wrongdoing. He appears to
be culpable in bringing the wrath of God upon the people in the matter
of the census (1 Chron. 21).[87] Knoppers concludes:

> that there are compelling reasons to recognize an additional dimension of
> David's legacy in Chronicles. The image of David as the model of a
> repentant sinner is a constituent element in the Chronicler's depiction of
> David.[88]

He sees David's repentance and intercession, as well as other actions
and personal qualities, as paradigmatic. Secondly, we noted above the
unity between the prayer of Solomon (2 Chron. 6.41-42 quoting Ps.
132.8-10) and the commands of David in 1 Chronicles 15–17. This
connection suggests that David's personal piety would involve singing

---

87. N. Bailey, 'David's Innocence: A Response to J. Wright', *JSOT* 64 (1994),
pp. 83-90 (in response to J.W. Wright, 'The Innocence of David in 1 Chronicles
21', *JSOT* 60 [1993], pp. 87-105); and G.N. Knoppers, 'Images of David in Early
Judaism: David as Repentant Sinner in Chronicles', *Bib* 76 (1995), pp. 449-70.
88. Knoppers, 'Images of David', p. 469.

and praying psalms, as would the recognition of his authorship of psalms. Knoppers concludes: 'The Chronicler simply has a broader conception of David's exemplary significance than modern commentators have recognized.'[89] The image of David as a repentant sinner, and to a lesser extent, a pious individual, certainly do not dominate Chronicles, but they do qualify the royal, military image.

To summarize, it would seem that even at the early stage of the composition of Chronicles the association of David with the psalms had taken on aspects that went beyond issues of authorship. He was still far from the model pray-er whom we see in later Christian circles. He had, however, been placed in a relationship with the psalms that would contribute significantly to the image that would appear later.

The Way Forward

One ought not overemphasize the way in which the study of the psalms in Chronicles might inform Psalms study generally. After all, the psalm texts in Chronicles provide only a small corpus for study. Nevertheless, an examination of them provides stimulus to take up with new vigor some old matters, such as the complexity of the history of the text of the psalms or the relation of *Gattung* to *Sitz im Leben*. It also urges further consideration of some matters that have not yet been discussed at great length and yet have played an important role in the lives of the faith communities through the centuries. The association of David with the psalms is such a matter. Above all, the study of the psalms in Chronicles puts before us the complexity that surrounds the use of such material in communities of faith. It also reminds us that it is precisely in such complex situations that texts like the psalms are imbued with life and, in turn, give life to those who read and hear them.

---

89. Knoppers, 'Images of David', p. 470.

Part III

TEXTS IN CHRONICLES

READING, READERS AND READING READERS READING THE ACCOUNT OF SAUL'S DEATH IN 1 CHRONICLES 10

James M. Trotter

Reading and Readers: A Methodological Statement

The advent of reader-oriented literary criticism in the last quarter century has resulted in an expansion of the conception of the 'meaning' of literary texts. Meaning is no longer limited to a product that can be derived from a text like the solution to a mathematical equation. In contrast to the formalist orthodoxy of New Criticism, which dominated the early part of the twentieth century, meaning is no longer understood as a static concept but as an event that occurs over time within the process of reading. This more recent theoretical perspective has transformed the value given to the event of reading. The creation of meaning during the reading event involves judgments, questions, discoveries and revisions of previous interpretations.[1] From a formalist perspective, the reading event is a non-event—meaning resides in and is derived from the text, and reading is only the procedure by which one extracts the textually determined meaning. This is an entirely static perception of reading. There is only one way to do it, in all times and in all places, and as long as one does it properly, there is only one meaning that can result. Reader-oriented approaches, particularly those at the antiformalist end of the continuum, remind us that reading is dynamic, that we are constantly creating meaning as we read. Meaning is not the end result of reading a text but is constantly formed and revised as we read.[2]

---

1. S. Mailloux, *Interpretive Conventions: The Reader in the Study of American Fiction* (Ithaca, NY: Cornell University Press, 1982), pp. 70-71.

2. S. Fish, *Is There a Text in This Class? The Authority of Interpretive Communities* (Cambridge, MA: Harvard University Press, 1980). Cf. W. Iser, *The Act of Reading: A Theory of Aesthetic Response* (Baltimore: The Johns Hopkins University Press, 1978), pp. 4-7.

This dynamic perception of reading not only highlights the importance of reading as a diachronic experience but also the important function of the reader in the creation of meaning. Reader-response approaches have brought into the critical consciousness the social, psychological and idiosyncratic aspects of readers reading and the way in which all of these aspects converge in the creation of meaning.[3] It is the unique combination of socially shaped reading conventions and individual experiences, which are given their particular shape by both psychological and social factors, that determines meaning rather than the words on the page. The words on the page cannot exercise a decisive control over the meaning that the reader derives from the text, because both their signification and the significance of their interrelationships with each other are determined by the reading conventions of the reader. In a very real sense, the reader constitutes the text.[4]

This antiformalist theory of the making of meaning can generate fear. The lack of external controls to ensure that the right meaning of the text is protected from the biases and idiosyncrasies of the interpreter or the interpretive community creates the potential for an infinite number of possible interpretations of any individual text. The fact is, formalist theories and appeals to authorial intention have never functioned as effective controls over the multiplication of interpretations. Only a brief survey of the history of the interpretation of any particular document is needed to demonstrate that readings proliferate as reading communities and readers proliferate. Antiformalist theory does not argue for the removal of constraints on the production of meaning but an observation that such constraints have never really existed.[5] In other words, reader-oriented approaches to interpretation are not a method devised to allow for the creation of multiple meanings but fall within a broad theoretical perspective that focuses on what happens when readers read.

Such an analysis of the interpretive process could also lead to despair that meaning can never be shared, and perhaps in some ultimate sense

---

3.   See, e.g., M. Steig, *Stories of Reading: Subjectivity and Literary Understanding* (Baltimore: The Johns Hopkins University Press, 1989).

4.   S. Fish, 'How to Recognize a Poem When You See One', in *Is There a Text in This Class?*, pp. 322-37.

5.   S. Fish, 'Introduction: Going Down the Anti-Formalist Road', in *Doing What Comes Naturally: Change, Rhetoric, and the Practice of Theory in Literary and Legal Studies* (Post-contemporary Interventions; Durham, NC: Duke University Press, 1989), p. 27.

this is the case, but it is a fear that is not finally realized. The social nature of interpretive conventions, which provides for a measure of commonality to readings within interpretive communities and the ability to communicate idiosyncratic experiences in socially constructed ways, provide for the possibility of intersubjectivity. Rather than acting as a barrier to shared meaning, idiosyncratic factors can function as catalysts to richer interpretations. In fact, the possibility of sharing insights derived from the idiosyncrasies of particular readings greatly enriches the range of possible interpretations produced by an interpretive community.[6]

A vital element in any reader-oriented approach to literary analysis is the identity of the reader. In most reader-response criticism the true identity of the reader, no matter how well masked by impressive jargon or theoretical argument, has been the critic her- or himself.[7] The difficulty with this is not the obvious truth that any reading that I produce will be my own, but that critical language often allows the critic to present such readings not as his or her own reading but as the reading of some theoretically constructed 'ideal reader'. In other words, the (perhaps) unintended result is the privileging of the critic's reading hidden behind a veneer of theoretical objectivity.

A valuable recent development in reader-oriented literary criticism has been an increasing interest in historical readers. If meaning results from the socially constituted conventions of the reading of a particular reading community, then the reconstruction of the reading conventions of past communities can provide important insights into the history of a text's reception. This move to investigate the reception of texts by historical reading communities, reception within specific socio-historical settings, has provided the opportunity for reader-oriented approaches to expand beyond the modern, ideal reader construct to the reconstruction of actual readers reading.

6. Steig, *Stories of Reading*, p. xiv. Note the similar argument made in L.E. Keck and G.M. Tucker, 'Exegesis', in *IDBSup* (1976), pp. 296-303: conclusions may differ due to 'varying sensibilities and insights' (p. 297); and 'Some exegeses are better than others, not simply because some exegetes are more knowledgeable, but also because some are more attuned to the subject matter' (p. 298).

7. S. Mailloux, 'Misreading as a Historical Act: Cultural Rhetoric, Bible Politics, and Fuller's 1845 Review of Douglass's Narrative', in J.L. Machor (ed.), *Readers in History: Nineteenth-Century American Literature and the Contexts of Response* (Baltimore: The Johns Hopkins University Press, 1993), p. 4.

Steven Mailloux argues that readings are rhetorical transactions that are shaped by particular socio-historical factors. He has called for a rhetorical hermeneutics that focuses on 'the cultural rhetoric in which readings are presented, circulated, adopted, and contested'.[8] This move to consider the socio-historically conditioned nature of textual reception represents a new and substantial additional move away from New Criticism's naive belief that meaning resides in the text, unaffected by cultural variations within and across historical eras. The recognition that conventions of writing and reading texts vary in different communities and that they continually change over time leads to the conclusion that the analysis of textual reception must be socially and historically specific. Operating from a similar perspective, James Machor has called for a theoretical approach that combines response and reception theories. This form of analysis, which Machor calls 'historical hermeneutics', allows for the situationally conditioned nature of interpretation.[9] Any reading must be a particularized reading, constructed from the reading conventions and socio-historical situation of a specific reading community. The reception of texts differs both diachronically and also across different interpretive communities synchronically. These approaches move beyond the limitations of a single ideal reader by combining the insights gained from a reader-response orientation with the variegated history of a text's reception. The critic's conception of the ideal reader is no longer the arbiter of how a text should be read.

8.   Mailloux, 'Misreading as a Historical Act', p. 5. Cf. S. Mailloux, *Rhetorical Power* (Ithaca, NY: Cornell University Press, 1989).

9.   'Such a reorientation needs to integrate response theory, which concentrates on the stages of hermeneutical processing, and the contextual emphasis of reception theory to create a historical hermeneutics that identifies specific reading practices and explores the role of interpretive communities in the way texts were constructed and made meaningful in a given era. For an era other than our own, such a turn would necessitate a close analysis of interpretive traces preserved in the archive, but in doing so, a historical hermeneutics would have to go beyond Jonathan Culler's call for a history of reception that merely surveys the legacy of responses to a particular text to reconstruct the codes that produced its various interpretations. Instead, such an approach would reconstruct the shared patterns of interpretation for a specific historical era to define the reading strategies of particular interpretive communities and to examine the impact of those strategies on the production and consumption of literary texts.' J.L. Machor, 'Historical Hermeneutics and Antebellum Fiction: Gender, Response Theory, and Interpretive Contexts', in Machor (ed.), *Readers in History*, p. 60.

Instead, the actual practices of historical reading communities shape the critic's understanding of the text.

Such a theoretical reorientation does not negate the previous observation that any reading will always be that of the actual reader. It is impossible for the critic to negate self so completely that the reading perfectly reflects that of another. In addition, the historical reader is a (re)construct(ion) that ultimately derives from the critic's interpretation (or 'reading') of the available evidence. Such a reconstruction will always be partial and provisional. This limitation, which is also true of all textual interpretations, does not alter the fact that a reconstructed historical reader is a substantial improvement over the ahistorical, ideal readers of earlier reader-oriented approaches or the reading-in-a-vacuum technique of New Criticism. The value of a historicized reader-oriented approach is not the ability to produce a final and unchallenge-able, objective meaning of the text, but the opportunity to open the critical process to the variety of socio-historical factors that ultimately make all reading subjective. As Machor indicates:

> Similarly, the purpose of a historically based reader-response criticism is not to restore the subjective/objective dichotomy but to collapse it by grounding the reading experience of fiction in an awareness of historical conditions, including the critic's own. In its interplay between the historical experience (re)constructed from the archive and the critic's own self-conscious enactment of interpretation, a historical hermeneutics would provide not an objective description of historicized reading so much as a Gadamerian 'fusion of horizons' that is always partial, provisional, speculative and thus open to the flux characterizing interpretation as an intertextual, historical and gender-based activity.[10]

Historicized reader-oriented interpretation provides a significant opportunity for biblical scholars. This theoretical perspective provides the possibility of overcoming the antipathy that has often characterized relations between scholars favoring the 'old' historical-critical approaches and those favoring the 'new' literary approaches. The best contributions of both, combined with a substantial contribution from sociological analyses, are necessary for the success of a 'historical hermeneutics'. This theoretical orientation derives from the point at which these diverse approaches intersect.[11]

---

10. Machor, 'Historical Hermeneutics', p. 63.

11. For a fuller discussion of these theoretical issues, see J.M. Trotter, 'Reading Hosea in Achaemenid Yehud' (PhD dissertation, Emory University, 1998), pp. 1-74.

Reading Readers Reading Saul's Death (1 Chronicles 10)

The story of Saul's death in battle with the Philistines represents a substantive turning point in the experience of reading Chronicles.[12] Most, if not all, readers, both ancient and modern, would be aware of the transition from genealogy to narrative. This transition functions as an important marker for the reader that the book is entering a new phase. The experiences of reading genealogies and reading narrative history[13] are quite different. Genealogies are one dimensional, providing the reader with a sense of chronological depth and continuity between the present and the past; but they lack the twists and turns of a plot and the development and resolution of tension that draw the reader into a story. This shift of genres functions as a signal to the reader that the complexion of the book has changed dramatically at this point. While it must be admitted that, from a reader-oriented perspective, the importance of this shift in genres might not be experienced by all readers: any reader who shares the conventions that permit the recognition of genealogy and narrative history as different genres will experience the important change that takes place at this point in the book.[14]

The fact that the Chronicles narrative begins with the last gasps of Saul's reign (literally) has consistently raised one question for readers: Why?[15] Starting the narrative with Saul's death seems, to say the least, a very unusual place to begin. In what follows, the shaping power of the

12. For the purposes of this paper, the text of Chronicles for the ancient reader(s) will be assumed to be basically coterminus with the MT of Chronicles. Although it is possible that Chronicles has undergone a substantial redactional history that includes significantly different versions, my primary focus here is on the reading of the final form of the book by ancient reading communities. It would be possible to use historical hermeneutics to analyze earlier versions of Chronicles, but the possible readings of these earlier versions of the book are beyond the scope of this essay.

13. The term 'history' is used here not in a modern, technical sense, but in recognition that ancient Yehudite readers would have believed that this narration was a representation of their national past.

14. Note the observations of one reader on the significance of this transition: 'The change of form at this point is an unmistakable indication of the author's conscious movement from the introduction of his work to its main body.' S. Japhet, *I & II Chronicles: A Commentary* (OTL; Louisville, KY: Westminster/John Knox Press, 1993), p. 221.

15. Cf. Japhet, *I & II Chronicles*, p. 221.

reader's expectations and conventions will be examined in dialogue with three recent interpretations of this text. Each of these interpretations represents different ways in which modern readers have understood the significance of the account of Saul's death as the beginning of the Chronicles narrative.

For Japhet the primary function of the narrative of Saul's death is to provide a past for the story of the kingdom of David. She claims that this chapter creates a continuum between David's reign and Israel's past, while it also functions as the turning point from prehistory, which is of no direct interest to Chr., to history.[16] As a result of this narrative, David's kingdom is depicted as both a continuation and a significant alteration of Israel's life. While this is an important observation, Japhet's comments are primarily descriptive rather than explanatory. Her description of how the narrative of Chronicles is different with the inclusion of the death of Saul is clearly true but ultimately unsatisfactory. How this inclusion alters the reader's experience remains largely unexplored. How is it different to read this book with this narrative in place? The genealogies alone would provide an experience of David's kingdom as the continuation of Israel's earlier history. How does the inclusion of Saul's death at the hands of the Philistines according to the desire of Yahweh change the experience of the remainder of the book in a way that the genealogies alone do not?[17] Clearly the presence of the narrative of Saul's death alters the reader's experience of the narration of the reign of David. Within the closed world of the narrative the inclusion of a story about a previous monarch means that David is not a beginning *ex nihilo* but rather represents the continuation of a preexisting monarchy. This observation does not, however, explain the altered experience of the reader. What is the significance of this fact? What is the effect of a narrative that indicates the existence of a previous monarch but that provides no details of the life or reign of this king,

---

16. Japhet, *I & II Chronicles*, p. 230. Note also Japhet's earlier remark: 'If the narrative were to begin with the assembly at Hebron, David's monarchy would have no past. Juxtaposing David's anointment with Saul's death creates a line of continuity, if not of succession, and that is why the chapter has been included.' S. Japhet, *The Ideology of the Book of Chronicles and its Place in Biblical Thought* (BEATAJ, 9; Bern: Peter Lang, 1989), p. 407.

17. Or, if we were to phrase the question in terms of authorial intention, 'Why was it important to the Chronicler to depict David as a continuation of a preexistent monarchy?'

with the exception of his death in battle? Japhet's observation is accurate but insufficient. Clearly the presence of this narrative means that the reader's experience of the remainder of the book will be different than it would have been without an account of Saul's death, but how that experience is altered by the presence of this text will depend on the identity and reading conventions of the reader.

S. Zalewski also views 1 Chronicles 10 as an introduction to the story of David. For Zalewski, however, the story does not simply provide for the Davidic narratives a past, a sense of continuity with the earlier history of Israel. He understands the chapter as a defense of David in relation to his replacement of Saul as king. The key to understanding this story, according to Zalewski, lies in the last two verses, which attribute the death of Saul to Yahweh (1 Chron. 10.13-14). Since Saul died at the instigation of heaven, David is innocent of Saul's blood.[18] He finds further support for this argument in the fact that the Chronicles account of the death of Saul—when compared with the account in 1 Samuel 31—appears to emphasize the end of the Saulide dynasty. The account in 1 Samuel indicates that many in Israel died as a result of the battle with the Philistines: 'So Saul and his three sons and his armor-bearer and *all his men* died together on the same day' (1 Sam. 31.6). In contrast, the summary of the outcome of the battle in Chronicles states, 'Thus Saul died; he and his three sons *and all his house* died together' (1 Chron. 10.6). Zalewski contends that Chr. made every effort to emphasize the legitimacy of the transfer of power to David and the Davidic dynasty by placing on Yahweh the full responsibility for the end of Saul and his dynasty.

This may well have been the intention of the author of Chronicles, but such a reading is not obvious from Chronicles alone. Zalewski's reading focuses on the differences between the accounts in Samuel and Chronicles and relies on the assumption that these differences are the result of Chr. working from the text of DtrH and consciously changing the story for a particular purpose.[19] Even if we grant Zalewski's assumption(s), he fails to take note of the fact that this possible reading of 1 Chronicles 10 is only available to a reader who knows the full

18. S. Zalewski, 'The Purpose of the Story of the Death of Saul in 1 Chronicles x', *VT* 39 (1989), pp. 449-67.

19. Cf. the substantially different reading of the relationship between these two texts in C.Y.S. Ho, 'Conjectures and Refutations: Is 1 Samuel XXXI 1-13 really the Source of 1 Chronicles X 1-12?', *VT* 45 (1995), pp. 82-106.

account of the reign of Saul from DtrH. Imagine a reader of 1 Chronicles 10 who does not have a copy of DtrH and does not know the depiction of the relationship between Saul and David presented there. It is not at all obvious that such a reader would interpret this text as a defense of David against charges of having been involved in the death of Saul or having inappropriately usurped the throne. Zalewski's reading of this text is a clear demonstration of the way in which the reader's knowledge and conventions of reading shape the text and produce meaning.

Unlike Japhet and Zalewski, who both posit a direct narrative connection between the account of Saul's death and the beginning of the story of David's reign, R. Mosis believes that the Saulide account is an independent unit that has little or nothing directly to do with the account of David that follows.[20] Mosis argues that the story of Saul is not the beginning of the Chronicler's history, which he believes begins with the reign of David, but is an independent unit that functions as a paradigm of exile and return. For Mosis the Chronicler presents Saul as the embodiment of many of the key flaws that brought disaster on Israel, and indeed he embodies the disaster itself. Leaving specific details of his reading aside for the present, this interpretation has much to commend it. As with Zalewski's suggested reading, however, this reading requires a community that understands the shape of ancient Israel's history in very specific terms. A reading such as that proposed by Mosis requires a community that perceives Israelite history within a schematic framework of exile and restoration. If this is not a dominant shape of the reading community's perception of Israel's monarchic and early post-monarchic history, then it is highly unlikely that a reader would read Chronicles in the way Mosis suggests.

These interpreters all share at least one common focus in their attempts to read this text. They all read the text with the goal of delineating or explaining *the intention* of Chr. They all read the text as if their methods permit them access to the mind of Chr. through the words on the page. Such a goal is ultimately impossible to achieve because authorial intention, like all other aspects of textual interpreta-

---

20. R. Mosis, *Untersuchungen zur Theologie des chronistischen Geschichtswerkes* (FTS, 92; Freiburg: Herder, 1973), pp. 17-43. Although they differ on some of the details, the readings of Ackroyd and Williamson are basically similar to that of Mosis. P.R. Ackroyd, 'The Chronicler as Exegete', *JSOT* 2 (1977), pp. 2-32. H.G.M. Williamson, *1 and 2 Chronicles* (NCB; Grand Rapids: Eerdmans, 1982).

tion, is construed by the interpreter. There is no universal, ahistorical, culturally neutral formula for deriving authorial intention from words on a page. If such a formula does exist, then why so much contention over the interpretation of texts? Reading could be described as a construing of the author's intention by the reader, but this is always contingent, shaped by the reading conventions of the reader.[21] As with all other aspects of reading, the way in which authorial intention is construed changes when the reading conventions change.

The variety of readings that have been produced by these different interpreters provides evidence of the veracity of the reader-oriented theoretical perspective. It is not the text itself that generates this multiplicity of readings but the multiplicity of readers. Their divergent reading conventions have generated a multiplicity of texts, that is, each of these readers has constituted a different text in the interaction of their socially constructed reading conventions, their own unique psychosocial make-up and the words on the page. Their readings tell us as much or more about them as consumers of the text than they do about Chr. as producer of the text.

Historical Readers Reading Chronicles

The original community of readers to which the author belonged and for whom the text was written is only one possible context for the reception of a text.[22] This 'original' context has clearly been the dominant focus within critical biblical studies of the last two centuries. Composite texts with a long redactional history have been examined primarily to separate the various redactional layers and then the 'original' words are interpreted in relation to the supposed 'original' context. This type of approach has produced valuable results and should not be rejected as inappropriate or lacking merit, but it has so dominated the attention of critical interpreters that the interpretation of the final forms of these documents within the communities that produced, copied, read and reread them has been almost entirely neglected. How

21. S. Fish, 'Working on the Chain Gang', in *Doing What Comes Naturally*, pp. 87-102 (100); S. Knapp and W.B. Michaels, 'Against Theory', in W.J.T. Mitchell (ed.), *Against Theory: Literary Studies and the New Pragmatism* (Chicago: University of Chicago Press, 1985), pp. 11-30.

22. A text may not necessarily be written for a community of readers to which the author belongs, but it is most often the case that authors write for their own community(ies).

were the texts of the Hebrew Bible read by these communities? How did these texts, which were accorded enough status to guarantee their continuous reproduction over the centuries, function within these communities? A historicized reader-oriented approach to interpretation, with its focus on readers rather than authors, on the contexts that produce meaning rather than on the words on the page, provides a method for dealing with these questions.

A historicized reader-oriented perspective differs from other attempts to read Chronicles not in its ability to generate the one, objectively *true* reading of the text, but in its focus on readers reading. From this perspective a multiplicity of readings is not evidence of a failure of some or all of the readers to arrive at the only true reading but simply the result to be expected when different human beings read. Since the focus is on readers rather than producers, interpretation is no longer tied to the moment of a text's origin. Any attempt to clarify what Chr. meant (intended) is necessarily dependent upon one's ability to determine accurately the date of writing. In contrast, by focusing on how a text is read by a particular community of readers rather than what it meant in the head of the author at its point of origin,[23] a historicized reader-oriented approach permits all contexts of reception to be considered as foci for critical inquiry. Since this approach is concerned with a text's reception rather than its production, it can appropriately be used to examine the reception of a text within any particular reading community, within any specific chronological period after the text's production.

A historicized reader-oriented interpretation requires a clear definition of the socio-historical period and the geographical and social boundaries of the reading community. The social history of the community must be reconstructed with as much data about their intellectual, political, religious and social structures as can be retrieved. All of these factors and more shape the way in which texts are received by any reading community. Historical hermeneutics is not so much a literary method as a theoretical perspective that recognizes the situational nature of interpretive practices and interpretations of texts. Space does not permit a full reconstruction of a particular reading community and their conventions of reading, but I would like to examine some of the important features of such a reconstruction that would shape a historicized reading of this text.

---

23. Something that we can never possibly ascertain with any degree of certainty.

Information regarding the literacy rates of the reading community is a vital factor in understanding the community's reception of texts. Such information should not simply estimate the percentages of literate and illiterate individuals but should include a nuanced analysis of the various gradations of literacy. William Harris has proposed three levels of literacy, each representing a portion of a continuum from complete illiteracy to the highly literate: professional literacy, craftsman's literacy and mass literacy (extending from the illiterate to the semi-literate).[24] The ability to read does not equate with the capability to produce or read complex literary creations like Chronicles. The production of a literate society requires the widespread availability of inexpensive texts and an educational system open to the vast majority of the population. Harris notes that no historical culture has achieved extensive literacy without the printing press.[25] The best estimates suggest that the skills necessary to produce and read complex literary texts would have been limited to approximately one per cent of the population of ancient societies.[26] Clearly literate individuals would have been a small proportion of the population of Achaemenid Yehud, and this consisted almost entirely of professional scribes.[27]

The limited accessibility of literary skills would have a significant impact on access to texts. This means that literary skills and the control of those with literary skills were sources of power. By effectively limiting the production and interpretation of texts to a small, literate elite, a substantial amount of power within the community is given to the literati and their patrons. This is especially true in the case of texts that are considered authoritative by the community. Tamara Eskenazi highlights three examples of the power of texts and, by implication, their interpreters in Achaemenid Yehud. First, messages from God come to the community through the reading of the written word, the book of the Torah (Neh. 8). Secondly, references to official correspondence function as a source of authority (Ezra 4–5). Thirdly, community leaders

---

24. W.V. Harris, *Ancient Literacy* (Cambridge, MA: Harvard University Press, 1989), pp. 7-8.

25. Harris, *Ancient Literacy*, pp. 12-16.

26. See J. Baines, 'Literacy and Ancient Egyptian Society', *Man* NS 18 (1983), pp. 572-99; J. Ray, 'Literacy in Egypt in the Late and Persian Periods', in A.K. Bowman and G. Woolf (eds.), *Literacy and Power in the Ancient World* (Cambridge: Cambridge University Press, 1994), pp. 51-66.

27. See Trotter, 'Reading Hosea', pp. 55-58.

assent to the covenant by signing a written document (Neh. 10.1-27).[28] It is especially important to note that when the texts are read to the wider community, representatives of the ruling elite are on hand to provide authorized interpretation (Neh. 8.7-8). By controlling access to and the interpretation of important religious texts, scribes and their patrons were effectively the gatekeepers to the divine.

As already noted, the reading community's perception of the history of Israel would play an important role in their reading of this text. What did they know of their past? What were the central ideological and theological constructs that gave shape to the community's knowledge of the past? Perhaps the most important factor in reconstructing the community's perception of its own history is the clarification of which literary texts were available to and known by them. As many of the treatments of Chronicles demonstrate, the reading community's knowledge of other textual traditions, and DtrH in particular, is a vital factor in reconstructing the reading context of Chronicles. Did the readers know DtrH? If so, was it known by some in the community or by everyone? This is particularly relevant to the reading of 1 Chronicles 10. It is highly unlikely that the readers of this text would have been familiar with the reign of Saul, about five hundred years earlier, without the textual traditions preserved in DtrH. Whether these traditions were known and in what form would have an important influence on reading this text. Unfortunately, there are many assumptions but few clear arguments about the texts that would have been known to these ancient readers.[29]

There have been many arguments regarding the relationship of Chronicles to DtrH. Whatever the true literary relationship between these two documents, it seems most likely—given the limited access to the requisite literary skills—that the small group of scribes who preserved and read the final form of Chronicles was the same group that

---

28. T.C. Eskenazi, *In an Age of Prose: A Literary Approach to Ezra–Nehemiah* (SBLMS, 36; Atlanta: Scholars Press, 1988), p. 5.

29. Two typical comments should be sufficient. 'In addition, an unparalleled editorial assessment of Saul's reign is appended in vv. 13-14. The reader's knowledge of the events of 1 Samuel is apparently presupposed.' Williamson, *1 and 2 Chronicles*, p. 92. And 'The narrative of the battle of Mt. Gilboa is introduced abruptly, the Chronicler taking for granted that the events which led to it were well known to the reader.' E.L. Curtis and A.A. Madsen, *A Critical and Exegetical Commentary on the Books of Chronicles* (ICC; Edinburgh: T. & T. Clark, 1910), p. 180.

preserved and read the final form of DtrH. It strains credibility to suggest that these two textual traditions could have been preserved entirely independently of one another, especially given the significant overlap in content between the two. This means that the scribal interpreters of 1 Chronicles 10 would have been familiar with the fuller account of Saul's reign given in DtrH. This is significant because it is only possible to read 1 Chronicles 10 as a defense of David in relation to the death of Saul, if one knows the earlier history of their relationship presented in DtrH. As a self-standing literary unit Chronicles does not make any connection between David and Saul beyond the fact that David came to the throne after the death of Saul. In fact, Chronicles moves directly from the death of Saul to the reign of David over *all* Israel (11.1-3). On the basis of 1 Chronicles alone, there is no reason to suspect David's complicity in the death of Saul or to read the attribution of Saul's death to Yahweh (10.14) as a defense of David. That the scribal interpreters would have been familiar with both traditions allows for the possibility that the account in DtrH could have shaped the interpretation of 1 Chronicles 10 in this way. It does not, however, exclude other possibilities.

It is impossible to determine whether the ordinary citizens of Achaemenid Yehud would have been familiar with the Saulide traditions of DtrH or 1 Chronicles 10. They could have known one, both or neither. This reinforces the powerful position of the literati in ancient societies. If it was to their advantage, the scribal interpreters of these texts could interpret them independently of one another or in relation to each other, or they could have kept the contents of both secret. The fact that Chronicles was produced during the Achaemenid period does suggest, however, that it served a particular political and/or religious function in the society that would make dissemination of its contents to a wider audience desirable.

The political and religious context in which Chronicles was (or is) being read would sculpt the reading in very specific ways. For example, a context in which the Second Temple existed as a widely accepted and revered aspect of communal life would result in a very different reading from a context in which the temple functioned as a symbol of religious and political strife in the community.

There are at least three periods after the imposition of Persian rule in which strife over the role of the Jerusalem temple in the life of Yehud could have shaped the interpretive conventions and expectations of the readers of Chronicles. The book of Haggai presents an apology for the construction of the temple that both castigates those who resist construction ('the time has not yet come'; Hag. 1.4) for living in luxury, while the temple lies in ruins (Hag. 1.4), and attributes economic hardship to their failure to build a new temple (Hag. 1.5-6, 9-11). Haggai's argument indicates that there was, at least among some segments of the population, resistance to the construction of the temple. In the aftermath of the temple's construction it is possible that opposition to the new Yahwistic temple may have continued. The anti-temple and anti-cultic rhetoric in Isa. 66.1-5 may preserve the arguments of this (minority) group that was opposed to the new temple. Finally, the construction of the Samaritan temple on Mt Gerazim, clearly challenging the centrality and uniqueness of the Jerusalem temple for the worshipers of Yahweh, could have shaped the reading of Chronicles and, in particular, its presentation of the first temple and its cult.

In each of these three periods Chronicles would have been read by the defenders of the Second Temple as presenting the founders of the Yahwistic cult and temple as specially chosen by Yahweh for that purpose. The fact that the cultic activities of the first temple, as presented in Chronicles, precisely paralleled those of the new temple would have provided a substantive defense against opponents or challengers (in the case of the Samaritans) to the appropriateness and centrality of the Jerusalem temple. In such a situation, read in relation to DtrH, 1 Chronicles 10 could indeed have functioned as a defense of David in the matter of the death of Saul. Although David is never directly linked to the death of Saul in Samuel, the bitter struggle between the two men and David's links with the Philistines would not be complimentary to David. It would certainly not help to establish the legitimacy of the Second Temple and its cult by linking them to a regicide as the cult founder. In this way, Chronicles, by presenting Yahweh as directly responsible for both the death of Saul and the choice of David (1 Chron. 10.14), not only absolves David of responsibility for a heinous crime but also presents him as an ideal choice for cult founder by virtue of Yahweh's election. In fact, Chronicles could have been produced for just such a situation. Chronicles could be a new account of the community's history that presents the founder of the Jerusalem cult in a much more flattering light than DtrH. It would have been relatively simple for the political and religious elites, the interpretive gatekeepers of the community's religious traditions, to have suppressed the earlier version in favor of Chronicles. It is important to reiterate, however, that such a reading is only probable in social settings in which the legitimacy of the contemporary temple cult is being undermined in some manner.

Perhaps a more interesting matter is how this text would have functioned in such socio-historical contexts if it were not being read in direct relation to the account of Saul and David in DtrH. Without the account of DtrH, there would be no need to defend David from possible involvement, directly or indirectly, in the death of Saul. If Chronicles had been the only or the primary narrative dealing with the period of the early monarchy that was known to the ancient readers, then the unsavory aspects of David's actions in these events would have been unknown. What does the account of the death of Saul add to the narrative if it is not functioning as a defense of David against charges of regicide? In a setting like this, Mosis's reading of 1 Chronicles 10 as a paradigm of exile and restoration becomes possible, but not the only possibility.[30] Such a reading fits the general pattern suggested by the interpretation of the monarchic period prophets in Zechariah 1. In Zech. 1.1-6 the fate of the ancestors, foretold by the earlier prophets whom they ignored, is called upon as a warning to the contemporary community. Failure to heed the warning of legitimate Yahwistic prophets lead the ancestors to disaster. This historical reading of the monarchic period prophets interprets these earlier texts, in light of the communal knowledge of their history, as a paradigm for shaping current practice.

The greatest difficulty with Mosis's reading is the complete disjunction that he posits between the account of Saul's death and the reign of David. Chr.'s summary of the death of Saul appears to make a direct link between these two events: 'Therefore the LORD put him to death and turned the kingdom over to David son of Jesse' (1 Chron. 10.14). Although it is conceivable that this statement could be read in some contexts without inferring any direct link between the killing of Saul and the appointing of David, it appears unlikely given the theological significance attached to Yahwistic texts by ancient Yehudite readers. These two events, as read by an ancient Yehudite, would be experienced as an integrally related pair of actions by Yahweh.

If ancient readers perceived a connection between the account of Saul's death and the inauguration of the reign of David but did not read

---

30. Mosis, *Untersuchungen zur Theologie*, pp. 17-43.

1 Chronicles 10 as a defense of David against complicity in Saul's death, how might they have interpreted this text? How does the account of Saul's death alter the ancient reader's perception of the remainder of the narrative of Chronicles?

Perhaps the most substantial difference that the presence of the account of Saul's death makes to the remainder of the narrative is to make David the continuation of the Israelite monarchy rather than its originator. Although he represents the beginning of a new dynasty, David is not the founder of the monarchy. This is a significant point for Persian period readings of Chronicles. From the perspective of Persian period readers, particularly readers of this book, the monarchy had been an abject failure. With the exceptions of David and Solomon, even the best Judahite kings had been guilty of crimes that brought punishment from Yahweh. Josiah is not a high point of the monarchy in Chronicles but another example of a king who was punished for disobedience.

The inclusion of the death of Saul in the narrative means that the reader sees David as the king, in a succession of rulers, who was specifically chosen by Yahweh to found the temple. In this way he is disassociated from the establishment of a failed institution and marked as the one king specially selected by Yahweh for the purpose of establishing the cult of Yahweh, which continues into the reader's present experience. Thus, the account of Saul's death does not defend David against charges of regicide but protects the cult founder from too close an association with the establishment of the corrupt and failed monarchy that no longer existed. By controlling access to the information contained in DtrH, the scribal gatekeepers, who read to and for the majority of the population of Achaemenid Yehud, had the power to facilitate such a reading of this text. In periods in which the temple cult was challenged by dissent or alternative cult places and practices, this reading would certainly be advantageous to those whose power and prestige was dependent upon the Jerusalem temple.

The preceding discussion only highlights a few factors related to the temple that might have influenced the reception of 1 Chronicles 10 in Achaemenid Yehud. The detailed socio-historical reconstruction of a specific period required for a historicized reading of 1 Chronicles 10 requires a much longer treatment than is possible in a single essay. This brief exploration indicates the type of factors that would shape the reception of this text and, hopefully, indicates something of the promise of historical hermeneutics for biblical studies.

THE DIALOGISM OF CHRONICLES[*]

Christine Mitchell

How do we understand the book of Chronicles as literature? This book, which can seem so pedantic, so relentless in its emphasis on temple, Israel and Davidic king, can also seem to be nothing more than a stitched together crazy quilt of mismatched textual pieces, as implied by its Septuagint title Παραλειπόμενα, 'what is omitted'. When doing literary study of the Bible, most scholars are content to ignore Chronicles in favor of the narratives of Genesis–2 Kings. Yet this book is one of the earliest exemplars of a text that shows its awareness of other written texts. It makes reference to numerous other written texts, such as annals, law, commentary and prophetic books, while Genesis–2 Kings makes reference very rarely to written texts other than annals or law.[1] Chronicles seems to be aware of books in narrative form other than itself (whether such books actually existed or not), which Samuel–Kings is not. If we assume that portions of the Hebrew Bible and the historical and philosophical texts of fifth-to-fourth-century-BCE Athens were the first texts to be composed as written narrative texts rather than oral ones, then Chronicles becomes interesting simply because it can do

*   An earlier version of this paper was read at the annual meeting of the Chronicles–Ezra–Nehemiah Section of the Society of Biblical Literature, 1998. Thanks are due to Robert Polzin, who read both versions. Support for this research has come from the Social Sciences and Humanities Research Council of Canada.
    1.   Samuel–Kings especially makes reference to written texts only in the cases of royal annals and the book of the Law: a book of the annals of the kings of either Israel or Judah is referred to over 30 times (e.g. 1 Kgs 14.19), and a book of the Law or covenant is referred to ten times (e.g. 2 Kgs 22.8; 23.2). Other books are referred to three times (1 Sam. 10.25; 2 Sam. 1.18; 1 Kgs 11.41). Chronicles includes the annals and law books (e.g. 2 Chron. 16.11; 17.9), as well as other accounts that are implied to be in narrative form: the commentary on the book of the kings (2 Chron. 24.27) and the records of various seers/prophets (1 Chron. 29.29; 2 Chron. 12.15; 33.19).

what few other texts in the Hebrew Bible can: reflect other written texts.

I would like to leave aside the minutiae of the issues of orality and literacy in the ancient world. They are not the issue at hand in this essay. What I would like to do here is examine the relationship of texts to one another within the Hebrew Bible, specifically the relationship between Samuel–Kings and Chronicles. I would like to examine this relationship through a different lens than those that have been trained on Chronicles up to this point. I shall not examine Chronicles and Samuel–Kings with regard to the question of sources, since it seems evident that they have much material in common, and for my purposes it does not matter which book came first or what the origins of their common material are.[2] Nor will I examine Chronicles as a proto-midrash on Samuel–Kings, since I think it has been shown that there are definite signs that midrash and other forms of post-biblical literature developed out of the trajectory for which Chronicles was the beginning.[3] Rather, I would like to examine Chronicles in its very textuality, its very existence as a written literary text in a tradition of written literary texts. To do this, I will draw on the ideas of literary theorists Mikhail Bakhtin and Yuri Lotman, first describing the work of each theorist before attempting to synthesize their work in order to develop a model to be applied to Chronicles.

Dialogism in Bakhtin

The use of the work of Mikhail Bakhtin in literary circles has exploded in the last 20 years, although there has been comparatively little work bringing the Bible and Bakhtin together.[4] Bakhtin's work was rich and

---

2. Although the consensus view is that Chronicles used a text of Samuel–Kings fairly close to the MT, a minority view holds that both Chronicles and Samuel–Kings used a common source (A.G. Auld, *Kings without Privilege: David and Moses in the Story of the Bible's Kings* [Edinburgh: T. & T. Clark, 1994], pp. 1-11).

3. For Chronicles as proto-midrash, embodying elements of haggadah, see M. Fishbane, *Biblical Interpretation in Ancient Israel* (Oxford: Clarendon Press, 1984), pp. 290-91. For the later developments in late biblical and post-biblical literature, see L.M. Wills, 'The Jewish Novellas', in J.R. Morgan and R. Stoneman (eds.), *Greek Fiction: The Greek Novel in Context* (London: Routledge, 1994), pp. 223-38 (223-25).

4. Exceptions include W.L. Reed, *Dialogues of the Word: The Bible as Literature According to Bakhtin* (Oxford: Oxford University Press, 1993); R. Polzin, *Moses*

varied, and for the purposes of this paper I will limit myself to drawing on his work on dialogism and heteroglossia. Dialogism is defined primarily in one of Bakhtin's early works, *Problems of Dostoevsky's Poetics*. There he examined dialogism in terms of linguistics, or more precisely, in terms of metalinguistics, which he defined as 'those aspects of the life of the word which...fall outside the bounds of linguistics'.[5] Dialogical relationships, for Bakhtin, are outside of purely linguistic study, that is, are a matter for metalinguistics. The word and the idea are by nature dialogical: the word and the idea want 'to be heard, understood and "answered" by other voices from other positions'.[6] The word and idea are also 'interindividual and intersubjective', existing not in 'the individual consciousness, but [in] the dialogical intercourse between consciousnesses'.[7] However, this rather abstract idea of dialogism can only be made concrete through linguistic formulae such as syntax and semantics; dialogical relationships are 'impossible without logical and concrete semantic relationships'.[8] Dialogical relationships thus cannot exist in the abstract; they must become concrete through the utterances of the author. The author uses his or her utterances to express a position, to which other utterances respond.[9]

Bakhtin developed his theories about dialogism on the basis of Dostoevsky's novels. We might wonder about the validity of using on biblical literature theories based on nineteenth-century novels. I would argue that Bakhtin anticipated that his theories about dialogism could have wider applications beyond the novels of this one particular author. Indeed, in his later works he expanded dialogism to include all novels

and the Deuteronomist: Deuteronomy, Joshua, Judges (A Literary Study of the Deuteronomistic History, 1; New York: Seabury, 1980); F.O. Garcia-Treto, 'The Fall of the House: A Carnivalesque Reading of 2 Kings 9 and 10', in D.N. Fewell (ed.), *Reading Between Texts: Intertextuality and the Hebrew Bible* (Literary Currents in Biblical Interpretation; Louisville, KY: Westminster/John Knox Press, 1992), pp. 153-71; K. Craig, *Reading Esther: A Case for the Literary Carnivalesque* (Literary Currents in Biblical Interpretation; Louisville, KY: Westminster/John Knox Press, 1995).

5. M.M. Bakhtin, *Problems of Dostoevsky's Poetics* (Ann Arbor: Ardis, 1973), p. 150.

6. Bakhtin, *Problems*, p. 72.

7. Bakhtin, *Problems*, p. 72.

8. Bakhtin, *Problems*, p. 152.

9. Bakhtin, *Problems*, p. 152.

(cf. his essay 'Discourse in the Novel'),[10] and towards the end of his life, he dealt with the even wider implications of dialogism in his essay, 'The Problem of the Text', where he described dialogism as:

> Confidence in another's word, reverential reception ... apprenticeship, the search for and mandatory nature of deep meaning, agreement, its infinite gradations and shadings ... the layering of meaning upon meaning, voice upon voice, strengthening through merging, the combination of many voices ... that augments understanding, departure beyond the limits of the understood ... [11]

If we take Bakhtin's thoughts on the subject as they developed, we could argue that dialogism could be applied to almost any literary text. However, even in *Problems of Dostoevsky's Poetics*, he began to generalize in ways that can be specifically applied to the Bible. He noted in his discussion of the dialogic that:

> The forms of actual authorship can be very diverse. A given work can be the product of a collective effort, can be created by the successive efforts of a series of generations, etc.—in any case we hear in it a unified creative will, a specific position to which we can react dialogically.[12]

What work does this describe if not the Bible as a whole or its component books like Chronicles? For Bakhtin, then, the ins and outs of the composition of the utterance (the book) would not matter, since the result is one specific position. This way of examining a composite text like the Bible as a whole or Chronicles more specifically can be very liberating: no longer is the interpreter bound to examine each block of text as determined by historical-critical scholarship. As long as we agree that the basic intent and message pervades the entire work, we can examine the entire work as one literary position.

Dialogical relationships can operate on the microlevel of individual words or speeches within a work (which Bakhtin later described as heteroglossia; see below), or they can operate on the macrolevel of relationships between entire works, as long as we can hear two voices

10. M.M. Bakhtin, 'Discourse in the Novel', in M. Holquist (ed.), *The Dialogic Imagination: Four Essays* (The University of Texas Press Slavic Series, 1; Austin: University of Texas Press, 1981), pp. 259-422.

11. M.M. Bakhtin, 'The Problem of the Text in Linguistics, Philology, and the Human Sciences: An Experiment in Philosophical Analysis', in C. Emerson and M. Holquist (eds.), *Speech Genres and Other Late Essays* (The University of Texas Press Slavic Series, 8; Austin: University of Texas Press, 1986), p. 121.

12. Bakhtin, *Problems*, p. 153.

operating. According to Bakhtin, there can even be dialogical relationships within one authorship, if the authorship is divided into two inner voices. And finally, Bakhtin pointed out that dialogical relationships are possible even between works in dissimilar media, as long as there is some kind of symbolic expression.[13]

Heteroglossia in Bakhtin is defined as the variety of speech types that make up the novel. This is how dialogical relationships (i.e. different positions) can enter the novel itself, through the differences in authorial and narratorial speech, the speech of characters, inserted genres and so on. The novel is inherently a dialogic form.[14] Again, what do we have in the Bible, and more specifically, in Chronicles, if not heteroglossia? Chronicles contains many kinds of speech, some of which overlap: the Chronicler's speech, the narrator's speech, the speeches of the various characters and the inserted sections that parallel the autonomous work of Samuel–Kings. With such a variety of speech types, Chronicles must be inherently dialogic: there must be a variety of words and ideas wanting answers from other positions.

But is Chronicles a novel? If we take Bakhtin's description of the novel in his essay 'Epic and Novel',[15] then Chronicles does in some sense appear to be a novel. For Bakhtin, the novel is distinguished by three characteristics: (1) its stylistic three-dimensionality (i.e. dialogism); (2) its ability to change the temporality of the 'literary image' (i.e. talking about the past as the past and not as some continuous 'now'); and (3) its ability to make the past contact the present (i.e. although the past is depicted, the starting point and concerns come from the present). The novel takes the form of dialogues framed by a story that is also dialogized.[16]

Chronicles has heteroglossia and dialogic relationships by virtue of its variety of speech types; it describes the time of the kings as the definable past, not in terms of some 'once upon a time' past; and its contemporary concerns for temple, Israel and Davidic king are depicted in terms of the past. Although in Chronicles the framing story seems to take precedence over the speeches of the characters, the basic form of Bakhtin's novel prevails. Chronicles can indeed be seen as an early

13. Bakhtin, *Problems*, p. 153.
14. Bakhtin, 'Discourse in the Novel', p. 263.
15. M.M. Bakhtin, 'Epic and Novel: Toward a Methodology for the Study of the Novel', in Holquist (ed.), *The Dialogic Imagination*, pp. 3-40.
16. Bakhtin, 'Epic and Novel', pp. 11-30.

novel or a proto-novel. Now, Bakhtin implied that the Bible as a whole was part of the epic tradition rather than the novelistic, a claim that I accept with some reservations. But Chronicles is not like most of the rest of the Bible: it is not a prose epic (as we might describe Genesis–2 Kings). In the same way, Esther, Ruth and Daniel are not prose epics but well-crafted stories expressing contemporary concerns. So, if we can accept Chronicles as being some kind of early exemplar of the novel, then we have taken the first step towards accepting and understanding its dialogic and heteroglossic relationships.

Textuality in Lotman

I want to turn away from Bakhtin toward the work of Yuri Lotman. Lotman certainly knew Bakhtin's work and in many places built his own upon it.[17] While the name of Mikhail Bakhtin is familiar to most by now, Yuri Lotman is still unknown in many Western circles. He was a professor at the University of Tartu (Estonia) and leader of the so-called Tartu School of Semiotics until his death in 1993. Much of his work has not been translated. However, some of it has, and I will be drawing upon some of this in order to refine and expand Bakhtin's concepts of dialogism and heteroglossia.

Among other things, Lotman was interested in textuality; that is, the form and function of texts. In his earlier work he defined the text's functions as transmission and generation: the transmission of the message and the generation of new messages. In order for the message to be transmitted perfectly, both the author and audience have to have wholly identical semiotic codes, which Lotman claimed was almost impossible. That gap between the transmissible and the untransmissible is what allows the text to create or generate new meanings.[18] Later, he added a third function, memory, which he described as the text's ability to condense cultural memory and to be interpreted—the text acquires new meanings through the history of interpretation.[19]

---

17. For the relationship between Bakhtin and Lotman, see A. Reid, *Literature as Communication and Cognition in Bakhtin and Lotman* (New York: Garland, 1990), especially pp. 36-37.

18. Y.M. Lotman, 'The Text within the Text', *PMLA* 109 (1993), pp. 377-84; Y.M. Lotman, *Universe of the Mind: A Semiotic Theory of Culture* (trans. Ann Shukman; Bloomington: Indiana University Press, 1990), pp. 11-17.

19. Lotman, *Universe of the Mind*, p. 18.

Lotman brought the audience of the text much more to the forefront: he claimed that 'as a generator of meaning ... the text needs an inter-locutor'.[20] This interlocutor could be an audience or a consciousness or another text. When the addresser sends a message to the addressee,[21] in a subject–object or what Lotman called an 'I–S/he' transmission, the message is transmitted in space.[22] However, when the addresser sends a message to the addressee in a subject–subject or what Lotman called an 'I–I' transmission, the message is transmitted not in space but in time. Lotman called this 'autocommunication'.[23] In I–S/he transmission the message is static, but in I–I transmission the message is dynamic: it acquires new meanings in the communication process. The original message is supplemented or has a new meaning imposed upon it, or the meaning of the message is transformed.[24] However, even in autocom-munication there is an audience, the new subject, for the message.

Not only did Lotman presuppose an audience for the text, he argued that the audience and text interact. For him, not only does the text have an idea of its own ideal readership, but the readership has an idea of its own ideal text. The text and audience must share an interpretive code.[25] Tradition is often one of the interpretive codes. Lotman defined tradi-tion as a system of texts in the cultural memory; any text is filtered through the code of tradition, that is, through other texts that serve as interpreters.[26] However, often an audience will change, and this will force a change in the way the text constructs its ideal readership: text shapes reader shapes text. The relevance of the foregoing to the rela-tionship between Samuel–Kings and Chronicles is, I hope, clear: when Samuel–Kings and its audience or a portion of it no longer sufficiently shared an interpretive code, such as tradition, then the audience reshaped its text and in effect generated a new one: Chronicles. Chron-icles was the result of autocommunication, a message sent through time to its addressee, the new writing subject.

---

20. Lotman, 'Text', p. 378.
21. Following Roman Jakobson's communication model (R. Jakobson, 'Linguistics and Poetics', in T.A. Sebeok [ed.], *Style in Language* [Cambridge, MA: MIT Press, 1960], p. 353).
22. Lotman, *Universe of the Mind*, pp. 20-21.
23. Lotman, *Universe of the Mind*, p. 21.
24. Lotman, *Universe of the Mind*, p. 22.
25. Lotman, *Universe of the Mind*, pp. 63-64.
26. Lotman, *Universe of the Mind*, pp. 70-71.

Finally, Lotman also dealt with one of the problems of Chronicles: the text within the text. He noted that 'The introduction of an external text into the immanent world has far-reaching consequences. The external text is transformed in the structural field of the other text's meaning, and a new message is created.'[27] This is fairly self-evident; in terms of the Samuel–Kings–Chronicles relationship, when a source text from Samuel–Kings is introduced into Chronicles, that source text is transformed by the text of Chronicles. What Lotman went on to say was that 'the transformation occurs not only within the entering text; the entire semiotic situation inside the other text is also changed'.[28] In terms of Samuel–Kings–Chronicles, not only is the source text from Samuel–Kings transformed, but the meaning of the text of Chronicles is also changed. This statement was anticipated by Vološinov/Bakhtin in *Marxism and the Philosophy of Language*, where it is argued (in the language of Lotman) that the other text (Chronicles) tries to break down the external text (Samuel–Kings), to obliterate its boundaries, while the external text (Samuel–Kings) tries to overcome the other text (Chronicles).[29] So, both the synoptic portions of Samuel–Kings–Chronicles and the surrounding text of Chronicles are changed in meaning by their interaction. Chronicles creates new information by the interaction of its synoptic and non-synoptic portions.

If we bring together the work by Bakhtin and Lotman that I have presented, we can summarize as follows: Dialogism involves the relationships between utterances, whether inside or between texts. The word or idea in an utterance is a position that can be answered by other utterances. Speeches and inserted texts are in a dialogic relationship and mutually shape each other and change each other's meaning. Also, when the utterance is an entire text, that text transmits its message not only through space but through time. The audience of the text receives

---

27. Lotman, 'Text', p. 378.
28. Lotman, 'Text', p. 379.
29. V.N. Vološinov, *Marxism and the Philosophy of Language* (trans. L. Matejka and I.R. Titunik; Studies in Language; New York: Seminar Press, 1973; Cambridge, MA: Harvard University Press, 1986), pp. 120-21. There is still considerable debate over the authorship of this work: some consider it the work of Bakhtin, others the work of Vološinov, while still others consider it more or less a collaborative effort. See, M. Holquist, *Dialogism: Bakhtin and his World* (New Accents; London: Routledge, 1990), p. 8; Reid, *Literature as Communication*, pp. 7-20; translators' preface (1986) to Vološinov, *Marxism*, pp. ix-xi.

the transmission and generates new meanings so that text and readers mutually shape each other, just as utterances or texts mutually shape each other. This is all leading toward a term that I have deliberately avoided so far: 'intertextuality'. Although the term itself was coined by Julia Kristeva in response to her readings of Bakhtin, he himself never used it. The closest he came to it was in the essay 'The Problem of the Text', where he described the text as 'a unique monad that in itself reflects all texts...of a given sphere. The interconnection of all ideas (since all are realized in utterances). The dialogic relationships among texts and within the text.'[30] 'Intertextuality' has become quite a catch-all phrase over the last couple of decades, so I would like to avoid it in order to focus on the more concrete aspects of dialogism as I have described them.

Dialogism in Chronicles

Now we can turn to the text of Chronicles itself. For this essay, I have selected 1 Chron. 10.1–11.9 as my sample text: the death of Saul, David's anointing and his capture of Jerusalem. Although 11.9 represents the end of a synoptic section (parallel to 2 Sam. 5.10), in the context of Chronicles, 11.9 is somewhat arbitrary as a terminus, since 1 Chronicles 11–12 is really a single literary unit.[31] However, I want to focus on Saul and David, and so I have omitted the accounts of David's mighty men in 1 Chron. 11.10–12.41.

At first glance, there is something that immediately appears to demonstrate the dialogism of Chronicles. Of all the commentaries, I could not find one that did not deal with the Chronicler's treatment of the death of Saul in comparison with the two treatments in the book of Samuel.[32] Almost all the commentaries structure their comments as an exercise in

30. Bakhtin, 'Problem', p. 105.

31. H.G.M. Williamson, *1 and 2 Chronicles* (NCB; Grand Rapids: Eerdmans, 1982), p. 96; S. Japhet, *I & II Chronicles: A Commentary* (OTL; Louisville, KY: Westminster/John Knox Press, 1993), pp. 232-33.

32. Commentaries I examined include: Japhet, *I & II Chronicles*, pp. 221-30; Williamson, *1 and 2 Chronicles*, pp. 92-96; R.L. Braun, *1 Chronicles* (WBC, 14; Waco, TX: Word Books, 1986), pp. 147-52; J.M. Myers, *I Chronicles* (AB, 12; Garden City, NY: Doubleday, 1965), pp. 77-82; E.L. Curtis and A.A. Madsen, *A Critical and Exegetical Commentary on the Books of Chronicles* (ICC; Edinburgh: T. & T. Clark, 1910), pp. 180-84; S.J. De Vries, *1 and 2 Chronicles* (FOTL, 11; Grand Rapids: Eerdmans, 1989), pp. 117-22.

comparative interpretation. Very few place primacy on the Chr.'s account or try to understand 1 Chronicles 10 purely in its context in Chronicles.[33] For the commentators, 1 Chronicles 10 cannot be understood except as it relates to 1 Samuel 31. Commentators intuitively understand, I think, that 1 Chronicles 10 is answering the position of 1 Samuel 31, and most devote the greater part of their comments to descriptions of the Chr.'s answer to Samuel's position. However, my aim is first to read 1 Chron. 10.1–11.9 purely in terms of itself, without reference to 1 Samuel 31 and 2 Samuel 5. I would like to show that 1 Chron. 10.1–11.9 can be read without Samuel and that it has its own literary logic.

Reading Chronicles on Its Own Terms
In terms of narrative time, 1 Chron. 10.1–11.9 operates in a disjointed sequence. The events are not recounted one after another. Instead, the narrative is punctuated by a series of flash-forwards and flashbacks. The first flash-forward (10.7) has the Philistines settling in the abandoned Israelite cities at some point after the battle at Gilboa. The second flash-forward is found in 11.4-9 and describes the capture of Jerusalem, which takes place only after the action of 12.38-40, but before the action of ch. 13, since 13.13 presupposes the capture of Jerusalem. Within this flash-forward is a flashback (11.4-5), in which David set and Joab won the prize for the capture. In addition, the action of 11.1-2 seems to be taking place at the same time as 10.8-12, while 11.3, David's anointing, might be understood as the first event that takes place after the action of ch. 10 is complete. In fact, this disjointed narrative sequence continues through most of 1 Chronicles. The effect is curious. Although the Chronicler understood the concept of temporality (the expression ויהי ממחרת ['on the next day'] is used in 10.8),[34] this mixing of temporalities has the effect of making all the events of 10.1–11.9 appear to occur at once. They are, in effect, all part of one event: the consolidation of David's kingship. This consolidation continues through 1 Chronicles until the end of ch. 12.[35]

33. An exception is De Vries (*1 and 2 Chronicles*, pp. 117-22), probably due to his form-critical approach.
34. De Vries, *1 and 2 Chronicles*, p. 118.
35. However, J.W. Wright argues that David's rule is not completely confirmed until 1 Chron. 14.2, after his first movement of the ark and his perception of his

The language used in this passage also serves to tie 1 Chronicles 10 to what follows. In 10.9, the Philistines raised up (נשׂא) Saul's head, and in 10.12 the men of Jabesh raised up (נשׂא) Saul's body. In Chronicles as a whole, outside of bearing arms and taking wives, נשׂא is used predominantly to describe the actions of lifting the ark or making offerings. Examples may be found in 1 Chron. 15.2, 15, 26, 27; 23.26; and 2 Chron. 5.4 of the levites bearing the ark or tabernacle, and in 1 Chron. 16.29; 18.2, 6; 21.24; 2 Chron. 9.1, 21; 24.11 of offerings or tribute being raised up. However, there are a few examples in Chronicles of נשׂא being used to describe booty being carried away by an army (1 Chron. 18.11; 2 Chron. 14.12; 16.6), while a body is carried away in 2 Chron. 25.28. The descriptions of these actions in 1 Chronicles 10 could be seen as making use of cultic vocabulary, or as using vocabulary loaded with cultic overtones that extend beyond the standard meaning of 'raise up'. As well as booty, Saul's head and body are sacrifices—Saul himself could be seen as a sacrifice. But since the Philistines carried away Saul's head and set it up in the temple of Dagon, Saul was sacrificed or made an offering to Dagon.

The word ראשׁ is also prominent in 1 Chron. 10.1–11.9. First, in 10.9, Saul's head (ראשׁ) was lifted up. But then in 11.6, in a multiple play on the root ראשׁ, Joab was made chief (ראשׁ) and commander for taking Jerusalem first (בראשׁונה).[36] Joab's headiness is contrasted to Saul's headlessness, both in the literal as well as in the metaphorical sense: Joab was now head of the people while Saul was not. Saul's role as military commander is removed from him here, as his role as worshiper of Yahweh was removed from him by his being sacrificed to Dagon in 1 Chron. 10.10.

On a related note, it is important to notice that only once is Saul described as king (מלך) in Chronicles, and it is in 11.2. Here it is the people who described Saul as having ruled (שׁאול מלך), using the verb rather than the noun to describe Saul. Because the verb is used to describe his action rather than the noun to describe his status, it could be implied that while he did act as a king, he may not have been one. Moreover, since it is the people and not the narrator who describe Saul as מלך, we might even wonder about whether they perceived his status correctly. In sum, it is as if Saul was never really king at all, and the

kingship. See J.W. Wright, 'The Founding Father: The Structure of the Chronicler's David Narrative', *JBL* 117 (1998), pp. 51-52.

36. Cf. Japhet, *I & II Chronicles*, p. 241.

one mention in 11.2 with its attendant ambiguities is there simply to emphasize Saul's non-kingship.

Moving from Saul's status to Saul's body, there is more to be said about the language of this passage. In 10.10, Saul's skull (גלגלת) was nailed up in the temple of Dagon, and in 10.12 his bones (עצם) were buried in Jabesh-Gilead. In 11.1, the people told David, 'Behold, we are your bone (עצם) and your flesh (בשר)'. In 1 Chronicles 10, it is clear that the Philistines sent Saul's head and armor on a tour around their land before laying them up in their temples. This would account for Saul's head being only a skull—some time had passed. After this period had passed, the men of Jabesh went to the battlefield and collected Saul's body, which likewise had been reduced to bone.[37] The flesh was no longer united with the bone at this point. Thus, when the people speak to David in 11.1, it is a contrast between the union of the flesh and bone of David and the people on the one hand, and the fleshlessness of Saul on the other. Saul no longer had any power at all—even his remains had dissipated.

Finally, there is the bridge of 10.13-14. In these verses, Saul is castigated for his unfaithfulness (מעל), his failure to keep the word of Yahweh, his consultation of a necromancer (אוב) and failure to seek (דרש) Yahweh. It has been often pointed out that מעל is a specific technical term for forsaking God, frequently used in Chronicles.[38] Similarly, דרש in Chronicles emphasizes the seeking of Yahweh and his commandments.[39] Saul is condemned in language common to the rest of Chronicles. It is possible to conclude, therefore, that the ideal ruler of Israel would not be unfaithful (מעל) but would seek (דרש) Yahweh, not other gods or necromancers. The classic formulation in Chronicles of this tenet is found, for example, in 1 Chron. 28.9: 'If you seek (דרש) him he will be found by you, and if you forsake him he will reject you forever'. A similar formulation is found in 2 Chron. 15.2, while 2 Chron. 15.13 states that those who do not seek (דרש) Yahweh should

37. Japhet (*I & II Chronicles*, p. 228) suggests that the men of Jabesh simply went to the battlefield and collected the bodies; it is important to notice their delay, which makes their efforts even less heroic (contra C.Y.S. Ho, 'Conjectures and Refutations: Is 1 Samuel XXXI 1-13 Really the Source of 1 Chronicles X 1-12?', *VT* 45 [1995], pp. 98-100, who sees the Chronicler as portraying the men of Jabesh as very heroic!).

38. Japhet, *I & II Chronicles*, pp. 229-30; Williamson, *1 and 2 Chronicles*, p. 94.

39. Williamson, *1 and 2 Chronicles*, p. 95.

be put to death. This was Saul's fate, although Yahweh killed him, not his fellow human beings.

It is interesting that Chr. chose to add 10.13-14 after the episode of 10.1-12, which did not show Saul having any of the characteristics for which he is condemned in 10.13-14. It is likely, therefore, that Saul is being condemned in Chronicles for his general attitude.[40] Here is an example of a dialogic relationship within Chronicles, an example of its heteroglossia. 1 Chronicles 10.1-12 presents one position: Saul, leader of his house (king, if we accept the declaration of 11.2), died in a battle with the Philistines, and his house died with him. He died because of a military event: for some reason, the army was not able to fend off the Philistines. Saul was defeated, and wishing to save whatever was left of his personal dignity, he committed suicide. 1 Chronicles 10.13-14, however, answers this position. These verses say: No, Saul did not die because of his military defeat; God killed him because of his מעל. Although the latter position intends to overwhelm the first, the first remains and, by its very presence, prevents the monologic vision of the second.

In all, this passage contrasts Saul with David and his associates. Saul is dead, mere bones, headless, sacrificed to Dagon and no king at all; while David is alive, flesh and bone, with Joab as head of the people, and he himself very much the king. The rest of 1 Chronicles will show whether David proved a proper king: whether he sought Yahweh and was faithful to him, or whether he deserved to die like Saul. Ultimately, David was a proper king—in 1 Chron. 29.28, 'He died in a good old age, full of days, riches and honour'; he did not die as Saul. So 1 Chronicles in fact could be read as being intended to demonstrate David's seeking Yahweh, that is, of his being a proper king. The rest of

---

40. A good deal of research has gone into trying to decide whether Saul is condemned for specific acts or his general attitude. For the former, see Myers, *I Chronicles*, pp. 81-82; for the latter, Williamson, *1 and 2 Chronicles*, p. 95; Braun, *1 Chronicles*, pp. 151-52. In light of the fact that his specific acts are not mentioned elsewhere in Chronicles, within a reading of Chronicles itself it seems more appropriate to regard these verses as an expression of Saul's general attitude. Contra H. Ringgren, who sees מעל as indicating unfaithful acts; מעל could also be read as indicating attitude: the actions may be expressions of the attitude. Ringgren himself notes that some uses of מעל in Chronicles are quite general (e.g. 2 Chron. 28.19; 30.7). H. Ringgren, 'מעל', *TDOT*, VIII, pp. 462-63.

1 Chronicles may be read in this way, but that is beyond the scope of this essay.

Once we have read 1 Chron. 10.1–11.9, it becomes clear that the passage fits perfectly within Chronicles. Its purpose is to demonstrate the unfitness of Saul and the fitness of David. This entire reading was done without reference to Samuel. Chronicles can make sense on its own literary terms—it does not have to be read with Samuel–Kings in mind. But what happens when we turn to Samuel–Kings, having already read Chronicles?

Reading Chronicles with Samuel–Kings

First of all, there is the issue of the Chronicler's *Vorlage*. Without going into too much detail, let me just say that I believe it has been well demonstrated that the Chronicler's *Vorlage* of Samuel was probably similar to the tradition preserved in 4QSamᵃ.[41] A mechanistic comparison of Chronicles to Samuel is worthless. However, if we look not at the individual words and phrases, but at the overall context and effect we are on safer ground. As an aside, I would like to point out that all of the features of 1 Chron. 10.1–11.9 that I described above are unique to Chronicles. In Samuel, time does not shift back and forth to the same extent. In 1 Samuel 31, נשא is not used with reference to Saul's head and body, nor is גלגלת used to describe Saul's head. Joab's chieftainship in 2 Samuel 5 is not emphasized using ראש as in 1 Chronicles 11. Saul is not described as מעל and in fact is often described as מלך in Samuel (by Yahweh in 1 Sam. 15.11; by other characters in 1 Sam. 17.55; by the narrator in 1 Sam. 17.56), which he is not in Chronicles. All of these features are absent from Samuel, and their presence in Chronicles has a definite purpose, as I have described.

In 1 Samuel, Saul lost his kingship to David because of his failure as a king. God changed his mind about Saul's being king in 1 Sam. 15.11 and 16.1, and David was anointed in 16.13. God no longer listened to Saul, even though Saul continued to seek him (cf. 1 Sam. 28.6).[42] The Chronicler's answer is that God did not reject Saul, but Saul rejected God. Saul did not seek God. God did not reject Saul because Saul was a

41. Cf. E.C. Ulrich, Jr, *The Qumran Text of Samuel and Josephus* (HSM, 19; Chico, CA: Scholars Press, 1978); S.L. McKenzie, *The Chronicler's Use of the Deuteronomistic History* (HSM, 33; Atlanta: Scholars Press, 1984); W.E. Lemke, 'The Synoptic Problem in the Chronicler's History', *HTR* 58 (1965), pp. 349-63.

42. Japhet, *I & II Chronicles*, p. 229.

failure as a king; Saul was doomed from the start because of his unfaithful attitude. The battle with the Philistines merely epitomizes and illustrates what happens to those who do not seek God. A reader who knows both Samuel and Chronicles can see the dialogue and tension between the two: rejection *by* God because of failure, rejection *of* God because of מעל.

To continue with the above example, I noted in my reading of Chronicles on its own that, within Chronicles, Saul seems to be condemned for his general attitude, for his מעל in a general sense. However, when we read Chronicles with Samuel, it is extremely tempting to try to see the charges against Saul in a more specific way: his failure to keep the word of Yahweh (1 Chron. 10.13) as a reference to his sparing of Agag in 1 Sam. 15.8-10 and his making of sacrifices in 1 Sam. 13.8-10; and his inquiring of a necromancer (1 Chron. 10.13) as a reference to 1 Sam. 28.7.[43] We do not need to choose between 1 Chron. 10.13-14 as referring to Saul's general attitude or to his specific actions, since both meanings are contained within the one utterance.

Finally, there is another example of the dialogism between Samuel and Chronicles, one that ranges a little outside of 1 Chron. 10.1–11.9. In 1 Samuel, Saul was from Gibeah, while in the genealogies of Chronicles (1 Chron. 9.35-39), Saul was from Gibeon. Gibeah is primarily associated with one thing in the Hebrew Bible besides Saul: the rape of the levite's concubine and the subsequent events in Judges 19–20.[44] Gibeah was a place of bad associations—one would think it would be perfect for Chr. But Gibeon was even more appropriate: the Gibeonites were not even real Israelites (cf. Josh. 10; 2 Sam. 21.2).[45] Not only that, but in 2 Sam. 21.2 we learn that Saul had even tried to destroy them. To Samuel's claim that Saul's ancestors were perpetrators of a great crime, Chronicles answers that Saul was in fact no

---

43. So Myers, *I Chronicles*, p. 82; Curtis and Madsen, *Books of Chronicles*, pp. 182-83.

44. Contra S.D. Walters ('Saul of Gibeon', *JSOT* 52 [1991], p. 75), who claims that Gibeah is meant to be associated with prophetic authority. Prophets are only associated with Gibeah in 1 Sam. 10.10, and priests with Gibeah in Josh. 24.33, while there are dozens of references to Gibeah as the dwelling place of Saul and the place of the rape of the levite's concubine. Hos. 9.9 and 10.9 make the latter connection especially clear.

45. Walters, 'Saul', pp. 70-71.

Israelite at all and—in a wonderful irony—was a member of a group he had tried to destroy.

The Chronicler's text can be read as simply showing another position while accepting that Samuel had a valid position as well; it does not have to be a correction or a replacement for Samuel;[46] it is more of a 'yes, but…' This way of looking at the Samuel–Chronicles relationship does not depend on one being composed first: the texts can be in dialogue if 1 Chronicles 10 used 1 Samuel 31 as a source or if they both used a common source.[47] This way of looking at the Samuel–Chronicles relationship also can accommodate Chronicles as a proto-midrash.[48] After all, what is more dialogic than midrash?

Conclusion

In this essay I have attempted to show that the theories of Bakhtin and Lotman can be fruitfully applied to Chronicles, using the example of 1 Chron. 10.1–11.9. Reading the unit first on its own and then in dialogue with 1–2 Samuel, we can see examples of dialogism within Chronicles and between Chronicles and Samuel. The theories applied to this unit of text could also be applied to all of 1–2 Chronicles and its relationship to Samuel–Kings and other texts of the Hebrew Bible. The reader of Chronicles does not have to know Samuel–Kings in order to get the messages of Chronicles. But the reader of Chronicles who also knows Samuel–Kings can appreciate the dialogue between the two, as well as the little ironies and playfulness that Chronicles has built into its text. The pleasure of reading is enhanced as we begin to understand Chronicles on many levels. It is not a pieced-together text; it is a text of complex artistry in the service of its messages.

46. Contra Fishbane, *Biblical Interpretation*, pp. 381-82.
47. Cf. Ho, 'Conjectures', pp. 82-106; Auld, *Kings without Privilege*, pp. 1-11.
48. Fishbane, *Biblical Interpretation*, pp. 290-91.

WHOSE SONG OF PRAISE? REFLECTIONS ON THE PURPOSE OF THE PSALM IN 1 CHRONICLES 16

Kirsten Nielsen

In the title of this article I pose the following question concerning 1 Chronicles 16: Whose Song of Praise? At first glance, the question seems simple enough. For the context in 1 Chronicles 16 tells us that Asaph and his associates were singing this song when David transferred the ark of the covenant to Jerusalem. In the Danish translation of the Bible the translators have thus called it: 'The Song of the Levites'. In the NIV, however, the inserted psalm is called 'David's Psalm of Thanks', and when reading the text itself, we sense that the purpose of the psalm is more comprehensive. Note, for example, the wide-ranging summons to praise Yahweh:

> Ascribe to the Lord, O families of nations,
> ascribe to the Lord glory and strength (1 Chron. 16.28).

So, whose Song of Praise is it? Is it that of David, the levites or all nations? We shall return to this. First, however, let us have a look at various scholars' interpretations of this text.

What Do Some of the Standard Commentaries Say about 1 Chronicles 16?

As my first example of a well-known commentary on 1 Chronicles, I have chosen the one by Jacob Myers in The Anchor Bible series. He emphasizes that the psalm is a compilation of known psalms. Verses 8-22 correspond with Ps. 105.1-15; vv. 23-33 with Ps. 96.1b-13; and vv. 34-36 with Ps. 106.1, 47-48. There is general agreement on what Myers points out, and I have nothing further to add. On the other hand, it is surprising that Myers, when referring to the contents of the text, merely says: 'for the interpretation of the hymn see commentaries on Pss xcvi, cv, cvi'.[1] But is Myers's assumption correct that the context of 1 Chron. 16.8-36 within the books of Chronicles does not change the meanings of these psalm passages? To address this question, I consulted several other commentaries on 1 Chronicles, but the results were disappointing.

I had expected scholars to be concerned about the context in 1 Chronicles (which is different from the context in the Psalms of David), and to ask why a piece of poetry appears in the middle of a prose narrative and what effect this piece of poetry has on the reader. However, none of the commentaries I consulted included these considerations.

In general, scholars are interested in the relationship between the psalm in 1 Chronicles 16 and the psalms from which it has been drawn. They examine why Chr. chooses what he does from Psalm 105 and why he changes this or that in Psalm 96. The general answer is that Chr. drops the themes that are of little interest to his contemporaries or do not serve the purposes related to the *Sitz im Leben* that he provides for the psalm in 1 Chronicles 16. Such is the perspective shared by Kurt Galling, Sara Japhet and Roddy Braun.[2] The Norwegian scholars, Sigmund Mowinckel and Nils Messel, point out that Chr. places the cultic act at the New Year festival, which they deduce from the *Gattungen* of the psalms that are reused in 1 Chronicles 16. It is thus the cultic *Sitz im Leben* of the text that is interesting for Mowinckel.[3] Finally, it should be mentioned that in the old *Handkommentar zum Alten Testament*, Rudolf Kittel discusses the possibility of concluding from the doxology in 1 Chron. 16.36 that at the time of Chr. there existed a collection of psalms ending with Ps. 106.48, where we find a similar doxology. About the psalm itself, however, we read nothing.[4]

In short, when a psalm appears in 1 Chronicles, the scholars noted above confine themselves to the questions, 'What is its origin? Did Chr. himself write it, or did he have some kind of *Vorlage*?' When such

---

1. J.M. Myers, *I Chronicles* (AB, 12; New York: Doubleday, 1965), p. 121.
2. K. Galling, *Die Bücher der Chronik, Esra, Nehemia übersetzt und erklärt* (ATD, 12; Göttingen: Vandenhoeck & Ruprecht, 1954); S. Japhet, *I & II Chronicles: A Commentary* (OTL; Louisville, KY: Westminster/John Knox Press, 1993); R.L. Braun, *1 Chronicles* (WBC, 14; Waco, TX: Word Books, 1986).
3. N. Messel and S. Mowinckel (trans.), 'Krønikeboken', in *Skriftene*, II (Det Gamle Testamente, 5; trans. S. Michelet, Sigmund Mowinckel and N. Messel; Oslo: H. Aschehoug, 1963), pp. 293-96.
4. R. Kittel, *Die Bücher der Chronik übersetzt und erklärt* (HKAT, 6/1; Göttingen: Vandenhoeck & Ruprecht, 1902).

questions have been answered, scholars may—as Mowinckel—take an interest in whether the *Gattung* of the psalm tells us something about the *Sitz im Leben* of the text, or—as Kittel—consider whether the doxology of 1 Chron. 16.36 can be used to date the closing of Book 4 in the Psalms of David. If they have comments on the text itself, these are intended to clarify where changes have been made in 1 Chronicles 16 on the basis of comparison with the *Vorlage* in the book of Psalms— and why. But what about the psalm itself and the fact that it is a poetic text that has been inserted into a narrative? This question must be raised, too, I think.

1 Chronicles 16 Read in Context—Then and Now?

As already mentioned, it is generally accepted that 1 Chronicles 16 has been composed from psalms that were already available to Chr. Watts, for example, notes that in the case of 1 Chronicles 16 we have to do with 'a medley composed of portions of three psalms: Pss. 105.1-15, 96.1-13a and 106.1, 47-48'.[5] Later in the chapter, Watts emphasizes that the simplest explanation of this medley is that it is the work of Chr. himself.[6]

What is important, however, is what happens when these portions of psalms are placed side by side in 1 Chronicles 16. Do we read the psalm differently when it is related to the narrative about David moving the ark to Jerusalem? And why did Chr. insert a psalm in the middle of the narrative at all? Why not simply say, 'David left Asaph and his associates before the ark of the covenant of the Lord to minister there regularly, according to each day's requirements' (1 Chron. 16.37)?

The answer to this question about why a psalm has been inserted in a narrative context may be found if we look at the text from a reader-response perspective and thus expand the context of the psalm to include the actual reader. We have, therefore, to examine more closely what we mean by reading in a context and determine precisely which contexts we have in mind.[7]

---

5. J.W. Watts, *Psalm and Story: Inset Hymns in Hebrew Narrative* (JSOTSup, 139; Sheffield: JSOT Press, 1992), p. 155.

6. Watts, *Psalm and Story*, p. 164.

7. On the possible values of such insertions for Chr.'s presentation, see the rhetorical analysis of R.K. Duke in this volume, 'A Rhetorical Approach to Appreciating the Books of Chronicles' (pp. 102-37).

Which Context?

As has been noted, the song of praise in 1 Chron. 16.4-43 is unique in having two different literary contexts. One is the narrative in Chronicles about the arrival of the ark in Jerusalem, namely, a narrative context. Here the psalm is regarded as belonging to Asaph and his associates. The other context is the book of Psalms, that is, a collection of poetic texts. It is striking, however, that none of the three psalms included in Chr.'s medley are ascribed to Asaph in the book of Psalms. Psalm 96 has no heading at all, and Psalm 105 only has a heading if we take the word 'Hallelujah' from the last verse of Psalm 104 (v. 35) and make it the heading of Psalm 105. It is true that Psalm 106 has a heading, but it says nothing about who has been singing the psalm, since it is a Hallelujah psalm.[8]

Further, it should be noted that the parallel to 1 Chronicles 16– 2 Samuel 6 does not mention that Asaph and his associates were singing, much less what they were singing on that occasion. Therefore, Chr. must have had his own reason for supplementing the narrative about David and the ark with a specific psalm to be sung by a special group of levites.

Excursus

In this connection it should be mentioned that Chronicles contains very few examples of poetic insertions. I would like to mention 1 Chron. 12.19 [*EVV* 12.18], where Amasai was led by the spirit of God to express his support for David in brief, pithy parallelisms:

> We are yours, O David!
> We are with you, O son of Jesse!
> Success, success to you,
> and success to those who help you,
> for your God will help you.

Another example is 2 Chron. 10.16, a short poetic utterance, which, unlike 1 Chron. 12.19, clearly rejects any solidarity with David:

> What share do we have in David,
> what part in Jesse's son?
> To your tents, O Israel!
> Look after your own house, O David!

8.   In the NIV, however, neither Ps. 105 nor Ps. 106 has headings.

This last utterance is also found in 1 Kgs 12.16 and—in abbreviated form—in 2 Sam. 20.1. Here Chr. reuses previous collocations, as is the case with his medley in 1 Chronicles 16. However, Chr. obviously does not feel bound by his *Vorlage* to reuse anything. There are several poetic passages in DtrH, for example, that Chr. does not reuse: David's lament for Saul and Jonathan in 2 Samuel 1; David's song of praise in 2 Samuel 22; the last words of David in 2 Samuel 23; and Isaiah's prophecy in 2 Kings 19.[9]

Following this excursus about the use of poetic passages in the books of Chronicles, we shall return to consider the function of the psalm.

The Function of the Song of Praise in 1 Chronicles 16

In his commentary on the books of Chronicles my Danish colleague, Kjeld Nielsen, gives the following description of the function of the inserted psalm:

> This cult psalm is the first psalm that is sung on the place where the future Temple is to stand, and in this connection it is interesting to note that the author of vv. 27 and 29 leaves out the allusions in the original psalm to the Temple, which, according to the author, was not yet built. The author thus camouflages his cult psalm to make it resemble—not a Temple psalm—but simply a hymn. This may imply that he also wishes to emphasize that the psalm can be used in the synagogue worship... What David does by letting the Levites sing is thus not merely to institute the cult in the later Temple, but also to establish the worship in the later synagogue. David thus becomes the founder *par excellence* of Temple cult as well as synagogue worship in Israel.[10]

The point of Nielsen's statement is that it is through Chr.'s reuse of old temple psalms that we gain access to Chr.'s theology and to the cult at the time of Chr. But why does Chr. do this by means of one specific psalm text? Why is he not content with v. 4, which notes that David appointed some of the levites (including Asaph) to minister before the ark, to make petition, to give thanks and to praise the Lord, the God of Israel? He might then have related v. 4 to v. 7, which explains that this

9. See also Watts, *Psalm and Story*, pp. 166-67, where he argues that Chr. derives from 2 Sam. 22 the idea of placing a psalm into a narrative context.

10. K. Nielsen, *Krønikebøgerne, Ezras Bog og Nehemias' Bog* (Danske Bibelselskabs Kommentarserie; Copenhagen: Danske Bibelselskab, 1995), pp. 41-42 (my translation).

was the first time that Asaph and his associates were appointed to praise the Lord. This would have given us sufficient information about David's establishment of the cult, and Chr. could have been spared the trouble of searching for psalms that were appropriate for use in synagogue worship but that did not so clearly evince the temple's existence. That Chr. prefers psalms that can be interpreted into his own age can be seen from his choosing portions of psalms in which praise plays a far more important role than sacrifice and that are, therefore, more suitable for the synagogue worship than for the pre-exilic cult.[11] Nevertheless, the question remains, 'Why depart from an exclusively narrative presentation at all?' That would have been entirely adequate to legitimate the cult of Chr.'s day.

One possible reason for the insertion of poetic material is that the citation of the psalm is proof that the levites did what David appointed them to do. Whereas the narrative itself may legitimate the role of the levites in the temple cult, the psalm may illustrate how carefully the levites pursued their duties. Hardly have they been ordered to sing for the Lord, when they begin to sing a specific song of praise. That this must have been an important motif for Chr. was demonstrated by Watts in his profound analysis of the language of the psalm and its narrative setting. The narrative explaining what the levites were ordered to do contains precisely the vocabulary used in the psalm. As Watts has presented it:

> Through its many exhortations to praise and the communal response at its end, the song shows the Levites leading the people in worship, precisely the role to which David appointed them. Specifically, David's order להזכיר ולהודות ולהלל, 'to bring remembrance, to give thanks, and to praise' (16.4) is fulfilled literally by multiple uses of this vocabulary throughout the medley and more generally by the singing of this and other songs before the ark.[12]

Watts also stresses (as did Kjeld Nielsen) that the psalm functions as a model for the worship that Chr. desires and that its function is to create continuity between the cult at the time of David and the cult of Chr.'s day.[13]

I quite agree with Watts in his assessment of Chr.'s intention, but I believe that we may reach a bit further. For whereas Watts emphasizes

---

11. Cf. Watts, *Psalm and Story*, p. 161.
12. Watts, *Psalm and Story*, p. 158.
13. Watts, *Psalm and Story*, p. 161.

semantic and thematic links between the psalm and its prose context, such links could also have been created through a piece of narrative. There must, therefore, be special reasons for presenting the poetry. Therefore, we shall proceed with a treatment of the psalm as poetry.

The Psalm as Poetic Insertion

The first thing I wish to say about the links between the poetry and its prose context is that at the moment when Asaph and his associates begin singing the song, there is a pause in the progress of events. Prose continues the story; poetry creates a standstill. This, however, does not mean that the psalm leaves the audience untouched or unchanged, for the psalm has been placed in the middle of the narrative about the ark arriving in Jerusalem. It is especially at this point that it is necessary to clarify who captured Jerusalem, and a hymn is suitable for this purpose. It can praise Yahweh as the one who chose Jacob, made the covenant with Abraham, gave them the land of Canaan and protected their prophets. Further, it says that Yahweh, who is to be praised, is also to be feared above all gods. They are idols and, therefore, the whole world must know about Yahweh's marvelous deeds, and all peoples must ascribe glory to Yahweh. Connected with David's reign over Jerusalem is also Yahweh's reign over the world. Consequently, Israel may ask Yahweh to deliver them and save them from the foreign nations. The following chapters thus also unfold what the psalm has anticipated: their victory over the neighboring nations.

That the psalm points forward in the narrative context can also be seen from the thematic links that relate the psalm to what follows. In this connection I wish to emphasize that the vocabulary found in the final prayer ('Give us victory, God of our victory, and gather us together and deliver us from the nations'; 16.35) is also found in the surrounding narratives.[14]

From a literary point of view the psalm anticipates the description of David's political victories, but the latter are interpreted as if the credit is due to Yahweh himself. This connection, however, could also have

---

14. Cf. Watts, *Psalm and Story*, p. 159, where he refers to the use of ישׁע (hiphil) in 1 Chron. 11.14; 18.6, 13, to נצל in 11.14, and to קבץ in 11.1; 13.2. Watts concludes, 'The medley thus reflects the military concerns and situation of the surrounding narratives'.

been created otherwise, as through a brief report that David asked Yahweh to help him against his enemies.

The poetic form chosen by Chr. implies that the prose is broken by a rhythmic text, full of parallelisms, describing what the right relationship with God should be and, by its narrow form, signaling that the world is an orderly place where, in fact, nothing is left to chance. The use of inclusio, namely, the use of parallel structures at the beginning and end, helps create a sense of unity. The psalm begins with the summons to give thanks to Yahweh, call on his name and make known among the nations his wonderful acts (in the past; vv. 8-9), and it concludes with the call to give thanks to Yahweh and to ask him to deliver his people from the nations, so that they may give thanks to his holy name and glory in his praise (vv. 34-35). However, this inclusio also follows the fundamental rule for any parallelism: that B is larger than A.[15] The perspective is expanded in part B, the end of the psalm, where present time pushes forward with the current need for Yahweh's intervention here and now and not as in the introduction, where Yahweh's acts (in the past) are the motivation for the present joy and song of praise.

This gives weight to the conclusion: the distress of the present time and the need for deliverance are accentuated and demand that the story move forward. Is Yahweh then going to intervene? As mentioned, the answer is given in the following chapters. And it now becomes obvious that the instrument of deliverance is King David![16] By including his medley, however, Chr. stresses that David is in fact (only) the tool and that thanks are to be ascribed to the Lord himself!

Last but not least, it should be emphasized that the poetry can make us, the readers, contemporary with the text. This happens through the direct requests to praise and thank Yahweh. The reader may feel that he or she is addressed directly, when it says:

> Remember the wonders he has done,
> his miracles, and the judgments he pronounced,
> O descendants of Israel his servant,
> O sons of Jacob, his chosen ones (1 Chron. 16.12-13).

15. Cf. J.L. Kugel, *The Idea of Biblical Poetry: Parallelism and its History* (New Haven: Yale University Press, 1981), p. 58.

16. Watts has emphasized that this is specific for this psalm. Usually poetic insertions in narrative contexts are used to characterize persons, whereas they play minor parts in connection with the actual plot. Watts, *Psalm and Story*, p 155.

Or as it says later in the psalm:

> Sing to the Lord, all the earth;
> proclaim his salvation day after day.
> Declare his glory among the nations,
> his marvelous deeds among all peoples (1 Chron. 16.23-24).

Not only the descendants of Israel but all nations are summoned to join in the offering of praise. These verses about the participation of all the earth in the song of praise take us to the part of the medley that originates in Psalm 96. The YHWH-*mālak* psalms thus become the intertext of the narrative about the ark's arrival in Jerusalem. And whereas the narrative context mentions the Davidic dynasty and its victories, the poetic text stresses that the praise is to be ascribed to the God of Israel, the king who has to be praised for ever. David may well play the role of the narrative's hero in Chronicles, but when the song of praise is heard, then Yahweh himself is praised as king—not just by Asaph and his associates and not just by Israel, but by all nations. It has, therefore, been possible here to reuse the old YHWH-*mālak* psalm to emphasize what will be decisive in postexilic time: that Yahweh himself sits on the throne and looks after his people.

By letting the song of praise appear in the middle of the narrative, Chr. also shows that the decree by David that the function of Asaph and his associates before the ark should last forever remains in force. However, the chorus has been expanded to include those of us who use the text at a later date. David's decree thus lasts beyond the time of Chr. Hence, any who use the psalm also become part of this eternal arrangement.

The psalm in 1 Chronicles 16 is, therefore, not just 'David's Psalm of Thanks'. Neither is it merely 'The Song of the Levites'. It is every reader's song of praise. The answer to the question 'Whose Song of Praise?' is, therefore, complex. The psalm is rooted in the book of Psalms; it is composed and inserted in Chr.'s narrative as an example of the song of praise of the levites; but through its poetic style it also becomes the reader's song of praise, which makes the reader part of the everlasting song of praise.

Conclusion

So, it seems that the simple question about the reader's reaction to a piece of poetry in the middle of an account of a past event has not been addressed in current commentaries on 1 Chronicles 16. I have certainly found support in Watts's discussion of 1 Chronicles 16 as 'a levitical medley' for my examination of the function of the psalm in the narrative context, but Watts is not concerned with the poetic aspects of the psalm either. He is searching for semantic and thematic links between the narrative context and the psalm. What he and others have not made clear, however, is that the poetic text addresses the reader and makes the reader contemporary with the arrival of the ark in Jerusalem. It thus draws the reader into the everlasting song of praise in a way that makes it impossible simply to replace the poetry with a piece of prose.

It is precisely this point that leaves plenty of room for the exegete who wishes to work with the role played by poetry in the Old Testament. Therefore, what I have done in this article is, first of all, to pose some very elementary questions and, hopefully, by this means to inspire others to take the poetic qualities more seriously, both when reading the book of Psalms and when reading a piece of poetry in the middle of a narrative context.

DAVID AND GOD IN 1 CHRONICLES 21: EDGED WITH MIST*

Noel Bailey

I hate Chronicles. In Chronicles I am a pious bore, as dull as dishwater and as preachy and insipid as that self-righteous Joan of Arc, and God knows I was never anything like that.[1]

Introduction

This article concentrates on 1 Chronicles 21, but it is not concerned with redactional or source-critical matters. It is primarily interested in gaps: Who is guilty? How many confessions does it take to appease God? What parts do the characters play in this census drama? After looking at these background questions, I will invoke the intertexts of Manasseh, Michel Foucault and Uzzah,[2] from which arise punishment, vengeance, terror and a David who is both more and less than a pious bore.

Sin, Guilt, Confession

Then David said to God, 'I have sinned greatly in having done this. And now, please remove the iniquity of your servant, for I have acted foolishly' (1 Chron. 21.8).

---

* With thanks to Professor Ed Conrad for a number of helpful suggestions.

1. The character David, in Joseph Heller's novel *God Knows* (London: Black Swan, 1985), p. 9.

2. Intertextuality as a method is too broad to be addressed here. I use it in the sense of juxtaposing texts that are related through an iconic equivalence. E. Van Wolde details this accurately: '*iconicity* ... denote[s] the principle that phenomena are analogous or isomorphic. Similar and different phenomena are not explained as being directly influenced by each other, causally or diachronically, but as being indirectly related to each other and having a similar or *iconic* quality or image in common. Where *indexicality* works on the basis of a succession of cause and effect, *iconicity* works on the basis of simultaneousness and analogy.' E. Von Wolde, 'Trendy Intertextuality?', in S. Draisma (ed.), *Intertexuality in Biblical Writings: Essays in Honour of Bas van Iersel* (Kampen: Kok, 1989), p. 46.

> David said to God, 'Was it not I who gave the command to count the people? And I am the one who has sinned and certainly done evil. But these sheep, what have they done? Yahweh God, please let your hand be against me, and against the house of my father, but do not plague your people' (1 Chron. 21.17).

The drama of the census in 1 Chronicles 21 is foregrounded in Chronicles in at least two ways: the relationship between the individual (David) and the nation is troublesome; as is the extent and direction of the punishment. Affairs both corporate and retributive are perplexing, with few answers to be found within the text.

The reason that the census incurs such a response from God will not detain us. In particular, the role of שָׂטָן and the actual census are separate issues, and this paper begins with the assumption that David orders the census, that it is taken and that there is a retributive response from the deity as a result of the event.

Japhet uses the word 'sin' to define Chr's perception of the census event,[3] theologically conditioning the signifier אַשְׁמָה ('guilt', 21.3). Furthermore, David—not the narrator—twice uses חָטָאתִי ('I have sinned') to describe his action (21.8 [qualified by מְאֹד, 'greatly'] and 21.17),[4] and אַשְׁמָה is itself used in Chronicles to denote religious guilt (cf. 2 Chron. 24.18). Since 'sin' is David's own description of his command to count Israel, by extension אַשְׁמָה certainly appears to take on religious freight (cf. 21.17, where David juxtaposes his expression of sin with the phrase וְהָרֵעַ הֲרֵעוֹתִי).

There is no obvious reason for the people becoming a target for retribution because of David's actions, and the commentaries generally exhibit confusion about this. Ackroyd, for example, suggests that Joab's

---

3. S. Japhet, *I & II Chronicles: A Commentary* (OTL; Louisville, KY: Westminster/John Knox Press, 1993), p. 377.

4. R. Alter gives one chapter of his book, *The Art of Biblical Narrative* (New York: Basic Books, 1981), to the importance of dialogue in narrative events and suggests that 'the primacy of dialogue is so pronounced [in biblical narrative] that many pieces of third-person narration prove on inspection to be dialogue-bound, verbally mirroring elements of dialogue that precede them or that they introduce. Narration is thus often relegated to the role of confirming assertions made in dialogue' (p. 65). Both times David acknowledges his sin, the narration confirms his assertion: the choice of punishments immediately follows David's first confession, and the command to purchase the threshing floor (an act of atonement) is collocated immediately to David's second admission.

claims in 21.3 reveal a 'conservative piety',[5] while Coggins refrains from evaluative comment, noting only that since it will bring guilt 'the stress is clearly on the wrongness of the proposal'.[6]

Elmslie takes the line of corporate responsibility by using Lev. 4.3 as an analogue and says 'the community is a unit, and the guilt of one falls on all'.[7] There is certainly an iconic and verbal similarity between Lev. 4.3 and 1 Chron. 21.3, especially in the collocation of אשמה with the verb חטא ('sin'): the first clause of Lev. 4.3 reads אם הכהן המשיח יחטא לאשמת העם ('if the anointed priest sins bringing guilt on the people').[8] Within the provisions of Lev. 4.3, however, expiation is to be made by the sinner, not by the people; therefore the people do not become *guilty*. They become *responsible*, and that is a different matter entirely. When Elmslie says, 'the guilt of one falls on all', it is uncertain whether he means that there is a metonymic transfer of guilt, or whether he is really saying that the people, although innocent, become objects of retribution because of the priest's sin. In its various forms, אשמה occurs only 19 times in the Hebrew Bible, and in almost every case it is attached to those who commit the offence.[9] Apart from Amos 8.14, only in Lev.

---

5. P.R. Ackroyd says that they 'may be seen as an expression of a conservative piety, perhaps originally in reaction against the development of what may be seen as undesirable governmental practices', which does not explain why the guilt should shift from David. P.R. Ackroyd, *I & II Chronicles, Ezra, Nehemiah* (TBC; London: SCM Press, 1973), p. 75.

6. R.J. Coggins, *The First and Second Books of the Chronicles* (CBC; Cambridge: Cambridge University Press, 1976), p. 108. On Joab's remark to David that all the people are David's servants, Coggins notes, 'the exact sense is not clear ... but in general Joab appears to be stressing the loyalty of the people without the need of a census' (p. 108). Many others do not discuss Joab's statement that David's decision will involve Israel: R.L. Braun, *1 Chronicles* (WBC, 14; Waco, TX: Word Books, 1986), p. 217; J.M. Myers, *I Chronicles* (AB, 12; Garden City, NY: Doubleday, 1965), pp. 147-49; M.J. Selman, *1 Chronicles* (TOTC, 10a; Downers Grove, IL: InterVarsity Press, 1994), p. 205; H.G.M. Williamson, *1 and 2 Chronicles* (NCB; Grand Rapids: Eerdmans, 1982), p. 144; I. Benzinger, *Die Bücher der Chronik* (KHAT, 20; Tübingen: J.C.B. Mohr [Paul Siebeck], 1901), p. 62.

7. W.A.L. Elmslie, *The Books of Chronicles* (CBSC; Cambridge: Cambridge University Press, 2nd edn, 1916), p. 131.

8. It should be noted that this addresses someone who has unconsciously sinned (כי־תחטא בשגגה; Lev. 4.2), though this distinction will hardly affect the argument.

9. Lev. 5.24 (*EVV* 6.5), 26 (*EVV* 6.7) 22.16; Ps. 69.6 [*EVV* 69.5]; Ezra 9.6, 7, 13, 15; 10.10, 19; 2 Chron. 28.10, 13; 33.23. 2 Chron. 24.18 is ambiguous: serving

4.3 and 1 Chron. 21.3 is אשמה used to describe those who are not directly responsible for the trespass. In Lev. 4.3 there is a visible cleft between the sinner and those whom the individual's sin may affect, and I suggest this can be used as an intertext to 1 Chron. 21.3.

Other examples of sin in Leviticus 4 are more individualistic in scope than 4.3: a 'chieftain's' (NJPS) unwitting sin requires an offering for forgiveness, but the nation is not apparently involved (4.22-26). Nor is it involved in the case of the unconscious sin of a person 'from the land' (4.27-35). Notice in 4.3 that the priest offers a sacrifice not for the sin of the people, but for his own sin; this leads me to think that the sin of which the *priest* is guilty—albeit unaware at the time of the offence—is different qualitatively, since it involves the nation in ways that the sins of others do not.[10] If so, David's sin in a theocratic environment is analogous, somehow being more serious than the sin of others differently placed in the hierocratic array and having the capacity to extend geographically beyond the person of the sinner. In Chronicles there is one fact that is singularly important: in almost every case it is the king or ruler who sins and/or the people; the sin of an individual who is not the king or ruler is insufficient to activate God's retributive intervention—the amorphous entity 'the people' is needed, usually in conjunction with the king, since it is the king who often leads (forces) the way for the people. In some cases there is a division between them, where the people forsake God in face of the king's piety. The differentiation does not, however, isolate the individual among the people.

Perhaps, then, the people in 1 Chronicles 21 do not become guilty themselves; instead, David's activity has the facility of drawing the people into its orbit. Since censuses of many descriptions occur in Chronicles and are hardly harmful,[11] I am suspicious that the census per se is the primary problem. Other kings' sins in Chronicles are (superficially) far more grievous than David's (e.g. abandoning Yahweh and following other gods); I wonder, then, whether the problem is not the

false gods is defined as אשמה, which brings wrath upon Judah and Jerusalem. But in 24.17 it is the leaders of Judah who persuade the king to forsake Yahweh, and it is unclear whether the antecedents of באשמתם are the leaders and king or Judah and Jerusalem. The quandry is resolved in 24.20, when Zechariah addresses all the people and includes them in his indictment.

10. By stretching the point severely, perhaps, the reference in Lev. 4.3 to the people is an elliptical and elastic remark that ranges across the following examples.

11. E.g. 1 Chron. 11.10–12.40; 23.6–26.32; 2 Chron. 2.17; 17.13-19 *passim*.

census event, but David. In other words, David, as founder of the cult and the effective constructor of the temple (aside from the nuts and bolts of its actual erection), is the one who should faultlessly embody the theocratic enterprise and is incapable of it, in which case the punishment is not so much of David's sin as it is an object lesson to David, and of David. It certainly anticipates the idea that no one is able to avoid sin (2 Chron. 6.36).

One Wrath or Two?

David's confession in 21.8 is semantically attached to the indeterminate event ויך את־ישׂראל ('and he struck Israel'). That this is an act of judgment or punishment discrete from, and hence additional to, the later acts of retribution recorded in 1 Chron. 21.11-12 is generally recognized by commentators,[12] though some see it as merely an anticipation of the later catastrophe. In the latter group, Williamson, for example, suggests, 'The whole verse [7] is a summarising introduction to the following paragraph, so that *and he smote Israel* refers to the pestilence of v. 14, not to some other and additional catastrophe'.[13] He gives no justification for this comment, unlike De Vries, who sees this verse as a prolepsis for the succeeding section and writes, 'while David may have been so conscience-stricken that he was aware of Yahweh's attitude (Joab had warned him of this in v. 3), Yahweh had not yet sent his angel when David began to pray'.[14] But De Vries seems to be doing two things in particular: (1) interpolating 2 Sam. 24.10 (ויך לב־דוד אתו אחרי־כן ספר את־העם, 'David reproached himself [lit., David's heart struck him] after he had counted the people') into this text; (2) connecting the textual cohesion to the appearance of the מלאך ('messenger'), in the sense that no punishment can precede this phenomenon. It is uncertain what role De Vries is giving the מלאך, and no reason for the connection is offered.

Harvey-Jellie, anticipating Williamson and De Vries, likewise sees repentance only after the pestilence: 'the Chronicler implies that David's repentance was awakened when he saw the Divine anger mani-

---

12. E.g. Japhet, *I & II Chronicles*, p. 379; Ackroyd, *I & II Chronicles, Ezra, Nehemiah*, p. 75; Coggins, *Chronicles*, p. 108.

13. Williamson, *1 and 2 Chronicles*, p. 145.

14. S.J. De Vries, *1 and 2 Chronicles* (FOTL, 11; Grand Rapids: Eerdmans, 1989), p. 171.

fested in the pestilence, whereas the author of Samuel shows how David was troubled by a guilty conscience (verse 10)',[15] though it is unclear as to whether 'pestilence' here is actually referring to the later disaster or simply filling out רד. Harvey-Jellie also offers the unusual harmonizing approach of having a single David, who crosses and exists in two narratives simultaneously; that is, 'the conviction of sin was due both to subjective [2 Sam. 24] and objective [1 Chron. 21] causes'.[16] However, the cohesion of the text ties v. 7 quite firmly into the preceding section;[17] David's self-attribution of guilt in v. 8 mitigates against seeing v. 7 as proleptic. The sequence of the text is clear: a smiting and an acknowledgment of guilt prompted by the event.[18] I conjecture that commentators who interpret this verse as an anticipatory summary of the later retribution do so under the influence of 2 Samuel 24: that is, there is only one punishment in the Samuel account. In the Samuel story David does not need an act of God to repent and so two discrete responses to the one sin in Chronicles converge into one, agreeing with the synoptic text. Chronicles, however, has its own voice, one that does not rely on a competing sibling for its semantic load.[19]

15. W.R. Harvey-Jellie, *I & II Chronicles* (CB; Edinburgh: T.C. & E.C. Jack, 1906), p. 139.

16. Harvey-Jellie, *I & II Chronicles*, p. 139. W.H. Bennett also conceives of 21.7 as a proleptic summary. In a footnote he writes, 'Ver. 7 is apparently a general anticipation of the narrative in vv. 9-15', but the text to which this note attaches refers only to 'some sense of the Divine displeasure' that fell upon David. W.H. Bennett, *The Books of Chronicles* (ExpB; London: Hodder & Stoughton, 1894), p. 280 n.1.

17. Myers states that how David comes to an understanding of his sin is unknown (*1 Chronicles*, p. 147) but ignores the spatially immediate collocation of David's assertion of guilt with the incident of God 'smiting' Israel. Nothing is allowed to intrude the narrative flow. To separate the two events is artificially to divide the narrative so that v. 7 is attached to the preceding verses and not to v. 8, the only way that Myers's view can be supported. See also my 'David's Innocence: A Response to J. Wright', *JSOT* 64 (1994), pp. 83-90.

18. So Japhet (although speaking redactionally): 'the Chronicler reveals his view that repentance must be catalysed by some active factor, explicitly referred to in the course of the story: a prophetic message, divine punishment or the like. David's unmotivated repentance [2 Sam. 24] calls for motivation, and this is provided by the smiting of the [sic] Israel in v. 7.' Japhet, *I & II Chronicles*, p. 379.

19. At a methodological level, Japhet's observations are notable. She accepts two punishments, but says 'the change [God smiting Israel instead of David's heart smiting David in Samuel] introduced by the Chronicler did not contribute to a

Not only are there two punishments, but the prophet's role is not to seek repentance—it is to relay God's choice of punishments. In fact, David has already repented, yet unlike other kings, there is no softening of the punishment, and it is only for the sake of the city (as metaphor?), rather than for David or the people, that the second punishment ceases before its time (1 Chron. 21.15). The prophetic role is limited (apart from the complication of Joab's cautioning voice), since Gad does little beyond act as God's mouthpiece;[20] there is certainly no explicit call for repentance in Gad's words, and there cannot be an implicit call for confession because David has already confessed—unless his first confession in some way lacked efficacy.

Some would argue that David does not confess quite enough. De Vries writes:

> In his prayer he does seem to take the responsibility upon himself, yet *hāṭā'tî mᵉ'ōd*, 'I have erred seriously,' in his confession, and especially *niskaltî mᵉ'ōd*, 'I have acted very foolishly,' in the request for absolution (v. 8), hardly express the kind of repentance that can avert the severe penalty that his transgression has earned.[21]

No particular reason is offered for this odd statement, and I assume that it is the later narrative, specifically the figurative bulk of the altar and presentation of offerings, that has prompted De Vries's comments. Selman takes a similar approach, commenting on 21.8, 'the reality of judgment is not diminished by his confession',[22] and on 21.17 he writes, 'David's own response [to the pestilence] is further repentance, finally accepting full personal responsibility for the census'.[23] I read 21.17 only as affirmation and embellishment of the points raised in 21.8, because 21.8 identifies the sin unambiguously as David's. In 21.17 David may be stretching the point for Yahweh's benefit, but it is the *same* point.

As an aside, David's polite and concise petition to God (21.8) speaks

---

smoother story, as this verse does not fully integrate into the narrative sequence'. Japhet, *I & II Chronicles*, p. 379. But if we read Chronicles synchronically, it *is* an integrated segment of the narrative; it is only 'rough' if the narrative of 2 Sam. 24 is expected as we read the Chronicles text.

20. Assuming, of course, that Gad correctly relays the options, since the passage of words between God and Gad is not noted (1.10).

21. De Vries, *I and 2 Chronicles*, pp. 171-72.

22. Selman, *1 Chronicles*, p. 206.

23. Selman, *1 Chronicles*, p. 208.

of taking away the עון. This is usually considered to be something like 'iniquity', establishing a link back to the census command, or to the census event itself, or to both. It is also reasonably a link to אשמה, so that 'your servant' transmits both 'David' and 'Israel'.[24] While 'iniquity' is sound and rational, there is the danger that isolating a healthy translation shuts the door, so to speak, on other options; as Eco remarks in his novel *Foucault's Pendulum*, 'the more ambiguous and elusive a symbol is, the more it gains significance and power'.[25]

In this case, another translation is feasible and presents an impressive list of precedents. Elmslie in 1916 suggested, without further comment, that עון should perhaps be rendered 'punishment', through analogy with Gen. 4.13 and 1 Sam. 28.10.[26] In other words, he seems to be suggesting that David, after initially confessing, then addresses the retributive activity of 21.7. This assumes that the 'smiting', from David's perspective—although forcing self-realization and confession—might be incomplete. Whether עון is translated as 'iniquity' or 'punishment', however, does not significantly alter the issue, so it can be left as a point of ambiguity.

Verse 13 transparently asserts a characteristic of God: mercy. The significant first unit of this verse, 'I am in great distress', has two possible points of reference: first, David is being forced into the untenable position of having to choose the disaster that will be applied without discretion over Israel (if the punishment implied by ויך ('he struck') is anything to go by), almost secondarily incorporating David, the only real 'sinner'; secondly, it confronts the equation of sin and punishment that David had thought resolved. The fact that David had repented (21.8) and sought the removal of the iniquity or punishment suggests that he expected his confession to be accepted. For God immediately to offer via Gad more extensive punishment for the same offence is disconcerting, and David has no recourse except to the concept of mercy.

---

24. Israel is occasionally described in poetic texts as a 'servant' (e.g. Ps. 136.22; Jer. 2.14), though I doubt the point can be stretched to accommodate Israel alone in this instance.

25. U. Eco, *Foucault's Pendulum* (London: Picador, 1990), p. 432.

26. To which I add Gen. 19.15; 2 Kgs 7.9; Jer. 51.6; Ezek . 4.4, 5, 6, 17; 14.10; 21.30 (*EVV* 25); 21.34 (*EVV* 29); 35.5; 44.10, 12; Ps. 69.27; Job 19.29. To quote just one example, when in 1 Sam. 28.10 the woman of Endor accuses Saul of entrapment, Saul responds by assuring her that no punishment will come upon her: חי־יהוה אם־יקרך עון בדבר הזה.

The punishments offered to David—famine, sword or plague—are not unusual; the trio occurs elsewhere in Chronicles. They are invoked by Jehoshaphat in 2 Chron. 20.9 as examples in his plea to God to spare Judah from an advancing military threat. Jehoshaphat likewise uses them as models when he says, 'Should evil befall us', and lists the three.[27] In Solomon's speech at the temple dedication, all three occur in a more comprehensive list of calamities (2 Chron. 6.28). This deadly triad of sword, famine and plague is very relevant when it comes to the matter of the severity of the punishment, because David has thrown himself upon God's mercy (21.13): God (through Gad) tells David to 'Choose a punishment', but David radically addresses God and says, 'Choose it yourself'. David bends it backwards, lacing it simultaneously with a call for mercy. Ironically, David sets up a binary opposition between the mercy of God and the mercy of humanity, extolling the first and inviting a comparison with the second through the adversative conjunction.[28] The death of seventy thousand soon shows God's mercy to be debatable, and we are left to wonder if David elevated the wrong standard, or whether there is any real distinction between the two.

There is further irony in that the three punishments are surrounded by the language of choice and desire: Yahweh 'offers'[29] three things to David and commands him to 'choose' one (בחר־לך; 21.10), to 'receive it/accept it' (קבל־לך; 21.11). The three being offered are not personal punishments, though, for any choice would involve the people of Judah, even though the language of proposition is specifically personal (אני נטה עליך, 'I offer you'; בחר־לך, 'choose'; ואעשה־לך, 'I will do it to you'; קבל־לך, 'choose').[30] David's earlier choice of the census is now mirrored by his 'choice' of a penalty. Initially, David entangled Judah in his census, a choice the people resisted without success (through Joab as synecdoche). The voice of the people, expressed in the objections of

27. It is fascinating that Jehoshaphat is saying that when misfortune arises (sword, plague or famine), then they are assured that by seeking God they shall be delivered. Within a doctrine of retribution, misfortunes would only have arisen because of sin; in other words, if they occur it is because God sent them.

28. וביד־אדם אל־אפל; 21.13.

29. So NJPS and RSV, translating the qal participle נטה (21.10). 2 Sam. 24 and other witnesses read the participle נוטל, and the NIV translates 1 Chron. 21.10 closer to this word: 'I am giving you three options.'

30. David's response is equally individualistic in orientation: 'let *me* fall (אפלה־נא) into the hand of Yhwh ... let *me* not fall (אל־אפל) into the hand of humanity' (21.13).

its strongest non-ruling representative, gives way to the privilege and power of monarchy (חֹזֵק וּדְבַר־הַמֶּלֶךְ עַל־יוֹאָב, 'the word of the king was strong over Joab'; 21.4), yet their act of resistance is ignored by Yahweh. Their act is, fundamentally, a positive one, for they come down on the side of Yahweh: they are essentially seeking Yahweh against the wishes of one who is busy forsaking Yahweh. However, retribution still comes to them: wrath for their faithfulness, an attack for their loyalty. In an astounding and grotesque situation, an anachronistic parody of a television game show that could be called 'Pick your Punishment', David is placed in an inescapable position of choice. This time there is no way to avoid the act of choosing; there is still, however, a further interjection of the people's voice, but their advocate is— ironically and too late—David (in 21.17).

But we move too far. David must accept the punishment, and by invoking God's mercy he seeks to avoid the sword of his human enemies (presuming this to be the referent of וּבְיַד־אָדָם אַל־אֶפֹּל, 'but do not let me fall into the hands of humanity'; 21.13).[31] David actually makes a choice: to let Yahweh choose from either the famine or the plague + sword of the divine messenger, and Yahweh chooses the latter. It is all something of a game. Punishment appears to be required for an infringement of the 'rules', as much of Chronicles would suggest, but this is almost masochistic; in no other case is punishment delayed in this tense and drawn-out manner. Another question, unanswerable but nagging, is raised: Did Yahweh choose the *lesser* of the two remaining forms of retribution?

Braun's concluding comments to his treatment of 1 Chronicles 21 are curious:

> Despite David's guilt in calling for a census of Israel, his sin leads to the designation of the threshing floor of Ornan as the place of Yahweh's choosing for his altar and temple. It is quite clear here ... that God's grace stands in the forefront—a point that David himself is at pains to make (v 13).[32]

It is true that David declares God's compassion to be great; whether he means it is not so obvious. Given that it comes from David's mouth as a response to God's demand that he choose a medium of destruction, there is a suspicion of wishful thinking. It may be an innocent descrip-

---

31. So, e.g., Williamson, *1 and 2 Chronicles*, p. 146.
32. Braun, *1 Chronicles*, p. 218.

tion of a facet of God recognized (hoped for) by David, but contextually it can be read as an affirmation that God truly is gracious, or as a sycophantic call on vanity, or bemusement that God *should be* gracious and that the request to choose a punishment contradicts this belief.

The interpretation depends on the antecedent of 'his compassion'. Upon what grounds does David invoke a compassionate Yahweh? Is it the earlier smiting in 21.7? Do we look further to Uzzah? Or, is it the times that God *is* actually with David? The antecedent is unknown, but the local context of 21.13 allows for a pointed, sardonic reading that calls into question the grace of God at the same time that it is literarily affirmed. Braun is useful again: 'That same grace of God which triumphed over David's sins and led to the establishment of God's house remains God's principal attribute available to human beings.'[33] Let me be clear here: this 'grace' that 'triumphs' over *David's* sin is exhibited through the mass slaughter of those who did not sin; a triumphant grace is oxymoronic under the circumstances.

Williamson's comments on 21.15-27 are equally extraordinary:

> Enclosed within the framework are the accounts of David's repentance (17) and purchase of the threshing floor (18-25), and God's acceptance of the sacrifices offered there (26). *The whole thus becomes a fine expression of repentance (17) consequent upon God's prior grace (15f.)* in a way which yet at the same time safeguards the real significance of man's response (26 with 27).[34]

But David does not repent as a result of God's grace. He repents because the messenger is still hovering with drawn sword (I will return to this).

Punishment: Why?

One particular question is raised here, and it is a question that is raised over all of Chronicles: What purpose does punishment serve? At this point I invoke Michel Foucault's *Discipline and Punish*,[35] which is basically a long discussion on the three 'modalities according to which the power to punish is exercised',[36] namely vengeance, correction and

33. Braun, *1 Chronicles*, p. 218.
34. Williamson, *1 and 2 Chronicles*, p. 146 (italics mine).
35. M. Foucault, *Discipline and Punish: The Birth of the Prison* (Harmondsworth: Peregrine, 1979).
36. Foucault, *Discipline and Punish*, p. 131.

discipline, a triad Foucault labels 'three technologies of power'.[37] Very briefly, 'vengeance' signifies a period[38] where punishment was a chastisement of the body, often as grisly torture, carried out in the public gaze.[39] Foucault notes that torture was systematically abolished in Europe in the late eighteenth and early nineteenth centuries[40] and that:

> whatever theatrical elements it still retained were now downgraded, as if the functions of the penal ceremony were gradually ceasing to be understood, as if this rite that 'concluded the crime' was suspected of being in some undesirable way linked with it. It was as if the punishment was thought to equal, if not to exceed, in savagery the crime itself, to accustom the spectators to a ferocity from which one wished to divert them, to show them the frequency of crime, to make the executioner resemble a criminal, judges murderers, to reverse roles at the last moment, to make the tortured criminal an object of pity or admiration.[41]

From retribution as vengeance, Foucault traces a move to where it is the conviction of the crime that is paramount: 'it is the conviction itself that marks the offender with the unequivocally negative sign: the publicity has shifted to the trial, and to the sentence'.[42] This is retribution as correction: 'from being an art of unbearable sensations punishment has become an economy of suspended rights'[43]—the aim of this suspension is to 'correct, reclaim, "cure"'.[44] This shift in emphasis meant that the body was no longer the chief object of punishment; instead, it was the soul: 'passions, instincts, anomalies, infirmities, maladjustments, effects of environment or heredity'.[45] Correction has two particular facets: 'to

---

37. Foucault, *Discipline and Punish*, p. 131.

38. Foucault's discussion is decidedly Eurocentric, beginning in eighteenth-century Europe.

39. Foucault begins his book with a matter-of-fact description of the torture that was to be inflicted upon a regicide and the application of those techniques to the victim. Foucault, *Discipline and Punish*, pp. 3-6. Torture as public spectacle was, in Foucault's words, 'a gloomy festival of punishment' (p. 8).

40. Foucault, *Discipline and Punish*, pp. 8-9.

41. Foucault, *Discipline and Punish*, p. 9; see also p. 130. Foucault also quotes Beccaria, who wrote in 1764, 'The murder that is depicted as a horrible crime is repeated in cold blood, remorselessly' (p. 9).

42. Foucault, *Discipline and Punish*, p. 9.

43. Foucault, *Discipline and Punish*, p. 11.

44. Foucault, *Discipline and Punish*, p. 10.

45. There is, as Foucault puts it, a 'substitution of objects', in which 'acts of aggression are punished, so also, through them, is aggressivity; rape, but at the

get all citizens to participate in the punishment of the social enemy and to render the exercise of the power to punish entirely adequate and transparent to the laws that publicly define it'.[46]

The third partner of Foucault's taxonomy is 'discipline'. While correction refers to a legal corpus and judicial machinery, discipline is concerned with docility, in the sense that a level of social homogeneity is sought that will delimit and constrain the individual.[47] Since discipline is concerned predominantly with institutional power in an act of human creation (in, for example, the discipline of a monastic or military life) rather than retribution, it need not distract us. Retribution as vengeance and retribution as correction are, however, very relevant, and I will discuss them through another intertext.

Manasseh and David

Retribution in Chronicles is firmly tied to the pursuit of Yahweh. The pursuit of other gods and other human (military) alliances normally draws upon itself God's wrath, either directly or though a human agency. The story of Manasseh in 2 Chron. 33.1-20 is a useful intertext here because it contains a pertinent element of Foucault's study and has an iconic similarity to the events of 1 Chronicles 21.

Manasseh does what is displeasing to Yahweh, and on a grand scale:

same time perversions; murders, but also drives and desires'. Foucault, *Discipline and Punish*, p. 17. Execution was not avoided, but detached from the horror of torture, so that the elimination of pain became a feature—executions were to be swift and, as far as possible, painless (pp. 14-17).

46. Foucault, *Discipline and Punish*, p. 129.

47. 'The art of punishing, in the régime of disciplinary power, is aimed neither at expiation, nor even precisely at repression. It brings five quite distinct operations into play: it refers individual actions to a whole that is at once a field of comparison, a space of differentiation and the principle of a rule to be followed. It differentiates individuals from one another, in terms of the following overall rule: that the rule be made to function as a minimal threshold, as an average to be respected or as an optimum towards which one must move. It measures in quantitative terms and hierarchizes in terms of value the abilities, the level, the "nature" of individuals. It introduces, through this "value-giving" measure, the constraint of a conformity that must be achieved. Lastly, it traces the limit that will define difference in relation to all other differences, the external frontier of the abnormal ... The perpetual penalty that traverses all points and supervises every instant in the disciplinary institutions compares, differentiates, hierarchizes, homogenizes, excludes, In short, it *normalizes*'. Foucault, *Discipline and Punish*, p. 183.

he erects shrines and altars to pagan gods, including their construction in the temple of Yahweh (33.3-5); he sacrifices his sons and becomes involved in a host of pagan practices ('soothsaying, divination, and sorcery, and [he] consulted ghosts and familiar spirits' [33.6; NJPS]). Chr. makes it clear that these activities are displeasing to Yahweh (33.6),[48] in language that corresponds to God's displeasure at the census (cf. 1 Chron. 21.7, ויֵּרַע בעיני האלהים, 'it was evil in the eyes of God'; and 2 Chron. 33.6, לעשות הרע בעיני יהוה, 'he did evil in the eyes of the Lord'). In Manasseh's case there is also a curious little appendix to the statement of God's outrage: Manasseh does these things 'in order to vex Him'. David's determination is not characterized in this frank way, though it could be read into the way he overrules Joab.

In both cases there is sin. In the Manasseh event the narrator is not reticent about condemning Manasseh's exploits before there is any hint of retribution. Whether or not David's command to count Israel is a sin is implicit only in Joab's remarks about Israel and אשמה; it is not until the census is effectively consummated that it is truly decreed as sin, and that happens only through the act of retribution, bracketed and confirmed by the narrator's assertion of Yahweh's displeasure and David's confession. Whatever is actually signified by David's command to count Israel, the command is a reflection of not seeking God, of forsaking God. There is little middle ground. Accordingly, the *type* of sin is less important than the *fact* of sin. David commands a census; Manasseh sacrifices his sons and actively pursues pagan gods. The only commonality is intent: in both cases the actions are *deliberate*. Ironically, David's sin is transparently less serious than Manasseh's in content, yet it is inverted as the cause of far greater and far more involved punishment.[49]

The contrast in these narratives regarding the people is stark. In

48. Of course the alert reader, or the one armed with a concordance, realizes that this is a reflection of prohibitions in Deut. 18.10-11. The close similarity between these verses means that those in Chronicles are almost in quotation marks, which would force a comparison if the earlier verses were known; but Chr. typically does not direct the reader elsewhere, nor hint to the reader that another text may be in operation.

49. The description of retribution in the story of Manasseh occurs in one verse (v. 11), which simply states that Yahweh brought the Assyrians against Manasseh and the people, and the Assyrians took Manasseh off to Babylon. It is matter-of-fact, functional. The retribution for the census involves significant numbers and specifics, which focuses more attention on the act of retribution and its scope.

1 Chronicles 21 the people are drawn into David's sin, but they are not themselves sinners. By comparison, the narrative in 2 Chronicles 33 leaves little room for doubt: Manasseh may have led the people into evil (v. 9), but they were content to stay there (vv. 3-10). In the latter instance retribution is inflicted only after both Manasseh and the people have ignored Yahweh (v. 10).

Retribution comes in both stories: Yahweh acts directly against Israel in 1 Chron. 21.7 and through the agency of the Assyrians in 2 Chron. 33.11. In both stories the repentance of the two kings occurs immediately after the acts of retribution, which highlights the efficacy of these punishments. Manasseh's contrition is a model of returning to Yahweh, in a small narrative laden with redundancy. Manasseh prays (חלה; 33.12), humbles himself greatly (ויכנע מאד; 33.12) and prays (ויתפלל; 33.13). After Yahweh grants his return to Jerusalem, he knows that Yahweh alone is God (33.12-13). David's repentance, although succinct, expresses both an acknowledgment of his wrongdoing (חטאתי מאד, 'I have sinned greatly') and a declaration of his folly (נסכלתי מאד, 'I have acted foolishly'; both 21.8).[50] In terms of content, there is little to choose between the behavior of Manasseh and David.

Manasseh's repentance leads to a period of construction and fortification, as well as a partial purge of foreign cults (33.14-17), and he and the people worship Yahweh—that is, there is peace and prosperity, a sign of the lack of negative retribution, thereby indicating a period of seeking God. David's repentance, on the other hand, is not met favorably; there is only a pronouncement of further punishment and David's resultant call upon God's mercy.

We come now to the problem of punishment as vengeance versus punishment as correction. Punishment on such a grand scale in 1 Chronicles 21 could be viewed as an overexpressed matter of correction; of course, the death of seventy thousand can be a corrective only for the survivors, and since the people are apportioned responsibility without guilt, then 'correction' is inappropriate and their death is simply that: their death. David is not personally punished for his transgression, unlike other kings (Uzziah, Jehoram, Asa), and so if the correction of David is at stake then it dehumanizes the population as

---

50. 'Folly' is used only one other time in Chronicles (2 Chron. 16.9), in the mouth of Hanani the seer, who describes Asa's alliance with Ben-hadad as foolish behavior (נסכלה); it is an example of forsaking Yahweh, and it is contextually feasible to read this interpretation into David's declaration of foolishness.

simply David's possessions, a tool by which David is 'cured'; the distinction between the responsible individual and those who stand apart from the transgression is blurred and ignored. The people are guilty only by association, and although David may be punished through the loss of his people, the absence of seventy thousand people does little to affect the context of Chronicles. We are left with vengeance—hierarchical space that exists and operates as a functional means to an end: the restoration of a situation where 'seeking God' is primary.

The terseness of the narrative in 1 Chron. 21.14 prevents, I think, the reading of retribution as a 'gloomy festival of punishment'. The description is concise and absolutely condensed, dwelling neither on suffering nor spectacle. Nonetheless, seventy thousand die, and in that sense this punishment *is* a spectacle. There is, as Foucault generally remarks, an ironic reversal of roles between the executioner and the criminal when punishment is violent.[51] Seventy thousand dead for David's crime is not correction but spectacle, a violent punishment confirming power and caprice (a foot ailment [Asa] or a brief bout of leprosy [Uzziah] would perhaps be sufficient). It is almost as if David is not to be equated with other kings, regardless of their behavior, as if he stands outside the (inconsistent) sphere of retribution that applies to them; certainly, no others are offered a choice of punishment. The loss of seventy thousand is a 'theatrical representation';[52] it is not a punishment that fits the crime. Cate writes:

> Unlike human anger, God's anger never gets out of control. It is simply His passionate reaction to human sin. The point clearly made by these books [historical books] is that God cares deeply about His people and, therefore, cares about their almost habitual disobedience and apostasy. Thus Yahweh's anger is real, but we must never forget that, unlike the gods of the pagans that surrounded Israel, the anger of Yahweh is never irrational. His anger always arises from His covenant love.[53]

It is a strange love indeed that permits the destruction of the innocent. Cate is treading a fine line here, because apostasy and idolatry are themselves choices for not-Yahweh. God's anger may arise from 'covenant love'; it springs concurrently, however, from the rejection of a people's right to choose. Retribution for apostasy and idolatry is essentially a

51. Foucault, *Discipline and Punish*, p. 9.
52. Foucault, *Discipline and Punish*, p. 14.
53. R.L. Cate, *An Introduction to the Historical Books of the Old Testament* (Nashville, TN: Broadman & Holman, 1994), pp. 163-64.

denial of freedom. It is not that the people are seduced or attracted to Yahweh worship—the people simply have no choice but to follow Yahweh.[54]

David's case is unlike Manasseh's. Manasseh's sin may have drawn the theatre of the public spectacle, but it is not vengeance for it ends with an adjustment of Manasseh's perceptions: 'Then Manasseh knew that the Lord alone was God' (2 Chron. 33.13). It is finally a matter of correction, instituting a situation where Manasseh's knowledge and will accord with the predominant social power, which is, in this instance, Yahweh. David does not seek after other gods, as Manasseh did. David's sin, very loosely defined as forsaking Yahweh, is deliberate,[55] but perhaps not cultic or religious. However, it is still indirectly a pursuit of that which is not-Yahweh, and David is 'corrected' of this misapprehension.

However, correction is only one aspect. It is arguable that correction occurs in the first instance of punishment. David's confession (21.8) is at the same time an acknowledgment and a plea for the reinstitution of the Yahweh–David (Israel) matrix. Since this relationship seems only to exist in Chronicles if the human side of the connection is in active pursuit of the divine aspect, and David is certainly fulfilling this function when he expresses his repentance, he has been 'corrected'. What is the purpose of another punishment, one seemingly wider in scope? Given David's confessions, what is the point of this excessive exercise? It is intemperate and pointless as an act of return. But it does demonstrate power. David is forced into the position of acting as one of the agents of vengeance for his own offence. It is he, the sinner, who is to decide the form of punishment over others—David is effectively twice the oppressor of his people, once of his own volition, and then when it is forced upon him. Since the sin has been punished and confessed, this new punishment serves as an illustration of the power of the God

54. Chr.'s theme of 'seeking God' has been explored in depth. See, e.g., G.E. Schaefer, 'The Significance of Seeking God in the Purpose of the Chronicler' (PhD dissertation, Southern Baptist Theological Seminary, 1972); C.T. Begg, '"Seeking Yahweh" and the Purpose of Chronicles', *Louvain Studies* 9 (1982), pp. 128-41. But what is the purpose of this performance? Continual retribution, notwithstanding its inconsistent application, is prevalent enough to force Israelite worship. 'Seeking God' becomes synonymous with 'seek God or perish'.

55. Assuming, as I have said previously, that David overruled Joab's objections while knowing that a census would be a trespass.

against whom David would transgress. And it is David who refuses the role of executioner. I can do no better than cite Foucault on the idea of vengeance as a demonstration of power:

> punishment is a ceremonial of sovereignty; it uses the ritual marks of the vengeance that it applies to the body of the condemned man; and it deploys before the eyes of the spectators an effect of terror as intense as it is discontinuous, irregular and always above its own laws, the physical presence of the sovereign and of his power.[56]

David's word 'is strong over Joab' (1 Chron. 21.4), an example of Foucault's putative ceremonial of sovereignty. It is an instance of David's ability to use his position and power to control Joab's (hence Israel's) actions. Yahweh takes David's own sovereignty and subverts it. In other words, there are always two active and conflicting sovereigns: Yahweh over David, and David over Israel. It is only when the two relationships merge that David loses his sovereignty and displaces Israel; or, at best, joins the people. The irony is that Yahweh takes on David's ceremonies and uses them not against David, but against Israel, an act of further displacement.

After the second act of retribution has been halted, David requests that the punishment be redirected to the person who started it all, that is, himself (21.17). Japhet notes that:

> [David's] request to transfer God's wrath to himself and his father's house has in fact no point at this stage of the story. The punishment of the people has already been executed, and a divine decision has just called a halt to any further chastisement.[57]

But Japhet is not taking David's point of view. From David's perspective, the withdrawal is temporary. God tells the messenger to refrain from further destruction (רב עתה הרף ידך; 21.15); a message that does not appear to involve David in its hearing. David only sees a heavenly figure with drawn sword (21.16), a hostile figure, with no indication that the destruction has permanently concluded. The fact that David and the elders (in sackcloth) throw themselves on their faces (21.16), quickly followed by David's second confession and plea, indicates not relief that it is over, but a *wish* for it to end (or be redirected). It is not until the altar has been built and the sacrifices accepted that the messenger is told to return the sword to its sheath (21.27). In other words,

---

56. Foucault, *Discipline and Punish*, p. 130.
57. Japhet, *I & II Chronicles*, p. 383.

during the time that David purchased the threshing floor, built the altar and made offerings to Yahweh, a messenger from God, known only for its destructive capabilities, is in sight, with drawn sword (it is, of course, figuratively or literally the sword that destroys: cf. 21.12).[58] From God's perspective, the position is also unclear. Since it is God who commands the return of the sword to its sheath, and God does not do this immediately, I speculate that God's 'repentance' (וינחם)[59] is actually conditional upon David's further confession.

In 21.17 David again acknowledges his personal sin and questions God about the direction of the destruction: Why, says David, must others be responsible for something they have not done (refuting notions of corporate responsibility)? Notice also that David's probings are ignored by God, as is his confession. Unlike Manasseh, David's humility and repentance are insufficient; they must be concretized in a cultic act of atonement, which is effectively another act of repentance. David, then, repents three times for the one sin, and it is only the non-verbal act of expiation that is sufficient.

Note also that although the people become responsible (as in Lev. 4.3), they do nothing—and are to do nothing—to restore the situation to its former state. It is only David who is to act, not the people, for it is only David's sin. The single act of repentance that God accepts is, like Lev. 4.3, one of sacrificial expiation. It is not enough for David to say, simply, 'sorry', as Manasseh does. Interestingly, Selman notes two types of אשמה: instances that invoke God's wrath, and others where 'expiation and/or restitution' are required.[60] He includes 1 Chron. 21.3 in the first group and Lev. 4.3 in the second. In one sense, both of these 'types' operate in 1 Chronicles 21, but in another sense the question is sidelined because it is not the אשמה that is important—it signifies the

---

58. See also Dion who notes that the second part of the story (purchase of the threshing floor and the sacrifice) 'is to be read in the light of this terrifying vision' of the angel with the drawn sword. P.E. Dion, 'The Angel with the Drawn Sword (II [sic] Chr 21, 16): An Exercise in Restoring the Balance of Text Criticism and Attention to Context', *ZAW* 97 (1985), p. 115.

59. As I noted, it seems that God's mitigation of the disaster is activated by seeing Jerusalem, the city, and not by the scale of destruction already wrought among human life. But since the messenger's sword remains outside its sheath (the metaphor of potential devastation) until after David's act of expiation, it is moot whether even Jerusalem would have been spared had David's response been one of non-repentance.

60. Selman, *1 Chronicles*, p. 205 n. 1.

responsibility of the group, not their act of trespass, so the restitution is for David's sin, and only indirectly for the group's accountability.

After purchasing the threshing floor and offering a symbolic confession that is finally recognized, harmony is expected. What we have, however, is further disruption, centering on David's fear of God.

David's Terror and the Fear of God

Socrates: The poet (Stasinus) sings—
  'Of Zeus, the author and creator of all these things,
  You will not tell: for where there is fear there is also reverence.'
And I disagree with this poet. Shall I tell you in what I disagree?
Euthyphro: By all means.
Socrates: I should not say that where there is fear there is also reverence;
for I am sure that many persons fear poverty and disease, and the like
evils, but I do not perceive that they reverence the objects of their fear.
Euthyphro: Very true.
Socrates: But where reverence is, there is fear: for he who has a feeling
of reverence and shame about the commission of any action, fears and is
afraid of an ill reputation.
Euthyphro: No doubt.
Socrates: Then we are wrong in saying that where there is fear there is
also reverence; and we should say, where there is reverence there is also
fear. But there is not always reverence where there is fear; for fear is a
more extended notion, and reverence is a part of fear; just as the odd is a
part of number, and number is a more extended notion than the odd. I
suppose that you follow me now?[61]

Some commentators work with the proposition that God chose the site
for the temple. Hanks, for instance, says 'of course, the Chronicler in
stressing the election of the temple site is but echoing the promise concerning "the place which the Lord your God shall choose" of Deuteronomy'.[62] In Chronicles, however, it is *David* who chooses the temple
site, not God, and this choice is because of David's literal fear of God.
Note the sequence: David buys Ornan's threshing floor, erects an altar
(21.25-26) and burns offerings (21.26), and the messenger (מלאך) of
God sheathes the drawn sword (21.27). The next sentence begins
temporally (כעת ההיא, 'at that time') and is problematic (the phrase is

---

61. Plato, *The Trial and Death of Socrates: Four Dialogues* (ed. S. Weller;
trans. B. Jowett; London: Constable, 1992), p. 12.

62. T.D. Hanks, 'The Chronicler: Theologian of Grace', *EvQ* 53 (1981), pp. 16-
28 (17). See also Japhet, *I & II Chronicles*, p. 389.

repeated in 21.29); 21.28 is often considered a protasis that has its apodosis in 22.1,[63] with 21.29-30 as a parenthetical aside.[64] The problem is whether there are two different sacrifices, because after David's expiatory offering in 21.26, there is mention of other sacrifices in 21.28. If 21.29-30 is parenthetical, then 21.28 and 22.1 should be read together in a translation such as, 'At that time, when David saw that Yahweh had answered him at the threshing floor of Ornan the Jebusite, when he sacrificed there, then David said...'[65] The option, taken by RSV, NJPS, NIV and by me, is to render 21.28 as a complete sentence: 'At that time, when David saw that Yahweh had answered him at the threshing floor of Ornan the Jebusite, he sacrificed there.'

Japhet suggests that the sacrifices in 21.28 are not the sacrifices of 21.26, although she adds that it is 'doubtful whether this passage indicates that the threshing floor of Araunah had already become a permanent place of sacrifice in the time of David'.[66] Japhet asks, on the assumption that God chose the site for the temple, whether the site should be seen as 'a divine choice and act of grace' or as 'a concession to human limitation and weakness?'[67] But she is drawing those questions from a historical issue framed away from the narrative (though determined by it): Why, when Gibeon was the sacrificial site, does David offer sacrifices elsewhere?[68]

I am more interested in the complication of David being in fear of God. David is terrified to go to the shrine at Gibeon, even though the messenger had symbolically and figuratively removed the threat of any punishment by sheathing the sword (21.27). It is not God's command that determines the site; paradoxically, it is the fear of God—not reverential fear, but terror (נבעת). The logical assumption in the narrative is that if David were not frightened, then he would go to Gibeon and resume sacrifices there; hence, it is only his fear that keeps him at the

---

63. E.L. Curtis and A.A. Madsen, *A Critical and Exegetical Commentary on the the Books of Chronicles* (ICC; Edinburgh: T. & T. Clark, 1910), p. 254; Braun, *1 Chronicles*, p. 215; Williamson, *1 and 2 Chronicles*, p. 151.

64. Curtis and Madsen, *Chronicles*, p. 254. Japhet, *I & II Chronicles*, p. 388, includes 21.28, to say that 21.28-30 are either an interpolation or parenthetical aside.

65. See Williamson, *1 and 2 Chronicles*, p. 151; Braun, *1 Chronicles*, p. 213.

66. Japhet, *I & II Chronicles*, p. 390. Chronicles is silent about whether David ever again went to Gideon, but Solomon certainly went there (cf. 2 Chron. 1.3).

67. Japhet, *I & II Chronicles*, p. 390.

68. Japhet, *I & II Chronicles*, p. 389.

threshing floor and that determines the new temple site. (And note that David chooses the site, not Solomon. David may have been barred from the task of building it, but not only did he prepare for it, he decided where it would be.)

Another intertext is useful here, because this is, of course, not the first time that David is afraid of God in Chronicles. In the first abortive attempt to transfer the ark David is similarly afraid (וַיִּרָא; 1 Chron. 13.12). To stress the point, note that these uses are *not* fear in the sense of being 'in awe'. They describe fear in the sense of 'terror' rather than reverence.[69] God had killed Uzzah for touching the ark; literally, in the narrator's words, 'breaking out' against him (כִּי־פָרַץ יְהוָה פֶּרֶץ בְּעֻזָּא; 13.11). But as in questioning God's justice in 1 Chron. 21.17, David also breaks out—in short-lived anger—after Uzzah's death (וַיִּחַר; 13.11).[70] There is another disruption of hierarchy here, because David's anger is a reply to Yahweh's anger (also וַיִּחַר; 13.11). In the face of sublimity, humility is expected, yet David answers his God with an equal emotion. The fact of David's anger seems to suggest that David is questioning the ethic of God striking Uzzah for preserving the mobile home of God from an unceremonious tumble,[71] so that 'anger' connotes

69. 'Fear not' occurs a number of times in Chronicles: 1 Chron. 22.13; 28.20; 2 Chron. 20.15, 17; 32.18, but in the sense of 'don't be afraid' (a sign of encouragement). Apart from expressing reverence, 'fear' is, according to Soebagjo, 'also used to denote the character of the Holy'. M. Soebagjo, 'The "Fear" of Yahweh in the Old Testament' (PhD dissertation, University of Edinburgh, 1982), p. 115.

70. RSV and NIV translate וַיִּחַר as 'was angry', but NJPS renders it as 'was distressed', which lacks the force and tends to wreck the contrast between David being angry and David soon being afraid. Like NJPS, Japhet detects a different nuance to the verb ('to be annoyed, to grieve') and suggests that 'David understands God's reaction as a sign for himself and therefore calls off the whole enterprise'. She cites Gen. 4.5; 34.7; 45.5; Jon. 4.1, 9 to support this nuanced use, but RSV, for example, translates each of these occurrences as 'anger/angry' (Japhet, *I & II Chronicles*, p. 280). Elmslie paraphrases David's fear as the sign that David 'began to be really reverent', under the semantic influence of Prov. 9.10. He is happy to note that David was 'not unreasonably—indignant about the tragic fate of well-intentioned Uzza', but is unable to credit David with true fear of God. Elmslie, *The Books of Chronicles*, pp. 394-95.

71. It is not clear why Uzzah's act should be classed as a sin. Japhet suggests that 'the very touching of a sacred object is sacrilege' or, less reasonably, that it was up to God—not humans—to protect the ark, and so Uzzah demonstrated 'mistrust' and 'disbelief'. Japhet, *I & II Chronicles*, p. 280. Whatever the case, Uzzah is given no chance to repent of his actions.

a *human* response to an act of injustice. Selman says that David's anger and subsequent fear demonstrate 'at a vital moment his inability to maintain the high expectations associated with him'.[72] I gather from this that if David had maintained the 'high expectations', then his response would have been a placid acceptance that Uzzah's death was either necessary or appropriate. Instead, the narrative presents a king who is precisely not placid. He is *angry* that Uzzah died, and his anger, to my mind, is understood only through a perception of the act as unjust or unnecessary.[73]

David's anger is quickly followed by fear, and as in 1 Chronicles 21 his response is the same: he flees from God's presence. In 1 Chronicles 13 he sends the ark (effectively the presence of God) to the house of Obed-Edom, and in 1 Chronicles 21 he is unable to come before God's presence at Gibeon, or, for that matter, to bypass the presence of God reflected in the figure of the heavenly messenger. David's later view of God taking Uzzah's life is also revealing. In 1 Chronicles 15, when David is again making preparations to transfer the ark, he remarks that God had 'burst out against *us*' (15.13), a sign that his earlier fear was not, in his eyes, misplaced.

David's questioning of God is never resolved, and the census narrative ends where it began, with an implicit disharmony between David and his God. His attempt to establish the reason and ground for an injustice remains unanswered, and finally it is fear, rather than reverence, that closes this story. Josipovici writes, 'It is events which teach. Mere introspection cannot reveal to us who or what we are.'[74] If the character and the reader could meet, David's answer to this statement would undoubtedly prove fascinating.

---

72. Selman, *1 Chronicles*, pp. 153-54.

73. Selman turns the ark into a physical manifestation of God that has its own power, in which case the ark itself generated the נכה that killed Uzzah. He proposes that Chronicles attests this 'dynamic holiness' by the dubious reference to Uzzah dying 'before God' (13.10).

74. G. Josipovici, 'The Bible in Focus', *JSOT* 48 (1990), pp. 101-22 (116).

UTOPIAN POLITICS IN 2 CHRONICLES 10–13[*]

Roland T. Boer

Introduction

It might be argued that in some fashion or other most if not all interpretations of particular texts have the at least unconscious aims of dealing with, on the one hand, the more immediate problems posed by the text in question (and thus offering a more persuasive reading of that text than other existing readings) and, on the other hand, of making this very interpretation an argument in favor of the method(s) being employed. Such interpretations then engage debate in two areas: methodology and understanding the text under examination. This is also the case with the interpretation that follows, for here I wish to make a plea for the importance of some neglected methodological considerations in the study of Chronicles, and I would like to argue that such considerations provide some important insights for the interpretation of Chronicles itself.

In order to focus the discussion more sharply, I will deal with a representative text from Chronicles, namely 2 Chronicles 10–13, which will be approached first by way of a consideration or 'metacommentary' of the major lines of scholarship on these chapters, a proposal for another way of reading that attempts to redress a singular lack of socio-literary studies of Chronicles, while holding onto all that is best from previous studies, and then finally, the reading itself, which might be regarded as a sort of interpretive prototype.

Interpreting Chronicles

Chronicles, it seems, must suffer the fate of one who lives in the shadow of a more famous sibling, Samuel–Kings. Studies of 2 Chroni-

---

*   An earlier version of this article was published in chapter 3 of my book, *Jameson and Jeroboam* (Semeia; Atlanta: Scholars Press, 1996).

cles 10–13, apart from the commentaries,[1] are defined by five major characteristics: (1) comparison of Chr. with DtrH; (2) a tendency to deal with the whole of Chronicles rather than with the more restricted purview of the chapters under consideration; (3) a focus on questions of purpose, theme and theology; (4) a concern with historical reliability that takes the specific form here of the possible use of these chapters to illuminate reconstructions using archaeological data; and (5) a dearth of newer critical studies, particularly of the literary or feminist variety.

The desire to move into the area of purpose, theme and theology, as well as to compare Chronicles with Samuel–Kings, is signaled by a comparison between the three traditional historical-critical subdisciplines. Redaction criticism fares the best, while source criticism, apart from the study of 2 Chronicles 13 by Klein[2] and the commentaries by Curtis and Madsen[3] and Williamson,[4] forms a backdrop to other concerns. While it is impossible to know whether unnamed documents lie behind the material unique to Chronicles, and while the connections with Samuel–Kings and other biblical material are obvious, it is rather credulous to accept Chr.'s references to other sources at face value.[5] These references take on a somewhat different significance in my own study. Form criticism is—given the interest in structure and form and in the social location of the forms—much more akin to the approach taken below, but it is relatively poorly represented in studies of Chronicles

1.   E.g. E.L Curtis and A.A. Madsen, *A Critical and Exegetical Commentary on the Books of Chronicles* (ICC; Edinburgh: T. & T. Clark, 1910); S.J. De Vries, *1 and 2 Chronicles* (FOTL, 11; Grand Rapids: Eerdmans, 1989); R.B. Dillard, *2 Chronicles* (WBC, 15; Waco, TX: Word Books, 1987); A.S. Herbert, 'I and II Chronicles', in M. Black and H.H. Rowley (eds.), *Peake's Commentary on the Bible* (London: Thomas Nelson, 1962), pp. 357-69; S. Japhet, *I & II Chronicles: A Commentary* (OTL; Louisville, KY: Westminster/John Knox Press, 1993); W. Rudolph, *Chronikbücher* (HAT, 21; Tübingen: J.C.B. Mohr [Paul Siebeck], 1955); S. Talmon, '1 and 2 Chronicles', in R. Alter and F. Kermode (eds.), *The Literary Guide to the Bible* (Cambridge, MA: Belknap Press, 1987), pp. 365-72; H.G.M. Williamson, *1 and 2 Chronicles* (NCB; Grand Rapids: Eerdmans, 1982); see also J.M. Myers, *I Chronicles* (AB, 12; Garden City, NY: Doubleday, 1965); Myers, *II Chronicles* (AB, 13; Garden City, NY: Doubleday, 1965).

2.   R.W. Klein, 'Abijah's Campaign Against the North (II Chr 13): What Were the Chronicler's Sources?', *ZAW* 95 (1983), pp. 210-17.

3.   Curtis and Madsen, *Books of Chronicles*, pp. 17-26, 44-48.

4.   Williamson, *1 and 2 Chronicles*, pp. 17-23.

5.   E.g. 2 Chron. 12.15; 13.22; see the timely cautions of Williamson, *1 and 2 Chronicles*, pp. 17-19.

generally, let alone for the four chapters that are the focus of this study. In its search for pattern and structure, form criticism quite naturally leads to other sorts of investigations, such as those by Allen on kerygmatic units,[6] De Vries on the forms of prophetic speech,[7] Throntveit on the forms of royal speech and royal prayer,[8] and Mason on the addresses, with a good dose of homiletic interest.[9] As might be expected, De Vries's commentary in The Forms of the Old Testament Literature series deals with questions of form or genre in great detail (as well as structure, setting and intention), identifying chs. 10–13 as part of an 'account' that runs through 2 Chron. 36.23. This account is characterized by four major schemas—reward and retribution, revelation appearances, dynastic endangerment and festival (only the last is not found in our passage)[10]—which in turn are made up of myriad molecular genres.[11] While these concerns are comparable to a limited extent to what is attempted below, my own analysis will suggest that such features (particularly a schema such as dynastic endangerment) point to deeper structural and ideological features.

Most historical critical research has been of the redactional variety, especially when under this expansive umbrella the relationship with Samuel–Kings and the theme, purpose and ideas that controlled the redaction process are included (theology does, however, claim a degree of autonomy, which will be respected on this occasion). In this study I am not so interested in the distinct ways in which Chronicles deals with the material, mostly from Samuel–Kings but also from elsewhere in the Hebrew Bible.[12] Too quickly, however, do the studies of 2 Chronicles

6. L.C. Allen, 'Kerygmatic Units in 1 & 2 Chronicles', *JSOT* 41 (1988), pp. 21-36.

7. S.J. De Vries, 'The Forms of Prophetic Address in Chronicles', *HAR* 10 (1986), pp. 15-36.

8. M.A. Throntveit, *When Kings Speak: Royal Speech and Royal Prayer in Chronicles* (SBLDS, 93; Atlanta: Scholars Press, 1987).

9. R. Mason, *Preaching the Tradition: Homily and Hermeneutics after the Exile* (Cambridge: Cambridge University Press, 1990).

10. De Vries, *1 and 2 Chronicles*, pp. 274-75.

11. For chs. 10–13, see De Vries, *1 and 2 Chronicles*, pp. 280, 284, 286, 289, 293-94.

12. On Abijah in 2 Chron. 13, see Klein, 'Abijah's Campaign'; D.G. Deboys, 'History and Theology in the Chronicler's Portrayal of Abijah', *Bib* 71 (1990), pp. 49-50; P.R. Ackroyd, *The Chronicler in his Age* (JSOTSup, 101; Sheffield: JSOT Press, 1991), pp. 311-43; T. Sugimoto, 'Chronicles as Independent Literature',

10–13 trickle away to be superseded by more general studies, whose significance for my work is less direct. Thus, the different portrayal of prophets in Kings and Chronicles is relevant,[13] but the whole question of the relationship between Chronicles and Ezra–Nehemiah is not.[14]

Apart from the relation between Kings and Chronicles, there is a second emphasis of redaction criticism that I am tempted to characterize as loosely ideological: those studies that resort to matters of intent, thought and theology in accounting for Chronicles' distinct perspective on Israelite history. This emphasis in fact breaks out of the redaction-critical mold to take its place in the related but independent area of theology. The most suggestive for my work are those that identify the major ideological or theological factors determining the composition of the 'parallel historiography' of Chronicles as the picture of the ideal or Utopian Israel under the direct rule of God in its own distinct and carefully delineated land.[15] Studies concerning prophecy to an 'ideal Israel',[16] eschatology, messianism and theocracy in Chronicles have a

JSOT 55 (1992), pp. 61-74. Text-critical studies are essentially comparative, making use of as much evidence as possible, particularly with textual cruxes such as 2 Chron. 9.31–10.3, where 1 Kgs 11.43–12.3 is brought in along with 3 Kdms 11.43–12.3, 24–25. See S.L. McKenzie, 'The Source for Jeroboam's Role at Shechem (1 Kgs 11.43–12.3, 12, 20)', *JBL* 106 (1987), pp. 297-300; T.M. Willis, 'The Text of 1 Kings 11.43–12.3', *CBQ* 53 (1991), pp. 37-44. The Chronicles material is, however, normally used as evidence in the discussion of the text in Kings; there are no major difficulties in the Chronicles text as such.

13. See C.T. Begg, 'The Classical Prophets in the Chronistic History', *BZ* 32 (1988), pp. 100-107; De Vries, 'Forms of Prophetic Address'; De Vries, *1 and 2 Chronicles*.

14. The older tendency to see Ezra and Nehemiah as part of the 'Chronicler's History' has been challenged over the last couple of decades. See, e.g., S. Japhet, 'The Supposed Common Authorship of Chronicles and Ezra–Nehemiah Investigated Anew', *VT* 18 (1968), pp. 330-37; D. Talshir, 'A Reinvestigation of the Linguistic Relationship between Chronicles and Ezra–Nehemiah', *VT* 38 (1988), pp. 165-93; H.G.M. Williamson, *Israel in the Books of Chronicles* (Cambridge: Cambridge University Press, 1977); and the survey in Mason, *Preaching the Tradition*, p. 9.

15. See especially Williamson, *Israel in the Books of Chronicles*; Williamson, *1 and 2 Chronicles*, pp. 24-26; S. Japhet, 'Conquest and Settlement in Chronicles', *JBL* 98 (1979), pp. 205-18; T.C. Eskenazi, 'The Chronicles and the Composition of I Esdras', *CBQ* 48 (1986), pp. 39-61; K.W. Whitelam, 'Israel's Traditions of Origin: Reclaiming the Land', *JSOT* 44 (1989), pp. 19-42.

16. De Vries, 'Forms of Prophetic Address', pp. 35-36.

bearing on this theological construct.[17] Part of this total picture is the problem of Chr.'s attitude toward the North. Some have argued for a reassessment of the long-standing consensus that Chronicles is essentially an anti-northern polemic,[18] though Knoppers asserts the older position. Knoppers locates a familiar problem, namely divine activity or sovereignty and human responsibility, or 'immediate divine retribution', that will be of interest in my reading of 2 Chronicles 10–13.[19] One factor contributing to the reassessment, particularly the pattern of mitigated punishment, will be that of 'immediate divine retribution'.[20] Various issues from these more theological studies will thus find their way into my own analysis.

Related to the theological approaches mentioned above are those investigations into the homiletic dimensions of Chronicles. Triggered by von Rad's idea of the 'levitical sermon',[21] both Allen[22] and Mason[23] have developed this line of interpretation further.

The continual insistence on dealing with Chronicles as a whole is best exemplified by the nonetheless important social-scientific studies of Weinberg, who in a series of articles has undertaken a statistical analysis of word frequency and usage in order to map the various com-

17. R.L. Braun, 'Chronicles, Ezra and Nehemiah: Theology and Literary History', in J.A. Emerton (ed.), *Studies in the Historical Books of the Old Testament* (VTSup, 30; Leiden: E.J. Brill, 1979), pp. 52-64; although see S.J. De Vries, 'Moses and David as Cult Founders', *JBL* 107 (1988), pp. 636-38 on the messianic problem in Chronicles.

18. R.L. Braun, 'A Reconsideration of the Chronicler's Attitude Toward the North', *JBL* 96 (1977), pp. 59-62 (see the references there to A. Noordtzij, R.J. Coggins and J.D. Newsome); Brown, 'Chronicles, Ezra and Nehemiah', pp. 56-57; Williamson, *Israel in the Books of Chronicles*; Williamson, *1 and 2 Chronicles*; Japhet, 'Conquest and Settlement'.

19. G.N. Knoppers, 'Rehoboam in Chronicles: Villain or Victim?', *JBL* 109 (1990), pp. 423-40.

20. See J. Wellhausen, *Prolegomena to the History of Israel* (Edinburgh: A. & C. Black, 1885; repr.; Gloucester, MA: Peter Smith, 1973), pp. 203-10; Braun, 'Chronicles, Ezra and Nehemiah', pp. 53-55; Deboys, 'History and Theology'; Dillard, *2 Chronicles*, pp. 76-81; Williamson, *Israel in the Books of Chronicles*, pp. 67-68; Williamson, *1 and 2 Chronicles*, pp. 31-33.

21. G. von Rad, *The Problem of the Hexateuch and Other Essays* (Edinburgh: Oliver & Boyd, 1966), pp. 267-80.

22. Allen, 'Kerygmatic Units', pp. 21-36.

23. Mason, *Preaching the Tradition*.

ponents of *das Weltbild des Chronisten*:[24] nature,[25] the total human person,[26] the human body,[27] the human psyche,[28] the designations 'we' and 'they',[29] war and peace,[30] social groups,[31] kingship and kingdom,[32] God[33] and king.[34] The significance of this series[35] is that the concern is with the wider ideological framework of Chronicles, a more comprehensive picture of the world out of which Chronicles arose. Such an interest is congruent with the approach used in my own study, although the modes by which the two approaches work are distinct.

Historical reliability remains an important issue in Chronicles research, particularly in regard to the detail of specific events—so often the temptation and direction of historical critical efforts. Tying the text so securely to the particular events that are immediately accessible to the people of the time, but that are so easily lost to those coming afterward, seems to me ultimately futile. Among recent works, Deboys has been particularly guilty of this, arguing for the presentation of an alternative theological position in the portrayal of Abijah in 2 Chronicles 13

24. A collection of J.P. Weinberg's essays in this connection has been translated by D.L. Smith-Christopher: *The Citizen-temple Community* (JSOTSup, 151; Sheffield: JSOT Press, 1992).

25. J.P. Weinberg, 'Die Natur im Weltbild des Chronisten', *VT* 31 (1981), pp. 324-45.

26. J.P. Weinberg, 'Der Mensch im Weltbild des Chronisten: Die allgemeinen Begriffe', *Klio* 63 (1981), pp. 25-37.

27. J.P. Weinberg, 'Der Mensch im Weltbild des Chronisten: Sein Körper', *OLP* 13 (1982), pp. 71-89.

28. J.P. Weinberg, 'Der Mensch im Weltbild des Chronisten: Seine Psyche', *VT* 33 (1983), pp. 298-316.

29. J.P. Weinberg, '"Wir" und "Sie" im Weltbild des Chronisten', *Klio* 66 (1984), pp. 19-34.

30. J.P. Weinberg, 'Krieg und Frieden im Weltbild des Chronisten', *OLP* 16 (1985), pp. 111-29.

31. J.P. Weinberg, 'Die soziale Gruppe im Weltbild des Chronisten', *ZAW* 98 (1986), pp. 72-95.

32. J.P. Weinberg, 'Das Königtum und das Königreich im Weltbild des Chronisten', *Klio* 69 (1987), pp. 28-45.

33. J.P. Weinberg, 'Gott im Weltbild des Chronisten: Die vom Chronisten verschwiegenen Gottesnamen', *ZAW* 100 (Suppl, 1988), pp. 170-89.

34. J.P. Weinberg, 'Der König im Weltbild des Chronisten', *VT* 39 (1989), pp. 415-37.

35. See Weinberg's works listed above. In addition, see 'Das Eigengut in den Chronikbüchern', *OLP* 10 (1979), pp. 161-81.

on the basis of alternative but reliable information and traditions.[36] A
comprehensive survey of the more abstract issue of historical reliability
is provided by Japhet.[37] It must be reiterated that invariably such studies
and debates seek to ascertain the degree of the reliability of the *content*
of the text, in contrast to the very different search I conduct on the basis
of form.

A more interesting aspect of the debate over historical reliability has
concerned the disciplines of archaeology and geography: this comes for
the researcher as something of a pleasant surprise, for these studies
reinforce the sense of the importance of space and its organization in
these chapters of Chronicles. Scholarly efforts thus far have focused on
two problems: the identification of the cities in 11.5-10 and the prove-
nance of the list.[38] In addition, some interest has also been shown in the
cities mentioned in 13.4, 19, with the debate there being over the
historical accuracy of the references to the capture of these cities by
Abijah.[39] While the interest is spatial, the specific identification and

36. Deboys, 'History and Theology'.

37. S. Japhet, 'The Historical Reliability of Chronicles', *JSOT* 33 (1985), pp.
83-107; Deboys, 'History and Theology', pp. 48-49; M.P. Graham, *The Utilization
of 1 and 2 Chronicles in the Reconstruction of Israelite History in the Nineteenth
Century* (SBLDS, 116; Atlanta: Scholars Press, 1990); P. Welten, *Geschichte und
Geschichtsdarstellung in den Chronikbüchern* (WMANT, 42; Neukirchen–Vluyn:
Neukirchener Verlag, 1973).

38. See V. Fritz, 'The "List of Rehoboam's Fortresses" in 2 Chr 11.5-12—A
Document from the Time of Josiah', in B. Mazar (ed.), *Y. Aharoni Memorial
Volume* (ErIsr, 15; Jerusalem: Israel Exploration Society, 1981), pp. 46*-53*; and
Rudolph, *Chronikbücher*, p. 230, who both argue for Josiah's time; and the debate
between N. Na'aman ('Hezekiah's Fortified Cities and the *LMLK* Stamps', *BASOR*
261 [1986], pp. 5-21; 'The Date of 2 Chronicles 11.5-10—A Reply to Y.
Garfinkel', *BASOR* 271 [1988], pp. 74-77) and Y. Garfinkel ('2 Chr 11.5-10
Fortified Cities List and the *lmlk* Stamps—Reply to Nadav Na'aman', *BASOR* 271
[1988], pp. 69-73), who date respectively at Hezekiah's time and the time to which
the list refers; also Z. Kallai, *Historical Geography of the Bible: The Tribal Territories of Israel* (Jerusalem: Magnes Press; Leiden: E.J. Brill, 1986), pp. 79-83;
M. Noth (*The Chronicler's History* [JSOTSup, 50; Sheffield: JSOT Press, 1987],
p. 58) refuses to date this older source.

39. See Y. Aharoni, *The Land of the Bible: A Historical Geography* (Philadelphia: Westminster Press, 2nd edn, 1979), pp. 350-51; W.F. Albright, *Excavations
and Results at Tell el-Ful (Gibeah of Saul)* (AASOR, 4; New Haven: Yale University Press, 1924); Klein, 'Abijah's Campaign', pp. 212-14; Welten, *Geschichte
und Geschichtsdarstellung*, pp. 11-15, 116-29.

location of place names is not as important for my study as the whole use of space itself in the text under consideration.

It is when we move away from historical-critical approaches that the supply of studies dries up almost completely: apart from the very occasional item, so-called literary studies of the more conventional sort of New Criticism or, as it is better known in biblical studies, rhetorical criticism—let alone anything that owes its methodological allegiance to structuralism or deconstruction or cultural studies—are noticeable for their virtual absence,[40] particularly with 2 Chronicles 10–13. Feminists, too, seem to find this territory less promising, given its energetic and uncompromising patriarchal nature and the absence of any immediate breaks or disruptions in such an ideological framework.[41] It is, however, precisely such a terrain in which I dare to tread, namely making use of newer critical approaches in the study of Chronicles. Yet I am not prepared, as some critics in the first flush of the newer literary approaches were wont to do, to regard all that has gone before as so much garbage to be consigned to the recycling bin. On the contrary, there are many points at which the studies noted above contribute to and intersect with my own reading: the significance of references to other 'sources'; the nature of form-critical study and the forms of literature; the redactional focus on the ways by which a picture different from Kings is presented and the theological or ideological factors that affect those alterations; the social-science concern with the total perspective; and the archaeological-geographical question of the organization of space. Each of these points resonates with certain aspects of the study to follow, although the direction taken is quite different from those covered above.

Following the suggestions of Fredric Jameson,[42] George Lukács[43]

---

40. But see the use of Aristotelian rhetorical principles in R.K. Duke, *The Persuasive Appeal of the Chronicler: A Rhetorical Analysis* (JSOTSup, 88; Bible and Literature Series, 25; Sheffield: Almond Press, 1990).

41. See, e.g., A.L. Laffley, '1 and 2 Chronicles', in C.A. Newsom and S.H. Ringe (eds.), *The Women's Bible Commentary* (Louisville, KY: Westminster/John Knox Press, 1992), pp. 110-15; M.-T. Wacker, 'Die Bücher der Chronik: Im Vorhof der Frauen', in L. Schottroff and M.-T. Wacker (eds.), *Kompendium feministische Bibelauslegung* (Gütersloh: Chr. Kaiser Verlag, 1998), pp. 146-55.

42. See works cited below (n. 45, 57, 60, 65, 85, 90).

43. G. Lukács, *History and Class Consciousness: Studies in Marxist Dialectics* (Cambridge, MA: MIT Press, 1971); Lukács, *The Historical Novel* (Lincoln: University of Nebraska Press, 1983).

and David Jobling,[44] I propose a mode of reading that adheres to its own terms but is at the same time sensitive to the contours of the text in question. In one sense 'method' emerges from the object or text itself, into which—as the latter is gradually unwrapped or unpacked—it should abolish itself again, with a few concluding remarks to justify its brief existence. As Jameson writes:

> [s]uch a squaring of the interpretive or hermeneutic circle (sometimes called dialectical criticism) will however necessarily be different on the occasion of every text, so that it is impossible to provide a model of the operation as can be done for 'methods' in general (this is not, in other words, a method).[45]

Generally, the approach followed below may be characterized as an investigation into the way in which formal, structural and linguistic features of narrative function as responses to physical, social and economic situations. Rather than attempting to 'solve' the problems of a text or to disambiguate or explain a text by banishing problems and difficulties to the realm of incompetence or corruption, this approach identifies the formal contradictions or anomalies of cultural products as indicators of deeper oppositions and contradictions that must be illuminated.

The only general feature of my analysis concerns the relationship between text and context: perhaps the best way to describe this relationship is in terms of a historical and social situation to which the text forms an active response. In other words, the text forms an answer to a particular question posed by the context of the text. Thus, for example, the situation of the Babylonian exile elicits a variety of responses ranging from Deutero-Isaiah to Lamentations. The outcome of this approach is that texts (and cultural products in general) are no longer regarded as passive reflectors of social conditions, as sources of easy and direct information, but rather they become 'active interventions' in problem-

---

44. D. Jobling, 'Writing the Wrongs of the World: The Deconstruction of the Biblical Text in the Context of Liberation Theologies', *Semeia* 51 (1990), pp. 81-118; Jobling, 'Feminism and "Mode of Production" in Ancient Israel: Search for a Method', in D. Jobling, P.L. Day and G.T. Sheppard (eds.), *The Bible and the Politics of Exegesis: Essays in Honor of Norman K. Gottwald on his Sixty-Fifth Birthday* (Cleveland, OH: Pilgrim Press, 1991), pp. 239-51; and other works by Jobling cited below (nn. 85, 87).

45. F.R. Jameson, *Signatures of the Visible* (New York: Routledge, 1990), p. 127.

atic social situations; texts play particular social and political roles in their contexts. In what follows, narrative form, ideology (particularly in terms of Utopian thought and libidinal investment), class and mode of production comprise the mental framework within which this text from Chronicles is reconstructed.

Textual Forms and Narrative Structure

I begin with the whole question of narrative structure or form, which limits itself to the boundaries of the text. This is unapologetically formalist, particularly in the tradition of Russian formalism and then French structuralism. The forms and structures of the text come under close scrutiny, since it is the form of the text, and not its content, that provides crucial hints and indications of the social and historical ground of the text. My search in particular is for the contradictory features of the text's form, which normally means that more than one structure or formal device in the text will be isolated, often as a dominant structure and then one or more subordinate structures in conflict with each other.

The narrator of Chronicles (for convenience: Chr.) organizes his raw material in four ways: (1) quotation or material parallel to 1 Kings; (2) recasting of sections from 1 Kings; (3) material unique to 2 Chronicles; and (4) a narrative type that I will designate as report. 'Quotation' refers to the almost verbatim copying, with some minor (and occasionally significant) shuffles and modifications, of a reasonable segment (i.e. more than a couple of verses) of the deuteronomistic text. Here 2 Chron. 10.1–11.4 reproduces without direct acknowledgment the text of 1 Kgs 12.1-19, 21-24. As a whole, this section of 2 Chronicles (10.1–11.4) follows the Kings text quite closely, yet the alterations made serve to marginalize Jeroboam and allow no room for the legitimation of anything outside Jerusalem and the Davidic line.

If we move along the spectrum from material close to Kings to what is more distant, the next mode of dealing with the raw material from Kings may be designated as recasting, whereby the text from Kings is reshaped, rearranged, expanded and condensed. There is a range of operations that come under the umbrella of recasting: those that are closer to quotation, quoting sections and expanding the account (2 Chron. 12.1-12); those that produce a complex rereading with more comprehensive alterations but also with snatches taken straight from the Kings text (the regnal formulae in 2 Chron. 9.29-31; 12.13–13.2; 13.22-

23); and those that thoroughly recast the Kings material without any quotation (2 Chron. 12.14-15; 13.5-9). This range works its way across from the vicinity of quotation to the borders of material unique to Chronicles.[46]

Relatively little comment is required for this unique material. It occurs in 2 Chron. 11.5-13, 16-23 (the account or report of the consolidation of the kingdom by Rehoboam) and 13.3-4, 10-21 (the battle between Ahijah and Jeroboam). This material provides the most direct and continuous evidence of the ideological content that controls the narrative in Chronicles. It will, therefore, be of great interest in the ideological discussion to follow. In both sections some heavy recasting is identified (11.14-15; 13.5-9), which indicates that at this end of the recasting scale it very easily slides into unique narrative.

Such intermeshing and overlay is characteristic of a narrative feature noted above—report—which is Chronicles' own contribution to narrative types (see pp. 372-79 below). It may be set in relief by a contrast between the two sections of unique material: 2 Chron. 13.3-21 has the nature of a full and even embellished narrative, while 11.5-23 is pared down until it resembles more a report or collection of reports than a full story. This latter text is a curious half-commentary, half-narrative that might best be designated as a collection of 'reports': summarizing statements of the features of Rehoboam's reign, somewhat reminiscent of the genealogical lists, interspersed with various comments and asides in 1 Chronicles 1–11. Indeed, 2 Chron. 11.5-10 contains a list of fortified towns, while 2 Chron. 11.18-23 is an expanded genealogical section.[47] In chs. 10–13 the report would seem to be characteristic of

46. It would be possible to describe the different ways in which Chronicles deals with the Kings text in terms of V.N. Vološinov's distinction (*Marxism and the Philsophy of Language* [Studies in Language; New York: Seminar Press, 1973], p. 5) within reported speech between citation (repetition), paraphrase (transformation), and an interaction of repetition and transformation. Thus, quotation becomes recitation, extreme recasting becomes paraphrase, and the lighter forms of recasting that include sections of the original text become the interaction of recitation and paraphrase. On Chr.'s literary techniques for recasting DtrH, see most recently I. Kalimi, *Zur Geschichtsschreibung des Chronisten: Literarisch-historiographische Abweichungen der Chronik von ihren Paralleltexten in den Samuel- und Königsbüchern* (BZAW, 226; Berlin: W. de Gruyter, 1995).

47. See B.O. Long, *I Kings, with an Introduction to Old Testament Historical Literature* (FOTL, 9; Grand Rapids: Eerdmans, 1984), pp. 4-8, on list, report, historical story and history.

material unique to Chronicles, although it by no means covers the nature of all that material.[48] Quotation, recasting and unique material, therefore, constitute the modes by which 2 Chronicles 10–13 deals with the text from Kings and constructs its narrative.

In the light of these organizing features, the structure of the narrative takes the following shape:

9.29-31	Formulaic close: Solomon to Rehoboam (recast)
10.1-19	Breakup of the kingdom at Shechem (quoted)
11.1-4	Shemaiah's intervention (quoted)
11.5-23	Rehoboam consolidates (unique, recast; report)
12.1-12	External threat to kingdom by Shishak (recast)
12.13-16	Formulaic close: Rehoboam to Abijah (recast)
13.1-2	Formulaic introduction to Abijah (recast)
13.3-21	Internal threat to kingdom by Jeroboam (unique, recast)
13.22-23	Formulaic close: Abijah to Asa (recast)

It is a tight narrative structure marked by several features. First, the narrative is encased and punctuated by the regnal formulae that pertain only to Davidic kings.[49] Secondly, within the first and last formulae are two major sections concerning Jeroboam: in the first (10.1–11.4) he wins a large part of the kingdom away from Rehoboam; in the last (13.3-21) Ahijah regains it all. Thirdly—and related to the preceding point—is the minimal formal tension in 2 Chronicles 10–13. The point at which the most tension might be expected is between the account of the division in 10.1–11.4 and its reinterpretation in 13.5-9. However, Chronicles diffuses any potential tension by placing the reinterpretation in the mouth of Abijah. Fourthly, the marginalization of Jeroboam in the content—reassignment as an internal threat, exclusion from regnal

---

48. In the light of what I will discuss a little later regarding Utopian narrative, I will tentatively suggest here that the report is a peculiar narrative feature that exhibits the warping force of a symptomatic tension between the narrative or story with its structural requirement for some form of historical progression and the verbal geographical description that inevitably leads to the construction of a mental map of an ideal and timeless world.

49. Whereas the closing formulae in 1–2 Kings are used for kings of both Israel and Judah, in Chronicles the closing formulae, indeed all the regnal formulae, are restricted to the kings of Judah. The significance of this would seem to lie in the contraction of formulaic legitimacy to the southern kingdom: it contains, as far as the structure of the Chronicles text is concerned, the only monarchy by definition. This status is indicated by the narrative trappings of monarchy—the regnal formulae.

formulae, no coronation—takes place at the formal level as well:
Jeroboam is not the center of the account (as he is in Kings and Kdms)
but he finds himself on the outer limits of the narrative.

Utopian Politics

What is most interesting for my purposes is the way 11.5-23 yields the
initial ideological construct of 2 Chronicles 10–13 with relative ease.
2 Chronicles 11.5-23 deals with the consolidation of the kingdom after
its breakup in the previous part (10.1–11.4). These verses, whose form
is that of a report, delineate the three major themes of the whole
account.

The first of these themes deals with the organization of the state for
warfare: 11.5-12 outlines the building, provisioning (food, oil and wine)
and arming (large shields and lances) of a string of fortifications that
covers a relatively small stretch of countryside. These verses have generated a good deal of interest for their archaeological and geographical
value. Although the origin of the list remains debatable, there is no
doubt that the list refers to genuine towns and their fortifications. The
historical accuracy of the list is not crucial for this study; rather I am
interested in the spatial features of the text. Before proceeding, however, a look at a map[50] may prove helpful.

There is wide agreement[51] about the location of the towns mentioned
in 11.5-12.[52] A number of significant points arise from the map. As
Aharoni makes clear, the strength and strategic placement of the
fortifications are impressive:

> Hebron, Beth-zur and Bethlehem are on the main highway down the
> ridge of the Judean hills. Etam, Tekoa and Ziph protected the approaches
> from the wilderness of Judah. Adoraim, Adullam and Socoh guarded the
> various routes to the Shephelah and Philistia. A continuous line of forts
> was built along the western boundary with Philistia: Lachish, Mareshah
> and Gath in the south; Azekah, Zorah and Aijalon in the north.[53]

50. Aharoni, *Land of the Bible*, p. 331.
51. Aharoni, *Land of the Bible*, p. 330; Fritz, 'List of Rehoboam's Fortresses',
p. *47; Kallai, *Historical Geography*, map no. 2; H.G. May; Revd. J. Day, *Oxford
Bible Atlas* (New York: Oxford University Press, 3rd edn, 1984), p. 69; J.M. Miller
and J.H. Hayes, *A History of Ancient Israel and Judah* (Philadelphia: Westminster
Press, 1986), p. 239; Na'aman, 'Hezekiah's Fortified Cities', p. 5.

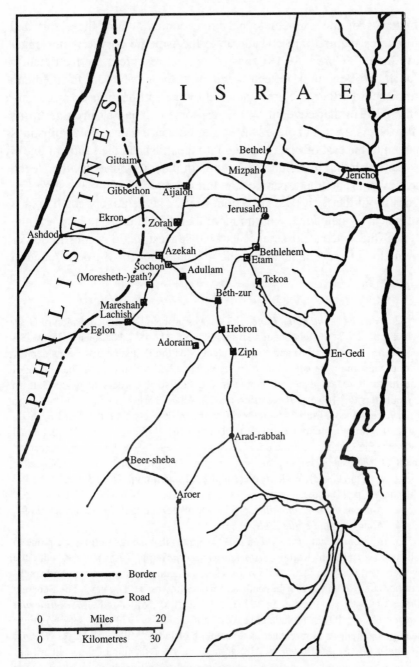

Rehoboam's Fortresses

(Reproduced from *The Land of the Bible* by Y. Aharoni. 1962, 1967. Used by permission of Westminster John Knox Press and Burns & Oates).

In terms of the immediate narrative context, then, the effort and resources required are considerable: the Israelite corvée is no longer available (2 Chron. 10.18) and so physical resources are restricted to Judah and Benjamin. Fifteen towns from these tribes are fortified and furbished. Further, the area enclosed by the fortifications is more constricted than that covered by the territory of Judah at any time in its history. As Aharoni notes,[54] the western defense line against Philistia is pulled to the east off the plain and into the hills, and the southern line is so far north that it excludes the southern plain (Shephelah), the Negeb and even the southern parts of the hill country.[55] Even the eastern line goes no further east than Jerusalem itself. This relatively small area is thus heavily defended, with no more than five kilometers between any two of the sixteen fortresses.[56] I would suggest that this constriction or reduction of space is related to the inflated numbers of troops found in

52. Aharoni (*Land of the Bible*, p. 330) sees problems with the location of Gath, which Fritz ('List of Rehoboam's Fortresses', pp. *47-48*), Na'aman ('Hezekiah's Fortified Cities', pp. 5-6) and May all identify as the Philistine town considerably further west in the coastal plain than the defence line which is at the beginning of the foothills (May places an indent in the Philistine borders to place Gath in Israelite territory [*Oxford Bible Atlas*, p. 69]). Aharoni argues that Gath would seem to have remained a Philistine city and that the most likely candidate is Moreshethgath (the prominent mound of Tell el-Judeideh). Although there is no textual evidence, he suggests that the original list in 11.8 read 'Moresheth-gath, Mareshah' and that 'Moresheth' fell out due to its proximity to 'Mareshah'. Kallai (*Historical Geography*, pp. 82-83), Williamson (*1 and 2 Chronicles*, pp. 242-43) and Dillard (*2 Chronicles*, p. 97) agree.

53. Aharoni, *Land of the Bible*, p. 330; see also Dillard, *2 Chronicles*, pp. 96-97.

54. Aharoni, *Land of the Bible*, p. 330.

55. Aharoni (*Land of the Bible*, p. 330) argues that the restrictions were due to Shishak's campaign. Kallai (*Historical Geography*, pp. 79-82) agrees with the western and northern restrictions but sees no difficulty with the eastern and southern borders extending well beyond the fortified towns. H. Donner ('The Separate States of Israel and Judah', in J.H. Hayes and J.M. Miller [eds.], *Israelite and Judean History* [OTL; Philadelphia: Westminster Press, 1979], pp. 388-99) thinks that the size reflects the weakness and isolation of Judah. Miller and Hayes (*History of Ancient Israel and Judah*, p. 238) argue for a strengthening of the southern hill country to avoid rebellion there without any intention to secure the borders. For Rudolph (*Chronikbücher*, p. 229) the cities comprise a second defence line, at least to the south.

56. So Donner, 'Separate States', p. 388.

Chronicles.[57] Thus, in 2 Chron. 13.3 a total of 1,200,000 soldiers line up for battle on both sides; they are then addressed by Abijah who stands on Mt Zemaraim (13.4). Unless blessed with extraordinary voice projection, no human being is able to address this number of people and no human crowd of such a size is able to listen in this way and understand what is said. Both cases, then,—small defended territory and large numbers addressed as though much smaller—illustrate the spatial or world reduction in operation in these chapters.

World reduction is a feature of Utopian writing of a more recent stamp, itself illustrating what I will later identify as disjunction. Here the most instructive example is that of Ursula Le Guin in *The Left Hand of Darkness*,[58] but especially in *The Dispossessed*,[59] whose work in these volumes:

> is based on a principle of systematic exclusion, a kind of surgical excision of empirical reality, something like a process of ontological attenuation in which the sheer teeming multiplicity of what exists, of what we call reality, is deliberately thinned and weeded out through an operation of radical abstraction and simplification that we will henceforth term *world-reduction*.[60]

In the novels under discussion, this affects sex, war, climate, biological diversity and food—in short, Utopia and scarcity are inseparable. The reasons for such reduction differ: for Le Guin world reduction or scarcity has its Utopian import in situations where overabundance and oversupply form the dominant ideological construction of what is ideal; in the case of Le Guin it is, of course, the consumer society of late capitalism.[61] For this text from Chronicles I will later suggest that the pressures of the notion of the *polis* play a crucial role in the context of the imperial ancient world.

To return to our text: finally, the fortifications form a rough U-shape or horseshoe, with variations allowable for landform and road systems.

---

57. On spatial reduction in science fiction, see F.R. Jameson, 'Science Fiction as a Spatial Genre: Generic Discontinuities and the Problem of Figuration in Vonda McIntyre's *The Exile Waiting*', *Science Fiction Studies* 14 (1987), pp. 48, 54.

58. U. Le Guin, *The Left Hand of Darkness* (New York: Walker, 1971).

59. U. Le Guin, *The Dispossessed: An Ambiguous Utopia* (New York: Harper & Row, 1974).

60. F.R. Jameson, 'World Reduction in Le Guin: The Emergence of Utopian Narrative', *Science Fiction Studies* 2 (1975), p. 223.

61. Jameson, 'World Reduction', p. 228.

In contrast to the heavily fortified western flank the northern stretch remains unfortified and unguarded, although this is remedied to some extent by the capture of Bethel, Jeshanah and Ephron in 13.19.[62] The significance of such a wide hole in an otherwise tight defensive system (Aharoni suggests plans of northern expansion)[63] is reinforced by Williamson's study[64] on the usage of the term 'Israel' in 2 Chronicles 10–13, as part of the more general usage of the term in Chronicles as a whole. Noting the slight changes in Chronicles (2 Chron. 10.16, 17, 18, 19; 11.1, 3, 13; 12.1, 6) over against the parallel passages in Kings, he concludes that 'Israel' is applied equally to both North and South. If spatial (the unguarded northern border of Judah) and terminological (the use of 'Israel') concerns are combined, then the conclusion suggests itself that the fortifications remain incomplete without the incorporation of the North into the ideological and spatial framework of the text.

This hole leads in to the second theme of 2 Chron. 11.5-23: the cultic and religious reinforcement of the enclave, which supports the conclusion of the previous sentence. 2 Chronicles 11.13-17 recounts the influx from the North of the priests and levites, purportedly not allowed to discharge their duties there. Religious orthodoxy and orthopraxis are more important than the traditional levitical pasture grounds and property rights (מגרשיהם ואחזתם; 11.14), which are surrendered by the priests and levites as they move south. These religious functionaries provide—through correct cultic practice—the religious legitimacy to Rehoboam in Judah. The priests even bring the faithful from Israel with them: for these people, the stated criterion is that they dedicate themselves to seek the Lord (הנתנים את-לבבם לבקש את-יהוה אלהי ישראל; 11.16). Thus, cultic correctness and spiritual zeal succumb to the centripetal force of Jerusalem and its now sacred territory. Although the subject of the verbs in 11.17 is unspecified, the position in the conclusion to this section of ויהזקו and ויאמצו makes it likely that they designate the strengthening

---

62. In order to fill in the gaps, particularly to the north, Kallai (*Historical Geography*, pp. 80-81) and Miller and Hayes (*History of Ancient Israel and Judah*, pp. 238-39) add the levitical cities (Josh. 21 and 1 Chron. 6), which they assume to have been established during the united monarchy of David and Solomon. Aharoni (*Land of the Bible*, p. 332) uses the levitical cities to extend the southern line.

63. Aharoni, *Land of the Bible*, p. 330.

64. Williamson, *Israel in the Books of Chronicles*, pp. 107-10; also Eskenazi, 'Chronicles and the Composition of I Esdras', pp. 42-45.

and securing force of all those mentioned in 11.13-16—priests, levites and the people who follow from the tribes of Israel. These people are even credited (through a plural הלכו ['they went'], which the LXX makes singular, in 11.17) with following in the way of David and Solomon, a role normally preserved for the king. Religious sanction is thus given to the state's preparation for war. The hint of something amiss comes with the limitation of three years (11.17) on Judah's security and strength (it would seem that לשנים שלוש refers back to both verbs and not merely to its immediate predecessor), but we will return to this later.

It is with the third theme—procreational prowess—that 'libidinal investment' makes its initial and quite obvious appearance. Libidinal investment and its related phrase, 'libidinal apparatus', are derived from psychoanalytic theory. The latter notion is a conjunction of structural and formal concerns with Freudian psychology: a libidinal apparatus is the way in which sexual (and thus political) energy or content is organized and structured in a literary or cultural product. This arrangement applies both to the originator of a text and to its reader. The structures of texts, therefore, become 'registering machines'[65] for the peculiar interests and obsessions of both author and reader, or 'pleasure grids' (my terminology) upon which those obsessions may be arranged. In comparison with libidinal apparatus, libidinal investment is the process of registering or loading the particular sexual and political energies onto that apparatus or structure. It would seem that the technical terminology is a more sophisticated way of determining why some texts are pleasurable and others are not.

Thus, in 2 Chron. 11.18-23 the sexual and procreational activities of Rehoboam are compressed: the first two wives, Mahalath and Ma'acah (who have acceptable royal pedigrees), are mentioned, as are some of the offspring (three from the first wife [11.19] and four from the second [11.20]). This restriction and control of the women, crucial for patriliny, subsequently enables the identification of the successor, Abijah, who is the first son of Rehoboam's favored second wife (11.21-22). Careful identification of the successor is important for the purity of the Davidic line, but this takes place in the context of more extensive procreational activity. Although not on the scale of Solomon's libido in 1 Kings 11

65. F.R. Jameson, 'Rimbaud and the Spatial Text', in T.-W. Wong and M.A. Abbas (eds.), *Rewriting Literary History* (Hong Kong: Hong Kong University Press, 1984), pp. 66-88 (72).

(the story does not appear in Chronicles), Rehoboam is credited with 18 primary wives (נשׁים) and 60 secondary wives (פלגשׁים), who produce for him 28 sons and 60 daughters. This constitutes a considerable level of procreational energy on the part of the women.

The explicit libidinal investment of these verses spills over into the other themes (initially the preparation of the state for war), for in 11.23 the commanders of the fortresses (previously mentioned in 11.11) turn out to be Rehoboam's sons, or at least some of them, since 28 sons must go into 15 fortresses. Although the syntax of 11.23 is difficult, it suggests that Rehoboam in his wisdom (ויבן) uses a strategy comparable to a more contemporary entertainment industry, dividing or breaking up (ויפרץ) his sons and providing channels of libidinal expression alternative to political conflict, namely much food (המזון לרב) and much sex in the form of a multitude of women (המון נשׁים). The linkage here between the two themes of procreation and military organization enables the extension of libidinal investment to the narrative construction of the heavily defended enclave as a whole. Here we find a particular form of libidinal investment that is the conjunction between family and state, sex and politics, which itself opens up the conjunction of politics and psychology at the level of method. In a more contemporary situation the sexual and the familial function as outlets for repressed political activity and expression, but in pre-capitalist texts such as the Hebrew Bible, the sexual or familial and the political are often explicitly connected.

Indeed, in the light of the classic Freudian connections between religion and sex, and with the relationship between procreational prowess and divine favor (characteristic of Chronicles as a whole), libidinal investment may also include within its domain the cultic and religious activity of 2 Chron. 11.13-17. This thematic link is made explicit in the description of the battle between Jeroboam and Abijah in 13.2b-20. The larger numbers (800,000) and the superior strategies (the encirclement or pincer movement) of Jeroboam avail for nothing against the cultic correctness of the priests who lead Abijah's forces, ready to sound the battle trumpets and summon Yahweh to their aid (11.11-12). It takes merely the battle shout of Judah during the battle to trigger the divine heavy artillery.[66] Since there is in this story a direct association between

---

66. The presentation of the battle is reminiscent of the story of the fall of Jericho in Josh. 2–6, where correct cultic observance, trumpets, shouting and the agency of Yahweh are found. Mason (*Preaching the Tradition*, p. 42) and Welten (*Geschichte und Geschichtsdarstellung*, p. 120) describe it as a 'holy war' theme,

war and cult or religion, and since procreation and war have already been related earlier, these verses therefore incorporate the third theme of 11.5-23 (viz. religion) within the influence of libidinal investment, which permeates from procreation through war to religion. Thus, in the light of these connections between the three components of the Judean enclave—war, religion and sex—it may be concluded that the fundamental relationship between them is that of libidinal investment itself.

This intense loading of the libidinal apparatus leads into some further features: first, standing over against the sexual, martial and religious centralization[67] in the restricted territory of Judah is an enhanced perception of the psychological and social Other. The dynamics and complexities of such an inside–outside, self–other relationship may be seen operating at various points in the text, all of which restrict any worthwhile activity to Jerusalem: the regnal formulae apply only to Davidic kings in Jerusalem; theological assessment is a right held only by the same kings; prophets relate only to these kings;[68] Jeroboam is marginalized by being denied kingship in the quoted material of 10.1–11.4, cast in a negative light in the recast version of the division in 13.5-9, and pushed towards the edges of the narrative structure; and the narrative structure outlined earlier shows that the basic concern is with the 'national security' of Judah. With such a focus, the urgent questions concern both identification of and modes of dealing with the other or the outside. How, in other words, may the enclave be subject to disrupt-

---

frequent in the addresses of Chronicles. These features also make their way into other texts that describe or give instructions for apocalyptic battles, particularly the Qumran War Scroll, in which correct cultic procedure ensures victory by the divine hand.

67. Williamson (*1 and 2 Chronicles*, p. 240) indicates that these themes of sex, war and religion are regularly used by Chr. in describing the results of obedience and disobedience.

68. Otherwise, there are two displacements that take place in this text from Chronicles: they are symptomatic of the displacement of prophecy itself in the world in which Chronicles seems to have arisen. First, virtually banished from the main narrative, the prophets have invaded and secured for themselves the domain of sources cited by the Chronicles text; they have moved from being active participants to observers, commentators and history writers (2 Chron. 9.29; 12.15; 13.22). The second shift or displacement concerns prophetic speech—namely, the exercise of narrative control and the mechanism of divine and human relationships—which has been transposed into a royal proclamation of the king, in this case Abijah (13.4-12).

ing features? How is it to deal with these threats and disturbances? These problems are raised by a narrative in which the kingdom is divided, is then secured and then almost collapses, only to recover.

One way to approach this problem is to examine the representation of various people inhabiting the textual space. Thus, the basic opposition between inside and outside is represented by Jerusalem and external enemies, in particular Shishak and his cohorts (Libyans, Sukkim and Cushites or Ethiopians; 12.3). There are also, however, those from the northern kingdom, the people and priests who emigrate to the southern kingdom for religious purity. Then there are those who are not precisely outside or part of the internal system, yet who threaten to tear that system down. These are the bandits, the guerrilla band, the 'worthless scoundrels' (אנשים רקים בני בליעל; 13.7), who gather around Jeroboam and constitute the internal threat to the kingdom, those who break it up but are then destroyed. Priest, people and bandits form a group that is not inside, but more inside than outside. Finally, there are those who have some connection with Jerusalem but have been away for so long that they no longer count as insiders, namely, the expatriots or Diaspora. Perhaps the best way to represent these complexities is with a semiotic square:

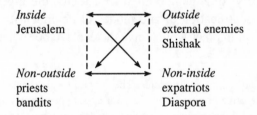

Inside
Jerusalem

Outside
external enemies
Shishak

Non-outside
priests
bandits

Non-inside
expatriots
Diaspora

The whole question of the disjunction has become much more complex in this light. What is of interest now is how this increasingly tangled contradiction works itself out in the passage under consideration.

The way this is attempted introduces us to an ideological construct that incorporates the others dealt with thus far: defense patterns, religious influx and procreational prowess—which themselves form a libidinal investment over against a looming Other—are all part of the Utopian rereading of Israel's history, a reinterpretation with the incorporated future dimension so characteristic of Utopian narrative. Indeed, for Jameson Utopian narrative construction itself requires significant libidinal investment, for it is the point at which social and personal liberation take place. On a more particular level, the strong demarcation of Utopian space and the rejection or exclusion of the outside are elements characteristic of Utopian narratives, particularly the disjunction between our own contemporary space and time and that of Utopia: Utopias appear as literal or figurative islands, independent and sharply separated from the Other in the form of the mainland, the place or planet of origin. The objection that the Utopian space in 2 Chronicles 10–13 is not entirely closed off (there is the gap to the north) does not hold, for such a feature is part of the ambiguity of Utopian narrative: that is to say, the strict demarcation carries with it an undercurrent of maintained or spasmodic connection with the Other that has been and is still rejected. In the same way, Rehoboam's defenses remain open to Israel in the north from whence the priests and people flow in.

This sharp relation of disjunction and connection is characteristic of Utopian construction: a Utopia requires a radical disjunction with this dismal world as a condition of its possibility, yet in order to be possible in the first place, it must find another way to re-open the connection. All Utopias, then, are incomplete in this sense, leaving themselves open to the world of reader, viewer or player ('Utopia' is now also a video game) in some devious way. This may be read as failure or limited success: in being bound to the here-and-now, such Utopias fail to achieve their goal of constructing the absolutely and qualitatively Other and thus exhibit the inability of Utopian thinking; or, Utopias may be mentally assembled only on the building blocks supplied by the present. In Thomas More's text—an inevitable reference, given the origin of modern genre by his book of the same name[69]—this dialectic continu-

69. Over against the philosophical and hermeneutical angles on the question of Utopia, More's text belongs to the literary dimension of Utopian thinking. More, friend of Erasmus and Christian humanist on the Roman Catholic side of the struggle with the Protestant reformers, apparently produced the book in stages. The primary layer became Book 2, being written while on a diplomatic mission to the Lowlands, and the other layers were written later to become the first and third books. This staggered origin, if we are to believe Erasmus's biography of More, finds an echo in the layering of dialogues and the variety of other literary devices such as declaration, persuasion and dissuasion, proverbs and enigmas. In the crucial Book 2, Hythloday relates, in the context of a framing dialogue in the narrative present, a dialogue he had in the past with a person who was reporting on an island (Utopia) recently discovered. It is precisely the formal tensions in the work that have secured its lasting importance, for it has a perceptive depth that unearths a host of unavoidable paradoxes of Utopian literature as such. However, in delineating the

ally replicates itself: the island was created at the command of King Utopus by the excavation of a trench that severed the link of the former promontory with the mainland; money is banned from Utopia but then used in foreign trade and in dealings with foreign governments; violence is excluded, only to be enthusiastically pursued by foreign mercenaries fighting the commonwealth's wars for it on the outside. This is the sort of contradiction—the trench is dug, but trade and war continue; the wall is built but is incomplete; the planets are separated by space, yet the spaceships do get through; the fortresses fail to enclose the total area—which appears in my reading of Chronicles. But the dialectic takes one more twist: despite the normally unwitting connection that remains open to our own world, More has bequeathed to us another problem of modern Utopian writing, or perhaps a problem of all Utopian literature, namely the absence of a means of transition from or transformation of the current socio-economic system. Thus, not only are there unexpected connections between the Utopian state and our own, but at the same it is impossible to see the way through to Utopia; for this we require the revolutionaries.

I would, therefore, conclude that the major ideological construct or ideologeme of 2 Chronicles 10–13 is that of Utopian nationalism, or— to avoid the associations of the term 'nationalism', since that designates ideological dimensions of the growth of the nation state in the nineteenth and twentieth centuries—Utopian politics. That a section of Chronicles should be fundamentally Utopian is not surprising in the light of those studies mentioned earlier that have focused on the eschatology, messianism and theocratic construct of Chronicles as a whole.[70]

major complexities of Utopian construction in 2 Chron. 10–13 in comparison with More's text, I run the risk of making eternal a genre whose features are tied to the specific sociopolitical context in which they have arisen. I would respond with the observation that the arrival of a new genre—More's Utopia is our example—is not without its cultural precursors, but more importantly, that the opening of one's eyes to the various contours of the radically new also opens one's eyes to examples and generic forms that provide a foretaste of what is to come.

70.   Braun, 'Chronicles, Ezra and Nehemiah', p. 59; De Vries, 'The Forms of Prophetic Address in Chronicles', p. 36; Williamson, *Israel in the Books of Chronicles*, p. 135. Rudolph (*Chronikbücher*, pp. xxiii-xxiv) is slightly off the point when he argues that Chronicles presents a realized theocracy with no future or eschatological expectation. His argument clearly falters when it becomes clear that a realized theocracy—insofar as that is a literary projection with the great unlikelihood of an historical referent—is as Utopian as eschatology proper.

The alternative designation of 'Utopian politics' is intended to discard some of the more theological associations of the former terms, to tap into more recent discussions of utopianism, to emphasize the political dimensions of such an ideologeme and to anticipate the location of this ideologeme in its respective mode of production.

Immediate Divine Retribution

However, there is a fundamental ideological contradiction in 2 Chronicles 10–13: the heavily fortified, pious and fecund Utopia of 2 Chronicles 11 virtually crumbles in 12.1-4 due to Rehoboam's disobedience. The fortified cities, closed to the south and the path of an invading Egyptian army, all fall as though they were nothing to the countless army (אֵין מִסְפָּר לָעָם; 12.3) of Shishak, due to lack of obedience and discipline on the part of Rehoboam and the people. The time scale itself is subjected to such a force: in a narrative organization that may be termed an 'ethical periodization', the security lasts for a certain number of years until Rehoboam's disobedience. It returns when he and the officers repent of their disobedience.

This pattern has been dubbed the doctrine of 'immediate divine retribution', which was mentioned earlier. It has been described as 'one of the most prominent and characteristic features of the Chronicler's theology',[71] which 'provides his dominant compositional technique',[72] although it was Wellhausen who first identified it in his *Prolegomena*.[73] The terms of this feature are previewed in 1 Chron. 28.8b-9 and then firmly established in 2 Chron. 7.13-14, where, as in 2 Chron. 12.1, it unambiguously applies to all the people and not merely the king. Such retribution, as is clear from the presentation of Shishak's invasion discussed above, is closely related to the questions of repentance and prophetic warning.[74] Immediate divine retribution—which now includes the cluster of retribution, warning and repentance—may be designated as the second major ideological unit, or ideologeme, of this text,[75] but it

71. Williamson, *Israel in the Books of Chronicles*, p. 67.

72. Dillard, *2 Chronicles*, p. 76.

73. Wellhausen, *Prolegomena*, pp. 203-10; see also Eskenazi, 'Chronicles and the Composition of I Esdras', pp. 39-61.

74. Williamson, *1 and 2 Chronicles*, pp. 31-33.

75. See the extent to which it controls the narrative in Dillard, *2 Chronicles*, pp. 76-81.

also creates significant ideological tension.

However, the initial impression of narrative control is short-lived, succumbing to a problem with the time scale. In 11.17 the emphasis through repetition is placed upon the three years of security enjoyed by Rehoboam and the people, yet it is only in the fifth year of Rehoboam's reign that Shishak attacks in response to disobedience at the third year (12.2). Such a time lapse places considerable strain upon the 'immediate' part of the retribution, even if the three-year schema is regarded as a typological device indicating the completion of a short space of time.[76] Such a rift suggests that this ideological unit has a subordinate and co-opted role. It has legitimacy but only under the direction of the text's controlling Utopian politics. In order to be a Utopia, it must have—apart from and even beyond martial strength, cultic purity and libidinal satisfaction—an obedient population and the favor of Yahweh. The lack of these indicates merely that the Utopia remains to be realized. The challenge to the Utopian formation presented by immediate divine retribution is therefore brought under control. Here, it would seem, the religious gives way to the political, but the significance of this must await later discussion.

The presence in 2 Chronicles 10–13 of immediate divine retribution as a subordinate ideological unit indicates a new function for the old and reworked theme from DtrH of divine reward and punishment for human activities: it may now be regarded as a subversive discourse within this text, threatening but not being able to topple the Utopia at the center. It has been reworked as an oppositional discourse seeking to undermine the ideological formation of the text.

A Question of Class

However, the presentation of Utopian politics and immediate divine retribution as merely ideological features of this text sells them short, for they also profoundly affect the way in which the various types of people or social classes operate. Of course, in work on the Hebrew Bible the question of class must remain both hypothetical and highly suggestive, but the following guidelines are useful. In the previous sections my concern was with ideology, which identifies a basic function

76. See M. Cogan, 'The Chronicler's Use of Chronology as Illuminated by Neo-Assyrian Royal Inscriptions', in J.H. Tigay (ed.), *Empirical Models for Biblical Criticism* (Philadelphia: University of Pennsylvania Press, 1985), pp. 207-209.

of human existence. In the words of Louis Althusser, ideology is the individual's imaginary relationship to his or her real conditions of existence.[77] That is, ideology is the way in which people understand their own individual and collective relationships to the larger realities of society and history. Ideology may, then, be negative or positive, and in its positive dimension it is very often Utopian. Ideology concerns the areas of beliefs and value systems, religion, ethics and so on. Closely bound up with ideology is the question of class, since the proper location for the production of ideology is class. By 'class' is meant the reality of social life, as that is determined by the one's position in the production process. The complex strata and subdivisions of class are understood as part of a more fundamental pattern of rulers and ruled. Each class and class subdivision justifies its respective position by the construction of ideologies. Conflict or contradiction are the essential characteristics of both class and ideology.

In this light I would suggest that in 2 Chronicles 10–13 the dominant class discourse is that of a ruling class. In other words, the Utopia constructed in these chapters, and presumably in the other chapters of Chronicles, is a ruling-class effort. The more obvious indicators of such a class location have been treated earlier: the fortifications and preparations for war take place at the direction of the king (and yet they require considerable labor); the class subdivision of religious professionals takes its place within the enclosed space of Judah; and the royal subdivision ensures its hold with an increase in its numbers and control over the fortresses.

Alongside these blatant expressions of class interest are those that tap into more wide-ranging Utopian desires. The first of these may be seen at a number of important points in 2 Chronicles 10–13, where the people form part of the collective whole of Judah and Benjamin. For instance, in 11.17 they join the priests in strengthening (ויחזקו) the kingdom and making Rehoboam secure (ואמצו). More importantly, as in 2 Chron. 7.14, it is this same group that follows in the way of David and Solomon (הלכו בדרך דויד ושלמה). The inclusion of the general populace is found again in 12.1 and 2, in which disobedience is assigned to both king and people: v. 1 asserts that Rehoboam and the people with him (וכל-ישראל עמו) abandoned the Law of Yahweh (עזב את-תורת יהוה); in v. 2 the plural subject of the verb works on the same assumption

---

77. L. Althusser, *Lenin and Philosophy and Other Essays* (London: New Left Books, 1971), p. 153.

(כי מעלו ביהוה). Although it is the officers and the king (שׂרי־ישׂראל
והמלך; 12.6) who are addressed and repent in 12.5-8, the point remains
that it is not the king alone who does so.

These observations are reinforced by Weinberg's study on social
class in Chronicles, in which he concluded that there is a constant
emphasis on the solidarity of many social groups with the king.[78]
Alongside this tendency to include ruling classes and the ruled as a
collective, there is a second, subtle designation of Utopian perspectives
on class. In this text and throughout Chronicles, as shown in Weinberg's study,[79] there is an effort to eliminate the realities of socio-economic differentiation. For instance, the terminology of poverty and
wealth—except in stereotypical formulae of royal power—and the
reality of property distinctions are systematically excluded from the
discourse of Chronicles.[80] These features—social solidarity and the
absence of class distinctions—point toward a desire to articulate the
image of a classless society, which is so important to many a Utopia.

The problem, of course, is that the excision of class references is so
often a ruling-class strategy of repressing class differentiation and
denying the presence of class conflict. Utopian demands for an end to
such inequitable differentiation and the resultant class conflict are met
not through any mechanism or process of redistribution but through a
discourse that represses the class distinctions, while leaving them firmly
in place.

There is the other ideological feature of 2 Chronicles 10–13 that
complicates matters. The ideological unit of immediate divine retribution, insofar as it poses a threat to the Utopian construct, undergoes a
double slippage in this text. On the first move, the ruling class in
Jerusalem is, after all, subject to an external and much more powerful
imperial ruling class: it may be argued, therefore, that the pattern of
immediate divine retribution and the dire threat it poses to the Utopian
territory of Judah is the text's way of registering the presence and
impact of this external, imperial ruling class. That such a threat is cast
in religious terms will be significant later on. The second shift in the
role of the punctual deity opens up the question of the ruled and
exploited. I suggest that what we have in this text is a subversive theme.
It gives all the impressions of being stilted, for which it is often criti-

78. Weinberg, 'Die soziale Gruppe', p. 94.
79. Weinberg, 'Die soziale Gruppe', p. 91.
80. Weinberg, 'Die soziale Gruppe', pp. 89-90.

cized. However, the direct and forceful nature of immediate divine retribution—to the extent of straining the narrative organization, as with Rehoboam's three (or five) years of favor—is precisely what suggests a non-ruling-class situation for this discourse. It gives voice to the direct challenge and threat posed by the ruled and exploited classes. The other characteristic that reinforces this argument was noted earlier: it is firmly located in a position subordinate to Utopian politics, a co-optation characteristic of the strategy of containment used by ruling-class discourse.

Thus far I have argued that the two contradictory ideological elements arising from the narrative structure of 2 Chronicles 10–13 are Utopian politics and immediate divine retribution, the former discourse giving expression to ruling-class aspirations and the latter playing the double role of reference both to the external imperial ruling class and to the subversive yet co-opted voices of the exploited classes.

'Political' Economy

By way of closing this analysis I would like to trace some implications of the ideological and class dynamics of what I have termed 'Utopian politics', for thus far I have expanded on the Utopian at the expense of the politics. Yet it is the former—particularly the Utopian construct outlined above—that leads into the latter by means of the question of space. In an earlier section I argued that the spatial arrangement of the fortresses was an important part of the Utopian politics of this text. Here such spatial factors play a different but related role. A striking feature—noted with surprise by Aharoni[81]—of the pattern of fortresses in 2 Chron. 11.5-10 is the restricted territory that is included. Indeed, apart from the maximum distance of five kilometers from fortress to fortress and apart from the northern gap, the distances measured directly from corner to corner yield the following results (based on measurements in both the *Oxford Bible Atlas* and Aharoni): 37 km from Jerusalem to Ziph on the eastern side, 30 km from Ziph to Lachish on the southern side, 40 km from Lachish to Aijalon on the western side, and only 22 km from Aijalon to Jerusalem in the north (although a slight opening is left). This is by no means an extensive territory: less than any of the descriptions of Judah (whether independent or under imperial rule) it resembles more the territory under the influence of a

---

81. Aharoni, *Land of the Bible*, p. 330.

powerful city state, or *polis*, such as Athens, Sparta or Corinth, or for
that matter any major city in the Hellenistic world. The implication, of
course, is that Jerusalem begins to be understood in the same fashion. I
would suggest, therefore, that the conceptual arrangement of the space
in 2 Chronicles 10–13, particularly 11.5-10, is that of the *polis*. This is
not to make any immediate claims that Jerusalem was a *polis* at the
time Chronicles was written, but merely that the cognitive map of these
fortifications is that of the *polis*.

The age of the *polis* is the age of what has been termed the classical
or ancient mode of production, in which the *polis* is the dominant form
of political and social life. It is here that the various formal, ideological
and class elements of the text are related to what have become known
as modes of production, the broad socio-economic situations under
which we live. Here history comes home with a vengeance, the basic
assumption being that at any particular point in history any number of
modes of production are in operation in varying strengths. Each mode
of production has characteristic sign systems—ways of thinking and
language that are distinct from any other mode—which show their tell-
tale traces and footprints in texts by a wide variety of means. But if
there are several modes of production in operation at any one time, then
there will be a number of sign systems functioning at any one time, and
those sign systems may be found in the cultural products of that era.

The introduction of the slave-based or ancient mode of production
into Palestine was probably slow over the Hellenistic period, perhaps
even at the latter part of the Persian period, but quite decisive after the
destruction of the temple and Jerusalem in 70 CE.[82] As the alternative
designation suggests, slavery was the fundamental factor of economic
activity for this mode of production, for Rome inherited from the Greek
world the universal use of slaves for work. Work—manufacturing,
farming, carrying, cleaning, cooking, rowing ships—was what slaves
did, but human beings did not work; they did other more useful things
such as soldiering, trade, reading, writing, participating in the legal
system or, above all, governing the city. Slaves formed part of the
economic and social structure without which the Greek and Hellenistic
worlds would not have been able to operate at all. The ability of the
Greeks and Romans to produce history writing, drama, poetry and,
above all, philosophy—the things that we count as the eternal gifts of

---

82. See N.K. Gottwald, 'Sociology of Ancient Israel', *ABD* VI, pp. 79-89.

the Greeks and Romans to us—were possible, because the historians, dramatists, poets and philosophers were freed from the work that the slaves did for them. But slaves were not regarded as citizens: only a restricted group of males were full citizens, and their focus was governing the city state, which was a distinct entity, covering a stretch of territory that included the temples, markets and government buildings of the city but also the surrounding fields and farms. 'Politics' is, then, all the business that pertains to one's *polis*, and for the person of the ancient world the *polis* was what gave a person identity and determined who that person was—if one was a slave, woman or child one wasn't much, of course.

This, then, is part of the conceptual frame that I am suggesting for this section of Chronicles, a set of possible ways of thinking about things, while systematically excluding others. The Utopian restoration constructed in the narrative of 2 Chronicles 10–13 is thus focused on the *polis* of Jerusalem and its limited territory of influence.

There is, however, an alternative 'politics' in this text whose symptoms center on that other ideological unit noted earlier. Immediate divine retribution is concerned with the workings of the divine in human affairs; indeed, its operation depends upon the assumption that the primary conceptual mode of understanding reality—in these few chapters reality includes family, cult, state and warfare—is the religious or the sacred. Bound up with this ideologeme is the emphasis on the cult in Chronicles as a whole[83] and specifically in 2 Chron. 11.13-17 and 13.8-12. Yet the main feature of this ideological unit is that in the distribution of favor and disfavor Yahweh acts as a despot granting favor to and withholding it from various subjects and subordinate rulers. It is not sufficient, however, to argue that the deity is understood in terms of the oriental despot, with the assumption that these two are distinct identities. Rather, it is often difficult to separate the two at an ideological level: the oriental despot and the deity are interchangeable and at times identical. This situation is characteristic of what has been termed the Asiatic mode of production, a highly centralized state that dominates society, politics and economics.[84] In the ancient Near East at the head and center of the state structure is the king or despot—the Asiatic mode of production is also termed 'oriental despotism'—in the

83. So Myers, *I Chronicles*, p. lxxv; Williamson, *1 and 2 Chronicles*, pp. 28-31.
84. N.K. Gottwald, *The Hebrew Bible in its Social World and in ours* (Semeia; Atlanta: Scholars Press, 1993), pp. 153-54.

image of whose body the dispersed collective unity is consolidated.[85] In the king or despot may be found the ideological center as well, which is expressed in religious terms:

> The whole ideology of the system owes its shape to the prominent role played in Asiatic society by the person at the summit of the political pyramid ... He tends to present himself, whether as high priest, son of heaven or son of God, as the intermediary between men and the divinity, or even as God himself . . . Asiatic tradition brings together the divinity or 'heaven' and the despot who rules the state; the exercise of power ... is at one with the orderly functioning of the cosmos.[86]

There is, therefore, a fusion of the political and religious dimensions of the despot as 'sole proprietor'.[87] The monarchy in Chronicles is if anything more highly placed than in the much more critical account of Samuel–Kings, and I would suggest that it is congruent with this perception of the imperial ruler in the Asiatic mode of production.

Yet, in contrast to the characteristic bureaucratic remoteness and arbi-

85. See F.R. Jameson, *The Political Unconscious: Narrative as a Socially Symbolic Act* (Ithaca, NY: Cornell University Press, 1981), p. 295; J. Frow, *Marxism and Literary History* (Cambridge, MA: Harvard University Press, 1986), p. 36. D. Jobling ('Deconstruction and the Political Analysis of Biblical Texts: A Jamesonian Reading of Psalm 72', *Semeia* 59 [1992], p. 17) notes, following L. Krader, that the Asiatic mode of production need not have a monarchy; it is just that no alternatives seem to have been pursued.

86. U. Melotti, *Marx and the Third World* (London: Macmillan, 1977), pp. 70-71, quoted in part by Jobling, 'Deconstruction and the Political Analysis', p. 17; see also K.A. Wittfogel, *Oriental Despotism: A Comparative Study of Total Power* (New Haven: Yale University Press, 1957), pp. 87-100; K.L. Younger, 'The Figurative Aspect and the Contextual Method in the Evaluation of the Solomonic Empire (1 Kings 1–11)', in D.J.A. Clines, S.E. Fowl and S.E. Porter (eds.), *The Bible in Three Dimensions: Essays in Celebration of Forty Years of Biblical Studies in the University of Sheffield* (JSOTSup, 87; Sheffield: JSOT Press, 1990), pp. 157-75.

87. See K. Marx, *Grundrisse: Foundations of the Critique of Political Economy (Rough Draft)* (trans. and foreword by M. Nicolaus; Harmondsworth: Penguin Books in Association with New Left Review, 1973), pp. 472-73. 'A part of their surplus labour belongs to the higher community, which exists ultimately as a *person*, and this surplus labour takes the form of tribute etc., as well as of common labour for the exaltation of the unity, partly of the real despot, partly of the imagined clan-being, the god' (p. 473). See further: D. Jobling, ' "Forced Labor": Solomon's Golden Age and the Question of Literary Representation', *Semeia* 54 (1992), pp. 18-19.

trariness of the divine-human despot of a fully functional Asiatic mode of production, the activities of the deity in 2 Chronicles 10–13 are both more stilted and efficient (if that is the correct adjective). Here Yahweh deals directly with the situation, bringing Shishak in for punishment (12.2), holding him back in response to repentance (12.5-8) and responding immediately to the shout of the people of Judah in the battle against Jeroboam's forces (13.15). Such efficiency is more directly threatening to whatever human activities are underway, forcing them to be accountable to the deity. It is also distinctly subversive to an older ruling order. This god comes closer to the *deus ex machina* of Greek tragedy who arrives on stage on a platform or glides down on a flying fox to set things aright at the end. Or, to use a different but related comparison from the political realm, the despot of 2 Chronicles acts more like the provincial governor of a different mode of production, in which the governor must move swiftly to maintain order as well as his (since they were all male) own position. Thus, despite all the conceptual trappings of the Asiatic mode of production, the semiotic grid in which the despot operates is that of the more efficient ancient or slave mode of production.

We are left, then, with an interesting opposition, between Utopian politics and the ancient mode of production on the one hand, and immediate divine retribution and the Asiatic mode of production on the other. Yet there has been enough to indicate that the former is clearly dominant: politics over religion, *polis* over despot, Rome over Babylon, ancient over Asiatic modes of production. I would suggest that 2 Chronicles 10–13 marks a less hostile and more comfortable stage in the transition from the Asiatic mode of production to the classical, from the religious or sacred cultural dominant to the political.

Another feature reinforces such a conclusion: the displacement of the prophets. The prophetic dominance in DtrH has been removed to the formulaic frames where they have become the authors of various works: Nathan, Ahijah, Iddo and Shemaiah have entered the scribal class, as it were. Apart from Iddo, the prophets have been removed from the narrative action in which they once participated to the regnal formulae of Chronicles that frame the comparable accounts now devoid of their presence. They have become mere spectators to events, their written words providing a retrospective coverage of events rather than a prospective direction to the narrative action itself. In other words, the prophets look back rather than forward. These are the signs, as Overholt has argued,[88] that the prophets have no programme with which to play; prophecy has ended and all that remain are the prophetic records that may be interpreted, applied and forged. The passing of the prophets is thus a symptom, or figuration, for the passing from the Asiatic to the ancient mode of production, the role of the prophets declining with the removal of the cultural form of the sacred from dominant to subordinate status.

Thus, 2 Chronicles attempts a reconstruction of Judah by presenting it in the past as a Utopian enclave and then uses that reconstruction as a model for a restored Judah. In doing so the text incorporates desirable elements from earlier modes of production, particularly the kinship structures of hierarchical kinship societies and the cultic emphasis of the Asiatic mode of production; even the subversive force of divine retribution against the ruling class is included. However, such a reconstruction is able to take place only in terms of the ancient mode of production. The signs of this are everywhere: the function of the deity, the nature of Judah as a powerful *polis*, the subordinate status of the deity and the religious domain as a whole. The double bind of 2 Chronicles 10–13, therefore, is that the attempt to restrain the tide of the ancient mode of production by producing a Utopian enclave is carried in the very terms of that newer mode of production: it is, therefore, achieving the transition in the very effort to resist it.

In this way 2 Chronicles 10–13 echoes one further element of Utopian imagination: in the more philosophical part of such reflection is the argument—despite the dangers of full-scale nostalgia—that Utopian aspirations are comprised of a combination of memory and hope, past and future, anamnesis and aspiration. But there is more here than a mere combination. Utopian thinking borders on the oxymoron, pushing to the edge of paradox and antinomy: 'Utopian thinking undermines society's attachment to the past for the sake of a desired future, while at the same time appealing to collective memory as a source of vision and motivation.'[89] The past is both denied as a source of the present status quo and also used as a source for a perception of an alternative form of

88. T.W. Overholt, 'The End of Prophecy: No Players without a Program', *JSOT* 42 (1988), pp. 103-15; see also A.C. Welch, *The Work of the Chronicler: Its Purpose and Date* (Schweich Lectures, 1938; London: Oxford University Press, 1939), p. 50.

89. E. Luz, 'Utopia and Return: On the Structure of Utopian Thinking and its Relation to Jewish-Christian Thinking', *JR* 73 (1993), p. 360.

social existence; while the future is tolerated not as a continuation of the present establishment but as the locus of the radically new society constructed out of restored pristine origins. Assumed here, of course, is the radical critique of contemporary social and economic structures. In drawing on Israel's past, particularly its monarchic and cultic dimensions, Chronicles constructs here a Utopia that embodies the ideals of a future Israelite state. Yet we must not think of Utopian narrative as merely the 'representation' of a perfect world or future society based on an ideal past with which to compare our own, but Utopian narrative is rather a collection of conceptual modes of dealing with our own society or at least the society in which the work is produced. The narrative is, then, in process rather than static, and that process is one of 'neutralization': Utopian narrative is not merely myth, understood in Lévi-Strauss's terms as a conceptual or imaginary resolution of a real social problem or contradiction, but is rather the logical inverse of this initial contradiction. There is a comprehensive inversion of the contemporary situation, which for our text is the ancient mode of production.

Conclusion

In this attempt to read 2 Chronicles 10–13 with the assistance of theoretical proposals from Jameson, Lukács and Jobling, I have argued that these chapters comprise a range of formal features in relation to the parallel section in DtrH, 1 Kings 11–14—quotation, recasting, unique material and report—that contribute to a new narrative structure that marginalizes Jeroboam and the prophets and focuses attention on Judah and its kings. Picking up the report in 2 Chron. 11.5-23, I argued that there are two conflicting ideological units, namely Utopian politics and immediate divine retribution, which themselves have some class echoes regarding rulers, ruled and imperial control. Finally, the implications for political economy were developed in terms of an opposition between Asiatic and ancient modes of production, particularly an attempt to recall the former in the context of the latter.

However, before this is conceived in terms of yet another historical reconstruction let me add the proviso that such a reconstruction must not so much be understood in more conventional terms as the social context in which the Utopian work is produced—and which may be reconstructed from data independent of the text and to which the text refers at particular points—but rather the social context—is produced by the text, 'borne within and vehiculated by the text itself, interiorized in its very fabric in order to provide the stuff and the raw material on which the textual operation must work'.[90] The social and historical circumstances of the text are, then, both generated by it and that to which it responds: the text carries its context within it. This, finally, is the status of my own suggestions regarding 2 Chronicles 10–13.

90. F.R. Jameson, 'Of Islands and Trenches: Neutralization and the Production of Utopian Discourse', in *The Ideologies of Theory, Essays 1971–1986*. II. *Syntax of History* (Theory and History of Literature, 49; Minneapolis: University of Minnesota Press, 1988), p. 81.

2 CHRONICLES 36.20-23 AS LITERARY AND THEOLOGICAL 'INTERFACE'

Magnar Kartveit

The book of Chronicles ends with a part of the edict of Cyrus. The last word is וְיָעַל ('and let him go up'; from עלה*), often used for immigrating to or entering the land of Israel (e.g. Gen. 13.1; 26.23; 46.4; 50.6-7; Exod. 3.8—all J). At the end of Chronicles our attention is brought to the theme of the land. A few sentences earlier the land is also in focus. We read that during the exile the land 'enjoyed her sabbaths'[1] (2 Chron. 36.21). A connection between the land and the sabbaths is known from the Priestly legislation (Lev. 26.34-35), but the idea that the exile was a long series of sabbaths is new. How is this to be interpreted? What is the function of these sayings about the land in the last verses of Chronicles?

As soon as we focus on the ending of Chronicles, we are in the middle of an old controversy: what is the relation of Chronicles to Ezra–Nehemiah? Rabbinical Judaism and medieval Christianity held that Chronicles and Ezra–Nehemiah had the same author—Ezra. L. Zunz (1832) maintained the idea of common authorship but suggested that the author was anonymous and designated him 'the Chronicler' (hereafter, 'Chr.'), who created the three books as one continuous work.[2] A 'light' version of this idea is that these books were composed by the same author, without originally forming one work. Discussion on this subject began again in earnest in 1968, and at the moment there is no agreement on where the work originally ended, in 2 Chron. 36.23 or in Neh. 13.31.[3] One of the points of interest in this connection has been

---

1. All translations are from the RSV, unless otherwise noted.
2. L. Zunz, *Die gottesdienstlichen Vorträge der Juden historisch entwickelt: Ein Beitrag zur Altertumskunde und biblischen Kritik, zur Literatur- und Religionsgeschichte* (repr.; Hildesheim: Georg Olms, 1966 [1892]), pp. 13-36.
3. S. Japhet began this discussion ('The Supposed Common Authorship of

2 Chron. 36.22-23, the introduction to and beginning of the edict of Cyrus. But v. 21 should also be brought into the discussion, since it has some characteristics that merit more attention than scholars have generally given them.

The opening words of v. 21 are clearly doublets to almost the same words in the following verse:

v. 21   למלאות דבר־יהוה בפי ירמיהן
('to fulfill the word of the LORD by the mouth of Jeremiah')

v. 22   לכלות דבר־יהוה בפי ירמיהו
('that the word of the LORD by the mouth of Jeremiah might be accomplished')

Even if the verb is different in the two cases, these phrases must be considered doublets and could not have been produced at the same time in this context. As the verb in v. 22 (לכלות, 'accomplish') is identical to the synoptic text of Ezra 1.1, the expression in v. 21 must be secondary, and an insertion made after v. 22 was part of the text. It is typical for insertions into a text that they repeat some of the existing text and expand upon it (see, e.g., 1 Chron. 5.1-3)—precisely the situation here.

The next part of 2 Chron. 36.21, עד־רצתה הארץ את־שבתותיה ('until the land had enjoyed its sabbaths'), is a subordinate sentence whose connection is not easily determined. It could be dependent on the opening word in the verse, the construct infinitive למלאות ('to fulfill'), but one would rather expect it to relate to a finite verb. We have finite verbs in the two main clauses of the preceding verse, the second one being closest to this subordinate sentence, ויהיו ('they became' [literally, 'were' and continuing: 'servants to him and to his sons']). If the sentence depends upon this verb, we have two subordinate clauses dependent upon the same verb, the other one being the clause following immediately after the second main clause in v. 20, עד־מלך מלכות פרס ('until the establishment of the kingdom of Persia'). The syntactical structure is different in the two subordinate sentences, but they both begin with the same particle. If they both depend on the same verb, they compete as syntactic parts following the verb and so are syntactic doublets.

Chronicles and Ezra–Nehemiah Investigated Anew', *VT* 18 [1968], pp. 330-71; *I & II Chronicles: A Commentary* [OTL; Louisville, KY: Westminster/John Knox Press, 1993], pp. 3-5) and has found substantial support from several quarters. See J.W. Kleinig, 'Recent Research in Chronicles', *CR:BS* 2 (1994), pp. 43-76.

If the subordinate clause in v. 21 is also an insertion in the context, it is not surprising that it has no clear connection to the existing text, or that the addition of it created a doublet. But there may have been a good reason for the somewhat unclear connection to the context: this sentence is an adapted form of Lev. 26.34-35.

If one compares אז תרצה הארץ את־שבתתיה...כל ימי השמה תשבת ('Then the land shall enjoy its sabbaths... As long as it lies desolate it shall have rest'; Lev. 26.34-35) to עד־רצתה הארץ את־שבתותיה כל־ימי השמה שבתה ('until the land had enjoyed its sabbaths. All the days that it lay desolate it kept sabbath'; 2 Chron. 36.21), the forms of the subordinate clause and of the immediately following main clause become understandable. The clauses were changed from sayings about the future in Lev. 26.34-35 to statements about the past in 2 Chron. 36.21, and an appropriate particle was added to introduce the 'quotation'. 'Appropriate', that is, if one had read the preceding verse first, because it imitated the form of the last part of v. 20; but *inappropriate* if one expected a continuation of the beginning of v. 21. It seems that Lev. 26.34-35 was condensed, the tense of the verbs was changed and an introductory particle copied from v. 20 in order to create two sayings for the present purpose.

The rest of the verse, למלאות שבעים שנה ('to fulfill seventy years'), bears a certain resemblance to Jer. 25.12, והיה כמלאות שבעים שנה ('Then after seventy years are completed'), and to Jer. 29.10, כי לפי מלאת לבבל שבעים שנה ('When seventy years are completed for Babylon'). Jeremiah 25.11-12 speaks of servitude to the king of Babylon for 70 years, and 2 Chron. 36.20 states that the captives from Jerusalem became servants to the king of Babylon. Jeremiah 29.10-11 promises that God will act against Babylon and bring Israel back to 'this place' after 70 years—something supposedly fulfilled as a result of the edict of Cyrus (v. 23). The final part of the verse is therefore probably an adapted form of similar expressions in Jeremiah, and the reference to servitude and return in 2 Chron. 36.20, 23 and Jeremiah prompted the use of the expression here. It is, thus, clearly secondary in this context.

The verb למלאות ('fulfill') in למלאות שבעים שנה ('to fulfill seventy years') is taken over from Jer 25.12; 29.10. The same verb also occurs in the beginning of v. 21 in a sentence that is a doublet to a sentence in v. 22, as we saw. Above, it was noted that לכלות ('accomplish') in v. 22 and Ezra 1.1 probably is the original verb and that למלאות in 2 Chron. 36.21 is secondary. The last phrase of v. 21 makes it possible for us to explain why the original verb was exchanged: the new verb was taken over from the expression at the end of the verse, למלאות שבעים שנה.

The corollary to these assumptions is that the interpolator created v. 21 by adapting sentences from Lev. 36.34-35; Jer. 25.12; 29.10. Further, he then had to introduce these adapting sentences by repeating לכלות דבר־יהוה בפי ירמיהו ('that the word of the Lord by the mouth of Jeremiah might be accomplished') from v. 22. Lastly, he changed the opening verb of this introduction, לכלות, to לכלאות on the model of the verb in למלאות שבעים שמה.

This explanation of the creation of v. 21 also accounts for the strange fact that the verse opens with a reference to God's word to Jeremiah and then goes on with a 'quotation' from Leviticus. Only after this 'quotation' comes the Jeremian part of the verse. One may ask why the Leviticus 'quotations' intrude into the context.

An explanation for this could be that the interpolator wished to reply to the question, 'Which prediction in Jeremiah is alluded to in v. 22?' When the interpolator of v. 21 checked the two texts that suggested themselves, Jer. 25.12 and 29.10, the word לשמה ('desolate') in Jer. 25.11, caught his eye. This word led him to a similar word in Lev. 26.34 and then to the whole of Lev. 26.34-35. Indeed, since the larger contexts in both Jeremiah and Leviticus speak about exile and the desolation of the land, there was every reason to combine the texts. Verse 21 probably started as a marginal comment on the text but eventually became part of the running text, thus creating the doublets.

This analysis of v. 21 gives us an impression of the literary technique of the interpolator. The use of adapted quotations from other parts of Scripture indicates that these texts had authority, but not to the extent that an adaptation was impossible. The connection of different sentences because of similar content or because of catchwords indicates that a link between them was presumed, and in this way it was highlighted. Finally, commenting on an existing text by bringing in 'answers' from authoritative Scripture means that the text could be clarified and its content explained.

This is not the place to draw further conclusions from these observations, but one might suggest that they have consequences for the relative chronology of biblical books and for the dating of Chronicles. If, for example, by the time of Chr. or of the interpolator, Leviticus and Jeremiah had attained a status where they could be quoted and adapted for the present purposes, then one would probably not consider a very late dating for Chronicles or its later strata.

If we assume that originally v. 20 was immediately followed by vv. 22-23, the text would then have read as follows:

> He took into exile in Babylon those who had escaped from the sword, and they became servants to him and his sons until the establishment of the kingdom of Persia. Now in the first year of Cyrus king of Persia, that the word of the LORD by the mouth of Jeremiah might be accomplished, the LORD stirred up the spirit of Cyrus king of Persia so that he made a proclamation throughout all his kingdom, and also put it in writing: 'Thus says Cyrus king of Persia, "The LORD, the God of heaven, has given me all the kingdoms of the earth, and he has charged me to build him a house at Jerusalem, which is in Judah. Whoever is among you of all his people, may the LORD his God be with him. Let him go up." '

This text moves uninterrupted from one element of the story to the next, in line with what we can read in the textually unproblematic parts of the *Sondergut* in Chronicles, and, thus, seems to be a genuine Chronistic text.

2 Chronicles 36.22-23, however, has a secondary form in Chronicles when compared to Ezra 1. The evidence for this is found in one of the differences between the texts. 2 Chronicles 36.23 has יהוה אלהיו עמו ('may the LORD his God be with him'), whereas Ezra 1.3 has יהי אלהיו עמו ('may his God be with him'). It is conceivable that one would substitute an exact designation for the God of Israel for a more general one, but the opposite procedure is improbable. This means that 2 Chron. 36.22-23 was copied from Ezra 1.1-3*, slightly altered and placed at the end of Chronicles.

The beginning of Ezra is, however, very strange: the book starts with 'and' (ובשנת). This would be understandable if the beginning referred to a preceding text, as in Exod. 1.1, but as the book now stands there is nothing to which it refers.[4] The Peshitta and Vulgate have omitted the 'and', but καί in the LXX testifies to the existence of the Hebrew conjunction.[5]

One could interpret the 'and' as evidence that Ezra 1.1 is not origi-

---

4. The assumptions in E.A. Knauf, 'Zum Verhältnis von Esra 1, 1 zu 2 Chronik 36, 20-23', *BN* 78 (1995), pp. 16-17, are ingenious but unsubstantianted.

5. W. Rudolph, *Esra und Nehemia mit 3. Esra* (HAT, 20; Tübingen: J.C.B. Mohr [Paul Siebeck], 1949), p. 2, refers to the facts without further comments; cf. M. Sæbø, 'Esra/Esraschriften', *TRE* X, p. 376.

nally the beginning of a book but became the beginning when Ezra–
Nehemiah was separated from Chronicles. This would also account for
the abrupt end of Chronicles and for the secondary character of 2 Chron.
36.22-23. The original version of the edict of Cyrus with its introduction
was left standing at the beginning of Ezra, and an adapted version was
used in Chronicles. The idea in Chronicles could have been to point the
reader on to the continuation of the work, but it could also have been to
provide the book with a conclusion that pointed to a future return or
immigration to the land.

We have no evidence or indication that Chronicles here originally
continued with the entire edict of Cyrus. Only the incomplete version is
attested. There is nothing in the rest of the edict to which Chr. might
have been opposed—to judge from the rest of the book. Therefore, it is
extraordinary that only a part of the edict was used. The ending of
Chronicles could have pointed the reader on to an independently existing Ezra, but then we have the surprising opening of that book. Despite
all the effort that has been put into proving the opposite, there still are
some facts that may indicate that Chronicles, Ezra and Nehemiah originally formed one book and that this work was split up.

When this split took place, the form of Ezra 1.1-3* was not so holy
that alterations were impossible, and therefore the small variants we
find in 2 Chron. 36.22-23 were made. By using a part of the edict,
Chronicles employs a literary device that might have given a hint to the
readers where more of the story was to be found, Ezra–Nehemiah. But
the last word of the book has associations of its own, as we have seen,
and these associations could be the reason for the rather abrupt ending
of the book.

We probably have three different stages for the last verses of Chronicles. The first stage was when the work existed without v. 21 but continued with the whole edict of Cyrus and then with Ezra–Nehemiah; the
second stage was when Chronicles ended with 36.20, 22-23 without the
continuation of the whole Cyrus edict in Ezra–Nehemiah; and the third
stage was when v. 21 was interpolated into the text.

Let us return now to the question 'What do these verses say about the
land in Chronicles?' It is essential to differentiate between these stages,
as each of them has a different—though not necessarily contradictory—
word to say. When Chronicles–Ezra–Nehemiah was one work, not
everything in it was smoothly and easily combined. Many modern
commentators have pointed to this fact. But material of different origins

was brought together, adapted and used for new purposes. If we here concentrate on the 'interface' of Chronicles and Ezra–Nehemiah, namely, on the edict of Cyrus, it has in its present form (Ezra 1.2-4) a reference to Cyrus as ruler over 'all the kingdoms of the earth', and God has 'charged [him] to build him a house at Jerusalem, which is in Judah' (Ezra 1.2). The building of the temple is, of course, the theme followed up in Ezra, but this connection of themes—the whole inhabited earth, Israel/Judah, Jerusalem and the temple—brings us back to the beginning of the book, 1 Chronicles 1–9.

In these chapters we first read about the genealogy and geography of the whole known world (ch. 1). This enumeration of peoples and places moves North-West-South-East, with Israel in the middle. At the end of the chapter the neighboring peoples to the west and east along with the Edomite kings are mentioned. In chs. 2–8, Chr. describes tribal settlements, starting with Judah, continuing to the south (Simeon), to the east (Reuben, Gad, Manasseh), to the north (Issachar, Manasseh, Ephraim, Asher) and ending north of Jerusalem (Benjamin). Israel with all its tribal areas is thus pictured as the center of the inhabited earth. Further, the tribal settlements are described in a circle that begins and ends in Jerusalem. Thus, Jerusalem is at the center of Israel. Chapter 9 enumerates the inhabitants of Jerusalem, especially the temple personnel. In this way the focus is on the temple as the center of Jerusalem. We get the impression that genealogies and land theology here are woven together to create a map of the world with ever smaller circles: world–Israel–Jerusalem–temple.[6]

Just as 1 Chronicles 1–9 is continued by the history of the southern kingdom, the edict of Cyrus is continued by the history of the Judean community after the exile—if history here is accepted as a general and not a modern term.[7] Both histories begin with a world-wide perspective and continue with a Judean and Jerusalemite view—if not with a focus on the temple. The main task for the Israelite kings is to look after the temple, and the temple and its community are also the main interest for Ezra and Nehemiah.

The next stage in the process was when Ezra–Nehemiah was cut off

6. M. Kartveit, *Motive und Schichten der Landtheologie in I Chronik 1–9* (ConBOT, 28; Stockholm: Almqvist & Wisksell, 1989).

7. For discussions on this topic, see M.P. Graham, K.G. Hoglund and S.L. McKenzie (eds.), *The Chronicler as Historian* (JSOTSup, 238; Sheffield: Sheffield Academic Press, 1997).

from Chronicles, and the edict of Cyrus was broken off in the middle, ending in a jussive, 'Let him go up' (2 Chron. 36.23). This verb evokes memories of the patriarchs entering the land and of the conquest under Joshua, as we have seen. In this way both the original immigrations to the land are remembered, and a third entering—after the exile—is permitted and urged by the Persian king. The purpose of this new immigration is the construction of the temple, as in the long form of the edict (Ezra 1.2-4). In the shortened form of the edict, though, God is not a provincial God of Jerusalem as in the end of Ezra 1.3b, but rather the God over all kingdoms in the world (2 Chron. 36.23). If anything was accomplished by shortening the edict, it was that God was depicted as a universal God, and the three different conquests of the land were noted.

But in a literary sense something else was obtained: an inclusio connecting beginning and end. As the book now ends in 2 Chron. 36.23, the themes world–Israel–Jerusalem–temple opened and closed the second-stage work. Form and content, literature and theology, were here used to highlight an important aspect of the history of Israel.

The third stage in the history of these verses came with the interpolation of v. 21: the understanding of the land taken from Leviticus 26 gives the impression that the people could start anew after the exile. The land had recovered from all the sins that its earlier inhabitants had brought upon it and was now ready for a fresh start with the returnees from the exile. The sins enumerated as possibilities in Leviticus 26 were atoned for by the 70 years for which the land was desolate, and a renewed people could now start in a renewed land.

Verse 21 is theologically oriented more toward the cult than is the case with the earlier text, which has a historical interest. The sabbatical years of this secondary material reveal an interest that we also know in the secondary material about the levitical cities in 1 Chronicles 6.39-66. There one can also see a growing focus on cultic matters.[8]

Verse 21 thus brings in aspects from a very different way of thinking about the land, cultic aspects rooted in the theologically fundamental saying of God in Lev. 25.23, 'the land is mine; for you are strangers and sojourners with me'. This cultic view of the land has a different orientation from that of the historical orientation. The land belongs to God, and rent should be paid for the borrowing of the land, rent in the form of tithes, first fruits, sabbatical years, 'jubilee years' and so on

8.   Cf. Kartveit, *Motive und Schichten*, pp. 159-63.

(Lev. 25–26).[9] By this idea in the addition, Chronicles is given one connection to the historical thinking and a new one to the cultic thinking about the land. It thus bridges the gap originally existing between the two and forms a stage in the ideological development where the two were combined.

In this cultic context one could think of several other texts in Chronicles. Suffice it to mention 2 Chron. 36.4, 8 (Jehoahaz and Jehoiakim) and what Chr. does and does not have to say about the end of the kings Jehoiachin and Zedekiah (also in ch. 36). All these were kings who died outside the land, and their deaths are not mentioned here because they die in a foreign (i.e. unclean) country (cf. 1 Sam. 26.19; Hos. 9.3-4; Amos 7.17).

A very clear expression of the cultic idea is present in 2 Chron. 34.3, 8, where Josiah 'purges' the land and the temple. Here, a term from the temple theology is used (טהר, 'purge') in connection with removing the idols from the land. A purged land and temple emerge in 2 Chron. 34.8—this is explicitly what 2 Chron. 36.21 implies by saying that the land 'enjoyed her sabbaths'.

The first stage of the 'interface' (2 Chron. 36.20-23) moves from an overall worldview to the particulars of the history of Israel. The next stage strikes a note of past history and future expectation. In the last phase of the text, the cultic aspect is the focus. Literary and theological interests go hand in hand on this road of textual development.

---

9. G. von Rad, 'Verheißenes Land und Jahwes Land im Hexateuch', *ZDPV* 66 (1943), pp. 191-204, repr. in von Rad, *Gesammelte Studien zum Alten Testament* (TBü, 8; Munich: Chr. Kaiser Verlag, 1958), pp. 87-100.

INDEXES

INDEX OF REFERENCES

OLD TESTAMENT

OTHER REFERENCES

INDEX OF AUTHORS